Q Clan:

The First Summer of the Korean Conflict, June–September 1950

A Lieutenant's Memoir

by

Ralph Derr Harrity

DORRANCE PUBLISHING CO., INC.
PITTSBURGH, PENNSYLVANIA 15222

The events, people, and places herein are depicted to the best recollection of the author, who assumes complete and sole responsibility for the accuracy of this narrative and assumes all liability for said work and indemnifies the publisher against any claims stemming from publication of the work.

ISBN # 0-8059-6748-6
Printed in the United States of America

First Printing

For information or to order additional books, please write:
Dorrance Publishing Co., Inc.
701 Smithfield Street
Third Floor
Pittsburgh, Pennsylvania 15222
U.S.A.
1-800-788-7654
Or visit our web site and on-line catalog at www.dorrancepublishing.com

This memoir is dedicated to all who served in the United Nations military force in Korea during the summer of 1950.

Contents

A Matter of Definition

At the onset of hostilities in (South) Korea and for some years following, the term "Korean Conflict" was widely accepted as all-inclusive, defining the three-year struggle as a limited engagement, distinctive from the all-out or victory-oriented missions mostly characterizing prior American military efforts.

Yet despite the distinction, the word "War" soon became more commonplace, supplanting "Conflict" when referring to or describing military and political sequences and complexities surrounding that three-year embroilment.

In May 1995, to clear the air—so to speak—an official term declaration was sought. A response was received from the Pentagon's Office of the Assistant Secretary of Defense:

> "This office researched the question of correct designation, either Korean Conflict or Korean War, and determined that KOREAN WAR is the most commonly used, generally accepted, and correct term...."
> (signed)
> Perry R. Dunn
> Colonel, USMC
> Deputy Director,
> Asian and Pacific Affairs[1]

And so, today and beyond, and historically, "Korean War" it shall be.

But for a brief moment still, since what follows is written as occurring at the instant, day by day, during that 1950 summer, the reader will be subject to the old term as it was and as continues to be fitting for those who were the first to fight in that place.

---

1 Letter of May 11, 1995, directed through the office of the Honorable Rodney Frelinghuysen, Member of Congress.

Preface

To this point in time, June 25, 1950, has not become an historic date emblazoned to "live in infamy." That spoken phrase, as every American schoolchild has or will come to learn, highlights the cassette image of a president asking for a declaration of war against the Empire of Japan. December 7, 1941, continues as the sole date of infamy in American history.

It might be said, nevertheless, that early on in 1941 most Americans sensed war approaching. The shock on December 7 was not so much the outbreak as the manner.

It was quite the reverse in 1950. Despite Soviet huffing and puffing in Europe and Red Army successes in China, few really anticipated a major military challenge to the status quo effected by America's destructive nuclear potential and a young, relatively potent United Nations organization. But surprise of surprises, a challenge was mounted and against a client state of the United States, the newly born Republic of Korea.

In slang parlance, the Republic (South Korea), in 1950, was an easy mark, a ripe rice stalk ready for cutting. True, the Republic's leadership stood voice-tall, mouthing matching rhetoric with their counterparts in the Peoples' Republic (North Korea) to the north, rhetoric that always seemed to climax with the cry, "Unification! By force, if necessary." The reality in the south, however, was a kind of Edgar Bergen/Charlie McCarthy performance, Edgar (U.S.) murmuring, "Now, now; mustn't, mustn't," and withholding important military hardware to prevent a restlessly petulant, often obstinate, and clearly feeble Charlie (South Korea) from making a run at the 38th Parallel.[1]

No Bergen/McCarthy act north of the parallel. It was a hard-eyed northern (NK) army that surged south on that June Sunday morning, demonstrating that their Soviet mentors were no comedians.

---

1 Harry F. Kern, foreign editor of *Newsweek* magazine, and Edward Weintal, diplomatic correspondent for *Newsweek*, writing in the July 3, 1950, issue, reported that both sides were itching for a scrap, the South being restrained by the United States by limiting ammunition supplies and refusing to turn over combat planes. See Harry F. Kern and Edward Weintal, "Significance of Korea: We Have to Put Up or Shut up," *Newsweek*, July 3, 1950, pg. 24.

At first, everyone who was anyone predicted that these northern peasant upstarts would get what for. But shortly, the United States and the rest of the West were struck dumb. The southern (ROK) army, and then the first Americans on the scene, both simply failed to bludgeon back the columns of simple grain farmers hard-welded into a driving, fighting machine. Embarrassment a half-world away followed.

So here we are, forty-five-plus years later, and the survivors of that first summer's battles are entering the evening of their lives. What can be reported now about these men and their efforts that has not already been placed in the record and on the printed page?

A number of writers have labored to inquire into the reasons for early military failures by United Nations forces as well as narrate the actions as they unfolded during the many months of a war that has come to be designated as the Korean Conflict. Where written endeavors have been honest in both inquiry and narration, the efforts are acknowledged with the deepest respect. Some might suggest that, by now, the ground has been covered quite thoroughly.

Yet the proposition is offered here that there is more to what already has been tendered in print. By way of offering implementation of this proposition, the reader is invited to discover an authentic recounting by a commissioned officer in the United States Army, an officer who served with the Occupation force in Japan prior to the outbreak of the Conflict and then assignment to the 24th Infantry Division Artillery from July 4 through September 30, 1950, the generally accepted time frame for the first United Nations combat phase in Korea.

Included in the recounting is a brief summation of certain national military policy facets that seemed to bear directly on the general preparedness level of the American Army by June 1950. Also included is a survey of certain features of the military training program effected within the Eighth United States Army (EUSA) in Japan during 1949 and early 1950, again as seeming to affect that Army as existing at the outbreak of hostilities.

And while the state of training is important in attempting to understand and evaluate early combat activity in Korea, so also is an awareness of both caliber and attitudes of the Occupation personnel as routinely perceived during the months that preceded combat commitment. These, too, receive consideration here.

These pre-Conflict examinations, brief and generalized as they are, are presented as observed and experienced personally by this writer. And it is understood that inferences drawn might be at variance with opinions held by others who also served in the Occupation either prior to or within the same time span.

Biographically, this writer served as an enlisted reservist with the 87th Division artillery in the European theatre during World War II. Following hostilities, he completed certain college-level and university requirements. Still drawn to the military, he volunteered in 1948 for a one-year period of active duty under a provision of the Selective Service Act of 1948. While on active duty at Fort George G. Meade, Maryland, he applied for and received an artillery second lieutenant's commission as provided for by Circular 330, 1948.

Continuing duty saw him ordered to Occupation service in Japan with the 7th Infantry Division at Camp Younghans, Jinmachi. Later, after the outbreak of the Conflict, he was sent as a battery filler officer to the 24th Infantry Division. Once on Korean soil, he was further assigned to the 13th Field Artillery Battalion, remaining with that unit thirteen months until rotation in July 1951.

He began, in May 1951, to jot down names and events that highlighted the course of operations during the early months of the Conflict, as remembered. As his primary assignment during those months was forward observation, serving with the infantry, he participated directly in or was privy to a number of early military operations undertaken by the 24th division. Thus, this narrative or memoir, if you will, has been set down, not from a command or staff point of view, but through the recollection and perception of one contending on the line.

The meager outline of 1951 grew slowly as relevant details, descriptions, and personalities emerged through correspondence sources, personal interviews, and library research, the latter most importantly being visitations to the New York City Public Library. And all the while, it should be noted, time had to be reserved for the normal pursuits of marriage, raising a family, and earning a living. There were many gaps before this writing effort reached a complete conclusion.

As stated above, this is an authentic/factual account. Much is included here, yet much is not. This writer was unable to witness every significant incident or event within the division's assigned sector of operations during that first summer of the Conflict. On the other hand, some important encounters not witnessed or experienced personally are recounted by others whose reliability was never in doubt.

Further, the reader may look forward to an account as free from unreasonable bias and braggadocio as is possible. War narratives (stories) too often, unfortunately, are descriptive of battles, movements, and individual struggles in a highly, almost unreal adjectival portrayal. Perhaps because warfare is often considered the ultimate in masculine enterprise, tendencies to exaggerate, particularly relative to the martial activities and achievements of participants reporting or being interviewed many months or years later, are all too common.

And finally, and very importantly, all personalities and events of the 1950 summer are perceived and discussed in then-contemporary fashion, not in the light of later uncovered evidence, hindsight, or qualification. Where additional information not known at the time of an occurrence has become available, or there is need for further explanation or identification, such becoming known after the fact and contributory to both sequence and reader edification, these are included within parentheses, end-of-chapter notes, or in the Epilogue.

This writer is very deeply indebted to the following individuals who assisted promptly and unselfishly in making this a complete and readable manuscript: Maj. Charles T. "Bill" Bailey, USA-Ret; Raymond J. Cody; Lt. Col. Dewey L. Coles, USA-Ret; Homer E. Dailey; Wilbert "Shorty" Estabrook; Col. Arthur P. Lombardi, USA-Ret; Herman F. Naville; Lt. Col. Ellsworth "Dutch" Nelsen, USA-Ret; Bernard Robinson; Lt. Col. David Rosen, USA-Ret; James Stavrakes; Lt. Col. Edgar E. Still, USA-Ret; Richard Stuben; and Col. Ernest P. Terrell, USA-Ret.

Also, gratefully, the following provided bits and pieces of information or proper direction or both: William Adkison; Robert E. Allen; William M. Allen; Edward J. Adkins; W. H. Burks; Herbert C. Carlson; Robert L. Edson; Maj. Jerry Fly, USMC; Joseph McKeon; Elmer E. Millsapps; Lt. Col. Rodolph Mullins, USA-Ret; and John Lee Tester.

Well, July 5 and 6, 1950, were terribly exciting, but anxious and lonely days for hundreds of men assigned to 24th Infantry Division infantry and artillery units approaching the shores of the Korean peninsula on Japanese-manned LSTs, a flotilla bringing Americans, for the first time since WWII, to anchor in a major battle zone. The generally existent American military posture, the Occupation milieu in Japan these men were leaving, and then a description of their advances to and their commitments on new fields of honor appear on the following pages, all as related by one of their number, a lieutenant of artillery.

PRELUDE

THE UNITED STATES PARED ITS MILITARY STRENGTH MASSIVELY FOLLOWING THE successful conclusion of World War II, and there were some who characterized the magnitude of this contractive policy as a "crime." As voiced, mostly anonymously, within the military establishment, the policy that vigorously reduced and economized, a policy that affected the Army in particular, was criminal. It was a policy that shrank the Army's personnel from 8,267,958 in September 1945,[1] to an authorized figure of 669,000 officers and enlisted as of March 17, 1948.[2]

That the reductions were achieved despite seemingly incontrovertible evidence of a continuing high level of Soviet military and political intrigue seemed inexcusable. Final proof that the effected economizing had damaging results lay contributorily in the relatively poor showing on the battlefield by the Japanese Occupation divisions, hastily mustered in 1950 to defend the Republic of Korea against aggression by the armed forces of the Democratic Peoples' Republic of Korea.

One might suggest that the policy of military reduction, with exceptions or allowances for routine maintenance, force redeployment, and further development of nuclear armaments and jet aircraft, began September 3, 1945. There was, on that date, no authentic national enemy. All Americans looked forward to a "Pax Americana" in concert with a hoped-for successful United Nations. What occurred during the remainder of 1945 and all of 1946 was the largest and most thoroughgoing military downsizing experienced by any world power.

By early 1947, however, a troubled air was noticeable in and about Western capitals, touching even the desks of American legislators imbued with "Fortress America" reasoning. While most in the West maintained a self-congratulatory stance over the success of the recent antifascist war, Soviet imperialism was actively consolidating political power in areas throughout eastern Europe under Soviet military occupation and seeking to make inroads elsewhere.

Of considerable concern was continuing economic hardship in western and southern Europe, the result mainly of a completely spent war effort, but also the destruction of much factory space and the inability in many areas to rebuild to thus create the capital necessary for employment and consumption.

While the United States initially had done little to help, the Soviets early offered their economic philosophy to the hard pressed. Rumania, Bulgaria, and

Yugoslavia had already turned eastward, albeit mainly the result of the Soviet military presence. Poland would soon follow. Italy tottered on the brink. Civil war began raging in Greece with control of the national politic as the prize. Occurring as these did within only two years after VJ Day, impact on the West was understandably disheartening.

Finally, faced with the fact of a dangerously surging Soviet and despite divided domestic leadership, the latter the result of the 1946 national midterm elections, the United States began clenching its policy-making fists, maneuvering to counter the Soviets.

A bill to bolster both Greece and Turkey was passed (May 1947). The Truman Doctrine was thus born.

Then, in a speech labeled by some as embodying the most unselfish deed in the history of mankind (June 5, 1947), Secretary of State George C. Marshall outlined an aid program, soon to be formalized as the European Recovery Plan, but would be dubbed by most as the Marshall Plan. Both the Truman Doctrine and ERP, truthfully, were anti-Soviet in concept, the former providing military assistance and the latter economic aid. Nations still struggling to recuperate from the war's effects, including those forcibly detained behind the Iron Curtain, would be recipients of ERP aid, assuming each would accept aid. Those nations within the Soviet sphere of influence refused the American offer, as it turned out.

At the same time, certain prominent military and civilian personages had begun urging Congressional approval of a bill, the policy embodiment of which was titled the National Service Training Act. This bill outlined a program of general military training for *all* young men, different in some respects from raw conscription, but accomplishing the same purpose. These spokesmen hearkened back to the 1939–1940 period when trained soldiery was scarce, despite the growing possibility of American entry into a major armed conflict.

Now again, advised these leaders, the world was in crisis, with a chance—remote perhaps—but a chance that war with the Soviet Union might break out. As that nation seemed not to have disarmed appreciably after September 1945, the United States could be at a distinct and perhaps fatal disadvantage should another war become a reality, our possession of the atom bomb notwithstanding.

Crash programs of economic and military aid abroad were one thing, of course, while enlargement of the military establishment was quite another. Republican and Democratic legislators joined in the spending necessary for the maintenance of European security and economic well-being, as the perception unfolded that the very future of Western Civilization hinged on what Americans would or would not do. But it was also not difficult for both parties to keep alive the spirit of niggardliness within those areas of the national interest where need had not been firmly established.

Such was the fate that met the National Service Act when, as a new and untested preparedness concept, it was introduced into Congress in March 1947. Hesitations, primarily economic, prompted postponement of the idea. Also, Congress desired additional time to evaluate evolving international developments as well as the emergence of a clear, favoring public sentiment.

Then, on February 25, 1948, after political rumblings from Eastern Europe had quieted considerably, the West was stunned to hear that a communist banner was flying for the first time over St. Wenceslaus Square in Prague, Czechoslovakia.

What passed for peacetime complacency was shattered as Americans began to inquire what must be done to stop Soviet assimilations. With Czechoslovakia, once a bastion of democracy among eastern European nations, now behind the Iron Curtain, the time clearly had arrived for a show of strength by the West and particularly by the United States. The Soviets were energetically demonstrating a total disdain of Western-style democratic institutions in general and the Yalta agreements in particular. The continued existence of a free western Europe was threatened in the aftermath of this latest coup.

President Harry Truman pointed the way for thought and action by warning Congress on March 17, 1948, that our armed forces must be strengthened, acknowledging that peacetime recruiting techniques had failed to bring the forces to authorized levels.[3]

The authorized level for the Army at the time was 669,000 officers and enlisted, a figure set to provide the nation with ten combat divisions at the ready, with allowance for special and supporting troops.[4] As the president spoke, Army strength hovered at 540,000.[5] Existing combat divisions were lowering to half strength. The Army needed an influx of 30,000 new enlistments per month to reach authorized levels. It was receiving only 12,000 to 24,000 per month.[6]

The president's speech had the effect, for the moment at least, of encouraging a rejection of defense economy policies. A new and dangerous era was unfolding and Congress was being asked to begin the task of reforging something of the military effectiveness that had been America's on VJ Day.

What resulted was not national service but what was felt to be an acceptable substitute, namely Public Law 759, the Selective Service Act of 1948. Opposition to national service from religious, labor, and education groups proved too strong. Further, as permanency was understood to be the key strength of the national service concept, the program might eventually cost a great deal more than its worth, as voiced by some of the plan's opponents. A temporary bulwark, as Public Law 759 was intended to be, would be more consonant with the times.

In brief, the new law provided for a twenty-one-month period of conscriptive service for all eligible men between the ages of nineteen and twenty-six. But as a measure emphasizing responsibility rather than coercion, the Army was permitted to enlist any eligible individual within the age category for a like period of time. The psychological compulsion to "beat the draft" was expected to be advantageous in implementing this provision. Enlistments for two-and three-year periods, as was the current practice, would be continued as a provision of the new law.

Secondly, civilian enlisted reservists of all ranks were permitted to apply for reentry to active service under the term *active duty training*. These men might volunteer for a period of active duty not to exceed twenty-one months. They would contribute initially by providing valuable nuts-and-bolts skills affecting the anticipated buildup and expansion of the Army, and then, upon active duty termination, return to their home communities and become cadre for reserve units, then being rejuvenated after muddling along since 1946 without much organization and without pay. It was reasoned that a sound reserve program would mean a stronger second line of defense during national emergencies, alongside the National Guard.

And finally, Congress authorized the Army to enlist up to 110,000 young men between the ages of eighteen and nineteen for a period of one year, after which each would return to his home community and join either an Army Reserve or National Guard organization to complete training. This measure also was termed "active duty training" and was included as an aid to building reserve components. It should be added that this new law forbade duty outside the continental limits for men in the one-year category.

Whatever the original intentions of its backers, the Selective Service Act was designed to *supplement* traditional procedures of recruitment. Principal responsibility for recruitment would continue to be placed on the inducement powers of the several services.

Interestingly, Congress seemed not to have listened to a future president as the debate over national service evolved. Approaching his final days as Army chief of staff in February 1948, Gen. Dwight Eisenhower argued that national service "must be a vigorously prosecuted activity in our preparatory processes until we can be assured that danger of global war belongs to history."[7]

But Senator Robert A. Taft, Ohio Republican and chairman of the Republican Policy Committee, completely disagreed. In a speech before the Lincoln Club in Denver, Colorado, that same month, Taft oracled that, "it seems almost too obvious that the next battle will be fought predominantly in the air." As a result, he concluded that national service would have little value for defense and would be contrary to the whole concept of American liberty.[8]

The new selective service law authorized the regular Army strength at 837,000 officers and enlisted, up 168,000 from the previous authorization of 669,000.[9] Kenneth C. Royall, Secretary of the Army, forecast twelve divisions drawn from the regular ranks, an increase of two. Six standby divisions would be readied in the National Guard and the reserve.[10] The nation thus would be assured of eighteen trained divisions on immediate call, at full strength, and equipped with the latest weapons for instantaneous battle commitment.

Almost immediately, expecting a large influx of new enlistments, particularly for the twenty-one month period, and needing to reopen a number of inactive facilities, the Army advertised for reservist NCOs to return to the active service for the maximum allowable time.

Many reservists volunteered for recall. A brief business recession during 1948 spurred the return of many family men. Some reservists were placed on cadre lists to refurbish and reorganize training centers. Others were assigned station complement duties for the direct handling of reception processing. Still others were earmarked for troop training cadres and shipped to various branch school centers, at which World War II combat skills, taught by the reservists, would be used to advantage in the training of recruits for line outfits. By the middle of September 1948, the Army was in the full throes of the first expansion process since the end of World War II.

With its enlisted serviceman problem solved, or so it thought, the Army next turned to acquiring additional officer personnel. Preparations for manpower increases revealed rank disparities among the active service commissioned. Termination of the recent war found many more captains and field grades endeavoring to continue than were needed. Lieutenants, on the other hand, always in need, were more apt to apply for separation.

The conventional sources for second lieutenants, the lowest officer rank, West Point, ROTC, and officer candidate schools continued to function throughout the postwar period. But even by 1948, the newly commissioned had not relieved the disparity. In fact, many of these merely replaced war-class officers who were resigning in droves to find places in a rapidly expanding civilian economy. As captains and majors do not command platoons, the time had come to resolve the problem.

Several Department of the Army circulars set forth qualifications whereby both Army active duty and civilian persons might be commissioned. One circular provided that certain enlisted personnel in the highest three grades might apply to be commissioned as second lieutenants. Commissions were awarded after appropriate examinations and board findings.

Circular 330, designed to tap whatever likely talent might be dormant in colleges and universities, provided for the commissioning of men between the ages of nineteen and twenty-seven, if two years had been completed successfully at any recognized institution of higher learning and a year of satisfactory military service also completed. Commissions in this category were tendered immediately following a favorable board finding, but were conditioned to the successful completion of a basic instructional course at a branch school.

And finally, some reserve officers in the grades of captain and below and members of civilian reserve units were permitted to apply for active duty. Now all that remained was for recruits to begin flooding through camp gates.

A flowing stream it was, but no flood. The enlistment rate heightened with men who either were not making it in the civilian economy or were intending to "beat the draft." By January 1949, enlistments were figured at 35,000 per month,[11] a figure greater than the 12,000 to 24,000 entries per month prior to the enactment of the new law. And yet by June 30, 1949, the Army's strength was only 658,000, eleven thousand below the pre-Act authorization of 669,000.[12]

Contribution by the draft, the core of Public Law 759, proved to be minimal, respecting the Army's strength figures. Only 30,126 draftees entered the Army during the two-year span of the law.[13] In matter of fact, drafting of men virtually ceased in January 1949, so there remained no expectation of reaching the strength goal of 837,000.[14] What happened?

Deep second thoughts seemed to have gripped high administration officials and congressional leaders. Despite repeated public comments to the contrary, an apparent new foreign policy conclusion was that the external threat to American interests from aggressive Soviet activities, heretofore perceived as extremely dangerous, was not any longer so perceived. This changed thinking was reflected in a portion of President Truman's January 1949 budget message, the portion pertaining to defense matters.

In the president's words: "The 1950 (defense) program gives priority to air power and to strengthening the civilian reserve components and continues to emphasize research and development and industrial mobilization."[15]

Secondly, the increased Army enlistment figures seemingly mesmerized many into believing that strength goals could be reached through volunteer recruiting efforts rather than with the aid of draft augmentation.[16] The drafting of men for military service during peacetime continued to remain controversial among large segments of the public, a major reason why the concept of national or universal service was never enacted into law. As the Air Force, Navy, and Marine Corps were achieving strength goals solely through recruiting, there was renewed pressure on the Army to accomplish the same by trying harder.

And thirdly, although not loudly proclaimed in leadership circles at the time, there was heavy pressure to economize at the federal level. In August 1949, the Senate Appropriations Committee told Secretary of Defense Louis Johnson to save a billion dollars any way he could.[17] This request, most probably, wrote *finis* to the 837,000 strength goal. And whether or not the request was cause and effect, the Department of Defense promptly embarked on a program to eliminate 10,500 "extra" reserve officers from the overall active military establishment, those considered excess to immediate requirements.[18]

So the goal to increase the active Army by two divisions was abandoned. That service would continue with ten divisions plus fifty-nine separate battalions.[19] With appropriate support elements, the Army's new authorized strength figure was set at 677,000 officers and enlisted, a figure only a few thousand more than that authorized at the weak point of March 1948.[20]

Failure to enact a genuinely compulsory manpower training program, plus the seeming unwillingness by both the administration and Congress to support sufficient appropriations to implement Public Law 759 to the fullest, precipitated the inevitable. Termination of the two-year enlistment program was announced. In October 1949, Secretary of the Army Gordon Gray informed all twenty-one-month men who had completed twelve active duty months that they would be offered separation beginning December 1. Approximately 30,000 were affected by this change.[21]

The enlisted reserve (recall) program ceased in early 1949. Also terminated was the company grade officer recruitment program outside active Army channels, with the greatest effect on those who had anticipated being commissioned under Circular 330.

By June, 1949 the Far East Command (FECOM) could not continue maintaining the outward appearance of full-strength combat divisions. These structures were reduced by one-third. Two battalions of infantry per regiment were retained rather than the normal three, supported now by a like number of artillery batteries, engineer companies, etc.

Authorization was granted to one combat branch to compensate for unit reductions. Whereas the number of howitzers in a normal support battery during WWII totaled four, or twelve howitzers supporting a three-battalion regiment, new tables of organization and equipment called for the addition of two howitzers per battery, continuing twelve howitzers within the new two support-battery artillery battalion.

Then in October 1949, Secretary Gray estimated that 630,000 officers and enlisted were the absolute minimum needed by the Army to carry out delegated responsibilities.[22] However, by March 1950, that minimum had ebbed to 596,000.[23] And it was in the same month that Secretary Johnson boasted before the House Armed Services Committee that he had saved not a billion dollars but a billion and a half from the defense budget for fiscal 1950.[24]

The agitation resulting from the communist takeover of Czechoslovakia had run its course. Fear of war was abating. Despite continued high international tensions, the nation, through Congress and key civilian advisors, resumed placing the value of the dollar foremost in defense considerations, provoking the respected *Army and Navy Journal* to comment editorially that the trend toward economy (as a national policy) results in a weaker, not a stronger, military establishment. "Important as it is to save money," the *Journal* counseled, "it is far more important to save the country."[25]

The *Army Times* also voiced misgivings. It warned that while many overhead units were being cut, combat units were not being strengthened proportionately. The *Times* further called attention to the fact that the ten combat-ready divisions about which the Army boasted were anywhere from 65 percent to 80 percent understrength, adding that "although Secretary Johnson's budget undoubtedly benefits (the nation), who will be the winner if our undermanned Army, Navy, and Air Force were ever called to the test?"[26]

Yet despite the clouded future toward which the Army seemed destined, two positive results of the 1948 expansion program were to become increasingly significant as the summer of 1950 approached. Many reserve NCOs, reaching the end of their voluntary duty periods, requested to be absorbed into the active Army rather than return to civilian life. It is no secret that strong elements of Eighth Army NCO leadership in June 1950 included remnants from the Army reserve active duty program of 1948–49. In the early stages of the Korean fighting, it was the older WWII NCO who often stabilized situations on the verge of becoming untenable, preventing outright panic in the ranks when officers fell or were incapacitated. For the active duty training program that provided for the recall of many of these veterans, a nation can be thankful.

In like manner, a significant number of commissioned platoon leaders and artillery forward observers in the active Army in Japan on June 25, 1950, were reservists, and many of these had received their commissions during the 1948–49 expansion planning.[27] Had the company grade officer recruitment effort not been in place during 1948, the officer shortage in these categories might well have resulted in more serious setbacks by the committed divisions during the opening weeks of the Korean Conflict.

In late spring 1950, apparently pleased with the administration's budget policies as related to defense concerns, Congress began considering a replacement law for the Selective Service Act, due to expire June 24. The new bill, to be known as the Manpower Registration Act, would continue compulsory registration of young men, but would not compel a draft except in the event of a national emergency on order from the president.

Dependence by the services on enlistment or inducement processes would be continued. The new act would be merely a registration and classification law.

If or when passed, the replacement law would have the effect of continuing to maintain two-thirds strength combat divisions. Should an emergency arise, it was felt that our nuclear stocks would be sufficient to deter an enemy (the Soviet Union) until an adequate, full-strength Army was mobilized. And although the Soviets had exploded a nuclear device in 1949, the United States was much further along in both testing and manufacturing atomic weapons. The position of this nation was, in a word, indomitable.

Still, on June 10, 1950, the *Army Times* pointed out editorially that the Manpower Registration Act without an included draft provision was not consistent with our need of preparation for national emergencies. The spur to enlistments contained in the previous law had worked well and should be continued. Not to continue the draft might be risking grave consequences in terms of lowered manpower and a resultant weakened military establishment. The paper called on Congress to keep the Army from deteriorating to the weak point of March 1948.[28]

In Congress there was much talk, but no final agreement. So on June 22, in desperation, two days before Public Law 759 was due to expire, the same act was extended fifteen days to prevent the nation from having no manpower law at all.[29]

Two days later, a hot, muggy Saturday afternoon in Washington, D.C., but a cool, rainy Sunday dawn fourteen hours and a new day in another part of the world, a brown-clothed platoon leader's ticking watch closed on zero hour. As it did, and with a deep-throated "*Mansei!*," the man led his fighters across a boundary line and onto a free nation's territory, triggering the first major conflict of the atomic era.

On the Way

Twenty-one newly commissioned second lieutenants comprised the first Special Associate Basic Artillery Officers' Course class that reported to Fort Sill, Oklahoma, on December 1, 1948, in conformity with provisions of Department of the Army Circular 330. Course training also began, or would begin soon, at twelve other Army branch schools.

An initial total or *tab* of the number of officers to be trained under this circular, as reported in January 1949, was 781. The largest tab of 200 was granted the Infantry School. The Field Artillery School's tab was 100. The fewest number of commissioned recruits, as appropriated, was the allotment for the Chemical Warfare Service School, a figure of twenty-five.[1]

Those branch schools that began course work prior to January 1949 were able to graduate three commissioned classes before defense economies during 1949 completely killed the program. And, although it had been reported unofficially that at least 500 commissions per combat branch as a goal would be tendered, the number finally completing branch schooling before termination of the program was closer to the initial tab figures.

If the Fort Sill course was typical, these young officers underwent an indoctrination that essentially was a review of WWII methods and techniques. A significant augmentation was the suggestion that nuclear weapons, coupled with strong air striking power, would pave the way for a smashing ground maneuver and quick victory over any or all enemies. That Europe might again be the site of the next conflict was never questioned, although some pause was given to the possibility of American cities being attacked for the first time.

None doubted for a moment that the Soviet Union would be the primary enemy, even as military instructors were still forbidden to mention that power by name except within the context of *ally*. A new term, "Aggressor," was coming rapidly into usage as synonymous with the national enemy, but it was only the very naïve who refused to associate Aggressor with the Soviets.

It took four months for these artillery fledglings to familiarize themselves with the duties, responsibilities, and technical grounding of their newly chosen profession. When the nest emptied, four were assigned to various Stateside posts; several drew European assignments; one was accepted for Marine Corps duty;

one volunteered successfully for the Air Force; one was selected for service on Guam; four received orders for South Korea, and the remainder were assigned to the Japanese Occupation. Of the original twenty-one, nineteen completed the course to remain active.

The designated port of embarkation for many assigned to the Far East was San Francisco via Camp Stoneman. And so, when the United States Army Transport *General W.F. Hase* slipped out of San Francisco harbor that April afternoon in 1949 to the strains of "Now Is The Hour," as played by the Fort Mason port band, the military aboard, some six hundred officers and enlisted, knew their destinations but contemplated only superficially the experiences they may encounter.

Despite an attitude of general detachment from world affairs that characterized this voyage for most, a number who traveled aboard the *Hase* on this particular trip may recall what might be termed a distinctly disturbing undercurrent that seemed to prevail wherever groupings formed to pass the time. Between alternating sequences of seasickness and shipboard hilarity, some uneasiness was noted, particularly among the civilian passengers. For aside from the military contingent, the *Hase* was transporting dependents of American military and civilian officials on duty in South Korea, and among these were several high-ranking United Nations representatives also bound for South Korea. This was the first movement of civilians into that country following the lifting of a thirteen-month ban due to unsettled internal conditions there.

Considerable dialogue took place during the first few days on board as to the state of affairs within South Korea and, by extension, the relationship with its northern counterpart. Several presumably well-informed officers of higher rank intimated that Gen. Douglas MacArthur had been in secret session with Syngman Rhee, the President of South Korea, concerning defense matters and personally had guaranteed the security of that country's northern border. If this was so, and there was no good reason at the moment to doubt that possibility, Occupation forces would be committed in the event of all-out hostilities between the two Koreas.

The talk suffered understandably in terms of unfounded generalizations and finally descended to the inconceivable. As few on the *Hase* knew enough background detail to continue an interest in the discussion, the subject gradually faded in favor of more exciting banter.

An event did occur, however, precipitated by the presence on the ship of the Korean-bound dependents and military, that had considerable significance for those who listened and remembered. Two high-ranking South Korean officials, bound for Seoul (the South Korean capital) from Washington and the United Nations at Lake Success, New York, were asked to address informally an assembled body of dependents and those military destined for Korean assignments. The charge given to these dignitaries was to orient the group as to general conditions within that republic, emphasizing people, customs, etc. The presentation was intended as an interim indoctrination for those whose lives during the immediate future would be in close proximity to Korean society.

The officials willingly obliged. However, if one listened for an illuminating discussion of what had been initially suggested as the main theme, one listened intently but in vain. What transpired was a strikingly explosive summary of the South Korean position in world affairs with very particular reference to the United States.

The statements made by these two diplomats (their names, unfortunately, are lost in the limbo of memory) provided a sharp insight into the popular logic of the Korean people as they attempted to understand the causes of their political predicament.

President Theodore Roosevelt, it was asserted, was responsible for the subjugation of Korea by Japan. By proffering his "good offices" as a measure to help settle the Russo-Japanese War of 1904–05, the resulting Treaty of Portsmouth, one provision of which permitted Japan a free hand in Korea, was his creation. The United States, through President Roosevelt's peace efforts, was therefore responsible for the ensuing absorption of Korea into the Japanese orbit of colonial domination.

More recently, at the conclusion of WWII, with an opportunity at last for reconstituting a totally independent Korea, the United States collaborated with the Soviet Union to establish a dividing line of authority (the 38th Parallel) between the two powers for the purpose of disarming Japanese soldiery. In doing so, the United States disregarded the "plain fact" that the Soviets were preparing to organize a permanent, competing government within their sector of authority and soon did so. For this state of affairs the United States must, again, be held accountable and should, therefore, prepare to aid South Korea in taking the initiative to reunify the peninsula under the democratic guidance of Syngman Rhee.

It was not a little difficult for many in the assembled group to stomach the accusation that their government was being held responsible for South Korea's woes, past and present. Roosevelt's position, as most who had studied the matter believed, represented a clear and simple recognition of an existent relationship between Japan and Korea. The Treaty of Portsmouth, as affecting Korea, in other words, was merely a confirmation of a certain status quo. More importantly for the time, the objective of the treaty was to limit competitive aggression between two world powers. That the objective proved successful, at least in the short run, resulted in wide acclaim and the conferral on the president of the Nobel Peace Prize.

The matter of the 38th Parallel, the agreed-upon dividing line in Korea that was established to facilitate disarming Japanese troops in preparation for Korean self-rule, was, of course, something else. Already, a rising chorus of criticism was being directed at the Soviet Union respecting its imposed Occupation policies. There was particular criticism concerning alleged hindrances of democratic (Western style) evolvement within the several Soviet zones of occupation. Evidence was being circulated to the effect that Soviet Occupation troops, rather than acting solely to maintain law and order until newly established governments, free of fascist taint, took hold, were actively supporting Soviet-style governing groups to achieve and hold power in the face of large opposition majorities, a policy the Korean diplomats were alluding to in their indoctrination session.

It was to be remembered, however, that the Soviet Union in 1945 was still a major partner in the Grand Alliance and, although very, very late in the war, that nation did declare war against Japan. It was in recognition of this declaration that certain policies respecting postwar relationships were agreed to. The military occupation of Korea north of the 38th Parallel by the Soviet Union was one of those agreements. It was, in matter of fact at the time, a "good faith" agreement, one of several that the United States, in particular, hoped would lead to an East-West cooperative stance in pursuit of common goals for the benefit of mankind.

All that was in 1945, of course. The *Hase* was plowing across the Pacific in 1949 carrying its burden of military and dependent civilians. The Americans on board didn't need reminding that the idealism embodied in "good faith" concepts was fading rapidly in the face of a belated recognition that the Soviets, as a rogue power now, were using their zones of occupation as springboards for attempted power expansion across Europe and, perhaps as the South Korean officials intimated, in North Korea. It was this understandably dangerous aggressor pattern that the United States, supported by western allies, was at the moment taking steps to counter.

Nothing was mentioned by the two diplomats about the fact that had Japan not attacked at Pearl Harbor or at other bases in the Pacific area, the Korean cities of Seoul and Pusan might yet be trembling to the measured tread of Japanese domination. It was the Pearl Harbor debacle and subsequently the First Cairo Conference of 1943 that gave birth to the declaration that Korea should be liberated and granted the opportunity to pursue a democratic future, a declaration initiated by an American president.

Needless to say, the noticeably jaundiced remarks by the two South Koreans were so galling that one of the more remarkable statements by one of them was probably lost on the many in the now hostile audience:

> "Everyone knows that North Korea is building an army of liberation. The aim of our government is to meet this threat and then counter with our own forces maintained through the help of the United States. Unification of Korea can only be accomplished by war. We are preparing for that eventuality."

The informal gathering broke up hurriedly at the sound of the steward's gong announcing a first call to dinner.

Coincident with the movement of the *Hase* across the Pacific, the United Nations, then in session, was being asked to consider certain questions relative to the military state of affairs in both North and South Korea. The Soviet Union, which had withdrawn the last of her occupation troops from North Korea the preceding December, now was calling upon the United States to do likewise in South Korea.

Then, on the tenth day of the voyage, the ship's newssheet carried an item to the effect that the Republic of Korea (South Korea) had formally requested the United Nations to ask all foreign troops to leave her soil.

Surprising as the request was, the reality was soon clear. By January 1949, the only American combat troops remaining in South Korea consisted of a regimental combat team and support units, and these were in the early throes of preparations to leave.[2] With the departure of these forces, only a group of military (KMAG) and civilian (AMIK) advisors, representatives of the foreign aid program, and a limited number of military support troops would be left.

For the military aboard the *Hase* bound for Korea, each succeeding day's news became increasingly propitious. As none really had looked forward to living on any part of Korean soil, reprieve at a late hour would be highly receptive.

Each waited impatiently for a change of orders. And then, for most, change came. When the *Hase* docked at Yokohama on April 22, only those dependents, civilian officials, a few Army officers, and a company of engineer replacements remained on board. The remainder debarked and then entrained for the Eighth Army Replacement Depot at Camp Zama and assignment in Japan. For these latter the future turned brighter on that particular day.

Preparation

If 1948 was crucial in that the Army's company-level officer needs were considerably secured, then 1949 was equally so in terms of tactical preparations. Within a month after the *Hase* disgorged its load of fillers and replacements at Yokohama, the Eighth United States Army, long in the lethargic grip of an Occupation atmosphere, roused itself to fresh challenges of preparedness and effectiveness.

This is not to say that serious military duties were only occasionally carried out during the preceding three years. Proper emphasis indeed had been placed on keeping troops physically fit and minimally proficient at the skill level for the rank held. Each would then become successful role models as benevolent defenders and protectors of the Japanese people and their new democratic governing experience. By the spring of 1949, however, faced finally with the reality of a successful Chinese communist revolution, commanders in the Far East Theatre of Operations were spurred to make their Occupation divisions "combat effective."

The first step toward combat effectiveness was taken not by theatre generals, but by the Department of the Army. Acting under the presumed influence of Congress, as interpreted by Secretary Johnson, the Army issued new tables of organization that reduced the number of combat units within line divisions by one-third. These reductions were the result of a thorough study of manpower needs which indicated quite clearly that, although the Selective Service Act of 1948 was expected to free thousands of regular Army personnel then stationed Stateside for overseas duty, the anticipated flow of replacements would not be sufficient to flesh out all existing units in the Occupation divisions.

So to compensate for the expected enlistee shortage, yet optimistically maintain normal combat effectiveness, each of the three divisional infantry regiments would now be comprised of two operational battalions rather than the normal three. Two firing batteries of artillery instead of three, plus a headquarters and a service battery, would constitute an artillery support battalion. Engineer, antiaircraft, and armor among other branches were similarly affected.

What resulted was a compression of officers and enlisted into six full-strength battalion combat teams within a division, rather than the normal nine teams, each battalion team considered capable of maximum effectiveness. The assumption was that in the event of a military emergency, missing battalions, companies, and batteries would be reactivated immediately, using cadres drawn from full-strength sister units. Unfortunately, some emergencies occur with such quickness as to impede immediate implementation of this core extension plan, the prime example being the hurried commitment of the 24th Infantry Division into the Korean fighting.

As a second step, the regimental combat team concept was to be prioritized where possible with direct support artillery, engineers, etc., moved to or near posts occupied by supported infantry. The moves would be permanent so as to permit continual realistic scenarios for training and maneuver.

Initial Occupation organization in Japan had dictated that artillery battalions be located near adequate ranges so that training might be more thoroughly supervised by artillery commanders and their staffs. Infantry regiments, on the other hand, were scattered strategically with Occupation responsibilities as the main mission. Division headquarters gathered support troops, such as signal, quartermaster, etc., and appropriated quarters in or near a large city close to the center of the designated Occupation zone. Such organizational placements, although pertinent to the aims and goals of Occupation, did not permit much in the way of teamwork above the battalion level.

The First Cavalry Division was moving toward RCT repositioning by June 1950. The 31st Regiment, 7th Infantry Division, with the 57th Field Artillery Battalion in support, became operational in and around Sapporo, Hokkaido, in late 1949. Had war in Korea not broken out when it did, the 17th Regiment, 7th Division, with the 49th Field Artillery Battalion in support, would have become operational at Camp Schimmelphennig, Sendai. That this change in training aim could not be carried out successfully in every Occupation zone was a matter of both facility and terrain.

Thirdly, and most importantly, a complex army-wide program of training for all units, with the objective of making each unit in each theatre as efficient as possible, was initiated in the early summer of 1949. Beginning with individual duty or military occupational specialty (MOS) training and testing, the program timetable next called for training and examination at company or battery levels and then battalion level operations. Regimental testing and maneuvering followed, but under unique and certainly difficult circumstances at times. The example of the 32nd RCT is illustrative in this regard, an early 1950 winter maneuver.

The 32nd Infantry Regiment, 7th Infantry Division, was located at Camp Haugen, a converted Japanese naval air base outside the northeastern Honshu city of Hachinohe. No suitable artillery range and maneuver area was available at the campsite. The regiment's direct support artillery, the 48th Field Artillery Battalion, billeted permanently at Camp Younghans in north central Honshu, the 7th Division artillery center, was required to make an overnight rail trip to Hachinohe for the maneuver.

The maneuver centered about Misawe Air Base, a critical stopover for many aircraft arriving in the Far East from the continental United States. Camp Haugen was but a few miles from Misawe, and sufficient bivouac and maneuver opportunities were present at the base for the combat team. Air Force commanders limited operations at the base to only the essentials during the several days of the maneuver, primarily to reduce the chances of air-truck accidents, portions of the runways being used for supply and communications purposes.

Two nights and a day were spent in bivouac for all troops, braving bitterly cold and snowy weather. Maneuver action began on the second day with simulated artillery fire and infantry reconnaissance. Simulated enemy attacks took place on the second day also. Counterattacking began at dawn of the third day. This action involved tanks (simulated), artillery barrages (simulated), and the overhead cover of the new Air Force jet planes (F-80s) from Misawe.

Infantrymen shuffled along several roads in columns; battalion and regimental officers raced back and forth in jeeps; the artillery fire direction center received "missions" from the forward observers (traveling along with the infantry); and, when there was a lull, observers were radioed to "think up some." The jets were in the air on schedule, zooming on the columns, some acting in friendly patterns and others as enemy, both simulating strafing.

There were several frostbite cases, a few hurt in vehicle accidents, and most cursed the weather. In general, however, a good, rousing maneuver in WWII tradition took place.

If there were any gains from the experience they were in the forms of (1) awe at the noise and speed of the new close-support jets and (2) the more conventional challenges of infantry and artillery officers adjusting to each other under particularly trying conditions. There was little doubt that this and probably other RCT maneuvers bordered on the questionable when measured in terms of adequate combat proficiency. Yet most felt that, although the beginning was certainly mediocre, subsequent operations would be much improved. None realized, of course, that this initial maneuver would be the last prior to the outbreak of conflict in June of that year.

Most RCT maneuvers were completed by March 1950, and the path cleared for the next training hurdle, one held by many to be necessary for all combat personnel in view of the type of fighting endured in the Pacific island area during WWII. Selected RCTs were to be detached temporarily and sent to Camp McGill, south of Tokyo and near the Yokosuka Naval Base. There, under both Navy and Marine tutelage, units would learn the principles of amphibious invasion tactics. An actual landing would be planned and implemented, concluding this phase of training.

The training landing site was to be at Chigasaki, on Sagami Bay, near the city of Hiratsuka, a site chosen by Gen. Douglas MacArthur as a principal invasion point in the projected invasion of Japan, had such an event been necessary. Elements of the First Cavalry Division, stationed in and around the Tokyo area, were the first to undergo this training while outlying units were to be scheduled later in the year.

Then, lastly, barring a change in training plans, division maneuvers would cap the cycle, certainly an ambitious climax given the severe shortage of maneuver space overall throughout Japan.

Following division maneuvers, the entire cycle would be repeated. It was theorized that each individual, during a normal tour of duty or enlistment, would experience at least two complete training cycles, sufficient to coalesce individuals and small units into competent orientation with both regimental and divisional roles in successful combat operations.

So in retrospect, to suggest, given the 1949–50 Eighth Army training program, that the first troops sent to Korea were inexperienced or green is a misstatement. Rather, it might be suggested that the men in these first units were *undertrained*. The Far East Command attempted with all its energy and facility to make the Japanese Occupation soldier as combat effective as possible. That this objective fell short in the implementation process was not necessarily the fault of the program. Despite the boldness of purpose that accompanied the initiation of the training cycle, there were serious limitations hampering execution of the program right from the start. A proper evaluation of the Army's showing in Korea at the outset ought not be made until due consideration is given to (1) the caliber of manpower present for duty and (2) the quality of training facilities available in Japan for Occupation troop use.

Basic to any army's success is the trained ability of the common soldier, the man who fires a rifle, pulls a lanyard, repairs a truck, or climbs a pole. The enlistee or draftee must become a skilled participant on the battlefield regardless of unaccommodating circumstances. No army can expect to engage in sustained operations successfully over a period of time without such men at the zenith of preparedness.

However, an army can give a fairly respectable account of itself initially if manpower is present in minimally acceptable quantities and better than half-trained. The abrupt baptism of combat motivates all but the most recalcitrant or weak to hastily complete the learning process. Such was the case during WWII when many fillers reached the fighting fronts directly from replacement training centers.

But WWII was unusual in that, it being a total war, manpower was drafted without predilection, the best along with the worst and all that lay between. The end result was a higher-than-normal proficiency in most every unit activated. Because this was so, the end of fighting was a tragedy for the Army. During the four years that followed, that service was virtually unable to attract outstanding men to its ranks.[2]

Contributory to this state of affairs was the roar of damnation voiced by countless ex-Army GIs when recounting their service experiences. A not-unexpected result was that many young men, hearing tales of woe and snafu from elder brothers, uncles, and cousins, felt that a hitch or career in the Army was a circumstance to be avoided at all costs.

By the spring of 1949, it was apparent to everyone that Army combat units were receiving a decreasing number of high school graduates. Educated youngsters, not culled out at Army or corps levels, were often detached somewhere prior to their reaching a company or battery. In fact, any enlistee with two years of high school and a reasonable Army General Classification Test (AGCT) score was usually earmarked for future responsibility and ordered to school for further training.

This is not to say that poor education is generally synonymous with inferior fighting ability. Indeed, many of the early (and often anonymous) heroes of the Korean fighting were young men with limited formal education. Native intelligence plays a greater role in the development of combat proficiency than most realize.

The real problem relative to manpower training during the pre-Korean Conflict period, and which emerged as troublesome in the early stages of the war, was the lack of qualified candidates for noncommissioned officer leadership among the enlistees of the period. Unlike the 1930s when men of average to poor formal education experiences but of fair intelligence were forced into the service out of economic necessity, becoming highly competent leadership cadre during the Army's expansion of 1939 *ff*, post-WWII saw a similar American remaining in civilian status taking advantage of the economic boom. As a result, although one might suggest that the post-WWII enlistee had a higher number of formal school years completed than was the case with his 1930s predecessor, a close observer might also discover that the native intelligence factor was not as high. In consequence, the demanding qualities of being articulate, the ability to deal with technical problems successfully, and a basic individual ruggedness of expectation, all requisites to the development of noncommissioned officer leadership, were not found in quantity within the 1946–50 enlistee group.

In addition to all of the above, it was also apparent that many enlistees of this period were products of less-than-complete home environments. In many homes, father was either in the service or working war plant shifts. Mother, also, was working, at least until VJ Day. What resulted for many was limited or, in the extreme, absent home supervision. Given the above, it would seem reasonable to argue that maturing boys, subject to lax home conditioning, might effect a failing, antagonistic complex, first at school, then within the community, eventually arriving at the door of a service recruiting office seeking entrance to that last economic refuge, one or the other of the armed services.

While it is always dangerous to generalize, much might be said for the conclusion that many enlistees of the 1946–50 period, suffering from a lack of moral nourishment at home, unable to find a niche in the civilian employment sector, and, later, drugged by an admittedly sensuous Japanese Occupation climate, proved poor matches initially, man for man, against soldiers of the North Korean Army.

Japan is a heavily populated nation. Dictates of both demographic and dietetic necessities, plus the age-old concept of land being the most important gauge of wealth, motivated the Japanese to carve out all accessible, productable soil. These motivations posed problems for Occupation forces when they acted to acquire land for military training sites. The Army could obtain abandoned Japanese military structural locations well enough, but larger land areas were needed for training purposes. Yet the political practicalities of coexistence demanded care and hesitation on the part of the Americans, so that in contrast to the easier availability of training and maneuver areas in the continental United States, sites for training and maneuver in Japan for combat units were severely limited.

The 11th Airborne Division Artillery, which initially had been based in northern Honshu, preempted a former Japanese naval air training station at Jinmachi and renamed the station Camp Younghans. A tract of mountainous land was requisitioned for training purposes near the village of Tateoka, about ten miles from Younghans. The artillery range actually was the near side of a mountain, but additional land beyond was included so as to limit damage to civilians and/or their property in case of observer or howitzer crew errors.

Four firing batteries could be accommodated within the surveyed limits of the designated points of fire. Maneuver to alternate positions was extremely limited, however. The requisitioning of both the range and the howitzer firing positions was recorded as war reparations, the Japanese government settling with the local residents as to compensation. All seemed well on the surface.

However, local farmers, planting their grain where able, often encroached on howitzer position areas. There were instances when the trucks and howitzers wheeled into a position lightly covered with new-grown grain stalks. Families often stood by, conveniently appearing as if they now faced starvation. So except for certain special tactical problems, held mostly during the nongrowing or winter periods, firing batteries occupied positions carefully and limited movement so as not to stir unnecessary local hostility.

Limitations in training space affected battalion and regimental operations. Battalion tests for the 7th Division Artillery were conducted at a site one hundred and fifty miles to the south, at Camp Weir. The First Cavalry and 25th Divisions were in better shape training-wise due to their close proximity to the Fuji maneuver area, a site that could accommodate a full division. The 24th Infantry Division had a central maneuver spot known as Mori which it used extensively, especially for artillery firing. The 7th Division had no central maneuver site, perhaps accounting for the fact that it would be the last division committed in Korea and then only after it had trained at some length of time at Fuji with many new personnel and Korean augmentations.

The matter of tank training and use deserves some mention here also. Much was made early in the Korean fighting of the imbalance in tank size as employed by American and NK (North Korean) forces. Where the latter suddenly confronted the Americans with Soviet-made T-34 medium tanks of thirty-plus tons, the best the Americans could muster was the light M-24 Chaffee, an eighteen-ton full-track vehicle. Why the disparity?

Actually, the American Army was not unprepared respecting the use of tanks in Asian warfare. The topography of large areas in the Far East dictates the employment of light vehicles for military purposes. Bridges were often infirm and roads narrow (1945–50 period).[3] Many rail tunnels were not wide enough to permit even the transport by rail of the M-24s. The larger, heavier Shermans and Pershings were not transportable at all by rail in Japan. Chaffee tanks available to the Occupation were kept close to maneuver areas or at camp tank parks. That the NK would use medium tanks in Korea, and successfully at first, was shocking to the defenders, particularly so considering the mountainous terrain and the deeply irrigated rice paddies that normally tend to keep such vehicles road bound.

One could say that the Chaffee tanks were not tanks at all in the conventional sense but converted WWII tank-destroyers. The overall design resembled closely the lightly armored M- 18 gun carriage developed late in that war to provide tank destroyer units with speed, maneuverability, and fire power, the first two characteristics lacking in the mainline TD vehicle, the heavier M-10 gun carriage. The fact that the M-18 turret was closed rather than open made its transformation to tank status a reality.

The Chaffee tanks were speedy and highly maneuverable, ideal for battle reconnaissance and peacetime needs. Not so much the tank-destroyer motto of "Seek, Strike, and Destroy," but the GI-inspired suffix, "and get the hell out of there," served well for those manning this particular vehicle during the early Korean action.

The M-24 was designed to oppose infantry assault troops and enemy wheeled and other light vehicles, but not designed to slug it out with medium or heavy tanks for a period of time from a parked position. It could fire a first shot, of course, but would have to move hastily to another vantage point before an enemy shell found its mark. Its armor, 12-38 mm, was an eggshell compared to the Sherman models: 12-108 mm.[4] The Chaffee was really effective only in quick-strike operations, and its availability to fight another day was dependent on how swiftly it could be moved to alternate positioning.

Finally, personal approach or attitude ought to be considered as a training limitation throughout the Eighth Army as existing prior to the outbreak of war in Korea. The most severe criticism leveled against the men comprising the Army has been that they were psychologically unprepared for fighting. This criticism is probably more correct than not. There was present in the Eighth Army the ability to fight, but not the will. There was no feeling for war. There was nothing of the hatred and strength of purpose which directed pre-Conflict orientation or propaganda campaigns can instill.

Additionally, the invincibility of American armed might during WWII had been stressed so intensely that the postwar soldier, feeling as a superior species in a superior army, did not always apply the vigor necessary to maintain battle-tested techniques and procedures. It is small wonder, then, that these same soldiers reacted with shock when the hitherto despised, scrubby, ill-educated NK came on to kill and continue killing until the Americans began thinking the unthinkable: the possibility of being pushed off the Korean peninsula.

Many in the Occupation force in Japan had been subjected to negative conditioning by soldiers returning from duty in Korea. Tales of filthy, substandard living conditions in the Korean countryside and of rank thievery in the cities prompted many to despise Koreans as inferior and their nation as not worth becoming upset over. The general attitude of the Japanese was little help. To these, Koreans were still the subject people. And so, admiring Japanese energy and taken by their outwardly demonstrated friendly and cooperative mask, and lacking any counteractive experience or guidance, the average Occupation soldier absorbed similar prejudices.

The fact that the Army limited commissioned duty in Korea to an eighteen-month tour seemed to be an official endorsement of negative attitudes. Transfers to Korea from Japan during the early Occupation period were considered in the manner of being punished or exiled. A chalked message on a blackboard in one of the transient officers' billets at the Zama replacement depot read: "Fear only three things: Gonorrhea, Diarrhea and Korea." Could a last-minute indoctrination, positive in nature, given as troop-carrying planes and LSTs left Japan's shores for the fighting area, have served to counteract some of this negative conditioning? It is doubtful.

Many among the first units in the Korean fighting assumed they would be treated at least minimally well should they become prisoners of war. This feeling no doubt prompted some to give up easily during the first few days of combat when faced with overwhelming odds. Only when word began passing that prisoners faced unreasonable brutality by their NK captors did the majority hesitate to surrender but found it expedient to leave engagement sectors earlier than tactically justified simply to avoid capture. The shock that registered when most realized that hope of remaining alive was more aligned with the concept of retreat than with remaining on the line was something to behold. Many found it difficult to adjust to this "no quarter" experience. Adjustment came ultimately, but not immediately.

The presence of civilian dependents in significant numbers in Japan also contributed to the negative conditioning of Occupation forces. Married officers and NCOs of the top three grades were permitted wives and children with them. So it was natural, as a result, that the lower unblessed enlistee grades would seek local consolation and companionship. There was a substantial liaison among the latter with Japanese women. Many enlistees, for all practical purposes, were married to these girls. Native ceremonies were performed to the satisfaction of all concerned. Evening *retreat* at many posts marked the escape home by many men of all enlisted ranks.

The upshot was, when the first divisions left Japan for Korea, it was as if a considerable number of men were suddenly dragged from their firesides to fight in a country and for a purpose, both of which had not the slightest bearing on their personal lives and immediate happiness. The first troops in Korea generally carried with them more thoughts of returning than of fighting, let alone dying for a cause that interested them not at all, however noble that cause was to Americans back home. Had North Korea not attacked until 1951, it is conceivable that the stepped-up training and maneuver program would have done much to offset this sensuous Occupation atmosphere.

Had some of the muscle really been cut from the Army by the unit reduction program of 1949? The answer must be "Yes," and spoken in the aftermath of the first thirty days of fighting in Korea. A full battalion of infantry was missing from each of three regiments in the 24th Division. Lost, basically, were three rifle companies, a supporting weapons company, and a headquarters and service company per regiment. Additionally, a battery of light artillery (six howitzers) was missing from each of the three direct support artillery battalions as was one battery of medium artillery, again, six howitzers from the general support battalion.

While the overall tactical shortcoming in Korea was insufficient lateral extension (only the simultaneous commitment of five or six American divisions could have provided a stable lateral defense line), the immediate problem was *maintenance of depth*. Shattered infantry units need breathers, time to rest, regroup, and pick up replacements. A three-battalion regiment normally provides for such relief: two up and one back, as the saying goes. During the first few weeks of combat, whole regiments leapfrogged each other, much as battalions normally do, and the withdrawals, when they occurred, extended further than normal distances as a result. An additional battalion per regiment might have permitted a battle line to have been held longer and in a more stable manner, a reserve being continuously available.

Curiously, much of the criticism directed against the fat-paring operations related to officer reduction policies rather than to unit eliminations. A common feeling seems to exist that a service loses more when its officer corps is pruned than when a ship is mothballed or a unit deactivated. This is not necessarily the case. As every efficient business periodically lets out a certain number of executives to strengthen its management structure, so the armed forces regularly employ methods to weed out its officer layers to provide advancement opportunities for the more promising of its junior officers.

By midsummer of 1949, the Army finally came to grips with a disproportionate number of captains and field grade in the ranks. It had been hoped that the adoption of national service would enable the retention of these officers because of their generally invaluable experience and war records. But national service failed as a concept and enlisted recruiting lagged. With Congress in the mood to make further defense appropriations cuts, the Army adopted reduced tables of organization, triggering the officer reduction program. The basic aim of the thinning process was to arrive at a more realistic ratio of command and staff slots to the number of remaining active duty units.

There were two phases of this reduction program. As implemented by the Eighth Army, the first phase began with a directive calling on all commanding generals to prepare efficiency reports on all officers within their respective commands. These reports would then be forwarded to theatre commands for analysis and process. Within a month's time, certain officers were ordered to inactive status.

After action by the local theatre commander, these same reports were forwarded to Washington where, with considerably more data available, a second list, all army-wide, was prepared. Officers failing to make the cut under this second scrutiny were notified of their pending inactive status. By April 1950, the schedule of partial demobilization of officer personnel was completed.[5]

As is the case with similar regroupings everywhere, there were inequities. Bias of one sort or another was bound to creep in as a factor in the final determination of fitness. There were some very able officers cut through no fault of their own. In the long run, however, in view of understood commissioned overstrength, a certain weeding was necessary and was accomplished.

Did this reduction program negatively affect the initial phase of the Korean Conflict? Not necessarily. (Lieutenant) grades 0-1 and 0-2 were less affected by the reductions, and these form the platoon leader and forward observer cores vital for combat success. That there were fewer of these grades in combat units when the war began was a concern either of regiment or division. Certain peacetime post positions overseas were filled by officers from the lower ranks, positions such as officers' club manager, special service slots, and the like. These positions were terminated immediately with the outbreak of war and the officers involved reassigned to their home units and primary specialties.

Did the officer reduction schedule mean that the Army permanently lost the services of the men affected? No, not entirely. Many reverted to enlisted status to retain continued medical benefits and retirement rights for themselves and for their families. Later, within a month or so after the conflict began, those who had held company grade rank prior to being cut were granted the opportunity to reapply for commissions. Few turned down this chance. Of course, some left the service, cutting ties completely.

To capsule, then, it was apparent that the Eighth United States Army, the occupying force in Japan at the outbreak of the Korean Conflict, seemed in the same relative position of a giant who, roused from a lengthy, almost drugged sleep, managed to gain a kneeling posture, barely commencing to stretch and to flex muscles in a minimally effective manner, when set upon in mortal combat. The ensuing struggle, considerably and unfortunately, at least in the initial stages, marred the military prestige of the American nation.

It Begins

It was a few minutes before 1400 hours on the afternoon of June 25, 1950, a Sunday. Warm mists of precipitation curled about the barracks and training fields at Camp McGill, a few miles from the city and naval port of Yokosuka, Japan, and some thirty-plus miles south of Tokyo.

Resting peacefully after a heavy noon meal were elements of the 5th Cavalry Regiment, First Cavalry Division, the 19th RCT, 24th Infantry Division, and the 32nd RCT, 7th Infantry Division. The latter two regimental combat teams had arrived but two weeks previous to undergo the amphibious phase of their training cycles.

In a large room of one of the several bachelor officers' quarters in the camp, several officers assigned to the 48th Field Artillery Battalion were quietly stirring as if in agony over the question whether to rise and go out into the mist or drift off to sleep again. The effort to get up seemed almost too much what with the soft tapping of raindrops on the tiled roof acting as a catalyst to induce continued relaxation.

Finally, one of the officers, a second lieutenant, yawned plaintively and then, reaching out, flipped a radio switch for the Armed Forces Radio Station, Tokyo. The program in progress was largely incomprehensible for the moment. Then a clear announcement was heard:

> "General MacArthur's headquarters announced this morning that about 0500 hours, Tokyo time, a violation of the northern border of South Korea by elements of the North Korean Peoples' Army was reported. It is not known whether any penetration of the border occurred, but unofficial sources claim that Kaesong, a South Korean city in the western sector of the 38th Parallel, has fallen. Heavy fighting is said to be taking place in several areas along the border between the two nations."[1]

The other officers in the barracks room were awake by the time the announcement ended. One or two grunted and noisily rolled over to continue their rest.

The Lieutenant switched off the radio and rose to dress. In a moment he had buttoned his raincoat and put on his garrison hat. Without so much as a glance at the others, he walked quietly from the room, closing the door softly behind him.

Misty dew dampened his face as he set a course for his parked jeep. *It's a lousy day*, he thought, frowning. A drive to Tokyo was out. Maybe he could wheel to Yokosuka. Damn.... He would be in this camp six more weeks.... Plenty of time remained for Tokyo.

Moisture began to seep down the back of his neck, and he quickened his pace.

With Bated Breath

The first few days of fighting, now that the so-called "border violation" was perceived to be a full-fledged invasion by the northern communist army, went badly for the South Koreans. After some counter-blows by the republic troops, notably by the 17th Republic of Korea Regiment, engagements that were publicized as somewhat successful, the defenders began falling back in disorder all along the front.

By the evening of the twenty-seventh, it was evident that the fall of Seoul, the capital, was but a matter of hours. Well-planned NK amphibious sallies along the east coast to the rear of ROK units limited resistance on the main coastal road. The NK army, it was projected, might soon commence a grand march along both the eastern coastal and central roads leading to the main southern port city of Pusan.

When the NK attack began, the ROK Army had eight infantry divisions comprising twenty-one regiments. An ROK division was somewhat smaller than the standard American division, there being fewer supporting units. There was also a cavalry regiment, many of the troops actually mounting horses, designed to provide flank security for units in combat. Other support bodies included six light artillery battalions (105-mm cannon howitzers) and twenty air trainers (ATs). No fighter planes (F-51 or F-80) were available to the Republic at the outset, nor was there any medium or heavy artillery.[1]

In short, the ROK Army had been organized along constabulary lines with no plans for making it an effective striking or all-purpose defense force. As their northern counterparts had done numerous times, the ROK Army constantly exhibited eagerness to attack. Fortunately, to the moment at least, the Republic's forces had been held in check to spare embarrassment to both the United States and the United Nations organization.

When the NK combatants moved on June 25, no one was quite sure of that army's strength. First reports indicated a highly mobile force in movement, a muster of well-trained and disciplined soldiers. Some Soviet propeller-driven support planes had been observed and recognized, and these were posing a threat to the evacuation of Seoul and other nearby population centers. There were also unconfirmed reports that a large number of medium tanks were being used by the NK to spearhead their drive south. If this latter was the case—and everyone was hoping it was not—the ROK defense might not be able to be maintained for long without outside assistance.

Rumors of all sorts began ricocheting among the Americans. First signs of troubled apprehension became audible on the twenty-seventh in the officers' mess and along enlisted chow lines. No one was as yet specifically aware of the cause of the outbreak of fighting, but a number, like the Lieutenant, who had been aboard the *Hase*, understood that both sides had been itching for a military struggle to finally determine total political control of the peninsula. The Lieutenant remembered particularly the South Korean official who implied strongly that war between the two governments in Korea was inevitable.

Some pause was given to the seeming coincidence of the NK attack with the visit to Japan of a number of high-ranking ROK Army officers. About six weeks previous, thirty-three officers arrived to begin a three-month visitation and inspection tour of American Occupation units.[2] The executive officer of a light artillery brigade, a Maj. Lee, had been a guest at Camp Younghans. A smiling, very likeable chap, Maj. Lee spent several weeks touring and observing training procedures.

On the date of the NK invasion, the major was at Camp Crawford in Hokkaido, visiting with the 57th Field Artillery. If the NK Army had wished to attack with considerable hope of instant success, a better time couldn't have been chosen, what with the absence of these key ROK officers. The officers were, of course, flown immediately back to South Korea.

In his musing about the coincidence, the Lieutenant recalled some comments made by Maj. Lee during the course of addressing an Officers' Call one afternoon at Camp Younghans. Lee's remarks focused mainly on weaponry.

Lee stressed the difficulties faced by the ROK Army respecting artillery. Medium (155-mm) and heavy (all mm above 155) artillery were nonexistent. The heaviest artillery available was the 105-mm (considered by the American Army as light direct support), and only six 105-mm howitzers were allocated per infantry regiment. This was in contrast to the American Army table of equipment, which called for an allocation of twelve howitzers per regimental combat team.

The howitzers given to the ROK Army were the smaller carriage type, officially termed the M-3, or cannons. These howitzers differed from the standard M-2 piece, used conventionally by the Americans, by shorter barrels and a shorter effective range.

Additionally, the South Koreans were given 75-mm pack howitzers, designed to be carried in sections by horses or mules, and 57-mm antitank guns. These latter had been deemed obsolete by the American Army very early during WWII, superseded by the three-inch or 76.2-mm barrels.

None of the above-mentioned weapons were present in the ROK Army in sufficient quantity, Lee reported, and the same held true for attendant ammunition.

In a summary statement, Maj. Lee warned the officers present that North Korea was preparing for war. "They are strong," he admitted, but "not as strong as we are." Further, he predicted, although the North might make initial gains should a conflict break out, the end would "never be in doubt."

The Lieutenant also recollected that very few Younghans' officers considered Lee's report and comments of serious portent. When the major left a short time later enroute to military bases on the island of Hokkaido, the significance of his Younghans visit had already begun to fade.

(It seems appropriate at this point to mention that neither the Lieutenant nor any with whom he came into contact in Japan were specifically aware of a so-called policy statement made by then-Secretary of State Dean Acheson that seemed to place South Korea outside the scope of American military support. Most knowledgeable individuals with whom the Lieutenant associated held that the North Korean People's Army (NKPA) attacked when militarily ready, taking into consideration the relatively weak state of both the ROK Army and the American Occupation divisions in Japan and the absence of key ROK Army officers who were, as detailed above, touring American Occupation facilities.

There are obviously other geo-political explanations holding validity as related to this discussion, and it is conceivable that Secretary Acheson's remarks gave the communist world added comfort when measuring the probable success factor. However, even without Acheson's remarks being considered, and hearkening once more to the atmosphere of extreme antipathy existing between the pair of Koreas, war probably would have broken out sooner or later. As one officer aptly put it, it was felt that South Korea could be conquered so quickly, what with the limitations placed on the security forces there that no country, the United States included, could possibly intervene in time to prevent the conquest.)

The often-buried assumed personal defense pact between Gen. Douglas MacArthur and the President of South Korea, Syngman Rhee, was exhumed once more, only this time none whispered "Humbug," so serious had the situation become. Some few were even noising the view that in the event of a major defeat for South Korea, the RCTs then in training at Camp McGill would embark immediately for the battle zone on the same ships that were being used for training.

Meanwhile, there was a brief run on the post library for books and other publications about Korea. As these were eagerly passed from hand to hand, the heretofore unaware began to absorb a clearer picture of Korea as a geographical entity and its relative position in the world community.

Those who read with historical perspective in mind discovered that Korea's culture is of direct consequence to its proximity with China. Korea had always been considered part of the Chinese empire, but was able to retain a semiautonomous position due in large part to its northern mountainous terrain and the general inaccessibility of the interior. Korea is a protégé of Chinese method and belief, with uniquely native innovations.

Japan first entered the Korean environment in 1522 when a somewhat brutal emperor named Hideyoshi embarked on an invasion of the Asian mainland. The invasion and subsequent occupation of Korea lasted only until 1528, but the experience was so threatening that, in mortal fear of further invasions and of the outside world in general, Korea withdrew from international contact and became the Hermit Kingdom. This isolation lasted until 1876 when, under pressure from the need of expansion to satisfy economic growth, Japan again forced open the Korean door. Japan continued as the dominant player in Korea's internal swirl until 1945.

Korean people are generally of a Mongol type with wide, flat faces, high cheekbones, and slightly almond eyes. North Koreans are a bit taller and whiter than their southern counterparts, a similar phenomenon occurring among the Japanese. The population figures showed an estimated total (1942) of 26,300,000 Koreans living throughout the peninsula.[3]

Korea is three-fourths mountainous, in similar respect to Japan, so that until 1900 at least, the nation was known as the most roadless, ground communication consisting mainly of footpaths and cart trails.

The South is more agricultural than the North, the latter having been developed by the Japanese into more of an industrial area because of the proximity of both raw materials and water.

There are few large cities, and most of these were so primarily because they served as control centers or judicial and legislative seats. Except in these larger communities, commonly accepted western conveniences were generally lacking.

Unusual interest was centered on the South Korean flag creation. The leading feature of the flag was a circular design comprising two perfectly mated outlines representing the primary forms of the world, the Yang and the Yin. The Yang and the Yin are the opposites of all things. The forms are colored red and blue. Four sets of three parallel bars in combination decorate the corners of the flag. These are derived from the Yang and the Yin and signify the four directions of the compass.

None reading these brief bits of geohistory, as one would a travel folder, felt any desire to "see Korea first," even as part of a noncombat stabilizing force, as some of the higher ranking officers were speculating would be formed. Shudders and twitches of uncertain anticipation were beginning to be noticeable as groups within the 32nd RCT sat about in bull sessions discussing probabilities. Fortunately for the state of mind, training continued as if no emergency was looming. In fact, after the initial surprise reports concerning the fighting, there were a number who dismissed the possibility of American troops being committed as not only unrealistic but impossible.

Meanwhile, American civilian refugees from South Korea, with some military aboard, began arriving at air bases in Kyushu and Honshu. Issues of the *Stars and Stripes*, the daily newspaper of record for the Occupation forces, were full of the experiences of these unfortunates. Some had been evacuated almost from under NK guns, having driven to Kimpo Field outside Seoul, and then running directly to waiting planes, car engines still idling. Most refugees carried only overnight necessities, leaving all else to the invader. The Lieutenant couldn't help but wonder, as he read the news releases, if among those being evacuated were some of the women and children who traveled aboard the *Hase* fourteen months previous in such a high state of excitement and relief at looking forward to being with husbands and fathers after a long absence. What now of these husbands?

Besides newsworthy evacuations from Seoul, other movements, of limited immediate news value but important to the state of affairs developing, were beginning. Route 1A south from Tokyo and every other major road used by the military in and around the Tokyo-Yokohama area were soon clogged with trucking. Heavy trailers, so-called "cattle hauler" trailers, low-boy trailers, and ordinary two-and-a-half-ton GI trucks were on the road moving supplies from ordnance depots and other warehouses to waiting ships and planes for ferrying to South Korean ports and airfields. This activity was in line with Gen. MacArthur's expressed desire that South Korea receive those supplies and materiel necessary and available to enable that nation to carry on with the defensive struggle. Ammunition, a critical item, was being flown over at this stage by a hurriedly organized airlift composed of all available cargo transports.

As a more rapid flow of developments swirled about the troops at Camp McGill, the general feeling was becoming one of hope that the supplies being furnished would be sufficient to bolster the retreating ROK army, making it possible for them to eventually mount victorious counterattacks. Many were reminded of a judgment made recently by someone of high rank that the 100,000-man South Korean Army was a first-rate ground army.[4]

There was a qualification to this judgment that did not reach the ears of some. The South Korean Army was, *relative to its size* the best, etc.[5] It seemed inconceivable that the force was being badly mauled in such a short time.

President Truman and his advisors must have recognized very early the seriousness of the situation because an announcement was made on Tuesday the twenty-seventh to the effect that American air and sea forces would be used to the fullest extent in support of the beleaguered South Koreans. If the Air Force and the Navy were to be so committed, the next logical step was the use of ground troops. The Occupation divisions waited with bated breath.

Suspension of amphibious training came suddenly on Wednesday. Without so much as a telephoned explanation, Navy and Marine instructors and support personnel departed to join their respective ships that were in the process of leaving Japanese ports to implement the president's administrative order.

With everybody at loose ends and waiting for something definitive to happen, someone called Camp Younghans. It was learned that the camp was in a highly nervous state. Northern Honshu's proximity to North Korea, plus the always anticipated possibility of a Soviet attack on the Japanese islands, had spurred camp authorities to place immediate emphasis on the safety of its civilian population. Evacuation plans had been dusted off, and several practice evacuations had already been executed. And rocket launchers (bazookas) had been mounted on the wings of small liaison/observation planes for defense against enemy fighters, should the latter appear over the camp.

Such panicky precautions were not apparent among the regiments and battalions at Camp McGill. Everyone sat tight, awaiting orders. Lt. Col. Joseph Massero, commanding the 48th Field, and his S-3, Maj. Lemuel Downs, huddled to complete plans for a possible return movement north. Lt. Col. Charles W.

Stratton of the 13th Field was presumed similarly engaged with his S-3, Maj. Leon B. Cheek, Jr.

Thursday, June 29, a rainy, terribly humid day, became the day of decision for the Eighth United States Army. Gen. MacArthur, disregarding poor flying conditions with an impetuous "We go," climbed into his plane and flew to Korea for a personal reconnaissance of the battle status. He landed at Suwon, thirty miles south of Seoul, and then motored north to Yongdungp'o, a city on the Han River just south of Seoul, where ROK forces were attempting to organize a defense line. Seoul was already in NK hands.

MacArthur first observed that not all available ROK troops were in the vicinity of the Han to man the new defense line. Hundreds were on the road south, either disengaged from the agonies of combat and preferring a defense line further south or perhaps desiring to wait a while longer before committing themselves to any combat at all. At the moment of his visit, with chaotic supply and communications efforts further hampering the South Koreans, the general recognized the situation for what it was—a rout. The Han River line could not be held. The line was already being flanked to the east. So secondly, he concluded coldly and dispassionately, only additional support in the form of ground forces would be of sufficient strength to contain the attacking NK.

Not one to be reticent about such matters, MacArthur confided to Marguerite Higgins, one of the correspondents accompanying him, that he would recommend to Washington that American Army divisions be immediately committed.[6] That this could be done was made clear by a special meeting of the United Nations Security Council the previous day. A resolution passed by that body called on all members of the United Nations to render every possible assistance in carrying out a cease-fire order. Correct interpretation of this resolution revealed the use of force as one measure of assistance.

And so, it happened. Gen. MacArthur's recommendation was approved. Orders arrived at Maj. Gen. William Dean's headquarters at Kokura, Japan, about midnight on the twenty-ninth. The entire 24th Infantry Division was to proceed to Korea without delay. Within minutes, messages were prepared for the camp commanders in the 24th Division Occupation zone: Camp Wood at Kunamoto; Camp Mower, outside of Sasebo; Camp Chickamauga at Beppu; and Camp Hakata at Fukuoka. It took slightly longer for the message to reach Camp McGill, but at about 0300 hours on the thirtieth, the men of the 19th RCT were called from their bunks to pack and entrain immediately for their home camps.

Until 0700 that morning, most of the rest of the men at Camp McGill were unaware of anything unusual happening. Then, acting on a rumor, the Lieutenant drove his jeep to the 13th Field bivouac area. It was entirely empty. He then drove to the camp RTO (Rail Transportation Office), and there he found the men of the 13th completing the lashing of equipment on flat cars. Other flats were being maneuvered into the rail yards, evidence of future rail movements. The men of the 19th Infantry Regiment had already left the RTO in coaches. The Lieutenant was able to speak briefly with Lt. Col. Stratton, who informed the Lieutenant that his battalion was on orders to go to Korea, as was the 19th Regiment and the rest of the division.

So now the question that heretofore had been on the minds of all the men in the Eighth Army was answered. Americans would be going to Korea to fight. That the first division to leave was the 24th seemed more a matter of geographical coincidence than demonstrated proficiency for combat operations. Officers sat in their CPs or orderly rooms in camps throughout Japan that morning and stared at the walls and floors. Little was said. What could be said? If the 24th was unable to stem the tide, another division would be sent. Which one? Maybe all would go. If geography continued to determine the order of commitment, the 7th Division would be the last called. This was a thought eagerly grasped by the men comprising the 32nd RCT at Camp McGill, but for some the comfort was short-lived.

About noon on that day, the telephone at the 48th Field headquarters rang, and the Camp Younghans' adjutant began speaking to an assistant adjutant with the 48th. The expression on the man's face told the story. It would be the beginning of many weeks and months of weary trial and agony for many; the beginning of the end for a few. The 24th Division was in dire need of filler officer and enlisted personnel, and until the remaining Occupation divisions were committed—if indeed this should happen—these latter would furnish needed manpower for the 24th to successfully carry out its mission.

The assistant adjutant finished talking and writing. He looked at the assembled headquarters staff. No word was spoken for a moment. Then, as the group knew he would yet hoped he would not, he began reading names. The combat pipeline had begun.

Pipeline

From the moment Maj. Gen. William Frishe Dean received his orders to the moment an infantryman in the First Battalion, 21st Infantry Regiment, fired the first shot in anger, there was no time to bring the 24th Division to a regular or wartime posture. Missing infantry battalions and artillery batteries were not restored. All that could be done in the few days of preparation and movement was to bring existing units to full authorized strength by use of filler personnel.

The immediate sources for these fillers were the three sister Occupation divisions. Within hours after the decision to commit, the Eighth Army imposed filler quotas of infantry and artillery officers and enlisted ranks on the First Cavalry, 25th and 7th Divisions, with emphasis on those whose military occupational specialties suggested company-level or battery-level training and experience and were currently performing duty on that level.

As it turned out, because of being in closer proximity to the 24th Division's home bases, the 25th Division became the major immediate supplier of fillers. The cavalry provided some additional men, as did the 32nd RCT at Camp McGill. The remaining elements of the 7th Division further north initially provided only a few. However, when that particular section of the pipeline began its rapid flow, valuable casualty replacements for units committed during the first days of fighting were gained. Later, when the 25th Division was about to be committed, the 7th became a prime source of fillers for that division.

The cavalry seemed not to have been cannibalized as were the other two divisions.[1] One apparent reason for this was the higher state of combat proficiency reached by that division, its proximity to excellent (by comparison) battalion and regimental-size training areas being major factors in this accomplishment. Also, constant stress on the cavalry being the "parade force" for both dignitaries and Japanese onlookers was a contributive incentive for the division's officers and enlisted men to look to their responsibilities with a greater degree of enthusiasm than was exhibited in the Occupation hinterlands.[2]

There had always been a certain amount of jealousy directed toward the cavalry during Occupation days. But the same might have been true respecting each of the other three divisions, had one or the other been stationed in and about the Kanto Plain. The cavalry, inhabitants of Camps Drake, Drew, McGill, and

Whittaker, "had it made," as those many outside the Tokyo hub constantly maintained. And the cavalry's continuous public relations struggle to present a hard-working, high-achievement, yet "one of the guys" image always had its detractors when one reflected upon that division's highly pretentious motto: The First Team.

It made little difference that the cavalry often struck back. Witness the following marching rhyme heard at Camp McGill as foot units from both the cavalry and the 19th Regiment passed each other on a road:

Up in the mountains, in relief,
We wipe our asses with a Taro Leaf[8]

Some of the more knowledgeable among the officer group held, and most probably correctly, that the cavalry was being kept as intact as possible for an impending, decisive operation, probably amphibious in nature, a theory that caused some chagrin on the part of others who now were being shuffled into the pipeline as quickly as it was possible to do so.

The three remaining combat divisions were not the only organizations called upon to provide fillers. Every separate unit or detachment throughout Japan felt the hand. Any officer or enlisted man with infantry or artillery training and who might be considered expendable was subject to orders as a combat filler or replacement. Many in these units, holding combat branch commissions or MOSs, had not seen line duty since arriving in Japan. These suddenly found themselves boarding the southbound Allied Express train to Kyushu within hours after the first call for fillers. Nor were officers and enlisted men in the Far East Command Headquarters and Eighth Army (EUSA) Headquarters immune.

In other words, in the early confusion, no one was really "safe." Even field grades, usually the last to feel the shake of the tree, were called upon due to last-minute organizational changes. Later, higher than normal casualties among officer grades saw a critical need for field grade replacements, the most publicized example being Brig. Gen, John Huston Church, from Gen. MacArthur's headquarters staff, as replacement commander of the 24th Infantry Division.

(This state of affairs would continue until the Pusan Perimeter was established, and then, with Stateside replacements filling the pipeline, stable wartime status returned to headquarters and service units, their officers and enlisted men remaining fairly secure from emergency combat drafts.)

A fairly large contingent of men from the 32nd RCT had been alerted for transfer and most left almost immediately, so that on Saturday evening, July 1, a full day after the alert, only three 48th Field officers boarded the southbound express at the Tokyo station. They were Capt. Paul J. Godsman, 1st Lt. John A. Anderson, and the Lieutenant. An officer from the cavalry, 2nd Lt. Arthur H. Books, joined the group. Books was late receiving his orders. Other cavalry fillers had left Tokyo the evening before. Destination for all was the city of Kokura, a large, primarily religious center in northern Kyushu, headquarters for the 24th Infantry Division.

The four reached Kokura on the evening of the third after a largely uneventful but very scenic train journey. They were met at the RTO by camp personnel and taken immediately to the replacement center, located within the division headquarters compound. On the way, the four learned that most of the division headquarters personnel had left for Korea that morning, that Maj. Gen. Dean had also gone, and that only a company of engineers, some military police, station complement, and replacement center personnel remained. The division stockade had been opened to permit most inmates, regardless of charge, to be returned to their respective units or become fillers elsewhere.

When the replacement center was reached, no "welcoming committee" was on hand to extend greetings. An orderly room sergeant casually suggested that the four go to the supply building and secure what necessary field equipment each presently lacked and would probably need.

The suggestion followed, the officers proceeded to the building, hoping to locate items such as field jackets and ponchos, items usually in short supply. They also would need steel helmets, helmet liners, carbines, and pistols, if the latter were in stock.

On arriving, they were taken aback at the sight of duffel bags full of clothing and other gear piled high, both inside and outside the small building. With a curt "Help yourself" from the sergeant in charge, the four began to pick over what once had been both government and personal property of scores of cavalry and 25th Division enlisted men who had already passed through this depot.

The usual army-issue clothing was here, of course, but so also were the knickknacks, keepsakes, and other residue of the Occupation. Pictures of American and Japanese girls, bamboo and leather goods, and assorted wrapped packages (giftwrap style) the latter to be taken home upon an enlistment expiration, all were present in profusion. Noted, also, was an occasional portrait painting of the soldier himself, a popular type of art in which so many Occupation youths delighted. It was clear that the men in transit brought all their belongings with them only to be told that except for combat equipment, personal clothing needed in the field, and assorted hygiene articles, gear so carefully toted to this building had to be left.

Now, gazing at the duffel piles, one beheld the work, the excitement, and the modest pleasures of Occupation duty scattered in debris. It could not be said that these men, young as most were, had not "lived." They had indeed "lived" as fully as their instincts and abilities permitted. But the immediate fruits of these experiences now lay in the gathering dust of this replacement center supply room. Unknowing at this moment, but clearer during the weeks and months to come, the passage of enlisted fillers through this typical but dank and dark supply room marked the beginning of the end of the Japanese Occupation.

With daylight of the fourth, Independence Day, the war picture was being clarified further. Camp Kokura had become Division Rear or Danger Rear, as the telephone code specified. Danger Forward had been established in the South Korean silk city of Taegon. Maj. Gen. Dean was organizing military strategy from his headquarters there.[4]

The 34th RCT, comprising the 34th Infantry Regiment and the 63rd Field Artillery Battalion, the first complete combat team to leave intact for the war zone, was, even at that moment, loading on trains at the South Korean port city of Pusan for movement north. A battalion of the 21st Infantry Regiment had been flown over earlier and, accompanied by A Battery, 52nd Field Artillery Battalion, was digging in on a hillside north of the town of Osan on the Taejon-Seoul highway.[5] The 19th RCT, having just returned from Camp McGill, was preparing for movement across the Tsushima Strait by LST.

While these activities occupied units of the division, the four officers sat at Camp Kokura awaiting further orders. While attending to such personal details as checking equipment, cleaning side arms, and writing letters, they learned of an unusual tragedy that had occurred just outside the camp the previous night. One of the stockade prisoners released from confinement had further been assigned to a remaining engineer company at the camp and was under area restriction. The soldier had broken restriction almost immediately. With a weapon he had managed to acquire, he invaded a Japanese dwelling, killing two of the inhabitants. Japanese police, arriving at the scene, managed to subdue the man and hold him for the military.

Since by moving but a few steps anywhere inside the replacement company area one could see the house wherein this act of depravity took place, an eerie quiet pervaded in that part of the camp's compound. The incident couldn't have happened at a more inopportune time. The majority of troops remaining in the camp were due to leave within hours, so that little time was left for the Americans as a group to demonstrate to the citizens of Kokura their own feelings of anger and dismay. Similar acts of violence had been committed in Japan by Americans during the years of the Occupation, mostly the result of imbibing too much native liquor or sake. Nevertheless, these were times when Americans needed the friendship of the Japanese people more than ever.

The Lieutenant soon learned that military authorities had promised unusually swift action in this case, a statement that went a long way toward mollifying the citizens of Kokura.

The sojourn at the replacement depot ended that afternoon. The four officers were given verbal orders to proceed immediately to Camp Hakata, headquarters of the 24th Division Artillery. The order seemed to mean that not all artillery units had left Kyushu and that there was a distinct possibility of being assigned prior to leaving for the battle zone. The four, now in fatigues, pistol belts, and boots and carrying side arms, entrained once more for a destination they now felt would be the end of the pipeline.

Camp Hakata bordered the city of Fukuoka, the nearest large port facility to Korea. This area, all of which originally was named Hakata, was the general invasion goal of the Mongols during the 13th Century when the *Kamikaze* nor Divine Wind blew to disrupt and destroy at least one of the attempts, thus preserving Japanese independence. A large naval station had been built near Fukuoka during WWII, a site now controlled by the American military and renamed Camp Hakata.

It was a warm, slightly foggy evening at Fukuoka when the four officers detrained. As most of the Hakata personnel were either enroute to Korea or leaving momentarily, the train was not met by any military. A call to the camp's headquarters elicited the reply that transportation would be forthcoming. With a few minutes to kill, the Lieutenant wandered out onto the main entranceway of the station and sat down on one of the steps.

Unlike in many American cities where, during preceding years, business enterprise began moving to the suburbs, the business shops in Japan were still centered about the local railroad station. Here in Fukuoka, as elsewhere in Japan, sake shops with their bright screen fronts, loud music issuing forth, offered diversion for the traveler, GI or Japanese. Gift stores and craft and clothing shops were just a few steps away. Marketing women, bustling along on their clogs, pausing now and then to bow and chat with neighbors and friends, predominated. Also, and creating noise and some disorder, were the three-wheeled motor carts dashing through the streets, scattering the unwary as the drivers, the really true race drivers in Japan, hurried about their errands.

A number of younger women were about too, some dressed immaculately in western garb. That most of those so clothed were friends of American soldiers was generally accepted. One thing about the Occupation GI; once he found a girl to his liking and the feeling was mutual, outwardly at least, nothing was too good for that girl in terms of clothing and standard jewelry.

Much was voiced among the Americans as to attitudes and expectations of American women vis-à-vis their Japanese counterparts. A generalization was often expressed that American girls expected showerings while Japan's maidens responded more surely to the receipt of necessities when offered as gifts. The reality, most agreed, was difference in form. Japanese women signaled needs and desires within a frankly romantic context, American women being less romantic and more forward. Thus, a second generalization was born, that Oriental women were superior to American women. Many an Occupation soldier upheld this second generalization as truth.

While the Lieutenant was musing, one girl detached herself from the evening throng and edged toward him, asking for cigarette. Without waiting for a pack to be produced, the girl moved closer and, in a whispery voice, invited him to share a "good time."

Now the expression "good time" was one of several standard gambits advanced by certain Japanese women to induce American soldiers into helping make a particular profession economically viable. Properly interpreted, one read the invitation as a two-fold one. It was either "long time," a hotel room, bath house, or the girl's cubicle where a pallet could be occupied at length and other activities generated; or "short time," again in the girl's room or in a vacant storeroom, but most likely in an alleyway somewhere behind a downtown building. A "short time" was most popular on weekday nights. A "long time" was preferred when the soldier was on a weekend or three-day pass.

Knowing that a laughing refusal might prolong her efforts, the Lieutenant resorted to gruffness, so the girl sauntered off in search of more amenable prey. She was gutsy, that one, because she knew that officers were forbidden to fraternize with Japanese women. However, her quest was understandable. Prostitutes at that time in Japan did not play for pleasure. Theirs was a serious business: to help fill the family larder or to augment work pay so as to attract a Japanese boy from a well-to-do family.

Suddenly, three Air Force transports roared over the city enroute to Atsugi Air Base not far away. The planes were returning from Korea. Realizing this, the Lieutenant's thoughts veered back to normal. Restlessness began to increase in anticipation of the still absent truck transportation. Then, just as he was about to suggest hiring a taxi, a three-quarter-ton truck pulled up. Duffel bags and lockers were loaded, and the four set off on the last leg of their journey.

Single officers or those married but unaccompanied by family were most fortunate at Camp Hakata. A large, two-story stone structure, erected originally for important Japanese naval rank, had been converted to a bachelor officers' quarters with attached bar and other recreational facilities. As the group had arrived at the camp in late evening, a duty officer, after taking names, directed the four to the BOQ and to report back in the morning. It was a simple task to find beds in the hotel-like interior as most of the officers billeted there had already departed. Once settled, the quartet wandered into the bar.

Most every officer left in camp and without dependents was in the BOQ bar that evening. The atmosphere was not unlike that on typical Saturday evenings at other Occupation posts except that fairly heavy drinking was in progress as the more than average number "Here's to you" salutations were downed. Although several women were observed in the club bar, the milieu was strictly male. Women, really, were as out of place this night as they would be later on the battlefield.

Perhaps it is being too psychological to use the term "escape" to describe what was happening, but any casual observer would be quick to note that, indeed, all involved were escaping, for the moment, the web of circumstance that had encompassed them all. The Lieutenant eventually would become acquainted with many of the men gathered there, but for the time being he was a stranger in their midst. Almost a stranger, that is. He headed for a telephone.

Back in October 1948, when Circular 330 was first published, another enlisted man at Fort George G. Meade along with the Lieutenant registered an interest in the commissioning program. He was Sgt. William J. Gibbons. Both Bill and the Lieutenant were enlisted assignees at Second Army Headquarters. The two even bunked in the same cadre room.

Both, ultimately, were commissioned and both chose artillery as a branch of service. They traveled together to Fort Sill and later sailed aboard the *Hase* to the Far East. Bill received assignment to the 24th Division while the Lieutenant went to the 7th. There had been a brief renewal of ties when the two met at Camp McGill, Bill being with the 13th Field, and now, on the eve of departure for Korea, this might be the last time for both.

The Lieutenant hesitated. Bill was a married man, living in the dependent area with his wife and young child. After all, with only hours until departure time for the thirteenth, would company be welcomed by a married couple? Oh well, he would take a chance. Bill could plead packing activity, and the hint would be taken and understood.

It was a pleasant visit. Ruth, Bill's wife, answered the phone and extended the invitation. Bill looked a bit weary at this hour, and no wonder. But such is the joy of married life. Beer was produced, and the three talked briefly of old times.

Inevitably, the conversation veered to the present. Bill volunteered a summary of opinion that had gained acceptance generally at Camp Hakata. No one expected the war to last any length of time. The moment our troops land, the NK would stop advancing. However, if by chance this did not happen, only a few weeks would pass until that army would be pushed back by our superior arms and air power. More particularly, we were being committed to boost the morale of the South Koreans.

As to the matter of personal preparations, Bill mentioned that he was taking fatigues and combat gear, also an old suitcase with two sets of khakis and several underwear changes. He expected to be gone no more than six weeks.

After but a short time, the Lieutenant caught the two looking at each other. It was time to leave. Love and devotion were overflowing, influenced by the rapidly approaching hour of departure. There were no cheery "Goodbyes" voiced, only "Take it easy" and "Keep in touch." The Lieutenant waved and then set his course for the BOQ.

The five-minute walk took the Lieutenant through a good portion of the officers' dependent area. Each occupied house was lighted in friendly fashion, conveying contentment to an outer world exhilarated by the warm, drifting, summer night air. Serenity, yes, but unreal. With absolutely no prior preparation and virtually no warning, one kisses wife and children "Goodbye," travels several hours by plane or boat, and then, upon landing, advances to mortal combat. The shock at this sudden turn of events, the Lieutenant had been given to understand, had unnerved some of the less stable among the dependents, and even at that very moment friends were gathered in some few homes to help ease troubled hearts.

The Lieutenant continued on. He began feeling a slight tug over the thought that, perhaps, within hours or days, there would be some now sitting behind the curtains of these brightly lit homes for whom the last moments of parting would become residual memory, permanently imprinted, the last clear reminder of a happiness never to be resumed. He kicked at the ground, trying to remove this speculation from his mind.

The next morning, July 5, the four reported to DivArty (Division Artillery) Headquarters. Anderson, because of his extensive motors experience, was selected to remain at Camp Hakata and assume command of the motor pool. The remaining three would be assigned later in Korea. DivArty was leaving Hakata that morning, so the needs of the support battalions could not be determined until after a Korean landing.

Meanwhile, the three would perform a chore of some importance. Additional weapons and prime movers were due at Camp Hakata from Kokura. These were 155-mm howitzers and M-4 tractors. They were destined for the 11th Field as replacement ordnance or, if losses proved negligible, become equipment for a third or C Battery. As the 11th Field was leaving Hakata that morning, and as none of their officers could remain at the camp, the three filler officers would take charge of the equipment upon arrival and load same aboard an LST leaving Fukuoka harbor that evening. Capt. Godsman would assume command of the LST until its scheduled docking at Pusan the following morning.

After issuing these instructions, the 24th DivArty ceased operations in Japan and, within hours, left for Korea. By noon on the fifth, Camp Hakata, except for dependents and station complement, was a deserted post.

Then, that afternoon, advance elements of the 25th Infantry Division arrived to begin a takeover of command and staff facilities. Their mission was obvious. Since that division's area of Occupation and associated defense centered on southern Honshu, north of the Shimonoseki Strait, its responsibilities were being extended temporarily while the 24th was tending to the Korean "police action." There was no inkling on this afternoon that the 25th, too, would go to Korea.

The arrival of the Lightning Division's advance party conveyed the impression that the 24th's mission was to be a temporary one, lending credence to Bill Gibbons's previous spoken thoughts on the matter. If the 25th was really slated for Korean action, that division's time and efforts would not be wasted in Kyushu. Morale among the dependents particularly lifted considerably that afternoon.

As the LST designated to carry ordnance equipment was to dock at 1900 hours, it was necessary to leave the camp area at least by 1800. A few minutes to that hour saw the arrival of a platoon of trucks from the division quartermaster company, each truck loaded with C-rations. The trucks, with trailers, would sail on the LST.

It was time to leave. The command to "Mount up" came from Capt. Godsman. With a roar of motors and yells of "Sayonara," the last Korean-bound 24th Infantry Division convoy moved toward the Camp Hakata main gate and the port of Fukuoka.

Kublai Khan in Reverse

The convoy moving toward Fukuoka stirred a tremendous dust cloud. It would have been bad enough had the column been composed of all wheeled vehicles, but the tracks of the prime movers pulling the heavy howitzers both dug and scattered the dirt along this unpaved road.

Japanese civilians hurried to the sides of the road to wave at the moving column. It was quite a relief to note the warmth displayed by these people, particularly after the dreadful incident at Kokura two days previous. Generally, it seemed, the Americans had made a fairly good impression here. There was, of course, wide word-of-mouth publicity given to the small criminal element within the Army. Yet most Japanese by now understood and were accepting of their Occupation status.

A cynical observation expressed by an individual later that evening and overheard by a number of men held that the real reason for the smiles and waves earlier was anticipation that the Occupation was approaching an end. Most who heard this remark were not convinced. The Japanese had no army at the moment. United States forces were the country's only protection. If Korea was lost, Japan would be that much more vulnerable to Soviet influence. Responsible Japanese were not looking forward yet to an end of the Occupation.[1]

At the moment, at least, there seemed to be intense satisfaction among the Japanese that the North Koreans were to become our adversary. The Japanese had always been contemptuous of the Korean, and a like feeling had been transplanted to many a GI. The burgeoning crisis at hand found both Japan and the United States on common ground in feeling toward North Korea, with the former indicating willingness to cooperate in any manner possible.

The Japanese-manned LST was waiting when the convoy arrived at the dock area. Also waiting was a small unit, the 442nd Counter Intelligence Corps team. Most of the men in this team were civilians, wearing military uniforms without insignia. An Army captain commanded the group.

Also waiting was the 24th Division Artillery Executive Officer, Col. James L. Beynon. Usual military procedure dictates that the executive officer accompany the extreme rear of the headquarters unit. In this instance, Col. Beynon's presence indicated that the group now embarking was to be the last divisional transport to the combat zone.

At the very last moment before departure, a jeep carrying John Rich, a reporter representing the International News Service, pulled up. Rich had just arrived from Tokyo to replace correspondent Frank Gibney, then listed as missing. Rich became the group's VIP, and all were glad he had chosen to travel by boat rather than by a short plane hop with the Air Force.

Loading took more time than expected, but by about 2100 hours everything was in readiness. Rich was already in his cabin, from which unmistakable sounds of a typewriter were heard. Col. Beynon turned over shipboard responsibilities to Capt. Godsman. The Japanese LST commander then gave orders to weigh anchor.

Shore lights were just beginning to blink over Hakata Bay as the LST slowly made its way toward Tsushima Strait. Squeezed between the ship's rail and a fender of a jeep chained on the top deck, the Lieutenant stood lost in thought. The full impact of his position was becoming clear at last. The trip through the pipeline had been so nonchalant that looming combat was all but forgotten. No sense of urgency or anguish had been felt.

Now, finally aboard this LST, with jeeps, trailers, howitzers, and trucks loaded with rations, reality had emerged. The other men, too, seemed in a similar frame of mind. Most of these were also along a rail, lighting up, saying little, and generally staring out onto the calm waters of the bay. The Lieutenant wondered what the men of Kublai Khan's armada thought as they approached Japan's shores centuries ago. The LST would pass over remnants of those ships, if any speck was yet extant deep in the mud and sand covering the floor of the strait. This craft was bound for the land of Kublai's preparations and a point of departure for his boats.

A bit of lightning flashed across the sky. It had been a hot day. The area was due for some cooling rain. As if these thoughts were a command, the bay seemed to take on a darker, more forbidding color. Perhaps a wind was stirring somewhere, a *kamikaze* perchance, just as happened in Kublai Khan's time.

The Lieutenant was still ruminating thusly when, with a slight roughening of the water, the LST cleared the bay and moved into the strait, twelve hours from the port city of Pusan and the Conflict.

ASSIGNMENT

SOMETIME ON THE MORNING OF JULY 5, PERHAPS AT THE VERY MOMENT THE THREE filler officers were being briefed concerning the LST movement, the first American soldier was killed during the course of an engagement with the NK Army at Sojong-ni, south of the town of Osan. He would not die in vain. Already others were moving up that dusty, pitted road north of Taejon, soon to demonstrate to the advancing invaders, by the shock of resolute battle, that a people must be permitted the right to retain an independent course of government.

Countless individuals had died within the span of human history endeavoring to achieve a self-determinate existence. Many more will sacrifice and be sacrificed in the millennia ahead. Significantly, that first American casualty symbolized a reaffirmation of the concept of unity, that a group of willing nations might join together to guarantee independence for another whose freedom is threatened by external forces. Kenneth Shadrick was the first American soldier to die under the banner of the United Nations in Korea, at the time the best assurance against external subjugation of free peoples.[1]

Now, the day after, the last units of the 24th Division approached the port of Pusan. The day dawned wet and windy. It had been exactly one week since Gen. MacArthur's visit to the battle-swept Han River area and his decision to recommend use of American troops. The weather, too, had come full circle. Rough seas in the strait had slowed the ship so that, instead of docking at 0700 hours on the sixth as planned, landing in early afternoon was projected. Seasickness had taken its toll. Most of the men, officers and enlisted together, became quite nauseated and sat or lay wherever. The Lieutenant had commanded the guard during the night, but, for all practical purposes, the guard was nonexistent.

With daylight, the men began to feel better. They came up onto the main deck, faces to the wind, to dissipate the sick feeling. The lurching and rolling of the LST became more rhythmic as the morning wore on and the waves subsided. Then, about noon, mountains were sighted and the jagged coastline of South Korea began to come rapidly into view.

No break could be discerned in the hilly coastal pattern at first, a pattern that seemed to jut out into the water and stretch every which way in crazy-quilt fashion. Soon, however, as the LST pitched closer, a definite cleavage appeared, and the outlines of a bay and adjoining city could be distinguished. Pusan had been reached.

The ship now glided into the harbor where other LSTs were moored. It soon became known that these, carrying the 11th and 13th Fields and the DivArty Headquarters, had also been held up by the storm, the units landing only that morning.

The Japanese captain, after a brief pause, steered the LST toward a concrete quay, aided by a large red marker some thirty-five yards or so inland. Then, with a scrape and a shudder, the LST came to a stop and anchored. With this, the 24th Infantry Division was wholly on Korean soil.

Once out on the quay and looking about, a dismal scene greeted everyone. Only a few buildings of any size were in evidence, and none of these showed signs of recent care. Two warehouses off to the left, probably erected by the Japanese, were the only visible maritime structures. A small Japanese freighter was docked next to one warehouse. It was the only ship in the harbor other than the LSTs.

One looked in vain for the stir of activity now that the Americans were committed. Preparations should have been underway to house supplies and improve the quay, the docks, and other port facilities. Little was being done. A few old laborers were digging what looked like postholes near the quay. The sight of this nothingness provoked a few Americans to spit derisively and turn away, muttering something about the "goddam gooks." Such was the landing at Pusan by some of the first American troops called to rescue the independence of South Korea.

Returning to the business at hand, Godsman gave the order to unload the ship. He had been briefed a few minutes earlier by a representative of the American Mission in Korea (AMIK), whose orange-colored jeep had been seen parked on the quay as the LST came to rest and anchored. The representative's job was to give the commanders of troops on the incoming LSTs information as to billets, available transportation north (or road details) and, finally, something about the military situation. In the case of this last LST, he merely provided direction for the vehicles.

During the unloading, a liaison officer from DivArty arrived and inquired about the filler officers, ordering them to report to the DivArty CP (command post) as soon as unloading was completed. It took only about fifteen minutes for the ship to empty and then, after signaling an "All Clear" to the Japanese crew, the three piled into waiting jeeps and headed to DivArty, a few hundred yards inland.

The first 24th Division Artillery Headquarters in Korea turned out to be a former Japanese Army compound. Several gray-brown concrete-plastered buildings comprised the extent of the billets and storage area. The facility was used at one time by elements of the American 6th Infantry Division during their Occupation stay in the vicinity and probably by some service troops during the evacuation of the 7th Infantry Division in latter 1948. Some ROK force trainees were billeted here now, drilling with U.S. Cal. .30 carbines. They seemed cheerful enough considering their immediate future and were friendly in their contacts with American servicemen.

38th Parallel
Kaesong
Seoul
Han R.
Inchon
Osan
Sojong-ni
Ch'onan
SOUTH
Chochiwon
RIVER
Kongju
Taejon
KUM
Nonsan
Kumsan
Yongdong
Kumch'on
KOREA
Naktong-ni
RIVER
Andong
Kunwi
PERIMETER
P'ohang-dong
Waegwan
Taegu
Kyongju
Kyongsan
Sangju
Hyonp'ung
Annui
Koch'ang
Kwanbin-ni
Ch'angnyong
Miryang
NAKTONG
PERIMETER
Yongsan
Chinju
Masan
Pusan
Hadong

Beyond the compound, on the bay side, was a rail line, along which several engines were engaged at shuttling small-size, four-wheel gondola and flat cars onto several sidings. Preparations were being made, obviously, for military units to load equipment for a trip north. One officer reminded an assembled group that one could conceivably board a passenger train in these yards and travel, without change, north into China, then the Soviet Union, across Siberia to Russia proper, eastern Europe, and then to Paris, the current military situation excepted, of course. Pusan to Paris rail service, for a short time, became a topic of idle conversation among the men lounging as a group inside the compound.

A remnant of the American Occupation was noted there in the compound. Empty tin cans were observed strung from barbed wire along the edges of the compound. It was explained that during the later stages of the Occupation, Americans endured considerable trouble with Koreans breaking into compounds to steal supplies and equipment. Harsh measures were often employed to stop these depredations. One warning device was the stringing of cans and unless the wind was gusting severely, a "tinkle" more often than not drew warning shots from a guard. The rusted cans had not been disturbed even though the Americans had been gone over eighteen months.

The afternoon still being a dreary one, the rainy spell not yet passing completely out over the strait, the men gathered about a huge fire in one of the compound yards. There they mingled and talked, some of what was anticipated, but mostly of WWII experiences, their immediate circumstances awakening fading memories. There was no loud or boisterous laughter or rhetoric. Conversation was mostly subdued, the voices of men trying hard to rationalize a situation full of apprehension and almost succeeding.

During the course of the chatting, the DivArty surgeon told the following story. A few days before, he had assisted in the examination of some soldiers leaving for the battle zone. One young GI approached the doc and told him he couldn't lower his arms, they being pressed against his chest as he walked. "Okay," the doc replied and began a normal examination, using his stethoscope. After nearly completing the routine, the doc made a sudden motion with his right hand in the direction of the boy's testicles. The boy shot his arms down just as quickly to protect them. "You passed," smiled the doc. "Next."

After a C-ration supper, Col. Beynon summoned the three filler officers to his temporary CP, which turned out to be a large window ledge in an inside corner of one of the buildings, there being no private rooms or furniture of any kind. He inquired as to the military specialties of each. None of the three had in his possession a personal 201 File in which was carried the Form 66 or record of previous service and assignment. Beynon was constrained to make assignment decisions based on brief interview.

After hearing from each, Beynon announced that Godsman and Books would remain with DivArty until needs of battalions already in the combat area could be determined. However, a vacancy in the 13th Field had just been reported, so the Lieutenant was assigned to that battalion. Beynon called his adjutant to arrange immediate transportation for the Lieutenant.

A brief word and handshakes comprised the "Goodbyes" among the three: no emotion, of course. The full impact of the Conflict was still not outwardly perceptible within the group debarking that afternoon.

A trip to the temporary billet of the 13th Field led through the main residential area of Pusan. The air had cooled slightly following the rain, although the humidity remained high. This latter condition helped waft acrid aromas peculiar to the Oriental manner of rural living.

Of the many references to Koreans made by returning servicemen, classic were tales of the putrescence that teemed wherever rural Koreans habitated. Particularly abhorrent was the widespread use of human manure as the common fertilizer. Although the Occupation soldier had become somewhat inured to the "odors of the evening," Japanese-style, the harsh raw odoriferousness of the Korean landscape was almost more than one could take at times, and on this particular evening the Lieutenant was somewhat sickened by the virility of it.

Adding to the generally dismal panorama of Korean life and society absorbed by the Lieutenant as his jeep sped through the streets was the grimy appearance of the garments worn by most Koreans, male and female. Tradition has it that the Korean male must have a clean white tunic every day. So through the centuries, the women of the families spent many late evening hours beating the husband's or father's clothing until the grime literally fled in agony, thus continuing to assure the male's community standing.

This evening, however, most tunics were of the dirty appearance, leading the Lieutenant to speculate whether the male was at last being toppled from his pinnacle by distaff resistance, or whether mother and daughters were just too tired these days to provide father with the spotless cloak of marital happiness and community success. Whatever the cause, men stood about in the streets smiling and waving, all wrapped in cloth seemingly blending in color with the earth at their feet.

In deference to the warmth, small children ran about clad in what might pass for short top blouses. The lower body remained open to the breeze, sunlight, and whatever else. Such scanty attire enabled these young ones to relieve themselves when either mood or nature dictated, and the sight of several doing just that in street gutters was not a little repugnant.

The smells, the dirt, and the teeming humanity that filled the streets this evening seemed to vindicate the "old hands" in their frequently expressed references to Korea as a questionable tour of duty.

(Yet, in all fairness, it ought to be noted that, while all of the above was apparent in varying degrees throughout the country, the first American contingent was decidedly prejudiced, having adopted returning soldiers' and Japanese intolerances toward both the Korean people and the land. Few of the Occupation force understood that the Japanese exploited Korea to an extreme, reducing that nation to a low pitch of economic degradation. Spirit and pride of the average Korean suffered as a result.

The Koreans resisted exploitation, of course, and their attitudes of resistance partially included a general disregard of acceptable moral and ethical standards.

As a result, this newly liberated people in 1945 found it difficult to adjust to roles of responsible behavior and leadership. In other words, it was impossible for the longest time for many Koreans to view American Occupation forces as different in experience from what was before. So habitual resistance continued, taking the form, as previously, of thievery and noncompliant approaches, to include basic sanitation and personal hygiene standards.

The American was often bitter in condemnation of the Korean, particularly for the thievery, and carried this dislike back to the States. What was not prominent and therefore little noticed by the average American soldier, was the small group of educated and group-oriented Koreans who had accepted and were practicing a generally Western ethical outlook. Having to deal daily with the sizeable common lot, the Americans evaluated accordingly. The first troops into 1950 Korea carried a similar evaluation.)

On the outskirts of Pusan, in a schoolhouse erected by the Japanese, ideal for a military command post because of an extensive, shrub-enclosed playground that now served as a motor pool, was located the 13th Field Artillery Battalion. The jeep driver stopped at the schoolhouse entrance, and the Lieutenant, pulling his V-pack beside him, stepped alone into the midst of a bustle of machines and men. He felt lost for a moment, a normal emotion, since the change from the familiar to the unfamiliar usually occasions some insecurity. In the service, security within an assigned unit is the prime goal.

While he was standing thus, an officer walked up, eyed him, and then, with outstretched hand, welcomed him.

"You a new officer here? I'm Dewey Coles. Bring your stuff on in and I'll introduce you around."

Feeling much better, the Lieutenant followed Coles into the building and into a room set aside as the operations center. There, several officers were at work over maps while others were standing and talking. No tension here, the Lieutenant thought. Second Lt. Coles led him to a major seated behind a small desk.

"Major, here is a new officer just reporting in."

With these words, conversation in the room virtually ceased. All eyes focused on the Lieutenant. Numbly, he stepped up to the desk and, in the best military manner he could muster, reported. Several seconds of silence followed as each man there took the measure of the newcomer. Then, as suddenly as it had begun, the silence ended and conversation buzzed once more.

The major introduced himself as Jack Kron, the battalion executive. An assignment sheet was produced and the following colloquy took place:

"What's your experience, Lieutenant?"

"Well, I've been an RO (reconnaissance and survey), an assistant exec (battery level), Ammo O (ammunition officer), and, of course an FO (forward observer)."

"Fine, an FO, just what we need. You go on down to A Battery and report as one of their observers. Good luck to you."

The Lieutenant saluted, turned heel, and left the CP with Coles. He doubted that Maj. Kron had heard him voice the other experience particulars.

Nevertheless, he was not really disappointed, as he understood that in the artillery, as in the infantry, new officers in combat situations are usually given line assignments to prove themselves before being tendered other, more choice positions. And, of course, as in many other occupations and professions, newcomers set off "bumping" maneuvers as they are positioned within tables of organization, effecting movement upward or outward of those previously assigned. So now the Lieutenant had reported and been assigned. The last hurdle was to become acquainted with his new organization.

Both lieutenants now made their way through the maze of vehicles to the A Battery CP. The CP turned out to be the front seat of a jeep. He was seated there, the CO, with his driver and another officer. The group looked up as the two officers approached.

Again the salute, and again the proper military manner of addressing a new commander. The CO dispensed with formalities in welcoming the Lieutenant into the fold. He introduced the other officer as 1st Lt. Robert L. "Tex" Fullen. Tex was, plainly, from Texas. He was a tall, somewhat lanky man, an ex-air corps officer who had desired a service career but could not undertake it until he transferred to an Army combat branch. Amenities over, it was recommended that the Lieutenant meet his observer section and see that all was in readiness for the morning.

The Lieutenant was anxious for this meeting in that, as an observer team would be very close, a certain apprehension always greeted a new member until he was accepted as a "regular." In this case the others would be accepting him not only as a "regular," but as one whose word was tantamount to command.

An artillery observer team operates on or near the front line, most normally with infantry. The team is attached to infantry and endures the dangers of front-line combat. Technically, the team is not under infantry jurisdiction to the point where it must perform rifle duty. However, cooperation is the key to infantry-artillery teamwork and success, and that observer group hewing closely to the infantry line commander's wishes and strategy is doing its job well.

Additionally, the artillery observer, the liaison between the men in his section and the infantry line commander, has the right to expect rigid obedience from his section members to all commands issued by him. Likewise, the same expectation dictated relationships between the infantry line commander and the observer and his section. As the ultimate success of the artillery group rested on the protection offered by the riflemen, the observer and his group cannot act independently and perform successfully the mission assigned it.

There was no cause for alarm. The section chief was Cpl. Columbus H. Thacker, a heavy-set and good-natured southerner from Maryville, Tennessee. Lum Thacker's stated ambition at the moment was a promotion so that his wife could join him in Japan following the Conflict. He assured the Lieutenant that all the section equipment was in the observer's jeep and ready for use.

Another southern boy in the group was Pfc. Charles Wallace of Hastings, Florida. Charles was only eighteen and had enlisted partly because an older brother and a sister both were in the service. He didn't plan on remaining longer than the three years of his enlistment. He was the radio operator, and his voice sounded good on the air, carrying a ring of authority, always an important qualification for the job.

The third soldier, the jeep driver, was a lad named JF Payne. The initials were really his first and middle names. A number from the south and southwest seem to be christened such. Payne hailed from Osceola, Missouri. He had volunteered for this assignment because observer missions were dangerous, and he liked being where danger was. He assured the Lieutenant that the assigned jeep was in perfect running order, it being one with very low mileage, and he promised to keep it that way throughout.

After speaking with Payne, the Lieutenant stood off by himself a short while to collect his thoughts and reflect over the day's happenings. He liked the observer team. Collectively, the group appeared, at first meeting, to measure up to the rather nebulous standard of common courage and efficiency. Now he pondered his immediate situation vis-à-vis informing his parents.

In letters written en route, he had not stated outright that his destination was Korea, but only that he had been transferred and for them not to worry. "Not to worry," or manifold variations of same, is perhaps the most overworked English language phrase during wartime. And, understandably, the recipient of such an admonition would begin to worry, sensing danger. In his pocket was a new letter headed "Somewhere in Korea." Receipt of this letter would make his circumstance official to his mother and father. There being no postage stamps available, and as it was too soon for free postage to be authorized by Congress, the men had been told to print "Postage Unavailable" on the envelope in place of a stamp and hope for passage through.

It was getting late. Movement north would begin tomorrow. Sleep was now of paramount importance.

The Lieutenant left the darkened motor pool and reentered the schoolhouse and into a room that passed for an auditorium where many in the battalion had gathered. Finding an open spot on the floor, he removed his fatigue jacket and lay down on a blanket and poncho, both contrived as a pallet. It would be a battle against group snoring, the stench of unwashed bodies, and the mosquitoes. He felt sure the mosquitoes would press their attacks without mercy.

The men were restless on their backs. One soldier muttered something loudly and stirred briefly, then sighed to sleep again. Home was far away, but for each, in this unpainted, odoriferous schoolhouse that night, home was closer in spirit than had been for many a previous month.

Moving Up

Writing in the Saturday Evening Post, correspondent Marguerite Higgins described the course of battle in Korea from June 25 through July 20 as a hit-and-run affair, the NK hitting and the ROK-American combination running.[1] There certainly was little need to conceal the manner used by the troops to break battle contact when such was prudent. It is not disgraceful to withdraw quickly when an escape by an individual soldier meant that reforming lines gained an additional rifle at a crucial defense point. NK agility and road mastery frequently did not permit the UN forces to withdraw by riding or marching in orderly fashion to a secondary defense line. Disengagement was often hasty, accomplished by pairs of strong, swift feet.

When Lt. Col. Charles B. Smith and his group of 21st Infantry were sent into the fray at Osan, it was felt that the mere sight of these Americans would translate into stiffened ROK resistance. The assertion that the ROK Army was the "best damned army" still lingered in the minds of some top brass. But the ROK retreat continued, and the NK, now brimful of confidence, quickly disposed of this initial American impediment.

NK assurance was no doubt disturbed somewhat when, on July 7, the 34th Infantry Regiment, supported by the 63rd Field Artillery Battalion, took a stand as the first complete combat team to face the onrushing northerners, allowing the 21st Regiment to withdraw through its lines. Division strategy was now focused. Regiments would leapfrog each other in delaying maneuvers until either the ROK Army could be bolstered sufficiently to hold a line or additional UN troops brought to bear.

Meanwhile, the 19th Regiment, whose motto was "First to Fight, Last to Quit," was preparing to move up and take its place on the line. Early on the morning of July 7, the artillery observers reported to regimental headquarters. The combat team had been alerted for a movement to Taegu, a strategic city about seventy miles north and west of Pusan and the hub of a major road net, from which pertinent battle assignments could be made. There was no immediate threat to that city, but intelligence reports had indicated that the NK might be in the process of splitting their main striking force so that any defensive relief unit had to be in a position to meet whichever NK drive posed the most dangerous to the American military effort. Thus the selection of Taegu as an ideal site for the positioning of a division reserve.

It was a foggy morning, the result of mist rising lazily from the dampness of the day before, and in the face of a sun that would soon radiate intense heat. The observer group, with 1st Lt. William A. Pate leading the three A Battery observer parties, and including the Lieutenant, and 2nd Lt. Charles T. Delorimier shepherding the three observer parties from B Battery, arrived at the regimental CP just as that building was being evacuated, regimental vehicles loaded with bedrolls and maps. The haze swirling about cloaked the men in a kind of eerie gray, contriving a pre-combat atmosphere as a much grimmer one than was the experience up to now.

The arrival of the artillerymen caught the regimental commander in the act of rolling up the last of his personal maps. The Lieutenant recognized the man from Camp McGill, a tall, youngish-looking man with gray fringes bordering an otherwise completely bald head and with a startlingly dignified bearing befitting his rank. The CO was Col. Guy S. Meloy, Jr.

Col. Meloy welcomed the observers, spoke a minute about the necessity of infantry-artillery cooperation, wished the group well, and then, as if in another world suddenly, abruptly turned away to occupy himself with other demands. The brief conference at an end, the observers saluted, turned heel, and left.

Outside the CP, the observers split. A Battery observers moved to the First Battalion CP while B Battery parties traveled to the Second Battalion. The command post for the First Battalion was nonexistent when the observer groups arrived. Orders had been issued for the battalion to leave at 0700, and it was then 0650. However, Pate managed to corner key staff officers for the moment and the observers were introduced.

As Col. Meloy had done, the First Battalion CO also emphasized the importance of artillery support for his men. But here, one received the impression that such support was to be considered necessary only because the manual prescribed it. The observers were warned not to risk casualties from friendly fire. In other words, when there is danger of hitting American troops, stop firing.

Later, after the conference ended, Fullen and the Lieutenant looked at each other and both spat in the dirt. Of course, there would be no friendly casualties, if such could be avoided. After all, the observers, too, would be on the line, and they certainly weren't going to commit deliberate suicide. Yet, in the course of an enemy attack, with infantry in danger of being overrun, if a curtain of artillery fire might save not only the position but the majority of men, what then? Would a few friendly casualties be worth it? The question remained unanswered for the moment, but the short meeting with the battalion CO was not a very auspicious beginning.

The plan of march to Taegu that morning called for an advance party traveling by road, of which the artillery would be a part, and a main infantry body going by rail. The advance group would take the east coastal road north and then, at the ancient imperial city of Kyongju, swing west toward Taegu. This routing, rather than over a more direct Pusan-Taegu highway, was chosen because ROK forces were having an extremely difficult time further north along this same coastal road. In the event of a major NK breakthrough or other dire emergency, the 13th Field would continue on to support the ROKs, at least temporarily, joining its supported infantry at Taegu at a later date. The column would be informed upon entering Kyongju if mission diversion was necessary.

At the IP (initial point of departure) finally, about a quarter-mile down the road, a sight greeted the observer parties that seemed as close a parallel to WWI and Paris taxicabs as could be imagined. Because the infantry service company trucks were loaded with ammunition and other supplies and no separate truck companies had as yet been transferred to Korea, the city of Pusan had been requisitioned to furnish such additional transportation as was needed for members of the advance party.

What was gathered was a collection of buses and trucks of such diversity that the scene could well have been staged by an ambitious producer in any movie lot. Yellow-colored buses of pre-1940 vintage and old, wobbly Japanese trucks, the latter left behind in 1945 when the Japanese Army folded its tents, were parked in motley array at a road intersection, their drivers jumping about, making last-minute adjustments to the moveable parts, mostly affecting the engines. To the dismay of the Americans, it seemed that none of the trucks and only a few of the buses would make the distance. GI drivers had already begun to appraise available space in their vehicles should stranded soldiers needed to be picked up along the way.[2]

There was little time to waste grumbling about these antiques that would form part of the convoy. In a short space, with all the men loaded, and a few grinning sheepishly as they waved to luckier comrades in the jeeps and three-quarter-tons, all vehicles began moving, if somewhat slowly and noisily.

A choking dust cloud began rising as the column wound its way through the outskirts of Pusan. Natives gathered along the streets and roads to cheer as the vehicles passed, making with what the Americans would soon come to know as the Korean symbol of encouragement: a circular motion of the right hand, ending with the pointing of a finger in the direction of north. The gesture would be repeated so often en route, as village after village was passed, that the ever word-resourceful GI began to reply, “You go. I’m tired.”

The Koreans were friendly enough throughout, and emotional highs were reached when the column passed schoolhouses with the children lined up along the road waving, cheering, and bowing, all in the same movement it seemed, and holding small handmade American flags. To these displays of friendship and gratitude the soldiers nobly responded, waving in return and tossing bits of candy and chewing gum. The motor march to Taegu was turning out to be a victory parade before the battle.

On the long drive to Taegu that day, several observations were imprinted in the minds of all who were part of that vehicle column. First, there was an awareness of the fierce hope aroused among the civilians as they watched the troops and vehicles pass. This had been the first such convoy seen by these villagers, the earlier units either having been flown over or moved north by rail, due to the necessity of getting those men to the front as quickly as possible. The almost fanatical cheering along the roadsides encountered by the Americans certainly was representative of a hope that NK forces would be stopped and the threat to South Korean independence erased.

Evidence of home defense activities was noted as the column progressed. Every hamlet of any size contained a police station and these, constructed originally of earth and stone, often with stiff plaster, had been lately reinforced with sod and timber. These were the village strongpoints. The police themselves were invariably in evidence, often in the vicinity of or supervising the construction of tank bypasses, where small stream bridges were deemed too hazardous for heavy vehicular traffic.

And then, Americans began to notice and become quite nettled about the fact that a fair number of able-bodied young men were either in the cheering ranks or working at bypass construction. It seemed to the Americans that, in the face of this a clearly demonstrated emergency, every eligible young man should be attached to an ROK fighting unit in some capacity. Muttering about this apparent malingering was heard the length of the convoy. Why should Americans be called upon to save South Korea when many Koreans appeared not to be interested in volunteering to save themselves? The enthusiastic cheering and waving by the populace soon began to take on the sound of jeering, or so it seemed. "Thank you for coming to fight our war for us," was the way one cynical GI interpreted the roadside commotions after having a bellyful of seeing native "shirkers" along the way. It would be some time before resentments aroused by certain sights and sounds along the road to Taegu that day would be dispelled.

In the middle of the afternoon, as the merciless sun was easing its ferocious glare and the men wearied almost to the point of sickness from the suffocating road dust, the convoy reached its destination, Taegu. That city at the time had a population of about 179,000. Besides its importance as a road net center, with associated trade and some manufacturing, Taegu was the primary university city of South Korea. Students were still walking about the campus when the Americans arrived, identified by the typical dress uniforms worn: dark jumpers by the girls and black tunics and caps by the boys. Although the school had been closed since the invasion, the students seen probably were residents of northern communities overrun by the NK.

There was a large airfield on the outskirts of Taegu, built originally by the Japanese and operated later by Occupation forces. It had been little used of late. But now, with both Kimpo and Suwon airfields in enemy hands, the Taegu field, plus one at Taejon, loomed as the two preeminent bases for resupply and other tactical purposes. C-51 transports were seen parked near a small hangar as the convoy passed by. The Lieutenant soon learned that an engineer battalion was on its way, scheduled to arrive within hours to begin reworking the field for jet basing.

Of particular import was the fact that the entire South Korean combat Air Force of four planes was based at Taegu, the pilots undergoing last-minute tactical training before being committed. The planes were standard F-51s, propeller-driven craft of WWII vintage. As the Americans rode past the airfield, the Korean pilots were in the air, diving, circling, and performing all the basic maneuvers learned by fighter pilots before being pronounced fit to tangle with enemy pilots of similar training. (As it turned out, these four planes would be the first *and* last fighters given to Korean pilots until later in the war.)

The 19th RCT advance party halted finally in front of a group of school buildings on the Taegu University campus. The Lieutenant was relieved to hear that the 13th Field had been assigned a building with a leak-proof roof and a good solid floor. But no sooner had he dismounted from his jeep and begun stretching his legs when 1st Lt. Pate walked up and announced that the observers and their parties would leave immediately for the infantry bivouac and remain there. With disappointed glances at luckier comrades, A Battery observers started toward the outskirts of the city. The infantry could always be counted on to organize a pup-tent camp, and this last opportunity would not be overlooked.

Happily, such dread was unnecessary at this time. When the First Battalion bivouac area was reached, a Quonset hut cantonment, a remnant of the American Occupation, built on a small plateau halfway up the side of a mountain, was to be the infantry camp site during this stop.

The Americans would not be alone here. Some ROK soldiers were moving about, members of the ROK 3rd Division Ordnance Company. That division had been assigned to the Taegu area prior to hostilities, and these men were now engaged in the job of repairing several of that division's pitifully limited allotment of vehicles.

The infantry kitchens arrived within a short time, and cooks and KPs began rattling pots and pans preparatory to serving the evening meal. Relieved but tired, the observer parties lay down by their jeeps to await the main infantry body.

The First Battalion, 19th Infantry Regiment, comprised about nine hundred officers and enlisted when it debarked at Pusan on July 5. If its C Company was any guide, each rifle company (there were three) contained close to one hundred and sixty enlisted men and six officers.[3] Each company had three rifle platoons plus a small mortar and machine gun section and the headquarters. The men were conventionally armed, the weapon of size being the 2.36 rocket launcher. None of the companies had the 57-mm recoilless rifle. The recoilless rifles were only just beginning to be standard issue in the Army at that time.

The 19th had had some maneuver experience prior to this commitment. It had completed RCT training and was undergoing amphibious training when hostilities broke out. Its home camp in Japan was Camp Chickamauga, at Beppu, Kyushu, some sixty miles from the Mori training area. Aside from its officers, it was doubtful if over three percent of C Company and perhaps ten percent of the entire regiment had combat experience, rear echelon duty excluded. It was a combat green, not a poorly trained regiment that arrived at Taegu that day.

As the Lieutenant was a newcomer to the combat team, he had not had the opportunity to observe the several rifle companies as to organization and training and hence state a preference for assignment. Both Coles and Fullen had earlier made their choices known. The newcomer was left with C Company. Not that the Lieutenant minded. One company was as good as another at this late hour. He was musing about what sort of people the officers in that company might be when a haze of dust at the foot of the hill signaled the approach of the main body. He would soon know.

The Lieutenant rose and leaned against his jeep while the infantry groups dismounted and marched to their respective quarters. Then, apprehensive yet determined, he walked over to the newly established C Company CP hut and began to introduce himself.

Commanding C Company on its arrival in Korea was a first lieutenant, Henry T. MacGill. MacGill was a West Point graduate, a member of one of the war classes. Young, slight, almost teenage looking, he was yet wiry and athletic, a talented leader of infantry. His was a southern smile, a southern voice, and a personality that welcomed companionship. Most impressive was a vast store of directed energy in every motion and word, spelling added confidence in his role as a military leader.

After initial amenities, the two spoke briefly of artillery. MacGill considered artillery support very necessary and did not wince when the subject of close-in fire was mentioned. He would welcome, he said, any fire that would both protect and aid the company in taking an objective. The end justified the means always, he felt, in a combat situation.

Later on at chow, the Lieutenant met the other five officers. The extravert of the group was its executive, 1st Lt. Edward F. Aldridge. He was a wit, never missing an opportunity to twist a conversation into a joke or backfire against the other fellow. Second Lt. James Stavrakes, or the Greek, as he was wont to call himself, commanded the first platoon. Stavrakes had the bearing of a troop leader. Well-proportioned, brusque, with a dry humor, his dark features masked a devil-may-care attitude.

Second Lt. Thomas A. M. Maher, who looked like he had just slipped out of a college frat house for a breath of fresh air, what with crew cut and ready smile, was the friendliest. Maher commanded the second platoon. Second Lt. Augustus B. Orr, the youngest officer, quietly resolute, academically serious in approach, commanded the third platoon.

And then there was George A. Lowe, a filler officer from the 32nd Regiment at Camp McGill. George, a first lieutenant, had recently arrived from the States and was waiting assignment with the 32nd when the Conflict began. He was the oldest of the officers. A chain smoker, George spoke profusely about his wife and children back home. He joined the company as its mortar section leader.

Several of the platoon sergeants arrived at the CP after chow, and they and the officers discussed the next day's operations. The regiment was scheduled to continue on to Kumch'on, a strategic town about halfway between Taegu and Taejon, and bivouac there in anticipation of further NK maneuvering. Everyone would be up at 0500 hours, with breakfast at 0515.

Within an hour after the meeting, the camp was quiet. All took full advantage of scheduled rest to better prepare for an onslaught each felt was only a few days away.

Shadow Boxing

When the camp stirred the next morning, it was learned that the Second Battalion, bivouacked in another part of Taegu, had been routed out much earlier and was en route to the east coast, where the situation had deteriorated so badly that no one knew the proximity of the NK. ROK forces were being shunted in that direction, but the reformation of their lines was yet to be completed, hence the urgency in sending 19th Regiment troops. The battalion traveled without artillery, as it was thought any commitment would involve a roadblock maneuver only.

For the First Battalion, the same funny Japanese buses and trucks were waiting, and promptly at 0700 hours, the advance party convoy, including the observers, moved out, heading for Kumch'on. The artillery batteries would remain in Taegu in march-order condition, ready to travel in whichever direction there was need. Meanwhile, howitzer roadblocks were organized on the minor roads leading to the city, measures of security not only for the city proper but also for the all-important airfield.

Although a distance only of about forty miles, Kumch'on was not reached until 1300 that afternoon. Several delays were encountered. The road being the main central highway, a swelling flood of refugees in cars and trucks met the American convoy. Each Korean vehicle was jammed with people and belongings. At intervals, the road was blocked.

A number of the automobiles undoubtedly belonged to Americans forced to evacuate the Seoul vicinity by air. The trucks were either privately owned or were properties of municipalities now overrun. No one inquired, but the guessing was that the drivers of the trucks were local mayors or headmen, using their positions in this hour of need. RHIP (rank has its privileges) was the dominant ethic now for these people. These were the lucky ones. They had been able to travel far beyond the main body of refugees, the latter on foot or in carts, at the moment clogging roads into Taejon, the largest city between Taegu and the advancing NK.

Once, during this motor march, an enemy YAK fighter was sighted, and the column halted while preparations were made to fight it off. The plane veered away in the distance, fortunately, but the sight of it generated some restlessness among the men. On July 8, contrary to what was being reported as published back in the States, NK air threats were being taken very seriously.

One of the first reports to filter back on the fighting then raging further north concerned shortages of small arms ammunition. At first hearing, this was a ghastly situation, fraught with danger and disaster. However, after sober reflection, the cause was understood. The first units carried what is termed a *basic load*, but then could not themselves arrange for immediate resupply. Such arrangements had to be made on a higher staff level. So, as basic loads were depleted sooner than anticipated, shortages resulted. The supply airlift, at the moment, was giving priority to ammunition of all types, and just about every other plane arriving at the Taejon airfield carried ammunition of some caliber.

Movement of artillery ammunition, on the other hand, is a slow process because of the weight and bulk involved. As Japanese LSTs were then being utilized for ferrying troop units and accompanying equipment, bulk shipments had to be handled through normal Japanese port facilities and cargo ships, unloaded at Pusan, and then reloaded on rail cars for the trip to the front.

The first full trainload of such ammunition reached fighting units about the same time that the First Battalion was on the road to Kumch'on. From that time forward, such supply arrived in a steady stream. As it was, another trainload of 105-mm ammunition, packed in steel containers, passed the column on the way north and a cheer went up. Morale, hovering between fair and good, shot up to excellent. The men had seen an ammunition supply train. It was a much more confident group that entered Kumch'on that afternoon.

Just as the observer parties were turning off the main road at the outskirts of Kumch'on to the one leading to a bivouac, a troop and equipment train passed. The unit being carried was the 24th Division Artillery Headquarters. The Lieutenant recognized 2nd Lt. Books among the other officers aboard. As the unit passed, the Lieutenant wondered who, in the long run, would be the luckier, they or he? Odd that DivArty waited so long at Pusan before moving north.

The bivouac was reached. The advance party had located a large schoolhouse just outside Kumch'on on the Sangju road, and it was anticipated that the battalion would remain there temporarily. All would have the opportunity to sleep under a roof once more. Infantry normally prefer the outdoors due to the nature of the work, but when no danger is apparent, the roof is welcomed.

Most of the men began reconnoitering the building for quarters. First Lt. Pate walked over and inquired as to the observers' plans. The observers shrugged, but Fullen indicated he would sleep in the courtyard unless it rained. The others agreed to do the same. The observers then wandered to their respective infantry company CPs. The main body was just arriving.

With the arrival of the main body, rumors began anew. It was anticipated that the Second Battalion would rejoin the regiment the following day. ROK forces were said to be holding a fairly steady line to the northeast. The major NK attacks were continuing along the main Seoul-Taejon highway where American units were in position.

The reason DivArty was late moving north was to allow priority for movement of the 11th Field. It was hoped that their 155-mm howitzers could counteract some of the effectiveness of the NK tanks which, according to reports, were Soviet-built and mounting 85-mm guns. A direct hit by a medium artillery shell could disable a tank. The situation sounded better with each passing hour.

About 0400 hours the following morning, a sudden burst of activity in the schoolyard roused the observer parties. Truck motors revved and companies formed. Within the hour, the main infantry body left for Kumch'on's rail station en route back to Taegu.

The observers soon learned that a renewed drive by the NK down the east coast during the night had altered the previously planned course of action. The entire 19th Regiment was alerted for possible combat in support of ROK units in that sector. The former advance party convoy left Kumch'on for Taegu several hours later.

The trip back down the road proved bewildering to those natives who only the day before had cheered the march forward. The same cheering and waving groups stood along the road berms, but this time their voices lacked the ring of sincerity. Uncertainty hung like a pall through the course of the march, and occasionally a storekeeper or business owner could be seen scurrying about gathering supplies should a quick evacuation be necessary.

The psychological effect of this retrograde movement might have been limited had not a trainload of empty flat cars approached on the rail line just as the motor column began its march. It was not really an empty train. Every available space on the flats was taken by refugees from the north. Here was an American column returning without attempting to do battle, and there was another full trainload of refugees. The fainthearted among the South Koreans that morning fairly jumped up and down with anxiety.

Once more back in the Quonset area, Coles and the Lieutenant decided to search for a place to bathe, a real honest-to-goodness bath. Most of the men by this time were becoming used to the odors of their unwashed bodies. Few had bothered to clean themselves completely since arriving at Pusan. The fact that none of the bivouac areas thus far were located near streams contributed no small measure to this worsening of individual BO. Enough was enough, both agreed.

An American dependent housing compound was located a short distance from the bivouac, used recently by families of the American Mission in Korea group. The two decided to go there.

It was learned, upon inquiry, that the huts in the compound had only just been vacated, the families evacuated to Japan, and the men either with ROK forces or with government units. For a modest tip (a package of cigarettes), one of the Korean houseboys would be happy to build a fire and thus provide hot water. What was not anticipated was that each hut contained a real bathtub. The houseboy needed only to heat water, pour same into two tubs, and the two officers could soak and clean at leisure.

The two wasted little time supplying the tip so that, within an hour, both were luxuriating in a state of unrestrained relaxation. Without a doubt, the two officers were the most contented Americans in Korea that afternoon.

Later that evening, it was made known that the Second Battalion would positively rejoin the regiment the next day. The east coast NK drive had been slowed, mainly through efforts by the American Navy, which was shelling both road and rail lines in NK-held territory.

That the regiment would soon leave Taegu permanently was signaled by the presence of some high-ranking Eighth Army officers. These were observed walking from building to building on the university campus staking out areas and erecting signs. Eighth Army headquarters would be established here in a few days. No suntan uniforms here. Officers wore well-pressed fatigues and shoulder holsters for their .45 pistols. In the jargon of the line, Eighth Army "commandos" were getting their first taste of dirt, such as it was.

So once more, on July 10, the same convoy moved along the road toward Kumch'on, and between the same line of civilians, now welcoming this "new" advance with signs, some stretched high across the road, much like victory arches, and with texts: WELCOME UN TROOPS TO GLORIOUS VICTORY; KOREAN YOUNG MEN'S ASSOCIATION FOR VICTORY AGAINST COMMUNIST AGGRESSION; THANK YOU FOR COMING TO OUR ASSIST (sic); and, finally, one that reached the heights, or depths, if you prefer, of incongruity: WE HOPE YOU ENJOY STAY AND BRING VICTORY.

Never did the antics of military strategy induce ulcers in so many people as did the movements of the past several days, but this time it was felt, among all who comprehended the situation, that the 19th was finally headed toward a battle commitment. Viewing the crowds of Korean civilians again lining the road, the Americans continued to be delighted at the natives' show of confidence in their arms. However, the men were becoming more inured to the roadside demonstrations, turning now to contemplatively assessing themselves as living entities, each seeming to realize, finally, the approaching proximity of combat.

A quiet began to settle on the convoy as many began to reflect on the rumors and rumors of rumors just beginning to surface concerning NK treatment of prisoners. Unconsciously, each set about to measure his own chances of survival as opposed to those of the other guy.

The waving, cheering crowds along the roadway became more of a blur as the distance to the front lessened.

For Real

That commitment was near became definite when the main body of artillery arrived at the schoolhouse outside Kumch'on that night. The battalion had been given a scare on the way when an unidentified person fired on the column. The commanding officer, Lt. Col. Charles Stratton, radioed for assistance, and C Company was sent out on trucks to convoy the column the remainder of the distance. There was much excitement and apprehension as the outcome was awaited, but it soon developed that there was no cause for further alarm.

It seems that in every war a prelude incident affecting a unit about to be committed for the first time is the accidental shooting of a civilian or fellow soldier by an overly apprehensive guard. When the 87th Infantry Division was first committed in Europe during WWII, one of the first casualties was an officer, assigned several miles to the rear near division headquarters, fatally shot by a jittery guard. The guard had challenged the officer in late evening as the latter stepped outside a command post and, not sure of the response, fired. It was a needless killing, but one engendered through constant training which guards in combat situations must effect.

Near the schoolhouse that night, a similar tragedy occurred. A Korean civilian walking along the road in front of the schoolhouse was challenged. Not knowing what was expected and not understanding English, he was shot and killed by one of the American guards.

Perhaps, had the artillery not been fired upon earlier, the guard might have been less nervous and the man spared. As it was, as the units left the area the next morning, they passed by the house where the man had lived. The soldiers witnessed a bereaved family gather about a husband and father, preparing for his funeral. A woman, obviously the wife, was screaming and raging at the troops as they passed. No one smiled. Each was aware of the circumstances. It was one of those things. Nevertheless, few failed to harbor some guilt over the incident.

The regiment spent only one night outside Kumch'on. A battle had been fought at Ch'onan by the 34th Regiment, and overwhelming pressure from the NK had forced the regiment to withdraw south to the town of Kongju, a Kum River bridgehead, where it dug in for another stand.

The significance of the Ch'onan encounter was the realization that the NK had taken advantage of a split in the main Seoul-Pusan road just west of the town of Chonui and were sending forces down both the main north-south road of western Korea and the Seoul-Pusan road, the latter toward Choch'iwan and Taejon. The 34th Regiment had been tapped to meet the western flanking threat while the 21st Regiment withdrew slowly toward Choch'iwan.

The 21st, newly reinforced and now fighting as an undivided combat team, met the advancing NK at Choch'iwan, and the fiercest battle yet of the young conflict was fought there. The outcome was foregone. The Americans could not avoid flanking hits, and so, after suffering severe materiel losses, withdrew toward the Kum River, about twelve miles north of Taejon. Of the two regiments already committed, the 21st was the more in need of regrouping. Thus, it was decided that the 19th Regiment would replace the 21st on the Kum River line, the latter dug in behind a length of river dike. A final stop for the 19th, prior to commitment, would be the city of Taejon.

Before the column organized for the journey to Taejon that morning of the eleventh, an infantry sergeant from the 34th Regiment drove into the schoolyard. For the men in the yard, including the observer parties, the sergeant was the first contact with other committed units since landing at Pusan. The sergeant had come to Kumch'on looking for clothing supplies. He was not reticent about the fighting thus far as he knew it.

The NK, according to him, had had little trouble penetrating the American lines of defense. There were too few defenders per square yard, he said. And although the NK seemed not purposely to engage in flanking operations, the defending companies were being outflanked naturally during the course of each battle.

Some prisoners had been taken by both sides, he continued, but some Americans had been killed after being captured.[1] Further, at least to his knowledge, no wounded GI was known to have survived after falling into NK hands.

Many American wounded had to be left behind because of the impossibility of taking them out. If one was wounded early in an action, that person was lucky. If the wound was received late, rendering the man unable to walk, there was virtually no hope for his safety. This latter situation, continued the sergeant, seemed to generate panic among the infantry, particularly during the late stages of battle.

It was most fortunate that the sergeant's words did not reach the bulk of the regiment. Some deteriorating effect on morale might have resulted. As it was, only some infantry officers and artillery observer parties were privy to this recital. A rumor about prisoners being killed had already been whispered about at Taegu, a rumor now fast becoming fact. All who were in the yard that morning agreed. This was becoming a different kind of conflict; no quarter asked, none given. Long after the sergeant departed the little group in the yard remained huddled, analyzing his words and speculating on chances.

The motor movement to Taejon should have been a normal one. It wasn't. During its course, a battalion of artillerymen, many still in their teens, finally learned something of the combat maelstrom into which they were moving.

Almost near the town of Okang-ni, where the road narrows and winds about some particularly high hills, the advancing column encountered the 724th Ordnance Company on its way south, the first full division unit the men had seen since arriving in Korea. Because of the road conditions and ordnance wreckers temporarily blocking the road at intervals, the men of the two units began talking back and forth.

The ordnance men appeared generally to confirm the essence of the report offered by the 34th Regiment sergeant earlier that morning. The 52nd Field had suffered an overrun by the NK several days previous, and some of its personnel were killed or captured. Infantry, upon retaking part of the artillery position, discovered that several artillerymen had succumbed from unnatural violence. One of the victims was a young officer, known by most of the 13th officers but not known by the Lieutenant. Further, declared at least two ordnance men, the NK were advancing on Taejon and there seemed little in the way to stop them.

The raw details of this intelligence hit the artillerymen hard. There was, obviously, no way to substantiate the hearsay conveyed by the ordnance men, so all had to be taken at face, given the indisputable fact that the 724th had been near battle action while the men of the 13th had not.

And while the information passed by the ordnance outfit was certainly sobering, another occurrence on the way seemed to offer the proof that was lacking so far. As the column reached the outskirts of Taejon, an officer approached in a jeep, a friend of a number in the artillery convoy. He quickly confirmed what he understood happened in the positions occupied by the 52nd Field. The officer calling out this intelligence to his friends appearing to be an excitable type, his information was met with greater dismay than had been the case with the ordnance personnel.

Well, from this moment on, there was little joking or laughter within the ranks of the artillery column. It might be said that the men in the battalion, in terms of their immediate mission, "grew up" in the space of a few minutes. And further, whatever each individual's thoughts concerning this Conflict, prior to knowledge of these brutal occurrences, each now became conditioned to think of two actions only: fight, but stay clear of the enemy's reach.

It might be added that, unlike the relatively unsuspecting commitment experienced by the preceding combat teams, the 13th Field was being given the advantage of learning beforehand what might be expected once in a combat stance facing the oncoming NK. And although these two meetings along this stretch of the Seoul-Pusan highway constituted, brief as they were, the only mental conditioning for combat on the part of the fourth artillery battalion to be committed in the Korean Conflict, the impact of the conveyed intelligence was close to overwhelming. It was a totally grim column that entered Taejon that late afternoon of July 11.

Taejon, the largest city nearest the approaching NK force, was teeming with both residents and refugees. There was hope (there was always hope) that the Americans might now be able to hold a defense line. Just where, no one was prepared to say, but the refugees still managed to smile as they witnessed the arrival of new combat units. Familiar cheers and arm waving greeted the arrival of the artillerymen. Artillery was the main necessity at this stage of the conflict.

Maj. Gen. Dean passed in a jeep and gave the column a wave. But he looked drawn. The strain of the past few days was telling. Much had been lost.

Just outside Taejon, on the main road north, was situated the airfield with its rows of Quonset huts. The 19th RCT would stop there for the night.

Activity on the airfield occupied everyone's attention. The arriving transports, with supplies, were literally the lifeblood at the moment for continued combat resistance. Each airborne load transposed into another hour or so of defense by ground troops, American and ROK. The GIs sat about and watched the action much as hungry individuals peer into bakery windows.

Earlier that afternoon, as the motor column was winding its way toward Taejon, a train of flat cars jammed with vehicles, equipment, and men of an engineer unit passed by. Waves and shouts were exchanged by the two groups of men in a fervor of camaraderie not normally demonstrated in a battle zone. These were the early days, however, when each knew the other was arriving to help. The units were all as firemen, rushing not only to fight but to rescue the trapped as well. This mission of urgency was so well understood that service and unit animosities were absent entirely for the time being. Now, although having arrived but a few hours previous, the engineers were already moving about the airfield with their dozers and graders. They would work most of the night where they could.

The moment the 13th arrived at the airfield, kitchens began preparations for mess. Sfc. Antonio E. Lucero, A Battery mess steward, supervised the heating of C-rations. There would be one can of solid food and a B-can of crackers, gum, coffee, and cigarettes per man. There was no other food at this stage. The C-ration was a standard combat ration, improved from WWII preparations to include more solid varieties. However, at the moment in Korea, only WWII mixtures were provided as quartermaster warehouses in Japan were being emptied of these long-stored items.

After chow, groups of men gathered about the vehicles to talk. Tension was perceptible in every voice heard. Some soon began picking out soft spots on the turf for sleeping. The sky to the north was already black. That the NK were looking at the same sky not so many miles away caused tugs of apprehension for many. Shortly, only a few rattles from the kitchens could be heard. Several trucks raced in the distance and a shot pierced the hearing, probably a jittery guard.

Planes were still landing by 2100 hours, although it was almost too dark to fly safely. Korean trucks and laborers stood by to unload planes the moment they stopped on the runway. Several transports arrived at the last moment carrying replacements, mostly officers. The planes did not remain long. Unloading was accomplished quickly and ramps cleared for succeeding flights. About 2115 hours, all flying activity ceased.

With darkness complete, the Lieutenant pulled his poncho about himself and lay down, his head resting on a dispatch case. He felt for his Bible, which he carried in the left fatigue jacket pocket. It was slightly bulky, but its presence was reassuring. He wondered, while doing this, whether through a miracle every prayer being said by the men this night could be magnified in sound. The ensuing roar might be sufficient to drive the NK back north. He chuckled cynically, not at the sacrilege of his thoughts, but because there were so many at that moment learning to pray earnestly for the first time. There are no atheists in foxholes, someone had said. How true.

For a moment, he, too, considered how to pray. There seemed but one simple answer. "Have mercy on us." Here, one ought not pray for individual safety or deliverance; one prays for mercy for the group—for all. "Have mercy on *us.*"

Thus composed and at peace with himself, the Lieutenant fell asleep.

The Last Mile

Another hot, muggy sun burst over Korea the morning of July 12. The droning of incoming cargo planes had earlier broken the morning stillness, the first plane landing about 0520. F-51 fighters went up about 0545, their buzzing take-offs conveying a sense of confidence to many. The pilots of these planes, comprehending the plight of the ground units already committed, were bending every effort to help.

Artillery spotter planes were lining up and becoming airborne. These L-5s, the bane of the German Army during WWII, would soon become feared by the NK. The spotters were the eyes of friendly forces and harbingers of that deadly harvester of human fodder, the light howitzer.

During the first few minutes the Lieutenant spent watching the action at the runways, he witnessed a near tragedy. An L-5 began taxiing along a concrete strip toward the take-off position just as an F-51 was in the process of landing. Unaccountably, the L-5 pilot turned to cross the incoming runway in front of the landing F-51. The fighter pilot hit the throttle and attempted to pull up to avoid the spotter. He was successful, but, unfortunately, one of the F-51 wings touched the ground, throwing the plane off balance. The plane veered to the left and cartwheeled, pancaking on its belly. Then, as the Lieutenant watched openmouthed, the F-51 pilot climbed from the plane and waved. A thin column of smoke began rising from the engine. There being no fire apparatus on the field, the plane was left to burn.

Word went out from the 13th CP shortly after breakfast that a motor movement to the front would begin about 1300 hours. Voices became increasingly sharp as the excitement mounted. Men now were willing to work at any activity just to relieve the tension. Supervisory noncoms no longer needed to prod. Proper incentive to perform duties learned in training materialized without orders. There was no lack of elbow grease as the howitzer barrels were cleaned and oiled once more; no gripes heard about cleaning rifles or carbines. All were conscious of what every fighting man from the prehistoric to the modern had learned: Equipment in A-1 shape might spell the difference between individual survival and demise. Moving parts had to work properly from here on or else.

Satisfied that Thacker was seeing to the equipment and with Payne lubing the jeep, the Lieutenant wandered over to the CP.

The 13th officers had been briefed the evening prior concerning the general battle situation. A newly arrived filler from the cavalry, Capt. Coleman L. Prescott, appointed Battalion S-2 (Intelligence), was explicit, mincing few words. The main NK force was about thirty miles to the north and moving southward rapidly. A battle line had been established about twelve miles north of Taejon, where the main highway crosses the Kum River. The 34th Regiment was in position on the left at Kongju, while ROK forces were grouped somewhere on the right. The 19th RCT would move forward to relieve the 21st RCT, now in position along the Kum north of Taejon.

As to the matter of tanks, the 24th Tank Company had been in action three days, incurring some losses. The NK were using heavier tanks, the closest estimate of numbers being about one hundred. Most of these tanks were thought to be on the road beyond the position held by the 21st. The atmosphere around the CP after the briefing had been anything but jovial.

Now at the CP once more, the Lieutenant had occasion to meet officer observers from B Battery for the first time. Second Lt. Edward D. Nattras had been in the second SABAOC class at Fort Sill. He was noticeably grim. As the Lieutenant was likewise, the two had something in common. Still, as he stated, "All I need to do is get up there and see what it's all about. Then, I'll be okay." He spoke for the quorum that morning.

Second Lt. Joseph A. Coomer and 2nd Lt. Raymond J. Cody were there as well, the other two observers from B Battery. Joe, like "Tex" Fullen, was an Air Force retread. Both, in order to remain in the military, had to choose a combat branch and both chose artillery.

An announcement about 1100 hours revealed that a demonstration of the new 3.5 rocket launcher would be held in a small canyon at the edge of the airfield and behind the 13th CP. These new launchers had just been rushed over from the States after it was learned that the smaller, conventional 2.36 launchers were proving ineffective against NK tanks. The first known KIA in the fighting was a member of a launcher or tank destroyer team that failed in its mission due to the smaller projectile type used. A larger launcher, the 3.5, had been perfected, but not yet gone into quantity production and consequently not available to ground troops as general issue. Another few months or so and the 3.5 would have been part of the normal equipment complement.

An infantry training officer, flown over especially for these training demonstrations, supervised the instruction. Several key infantry sergeants were permitted familiarization firing of the launcher, the sharp explosions noticeably pleasing the assembled group.

Each rifle company was to be equipped with two 3.5 launchers and six projectiles. Regimental orders were issued to the effect that the loss of any launcher under avoidable circumstances would result in court martial for the offender responsible. Above all, unused projectiles were to be saved at all costs, as this type of ammunition was considered the most critical item of supply at the moment in Korea.

After an informal lunch of pork and beans, C-ration variety, 1st Lt. Pate appeared with the news that the observer parties should join the infantry companies immediately. Zero hour had arrived.

There was little talking as Payne brought the jeep around, and the Lieutenant, with Thacker and Wallace, climbed in. Coles and Fullen, with their men, were already leaving the area. Most of the men in A Battery paused to watch the observer groups leave. There were whispers already that the observer sections would sustain casualties before the fighting ended. No one waved or smiled as the jeeps sped away on the dusty road.

This funereal atmosphere prompted the Lieutenant to wax cynical as he remembered an incident months earlier when the 48th Field was undergoing a battalion test. The officer in charge of the firing made the statement that only experienced officers would observe and fire the missions as called for. As he put it, "We don't want to lose any points by allowing second lieutenants to waste a few rounds." Where, now, were these experienced officers, the Lieutenant wondered?

The infantry had already mounted their trucks when the observers arrived. MacGill, Aldridge, and Stavrakes were waiting in a jeep, and all waved heartily. A few remarks broke the tension, and the four were soon joking about nothing in particular. All were impatient. They had come this far. They were anxious to move on to the starting line.

At about 1255, MacGill signaled the Lieutenant, and the two jeeps started forward to join the advance party. The battalion commander strode out from his CP carrying a map case, mounted his jeep, and then waved the column forward. Gears ground. A choking dust cloud began to rise into an already overheated atmosphere, topped by a ferocious sun. Several supply men being left behind stood on the road.

In a few minutes, the airfield was no longer visible, and the road began to wind between hills once more, leading the men of the 19th Regimental Combat Team to what would become their first field of honor in this new Conflict.

Into Position

Much was expected from this last 24th Infantry Division combat team. More time had been allotted it to evolve appropriate maneuvers peculiar to the Korean terrain. The men of the 19th RCT had a few more days to condition themselves for battle. Now the test was at hand. The future course of strategy by Eighth Army might turn on how the 19th performed in this a first hour of trial.

The defensive position which the 19th was slated to man was a near-perfect one, tactically speaking. The road leading north to the Kum River passed, finally, through a portal or gap between two hills and then entered onto a wide, semicircular plain of rice paddies and earthen dikes. Hills extended east and west from the road at the south edge of the plain, and one could observe a fairly clear 180° from these hills.

On the northern side of the river, which the NK would occupy, the terrain was much the same, although broken by tree patches and small settlements. The overall panorama resembled the fitting together of two soup bowls.

Some topographical imperfections on the enemy side were immediately noted, with tactical implications. Just across the river, to the right of the road as it led from a long concrete bridge, was a small, wooded hillock, in the center of which nestled a tiny hamlet, a placement that some were sure would be of concern to the defenders. Also, several small villages dotted the landscape beyond the river, settlements in and around which the NK might hide or camouflage heavy guns.

Perhaps the most serious defense problem presented was the depth of the river. This had been an unusually hot and dry summer. Rivers everywhere had fallen to dangerously low levels. It looked as if the Kum could be traversed by wading at any given point in front of the defenders.

However, for better or for worse, this was to be the point of battle contact. And as the advance party vehicle column stopped at the edge of the plain, just beyond the gap, a feature identified on the battle map as Taep'yong-ni, the men of the 19th saw, for an electrifying first time, remnants of the 21st Regiment dug in like moles behind a massive dike fronting the river and supported by two light M-24 tanks, one on each side of the road at the bridgehead, emplaced in the dike with only the turrets exposed.

Just as the 19th column halted, several trucks from the 3rd Engineer Battalion, carrying infantry, sped across the bridge from the north. The men had been engaged in mining bridges and otherwise preparing obstacles along the road beyond the river. The trucks came abreast of the 19th column and stopped, the men dismounting. Then, in what appeared to be a weary, agonizing moment, the dust-covered men comprehended the significance of what they saw, that their eyes had not deceived them. They were looking at fresh troops, men sent to relieve and carry on the struggle.

Almost unanimously the tired men of the 21st gave what soon came to be known as a "Thank God" cheer—softly, firmly, but not histrionically. The Lieutenant would encounter this response a number of times during ensuing weeks.

Having dismounted, these soldiers of the 21st Regiment piled onto several house porches nearby and began a noisy wind-down. During this brief interval, the Lieutenant glanced closely at the uniforms worn by the men being relieved. Most, of course, were wearing the conventional HBTs, but few had steel helmets or helmet liners, wearing HBT caps instead. One or two wore khaki outfits and several sported khaki caps. A few wore trousers cut off at the knees or higher. All, however, wore rifle belts and canteen covers with canteens.

One soldier, sensing the Lieutenant's curiosity, volunteered that clothes are where you find them. When fatigues (HBTs) are torn and useless, you wear whatever is available. Duffel bags had been indiscriminately ripped open by supply personnel and appropriate clothing confiscated and distributed as needed. Also, steel pots were too heavy to wear in the heat, as were long trousers. The 21st was reaching the bottom. The 19th had arrived just in time.

While the Lieutenant continued to stand along the road, several 52nd Field jeeps approached and stopped. Two officers climbed out and stretched. Quick glances brought smiles of recognition from all three. Capt. William Jackson and 1st Lt. Harry L. Rogers, both formerly with the 49th Field at Camp Younghans, now with the 52nd Field, were welcome oases to the Lieutenant at this stage. The two now functioned as artillery liaison officers with the 21st and looked quite weary as they paused on the narrow road for quick smokes.

It was the old story, they said, "They hit, and we run." The NK possessed too much in the way of firepower and stamina. (This was the first mention of comparable fighting qualities.) The Americans had been unable to maintain prolonged fighting, partly due to less-than-adequate physical conditioning.

Furthermore, although ammunition resupply was arriving at the front now, continued supply to the men on the hills usually stopped during an attack. So when the supply on hand was depleted, there was little else to do but fall back. Leaving a position often meant abandoning the wounded. Only those lucky enough to have been hurt early on in the fighting had a good chance of being brought out. Once a line wavered, it was usually every man for himself. Both officers held high hope for the 19th and said the word was being passed that the 19th would stop the NK advance.

The two were off. While engaged in the brief chat, the Lieutenant noticed how eager he was to get information about anything having to do with the

Conflict. He reasoned that any news, good or bad, was soothing and part of the mental conditioning taking place. As most in battle crave information, it is usually expedient for a commander to inform his men about any relevancy as completely as possible so that each can prepare for inevitabilities. Morale was better when information was forthcoming; very low when it is not.

First Lt. MacGill returned from a reconnaissance about this time and reported that he had located the C Company position. The remainder of the First Battalion began arriving and the men dismounted. Second Lt. Stavrakes organized his platoon and began leading it forward. Telling Payne to follow in the jeep when he could, the Lieutenant began walking with the company column, figuring that he would be doing a lot of walking soon, and he might as well get used to it.

The position was about a mile from the main road, as the cart trail the men were following wound its way. During the march, MacGill told the Lieutenant that the defensive rim would be manned by one battalion only. The Second Battalion of the 19th would remain in reserve and go into position along the rear flanks so as to broaden defenses, but without entering direct battle contact unless absolutely necessary. The strategy was to permit the First Battalion to fall back through the Second, if such became expedient. The defensive front was two miles, crow flying distance. C Company was positioned on the right, B Company on the left, and A Company in the center. There were defensive gaps, but few expected a wide frontal NK attack over the broad area of flat and muddy paddies.

The men in C Company marched the distance with full pack. There were three halts for rest, unusual for such a short distance, but few were in any real shape. First Lt. Aldridge got the men going each time until, after much puffing, a rendezvous was reached from which platoon sergeants went off to stake out platoon positions.

Noting the general direction of the company site, and noting also that the last few hundred yards led over a narrow cow trail, the Lieutenant turned back to a small settlement that marked the terminus of the cart trail and where a rear company CP would be organized for supply purposes. He first instructed Payne to remain at this location with the jeep and trailer. Then, with his section gathered around, he made another decision. He would rotate Thacker and Wallace on the line so that each would get some rest and, at the same time, become more mentally adjusted to the fact of combat. With wire not yet laid to a forward switchboard, radio would be the primary means of communication for the time being. So Thacker and the Lieutenant, securing their Set Complete Radio (SCR) 610 on packboards and with extra rations and other equipment, started along the narrow path to the company battle position.

The selected observation post (OP) was on a high knoll back from the main line of resistance (MLR). The MLR that 1st Lt. MacGill set up was right along the river, as he had the notion that the NK would wade the river and attack head on. He wanted the OP on that line, but the Lieutenant persuaded him to settle for a higher ground OP.

Something bothered the Lieutenant, something that didn't seem quite right so far as the position layout was concerned. The platoons were scattered on three small hills all right, but a larger hill to the rear and overlooking much of the company was not manned at all. For now, however, his faith in infantry tactics was consummate.

With all companies in position and communication trenches dug, evening fell along the Kum River and on the men of the 19th behind it. The 21st had long since departed. The sight of those men had been particularly touching. Most, mainly those who had manned the dike position, were gaunt, brown-burned, and physically spent.

Their commander, Col. Richard W. Stephens, seemed at great pains to exude optimism, dashing about in his jeep and never failing to stop and speak with or nod in respect to officers under his command. His presence was noted as one not wearing a steel helmet. Those who wondered about this were informed that this was his way of instilling confidence. Now the 21st, the first troops into Korea, had retired to rest and regroup.

A sudden, sharp explosion shattered the stillness, and the Lieutenant looked up in time to see a cloud of black smoke rising at the bridge site. The cement bridge crossing the river had been blown as a defensive measure. This also meant that the men and vehicles of the 21st had been fully accounted for.

With the bridge destruction still in mind, the Lieutenant recalled seeing a woman earlier, the first American woman since leaving Camp Hakata. She was outfitted in khakis, much too big for her it seemed, and was standing along the main road beyond Taep'yong-ni, talking with an officer. Most of the men in C Company saw her and remarked about her presence. Someone asserted that she was a news reporter. A sergeant with more mouth than sense ranted sarcastically that she ought to be home, wherever that was. He really didn't mean what he said. The Lieutenant noted that he was one of the last in the marching group to look back to where she was standing.

Thacker was already dozing. It had been a physically draining day for him, and he wasn't used to the exertions.

Summer evenings are enchanting in Korea if little else about the country is. A cautious breeze soothed the Kum valley, and a slight, picturesque mist rose from the moving water. Korea is known as the Land of the Morning Calm. One could not be far wrong by substituting Evening Calm.

The rice paddies were fading to black in the distance. Only the sand along the river continued to reflect the vanishing evening light. Soon that, too, would blend with the darkness.

No moon this night, either; every man would be nervous and trigger-happy. A shot already had pierced the silence somewhere off to the left. A youngster, perhaps, frightened by a field animal running past, had fired.

The NK were not expected for another day, and all had been told to get as much rest as possible. The night encompassed the Lieutenant within minutes.

THE KUM RIVER FIGHT[1]

BEFORE LEAVING TAEGU THE LAST TIME, THE LIEUTENANT BARTERED A PACK OF CIGARETTES in one of the stores for a piece of red cloth. He then tore the cloth into narrow strips, giving a strip to each member of his section. Each tied the strip around the back of the pistol belt. The red cloth strips would identify the wearer as artillery, minimizing any confusion in the mingling with infantry.

The morning of the 13th opened with artillery registrations and check-pointing. Infantry on the line observed the ensuing explosions, particularly the wallop from the 155-mm shells. George Lowe placed and registered his 60-mm mortars, and the enlisted observer from the heavy weapons company registered 81-mm mortars, fairly close to the forward trench positions.

The now-first platoon leader, 2nd Lt. Maher, displaced his men further to the east along the river in case the NK should make a wider frontal assault than expected. This right or east flank represented, at the moment, the most serious threat to the company's security.

The entire basin remained quiet most of the day. Some smoke was seen to the north in late afternoon and, near dusk, machine gun fire was heard, the speculation being that American stragglers had been caught. By dark it was felt that the NK, probably aware now of the new American battle line, would shortly position themselves.

A sharp crack about 0700 the following morning justified the feeling of the previous evening. With a low whistling sound, an 85-mm shell soared over the American lines and exploded somewhere along the main road south of Taep'yong-ni. This single round was followed by a bombardment which, lasting several hours, did considerable damage to both the road and wire lines strung alongside. Vehicle traffic was severely disrupted.

Friendly artillery quickly countered. One after the other, the observers requested fire on the several hamlets and copses across the river on the chance that NK guns and/or tanks were hidden at these spots. Most reported sightings of such weapons or vehicles were illusory, the result of continual pressure to neutralize as many NK guns as possible. Nevertheless, in the process, much damage was probably done, if not to guns and vehicles, to personnel and materiel that may have been bivouacked and stored in the hamlet areas. There being no shortage of artillery ammunition at this stage, both sides ended the day engaged in artillery duels.

First close-in air support was received on the fourteenth. The four ROK F-51s, whose pilots were in training at Taegu while the regiment was bivouacked there, the whole of the ROK combat Air Force at the moment, had been ordered to assist the 19th Regiment. The pilots flew in pairs, strafing and rocketing the hamlets and other suspected gun locations on the NK side of the river. The red and blue symbol of the South Korean republic glistened bravely on the undersides of the wings.

Although the C Company men were happy to see the ROK plane action, there was some adverse comment when the pilots proceeded to strafe groups of civilians running along a road in an attempt to escape burning houses. This strafing was particularly noticeable where a road across the river wound to the river's edge and bordered a high, jutting cliff immediately across from the company's position. As the ROK planes swept down, the civilians, mostly women and a few older men, threw their hands up as if in supplication. Machine gun bullets spat and individuals were seen to stagger and fall, one or two rising to stagger on.

Perhaps this type of conflict justified this and other similar attacks. There was already some question as to whether female refugees ought to be considered harmless in the light of recent startling disclosures that some women had been caught allegedly carrying war materiel for the NK. Yet, even if this latter were true, some decency seemed to be expected on the part of the side committed to democracy and justice. It was difficult for the Americans to witness these attacks and condone their necessity.

The Australians came into view that day. This United Kingdom Commonwealth became the first assisting United Nations member behind the United States to support the UN resolution calling for the use of force to support the Republic of Korea. The Australian contribution at this stage was a group of planes and pilots, their plane being the American-built F-51. Cheers went up along the American line with the recognition of the Australian bull's-eye on the wings.

But the real thrill was reserved for the American jets whenever they flew over the basin to strafe and rocket. Fighter bases in Japan had been reequipped with the new F-80 Shooting Stars prior to the outbreak of the Conflict in Korea. The previous standard F-51 had practically disappeared from the skies. The line troops felt confident that there was no real challenge to our jets for close-in support.

(The jets ran into trouble in Korea, however. The nature of the Korean topography limited their effectiveness as close-support vehicles. A fast-moving plane is more effective in the bombing, strafing, and the harassment of open targets. The propeller-driven F-51 proved the better as did the Marine Corsair later for close-in support in Korea, the jets soon shifted to enemy area reconnaissance, war-making potential, road movement, and enemy aircraft.)

The longer C Company remained in position the more it was felt that serious flaws in the defense plan outweighed any advantage gained. It was true that a fairly wide river separated the two contenders. Also, directly across the river, a high rocky hill extended almost to the river's edge, precluding mass enemy movement from that point.

On the other hand, the depth of the river remained a question mark. A few of the more adventurous had actually waded the Kum at several key places. And further, to make matters worse, instead of meandering from a generally easterly direction, the river flowed westward from behind hills to the right of and beyond the first platoon. No one knew if friendly troops were in that general area or whether it had become a potentially unguarded and fatal flank. A quiet feeling of apprehension permeated the position as the men continued to evaluate the situation.[2]

As the Lieutenant watched that afternoon of the fourteenth, small groups of civilians crossed the river off to the right at what appeared to be a ford. Little was done about this. There were too few for concentrated artillery, and the company could not spare men to rig a guard continuously at the ford and the immediate shoreline without weakening an already strained position. The Lieutenant did register a concentration at the ford, ready to fire a volley in the event of suspicious activity.

And then, both officers and senior NCOs, more and more, began to turn their heads and gaze with anxiety at the hill directly to the rear. Whichever force dominated the hill dominated both the infantry position and that portion of the river bordering. At intervals during the fourteenth, civilians were spotted walking along the ridgeline, occasionally pausing to watch the Americans. MacGill ordered them away, but many in the company thought them to be merely villagers looking after deserted hamlets while the inhabitants were in refuge. Each village seemed to have one or two such men designated as watchmen for the duration. However others in the company were already visualizing an impending NK encirclement and felt that the so-called civilian onlookers were really advance elements of the NK, ferreting out the company's strong and weak points.

The Lieutenant left the hill that afternoon and made the trip to the forward switch location in search of telephone wire. The distance to the C Company position was so great that the original wire-laying team ran about 250 yards short. Ground communication was vital as a substitute for radio contact, should the latter fail.

Payne drove the Lieutenant along the cart trail to the main road. Upon arriving, 1st Lt. Pate gave out the bad news that no new wire could be had. NK artillery had torn communications so badly that all available stocks were being held in reserve for future repair needs. However, if the Lieutenant could pick up sections of used wire along the road and then splice the ends together, he was welcome to as much as he could carry. This was the only alternative. A good hour and a half was spent searching. Finally, a sufficient amount was gathered.

Before leaving the CP area, the Lieutenant spoke briefly with the Headquarters Company commander, 1st Lt. Jim Ruddell. Along with several guards, he was on the road anxiously looking toward the river dikes. Clearly, the headquarters men were experiencing nervousness not shared by their line compatriots. However, the former had undergone a heavy siege of shelling, a trial C Company had not yet endured, so the nervous atmosphere was understandable.

The Lieutenant and Ruddell continued talking until the sky began to darken.[3] The Lieutenant would have to start back and hurry before complete darkness.

Before leaving the position that afternoon, the Lieutenant had inquired as to the password for the evening. He had been assured that it would be the same as the evening previous. This was stupid, of course, but was accepted because there was no other answer. Now, near the rear company CP, where several heavy mortars had been placed, he learned that the password had been changed.

The Lieutenant became apprehensive. He had been told earlier that the first known artillery observer team casualty was a victim of friendly fire. Several nights previous, a soldier in the 34th Regiment, hearing a noise, fired blindly into the darkness. At daylight, it was discovered that the artilleryman was the one hit. For some unknown reason, the man crawled out of his OP hole, and the accompanying noise alerted the overly nervous soldier to fire without challenge. This bit of information hurried the Lieutenant as he trudged up the darkening path toward the company position.

The Lieutenant strayed several times and had to retrace his steps. It had become so dark that, at intervals, he had to grasp the company telephone wire to keep from making a fatal directional error. A tremor of fright rose in the pit of his stomach as he realized he was becoming fair game to be hit as an NK infiltrator. He stopped once to reassure himself and to listen. He heard voices and recognized them as American. He was near the second platoon and on the right path. He could now make out the outline of his hill. He would be on the OP in a moment.

At that instant, a sharp rattle of automatic carbine fire broke the stillness, fire from near the crest of the OP hill, shocking the Lieutenant into panic. Tracers showed the direction of fire to be down into a gully to the Lieutenant's right. Regardless, however, the tragic incident involving the first observer casualty flashed before his eyes, and he was determined not to become the second such. A path led off to the left. Falling to his knees, he began crawling along it.

After crawling about ten yards, he stopped and sat, awaiting the next development. It came in the form of rain. The quickly darkening sky had forecast precipitation. There were now two alternatives: brave the trigger-happy guard on the hill in the hope that the new password was authentic, or stay where he was, rain or no rain, and take his chances on not being noticed the remainder of the night.

In that moment of indecision, the Lieutenant crawled a few feet toward the base of the hill and immediately saw what looked like a depression just off the path that might shelter a man from the elements. In one lunge, he squeezed himself into the depression and, sweating heavily, which began attracting varied species of night bugs and flies, proposed to wait out the night.

It was a long night, or so it seemed. As expected, his presence drew creeping and flying objects, so that his body became host to a mass of organisms. But he dared not move or make noises to alleviate his discomfort. And, in addition to this misery, frequent sounds in the nearby grass and bush growths, probably by little field animals, raised the fear of friendly patrol action.

The Lieutenant felt that his approach had been heard by some in the company, so he became very anxious over his being an object of search. If indeed a search would begin, a defensive shot aimed at a suspiciously supine figure, one who might utter the wrong password, would be justified. He clamped his jaws and shut his eyes at the thought.

After what seemed like forever, the morning of the fifteenth dawned. The rain had ended after only half an hour, so there was limited discomfort from being wet. The Lieutenant had been in the open-sided crevice about five and a half hours. After becoming used to the creeping over his body, he had dozed periodically, emerging somewhat refreshed despite the harrowing experience.

Waiting until it was light enough to be recognizable, the Lieutenant crawled from the crevice and stood up. He discovered himself to be at the exact base of the OP hill. Contrary to initial fears, no GI was within twenty yards of where he had remained. The firing incident had taken place halfway up the hill, in the company headquarters area. Now, secure in his presence within the position, he began walking up the hill.

He paused at the CP shelter to inquire about the incident. He was told that a patrol had been observed returning to the position, and a guard, hearing as well as seeing movement but not hearing or understanding the password, had fired, killing a Korean civilian the patrol was bringing in for questioning. There were no other casualties or damage. No one mentioned anything about a suspicious person being at the base of the hill. The Lieutenant saw fit not to mention his being there. He then continued on to his lookout position.

With the advent of another day, battle contact resumed. Several F-80s came over and disappeared beyond the enemy horizon. A few rounds from the NK batteries whistled in the direction of the main road and the First Battalion CP. Wallace came up and relieved Thacker. The Lieutenant asked the former to take the new wire and complete stringing the OP phone line. This was accomplished by about 1030 hours, telephone communication completed to forward switch for the first time.

All knew that the NK would attack soon. It had been learned that the 34th Regiment had, once more, been hit the previous day. News of the battle trickled in. The 63rd Field had been ambushed about noon, just as the men began lining up for chow. Some were swimming in a nearby stream.

The primary target was the Headquarters Battery. The 63rd suffered heavily. Much equipment was abandoned. With artillery effectiveness reduced to near zero, the infantry companies were forced to withdraw.[4]

The effect of this weakened left flank prompted the 19th Regiment to reconsider the tactical plan. Although some officers felt that the regiment ought to attack across the river if there was no action by the end of the sixteenth, MacGill mentioned the possibility of a general withdrawal to new positions, this to prevent the regiment from being outflanked from the west. July sixteenth was expected to be the day of tactical decision.

The afternoon of the fifteenth saw a cloud of aircraft wing in and attack the enemy side of the river. Many fires were ignited and burning hamlets cast reflected light long after sunset. Sounds were heard which few doubted rose from injured civilians or enemy soldiers. The men in the forward trenches gazed silently, but gave no indication that they heard. They heard, nevertheless. Already, certain cruelties were being accepted as standard by these so-called green troops. They were learning the essentials of their profession.

General supplies and ammunition, mostly the latter, were brought up to the line. First Lt. Aldridge had boasted that C Company was the best supplied in the battalion. To facilitate movement of ammo boxes, an ox, newly discovered, was commandeered. With boxes strapped to its sides, the ox made the trip at least half a dozen times that day, the sight of this ancient mode of transportation affording the one bright spot in the growing atmosphere of tension.

About 2000 hours, MacGill called the Lieutenant forward and told him of his expectations of attack. Were the artillery concentrations ready? Could defensive barrages be fired at a moment's notice? Mac was reassured. He then gave a general order for guarded sleeping through the night.

It was 2115 hours. The planes had gone and everyone was settling down. Wallace brought coffee from the company CP. The Lieutenant began reading a letter given to him by Thacker to be censored. He tried not to read too thoroughly.

Suddenly, it seemed that an extraordinary amount of firing, relatively close in, was beginning on the enemy side of the river. The Lieutenant lifted his binoculars and began scanning the opposing rim. In seconds he located the source of the firing. Grabbing his radio microphone, waiting precious moments while the set warmed, he almost shouted, "Apparatus Charlie, this is 4-2. Emergency message. Enemy tank attack along the main road leading to bridge. Six tanks spotted, possibly more. Request other observers be notified to fire as they are closer. Over."

The NK attack had begun. The Lieutenant was too far to the right to observe and conduct accurate fire on this enemy column. Clouds of smoke soon billowed up. Through the haze and squinting intently, he finally saw these vehicles not as tanks but gun carriages, self-propelled, the guns being fired as the carriages slowly moved toward the bridge.[5] No one watching was unaware of the limitations of this NK maneuver. The bridge itself was unusable, and the water probably too deep at this point for the carriages to cross successfully. The whole scene appeared as a diversionary tactic, but one taking its toll in American casualties and fouled communications.

Artillery quickly began to zero in. Both Coles and Fullen presumably were registering on the column. High explosive and white phosphorus shells began bursting on or near the vehicles.

Then, with a loud whine, an F-80 jet shot into view. A muffled cheer went up. There must have been an awful scramble somewhere when word went back of the NK armored movement. Only about eight minutes elapsed between the first sighting and the arrival of the first of four jets.

There was barely enough daylight to see moving ground objects from the air, but the pilots sized up the situation. Then, one by one, they circled down to strafe and rocket the column. Five passes were made. There was no light after that. But the column was stalled, and a number of enemy had hurled themselves into ditches along the road. There may have been twelve NK vehicles in all. The jets set three afire, while the artillery probably disabled another two.

Of significant import that evening of the fifteenth was the near sacrificial effort on the part of the jet pilots. Flying in closing visibility and endangering their own selves in the circling and diving maneuvers, their response and total mission immersion endeared the Air Force command to every soldier on the line, demonstrating how close the bond was between the two services during this early phase of the Conflict.[6]

A lull settled over the line. The remaining gun carriages reversed track and moved into the "island" area just north of the bridge site. No further firing was heard from them. It was thought that their engineers might try to get these vehicles across the river using the water-bridge technique: use of stones to build up the river base to about a foot or so below the surface. If the NK could succeed with this plan, an attack down the main road, with tanks and gun carriages leading, would split the line and leave flanking companies to withdraw in some disorder.

Uneasy darkness encompassed all. Flickering flames from burning hamlets reflected in the faces of the American defenders. The night would be long, but it had to be endured.

About 0330 hours on the morning of July 16, the inevitable happened to C Company. The sixteenth was a Sunday, but few realized it. It was exactly three weeks from the day the first NK attack began. Now, from the area of the ford, up river, the very spot that produced misgivings earlier, the NK came. An estimated battalion carried the enemy banner. Their immediate objective was to push in the first platoon, strung out along the river, envelop it with as few casualties as possible, and then attack the main position by climbing the OP hill, thus splitting the company. Seizure of the OP hill would enable the NK to command the position by overwhelming the company's CP and mortar area and then firing on the rear of the remaining platoons which were situated along and near the river, effectively trapping the men against the river. The NK almost succeeded.

Well-placed BARs (Browning automatic rifles) and just plain guts of the American defenders upset the NK timetable. The NK swarmed on the beach in front of the first platoon. Force of numbers beat the defenders into trench contact, knives and bayonets used. To say that forty or so men stood off a battalion of enemy is perhaps stretching a bit, but the NK lost valuable time where it had expected easy success. When the situation proved hopeless, 2nd Lt. Maher called out to his men, to those who could, to withdraw to the main company position. No sooner had he so urged than an enemy bullet struck and killed him.

Prior to this moment, it was virtually impossible to adjust supporting artillery fire because the exact location of Americans and NK, in the swirl of contact, was lost in confusion. However, company mortars and rounds from the heavy mortars were noticeable in effect along the river's edge.

Meanwhile, the remnants of the first platoon were heard struggling to reach adjoining trenches. As they reached those trenches they were heard yelling, "Don't shoot, for God's sake, we're Americans." It was well that their voices could be heard because everyone was primed to fire at anything moving. The main attack was imminent.

The NK had to hurry. They had hoped to accomplish the enveloping operation before daybreak, before planes and accurate artillery could be brought to bear on them. Their jabber could be heard plainly now. The Americans were straining to see. Now was the time for artillery.

The Lieutenant had been in communication with forward switch. He was silently thankful that he had taken the time on the fourteenth to secure wire for the phone line. Wallace had not been able to rouse anyone by radio. The 13th Field commander, Lt. Col. Stratton, was receiving the Lieutenant's messages at the regimental switchboard. The Lieutenant asked for a concentration in direct line, he figured, with the enemy's shouts as they approached. The command was relayed, fired, and the round burst where it could be seen.

Suddenly, as he was about to adjust further, a white, glaring light flared from the bottom of the OP hill. He ducked instinctively and, for a brief second, felt the urge to run. Was this *it?* Leaning weakly against the side of his hole, he managed to control himself enough to comprehend what the light was. He saw that the NK had positioned an A-frame, on which was plastered phosphorus or some similar substance designed to illuminate an objective close up and possibly blind defenders. As the brilliance of the flare outlined every nook and cranny of the hill, this was certainly the prelude to the main attack.

Forgetting for an instant that Lt. Col. Stratton was on the phone, the Lieutenant pleaded anxiously for the next adjusting round. Time was short. Only the artillery could save the company position now.

Stratton tried to calm the Lieutenant. He insisted that "everything was going to be okay." The round came in, a good one, a line shot, but still too far out to be effective.

The Lieutenant was sweating. Should he take a chance and drop all the way, or should he adjust slowly? The NK voices were now very clear, and the flare still burned. This was no time to experiment. He whispered hoarsely into the phone, "Drop 100 (yards) and request three volleys."

The line to the 52nd Field, the battalion firing the mission, was open by this time, and Capt. Carl C. Simpson, Assistant S-3 of the battalion, was listening to the Lieutenant's messages as well as to the relayed fire commands. Without waiting for Stratton to repeat the last fire request, Simpson broke in to warn that the command would place the rounds below the No Fire Line, meaning onto friendly troops. Hearing this, the Lieutenant almost yelled that the NK were at that moment attacking and that there was no No Fire Line. Perhaps it was the intensity of the Lieutenant's voice or perhaps it was dread of repercussion if no artillery was used at all. Whichever, the mission was fired.

They came, these rounds, whistling and close, with an authority that only those on the receiving end can fully appreciate and fear. The bursts extended from the base of the OP hill toward what formerly was the first platoon position, a near perfect curtain confronting the NK line of advance. The burning A-frame was knocked over. Complete silence followed.

Then the jabbering resumed and more shouting heard. Determined not to waste time, the Lieutenant called for five more volleys. The 52nd complied and the volleys arrived, writing *finis* to this particular NK effort.

The NK fell back, returning to the river beach, and the line was quiet once more. First streaks of dawn began appearing, and sighs of relief echoed among the holes and trenches. MacGill began a hurried tour of the position, calling encouragement to everyone. As his phone was out of order, he asked the Lieutenant to call and convey to the battalion CO the message that under present circumstances the company would have no difficulty holding, but that some assistance would be necessary if the NK attack continued after 0700. The time of the message was 0505 hours on the morning of July 16, a Sunday.

Few were worried. The planes would be up soon, and the remaining NK would slink back across the river. If matters should get rough, the Second Battalion would move up to assist. Men hurried about with confidence. A realignment of the position was begun to compensate for losses from the first platoon, this to minimize the danger of an exposed right flank.

Then, just when group optimism was approaching a peak, a bullet from an enemy sniper cracked into the position, not from the front or side, but from the rear. Another round was fired, then another, and soon a chorus of cracks, causing a new level of bloodshed.

What was becoming despondently apparent now to everyone was that the NK had occupied the hill to the rear of the position, the same hill that had stirred apprehension earlier, and begun to harass the exposed rear flank with rifle fire. The company headquarters and mortar personnel were trapped in their holes.

The Lieutenant, at the first sounds of enemy fire from this new direction, had Wallace take the radio to the unexposed side of the OP hill, where it was proposed to reestablish the OP. Both began digging in in anticipation of further NK assaults.

Before digging could be completed, however, NK rifle fire became very intense. Wallace jumped into a well-dug machine gun pit on the very top of the OP hill. The Lieutenant flattened out in his own half-dug slit trench. Others scurried about or began digging new holes along the face of the hill, away from the NK firing.

Shortly, during a lull in the firing, the Lieutenant dashed around the hill to where his telephone still remained, hoping to bring it to his new lookout. To test it before taking the extra time to pull on the line, he rang several times. The line was dead. It apparently had been cut. This setback left him with only the radio. But now, trying to send messages, he discovered he could receive but not send. Here, at a critical juncture in the fighting, he was without communication. C Company was now cut off from the rest of the regiment, physically and in terms of communication.

Most were hopeful that the NK firing would soon cease. After all, it was getting light and planes would be up. The pilots surely would erase any enemy seen moving about. Shouts of Americans calling to one another were heard from the exposed side of the hill. The Lieutenant heard several times a report that NK were observed dressed in GI clothing, taken perhaps from bodies of men killed only a few hours earlier.

Once, a shout was heard that some NK wanted to surrender. A white flag was being waved. A corporal said he would go over and investigate. He went, but was shot in the open. The white cloth was a ruse to frustrate the American defense.

The morning dragged on. Few had bothered to eat anything, but then few were hungry. About 0900, the NK began to mortar the OP hill. Most rounds fell on the rearward side, the side facing the NK, and onto the tragically exposed men crouched in their holes. Only one mortar was used. After about fifteen rounds, at three-or four-minute intervals, this ceased.

Being mortared was a tremulous experience for the Lieutenant. When it began, he was literally bounced out of his trench. This caused such a shock that he lay there during the next half-hour as tense as a body could be. He actually heard, during those brief seconds before impact, the awful *hiss* of the shell coming down. In the instant of hearing, he would turn against the side of his trench, place his hands over his steel helmet, and just "hang" until the round exploded. Then he would roll over on his back to await the next one.

Through shouts, he learned of casualties on the exposed side. Even the company medic was shot while trying to give aid to a badly wounded man. Someone would make a break for it every once in a while and would come running and rolling up and over the side of the hill. These filtered along the forward hump that led to the river. One didn't make it and sprawled grotesquely down a knoll and into a clump of bushes. He didn't even moan.

There were no outward manifestations of panic. Most knew that in previous wars and in similar situations, units were always objects of intense rescue efforts. None felt neglected, even as the hour grew late. The Lieutenant earlier had rejected an inclination to leave the position. As befitting his particular role, he could have approached 1st Lt. MacGill concerning a need to secure replacement communications equipment. Yet to leave the position, albeit with a well-grounded excuse, might present the appearance of a timorous approach to duty, and the Lieutenant chose not to play that game. He would remain with the company and carry out, as best he could, any role assigned him by MacGill.

(What the men in C Company did not know during the morning of their ordeal were the attacks mounted against the center of the line, against A Company. The center was breached, with fighting raging in the command post area, the hamlet of Taep'yong-ni, and the NK were twice repelled. And over on the left, NK guerrillas got behind B Company, dispersing only after the company began firing to the rear.)

Meanwhile, MacGill sent Sfc. Otis Loomis back to the battalion CP for instructions.[7] (Loomis reached the CP just after one of the breaching attacks. He was allegedly told that C Company would have to fight its way out as best it could, as the other two line companies had their hands full. Loomis was unable to return to the position, so the men remaining did not as yet know of their hopeless situation.)[8]

Stretching in his slit trench during a lull in the firing, the Lieutenant felt the end was coming. Although he had no way of knowing about the fighting at the center of the line, he was aware, if others were not, that the nearest infantry company was a good one-quarter of a mile away and that chances of help arriving were now slim.

He was becoming more aware of the man in a trench near his. He was a BAR man who had not once fired his weapon. The Lieutenant had lent his shovel to the man a while back and now, as the man's head occasionally popped over the escarpment of his trench, his face conveyed the image and pallor of death.

Gazing at this projection of stark terror, the Lieutenant began to muster his own courage. It is one of the phenomena of being human, that once the individual decides to face danger as reality, fear subsides and the mind turns clear so as to advise the body of the next course of action. The Lieutenant's faith in himself took hold, and he began planning for what lay ahead.

The time was about 1300. Hope of rescue had faded. Furthermore, not one plane, fighter or spotter, had appeared over the position, to the anger of many of the men.

Now the NK were observed engrossed in more than the usual engagement activity, as if preparing for another onslaught. Five bullets remained in the Lieutenant's pistol. If it came to that, four were for the NK and the fifth for himself. He had never thought of suicide previously, but the now documented cruelties and deaths inflicted on prisoners by the NK made him feel that death by one's own hand was preferable. He arrived at the decision to place the barrel in his mouth. It would be much simpler that way.

Another firing lull occurred. Word had been passed to conserve ammunition. A break was due any time, now.

It came. From the river's edge, the high, clear voice of 1st Lt. MacGill was heard: "Fire and fall back!"

Nothing happened for an instant. In that short space of time, the picture of retreat flashed through the company's survivors. The Lieutenant had seen, earlier that morning, American troops behind a high dike just to the left of the position. The dike, extending south and away from the river, joined the main frontal dike as a side protective bulwark of the paddy plain. There, logically, was an excellent fall-back site, placing men in the direction of friendly forces.

A curtain of fire began welling up along the irregular line. Someone shouted, "This is it," and then tumbled backward down a small ravine. That was the signal.

The Lieutenant yelled at Wallace. He heard an answering voice. Wallace would be ready. The Lieutenant looked once more at the objective dike, yelled "Let's go," and then, leaping over a mound of refuse dirt, half rolled and half stumbled down the OP hill.

He came to rest at the foot of the hill, surprised to be alive and unhurt. His helmet had fallen off, and he had dropped his pistol. He retrieved the pistol, but left the helmet. It might get in the way. Others were coming. It was a mass of legs, arms, and dust down the hill and onto the paddy area. Shouts and grunts pierced the air.

Everyone paused at the foot of the hill to consider the next step. There was no company officer about. MacGill was at the river's edge. One had been killed. Aldridge was somewhere in the rear, and no one knew where Orr, Lowe, or Stavrakes were. Decisions were made in fleeting seconds by the confused men and with those decisions went life or death.

The Lieutenant called for the men to go to the dike. Only about seventy-five yards separated the OP hill from the dike, although the path was narrow and precariously edged several paddies. Other shouts of "To the river" were heard. Several had already started that way. It was difficult to stem what appeared to be the simpler and more reasonable course.

Only two men followed the Lieutenant as he headed for the dike. It was run all the way. The three skirted several small earth mounds and then broke into an open space that wound behind the company position, where the Lieutenant had spent that harrowing night in the scoop-out.

Suddenly, in the corner of his eye, the Lieutenant glimpsed several figures in brown uniforms. They were about forty yards to the left and about five yards apart. They were NK. This, apparently, was the group MacGill had seen when he ordered the surviving company to fall back. An enemy encirclement maneuver had begun.

Seeing the running trio, the NK leader gesticulated wildly, pointing with both arms. A series of shots cut through the air. The Lieutenant's eyes remained on the dike; only a few more strides to go. A bullet splashed onto the paddy path in front of him; close, but not close enough.

The dike was reached. The Lieutenant flung himself at the top and onto his belly to roll down the other side. There was no stopping, now. He resumed running at a slight diagonal from the dike, first along a paddy wall and then along a small, dried-up stream bed.

The NK had reached the top of the dike, too. They continued firing and a bullet zinged through the air near the Lieutenant's head. He was tiring fast, and his arms tightened alarmingly. Blood rushed through his body at express train speed, sweat streaming down his face. Then breathing became difficult, and he had to slow down. At the moment he slowed, the NK firing ceased. He turned around and saw that the other two soldiers were still with him. One had been struck in the shoulder, but he would make it okay. The trio continued on, trotting.

There was no turning back. The presence of the NK so close around the position could seal the doom of those who had turned toward the river. The three faced in the direction of A Company and the main road.

Then, as they continued, another threat loomed. A group of military had been resting along the backside of the large frontal dike about three hundred yards away. As soon as the running trio came into view, this group rose and began walking. The path of march of this group and that of the Lieutenant and his two companions would momentarily cross.

Because of the weariness it was difficult to focus clearly, so that for several moments, the three thought they were looking death in the eye once more. However, as the distance lessened, the familiar green of the fatigue uniform reflected through the dusty air. The group turned out to be a platoon from C Company, to include 2nd Lts. Orr and Stavrakes.

(Stavrakes had been sent back to the Battalion CP when Sgt. Loomis failed to return. The former's mission was one of seeking both information and assistance. Upon his arrival at the CP, however, he was informed by the battalion CO that the situation had deteriorated considerably and that it was "every man for himself." Furthermore, he informed Stavrakes, word had already been sent to the company to withdraw. Loomis, apparently, was carrying this latter message when he disappeared.

Stavrakes then tried to return to the position, but was unable to do so. He did encounter the platoon sent out by MacGill to cover a possible withdrawal and remained with that group.)[9]

Now, observing the manner of the trio's escape, both Orr and Stavrakes deemed it useless to wait any longer. MacGill had delayed too long. He was being encircled. He and the men remaining in the position might be able to fight their way out for a short distance, but they were too far away from friendly troops and a protective hill mass to effect a successful withdrawal. There was only silence now from the direction of C Company.

For a long moment, the Lieutenant stared at his former OP hill and then, with the others, the immediate survivors, began walking toward the A Company position and the hill fronting Taep'yong-ni. They arrived just as the men of A Company were leaving forward positions and struggling up the fronting hill. The men from both companies intermingled. A general withdrawal from the Kum River line had begun.

The Lieutenant was continuing on sheer willpower by this time. Under normal circumstances the body would have rebelled, what with lack of nourishment and associated mental strain. But the drive for survival spurred him on, as it did others, and it would be many hours before he would recognize just how much he was suffering.

Moving up and over the hill then descending into Taep'yong-ni were a number of walking wounded. The position of A Company, which had been on the forward base of the hill beyond Taep'yong-ni (the company had originally been along the frontal dike, a position abandoned on the fifteenth), had been unusually hard hit in the course of the NK breaching attacks that morning. One red-haired fellow, badly wounded about the face, was being led and helped in his efforts to climb the hill. He was weak from loss of blood and was in a state of shock. Periodically, he would turn and call out to the NK as "those goddam dirty bastards." Men looked at him, but said little. If outbursts such as these helped him continue to walk, it was all right with them. At this stage, one had to keep moving above all else.

At the top of the hill, most turned to look toward the river. There, off to the left, at a distance of probably four hundred yards, crouched in ditches, were several squads of NK. These were part of the group beaten back earlier and now waiting for another chance at the Americans. Several .50-caliber machine guns from D Company were mounted on a hill to the left of the main road and were being trained on the NK group. The firing was covering the withdrawal. Once the infantry remnants reached the main road and begin marching back, the firing would cease and the battle end.

The survivors from the battalion were gathering in a sort of final rendezvous in the hamlet of Taep'yong-ni before commencing a march to the rear. There was now no battle line. There was little or no leadership. Several officers from A Company were about, as were several from battalion headquarters, but these were ineffectual for the moment.

A platoon equivalent from C Company had gathered around a well and were refreshing themselves. Sgts. Ray Point and Chester Van Orman led this group. Second Lt. Orr told the Lieutenant that he had led George Lowe, who had been wounded, out of the position quite early that morning, then he had had great difficulty returning. All the C Company officers were accounted for except Aldridge.

The Lieutenant learned that B Company had already withdrawn and gone down the road. That unit had not been as hard hit on the line as had the other two companies and therefore was better organized in the withdrawal.[10]

As the Lieutenant stood there on the road munching a peppermint mound someone had discarded, the men from the C Company supply section appeared. Thacker and Payne were with this group. They told of a guerrilla attack earlier. During the course of the engagement, lasting about an hour, the heavy mortar platoon, located in the vicinity of the company supply hut, was scattered and their mortars destroyed. Survivors began making their way gradually toward Taep'yong-ni.

One of the mortar men had commandeered Payne's jeep and drove it along the cart trail to Taep'yong-ni. Payne looked about the hamlet for signs of it, but without success. It was gone, probably, with the B Company withdrawal.

No one knew where the battalion or regimental staffs were. All staff organization apparently had disintegrated after the fire fights during the morning.[11]

As witness the intensity of the battles, broken carbines, rifles, and Soviet firearms were scattered about. There were no dead or wounded in the open. These either had been moved to the rear or piled somewhere to prevent a general gathering of flies. The smell of death hung heavy, however. One soldier was engaged in breaking several discarded Garand rifles against a pole. The machine guns were still firing. Mortar personnel were dismantling the few mortars still in evidence.

First Lt. Aldridge now appeared, driving the C Company jeep. He had picked up "Red" and another man and began driving down the road to the rear. He saw the Lieutenant and motioned him to hop in. The Lieutenant rejected the invitation. He would walk along with the rest of his section when a column was formed.

A shout went up to "Move out." Officers from A Company had managed to organize men into two columns. The Lieutenant called to both Thacker and Payne to fall in. Then, waiting until the column was well underway, he edged in.

Someone yelled, "Five yards." This would be a normal march interval. It also meant that the withdrawal would be an orderly one. Everyone felt better. A truck column was in view about a half-mile ahead. None felt lost or neglected now. A few were even joking. This dismaying affair would soon be over.

Roadblock

Almost as suddenly as they began moving, the marching columns halted. Like a wave, the two files merged into a ditch and high grass to the left of the road. None knew what had happened. Then the word came: An NK machine gun had begun firing on the leading elements of the column from a hidden spot somewhere on the side of a hill to the left of the road. The weariness returned. The men looked at each other. Roadblock!

The road away from Taep'yong-ni led through a river valley, a chain of hills on both sides. There were cultivated rice paddies on the right, and there was a stream with diked banks about two hundred yards across the paddy fields. Breaks in the hilly chain appeared about every quarter-mile or so, where narrow valleys or gullies, often cultivated, branched away from the road, offering ideal entrenching positions from which harassment of walking troops or moving vehicles could be effected.

It was at one of these breaks, about three hundred yards south of Taep'yong-ni, where the road broke into the open for about one hundred and fifty yards, that the NK had organized a machine gun nest designed to cause confusion and fear and, they hoped, force withdrawing units to break up into small, disorganized groups, making it easier for these to be eliminated or captured further down the road.

The NK gunner had chosen the spot well and cunningly camouflaged it. Then, waiting until the lead elements of the withdrawing columns were well out in the open, he opened fire. Casualties occurred during the first seconds of bewilderment, and these were lying in ditches at both sides of the road. Men who had started out in the open but escaped being hit were now grouped together by a little hut on the left, most sitting and waiting.

Several bazooka teams were hurriedly organized in the effort to wipe out the nest. Officers twice urged and threatened men to mount an assault on the hillside where the gun was located. Each time the assault effort was made, however, the chatter of the gun ceased, so its location continued unknown. No one led an assault group the entire way up the hill. Perhaps had that been done, the nest would have been discovered and the roadblock eliminated, but such was not to be. The men just were not willing and the leadership insufficiently organized to accomplish the task. After the second assault group returned to the road, the NK gunner resumed firing.

Almost immediately after the second group descended to the road, a jeep roared into view from the direction of Taep'yong-ni. Someone said, "It's the colonel." It was, indeed, the regimental CO, Col. Meloy. He appraised the roadblock situation and then assured the men standing about that he would secure help at once, there being no communication to the rear now except in person. He stepped back into his jeep, and his driver zoomed off across the open space. The NK gunner fired on the jeep, but the Colonel and his driver made it and were seen to stop on the other side. This display of courage gave momentary heart to the still stranded men.

Shortly, however, desperation began to take hold. A few men slipped into the putrid rice paddy water and began crawling toward the stalled vehicle column observed in the distance, using the built-up roadbed as a shield. For the majority, though, crawling in the paddies was a final alternative, and they chose to wait longer for something else to happen.

Suddenly, a burst of firing from the rear of the stopped vehicle column ahead erupted. Someone had fitted a machine gun to a truck ring mount and begun firing at the trapped men at the roadblock. The soldier apparently thought he was aiming at advancing NK. Several men immediately fell from the fire. Frantic waves and shouts proved useless, so the men waiting at the roadblock dove for any kind of cover.

The Lieutenant had been sitting on the side of a dirt mound behind the small straw and bamboo hut at the edge of the clearing, just out of sight of the NK gunner. When the friendly fire began, and it became evident who the targets were, he began digging into the dirt with his hands. Working furiously, he scooped a shallow slit trench and then slid in, hugging low.

Others about him were reacting incredulously. After the first dive for cover, several were seen not to have moved at all, these seemingly in the first throes of shock. A cry of "Medic" was heard, and a few feet away a green-clad figure lay prostrate. Blood oozed from a hole in the neck. No one so much as moved. The man was beyond help.

A young soldier sitting against the backside of the hut, facing the Lieutenant's slit trench, took a bullet in the shoulder. He didn't move, but his face took on the color of ashen gray.

Firing from the stalled column stopped after only a minute or two. Somebody evidently convinced the gunner that he was making a dreadful mistake.

Several jeeps from Taep'yong-ni arrived at the roadblock. These were D Company vehicles, carrying men who had manned the heavy machine guns covering the general withdrawal. There was no blocking action now. The D Company men were surprised at the situation, but quickly offered a solution: ride through. No one moved for a moment because to ride through meant sure death for one or more. Then, in the next instant, there was a rush for the jeeps. "Get it over with" was the imperative taking hold.

Each of the jeeps pulled a quarter-ton trailer, so the men who couldn't fit into the jeeps flattened out, face down, on the trailer tarps, legs dangling behind. Soon, all was in readiness. There were five jeeps with trailers. The Lieutenant was flattened, a man on each side of him, on the third jeep trailer.

He felt the jeep engine start up and the vibration as the jeep began to move. The throbbing became frantic. He held tightly to the tarp and closed his eyes. It was too late to pray. His mind became a blur of apprehension. The NK machine gun renewed its chatter.

Then the jeep stopped. The Lieutenant waited a moment and quickly found himself alone. The jeep motor for some reason stalled in the open space in full view of the NK gunner. The others were leaping to safety in the ditches. The Lieutenant followed in one tumbling motion. He was still alive.

Once in the ditch on the paddy side, the Lieutenant began looking around, taking cognizance of his new situation. He discovered he had landed beside someone. Then he heard a voice whisper, "Hello, buddy." He looked closer and his jaw dropped. He had splashed into the water beside Columbus Thacker, his recon corporal.

"Thack," he immediately cried and reached for his hand. But there was something peculiar about Thacker's movements. He rolled his head slowly; his eyes appeared glassy; his voice high and thin. The Lieutenant peered more closely. Then he saw the tell-tale stain of blood on the left side. The two looked at each other. Both knew the truth. There was a long moment. The Lieutenant could only hold the hand tighter. Thacker's response came the only way a dying man can manage: "Dear God."

It came out. Thacker, responding to the Lieutenant's urging to move into one of the two withdrawing columns, had taken a place near the lead group. He was in the open when the NK machine gun began firing and was the first man hit. He had been lying in the ditch a little more than an hour. A medic was with him, doing what he could to staunch the blood flow, but that wasn't enough. He needed a doctor.

During the next few minutes, the Lieutenant and the medic formulated a technique to get Thacker out of the ditch and back to safety. With the medic pushing and the Lieutenant pulling under the shoulders, the two managed to float the big man and edge him back toward where the majority of the men still waited. It was hard work and Thacker was in agony.

Finally, after about fifteen minutes, some safe defilade was reached. Both the Lieutenant and the medic were virtually swimming in the paddy, pushing at the muddy bottom with their boots to move their charge. Reaching some weeds, the Lieutenant looked up and saw several tankers peering down at him. The leader, a sergeant, gave an order for his men to reach down and help Thacker up and onto the road so that he could be evacuated in the tank. The M-24 had been the last vehicle away from Taep'yong-ni, covering the final troop withdrawal. Thacker was finally pushed up and onto the side of the road, and the tankers started to turn him over.

Then sharply, up the valley from the direction of Taep'yong-ni, came the cry, "Here they come!" There was no hesitation about personal safety now.

"They" meant only one group—North Koreans. Some of the backed-up infantry took off on a dead run through paddies, water and mud, to the other side of the valley and the stream dike. A few began running down the road toward the motor column, and one or two were cut down. The tankers reacted by shouting to both the medic and the Lieutenant to get out, that they would take care of Thacker.

The Lieutenant surveyed his situation for a final time and decided his best bet was to crawl through the paddies to the still-stalled motor column, using the dirt paddy walls as protection against the enemy gunner. With several others, he plunged into the stinking water and began to propel himself forward.

The little group moved steadily. The sun continued to beat down. Thirst had been bothering the Lieutenant for several hours. Finally, he opened his mouth to let paddy water rinse the inside. He did not swallow. The rinsing alleviated his suffering somewhat. Also, unable to sling his pistol in the manner of a rifle, he had to place it in his pocket. It was now quite muddy and perhaps unusable. What mattered now was to keep going and keep his tail down. He kept as close to the dirt bank as possible and talked and swore to himself to maintain his strength of purpose.

It was difficult to maintain proper direction. Paddy banks aren't laid out in precise measurements. Also, when reaching a paddy jointure, one had to time a movement up and in full view of the NK gunner before falling onto the next paddy and behind the next bank.

The group soon found itself at the edge of a paddy with a petered-out bank. Two men had already reached this point and were sitting there in the water, waiting. They had refused to backtrack. The Lieutenant and his group, on the other hand, did not hesitate but turned back, realizing finally that their only hope lay in reaching the other side of the valley. Fortunately, they discovered they could crawl in that direction at an angle, considerably reducing their chances of being hit.

At last, after what seemed like hours sloshing about in the paddies, the group reached a crucial point of departure. The bank they were following ended about twenty-five yards short of the stream dike. All now paused to gather strength for this final dash. The vehicle column was still on the road, not moving.

Several F-80 jets had appeared earlier and had strafed the stream side of the valley, proof that enemy activity may have been spotted there. An ROK F-51 also appeared, and this plane, instead of following the lead of the jets, which strafed the hill mass only, began strafing the valley and stream in front of the Lieutenant and the group with him. Strafing for all it was worth, the F-51 roared up the valley, made a turn, and then started back down. This time, however, there was no firing. The Lieutenant wondered why.

Two men made the break in front of the Lieutenant. They made it safely. It was his turn. With pounding heart, he crawled as far as he could and then, standing up heavily, he too made the dash.

The NK gunner, meanwhile, had seen the running men. Bullets began cracking through the air. The Lieutenant was afraid his luck was about to run out. But the dike was reached and, as he did earlier that morning, he threw himself at the top and rolled over and down the other side. He continued to run across the rocks that dotted the stream bed. The thumping in his arteries was terrible. Sharp needles were felt in his extremities, and his legs were like dead weights. But he forced himself on and finally gained the far side of the stream and the protective boulders ringing the base of the hill.

Pausing to measure his predicament, the Lieutenant noted several wounded and dead Americans, casualties caused by the pilot of the ROK plane. The pilot was so intent on relieving the pressure on American groups along the road that he fired on these men, thinking them to be NK. That the plane finally veered away was due to several brave souls who stood in the open and waved.

One man continued huddled behind a large rock looking at the sky, even though the ROK plane had disappeared. Another man, a C Company sergeant whom the Lieutenant recognized, sat with one hand on his upper chest and muttering, "This is it!"

Instinctively, the group with the Lieutenant did not hesitate and began climbing the hill bordering the stream, taking care to walk diagonally to conserve strength, continuing on just short of the ridgeline.

The Lieutenant looked at his watch. It had stopped at some point while he was sloshing about in the paddies, showing the time as 1851 hours. Several jeeps were still parked on the road at the roadblock site, men standing near them. There was yet no sign of the NK. The cry of danger may have been a false one. Whatever, it had resulted in a final disintegration of the First Battalion. For this body of men remaining, the concept of "every man for himself" finally became fact. The only organized unit within reach was the motor column, and in the mind of each struggling infantryman, that column represented a certain haven.

As the little group moved along the hill, the sound of a plane other than a fighter was heard. Everyone stopped. The plane was a B-29.[1] Within minutes the sounds of heavily crashing bombs were heard. The target undoubtedly was the "island," the rendezvous of NK tanks and gun carriages. By bombing the "island" it was hoped to slow movement of wheeled and tracked vehicles once the Kum was bridged by the NK.

Walking more rapidly, the group noted a bend in the stream, beyond which was a lately occupied artillery position. This was where part of the 52nd Field had been in place. Drawing closer, the group saw a soldier, previously a forward defense post rifleman, slumped dead over the leading edge of his hole. Other sprawled figures were nearby. Scattered debris identified the position as having been evacuated in a hurry.

The stream bend was reached and the group began descending. As they recrossed the water, they saw that the motor column was mostly artillery, comprising vehicles of Headquarters and B Batteries of the 52nd Field. There were also vehicles from the 19th Medical Detachment, and these mounted wounded on stretchers.

Just off to the left of the road was a small hut being used as an aid station. Some wounded lay on stretchers scattered on the ground surrounding the hut. Medical personnel were attending to the more seriously wounded among them. A badly wounded soldier lay on a jeep stretcher, and a buddy had attached a small tree branch to the side of the stretcher to act as a shade from the sun, yet above the horizon.

The Lieutenant felt the approach of complete exhaustion. His dirty, matted hair, combined with grimed face and muddy, smelly fatigues, caused several to stop and gaze. He walked up to a jeep where several medics were lounging and asked if he could be given a C-ration can. One of the medics gave him a can of franks and beans. He still had his can opener, but lacked a spoon. Casting about on the ground, he found a small flat stone. Then, for the first time that day, he sat in a state of complete relaxation and ate. Sounds emanating from the head of the motor column indicated that one of the battery howitzers was being aimed and fired at a suspected guerrilla position holding up the column, but the Lieutenant wasn't worried. There were too many soldiers around for a final debacle-like encounter to take place.

After finishing the beans, the Lieutenant asked for water. He began to feel better but was growing tired. Getting up, he moved his tortured limbs down the line of medical jeeps looking for Thacker and Payne. He could not locate either one.

Other escapees from the roadblock were arriving and talking in hushed tones. There may have been two hundred or so men who started back from Taep'yong-ni earlier that afternoon. No one could estimate the number still surviving, but there were fewer than at the start. Some of these were just sitting around with blankly staring expressions. One or two lay sleeping in truck beds.

The Lieutenant found Coles. The two had lost track of each other at the roadblock. Coles reported that he had been with the first jeep across, lying on a trailer tarp. Several men with him were wounded in the dash, one in the buttocks. Hearing this, the Lieutenant, despite his discomforting experience, felt thankful the way things ultimately turned out. Stragglers were still limping or jogging in from across the valley. None arrived along the road by the NK machine gunner.

Then, the word was passed down the line to everyone: "Load up." A motor dash was to be attempted. All wounded on the ground were loaded aboard the medical jeeps. A captain rode down the line urging everyone to climb aboard the vehicles. Once rolling, he said, fire rifles and carbines in the direction of a high hill across the valley. A tank will lead the way. Stretcher jeeps should proceed to the head of the column. If the dash turned out to be a successful one, these would be the first vehicles to break out.

The Lieutenant had no usable weapon when he mounted a truck, but volunteered to load clips. Most weapons being readied in his vehicle were carbines. Motors revved. Men became tense once more. The column began to move, but as it did a mortar shell burst with a fiery blast several yards off the road. Groans were heard, but none were known to have been hurt.

For a minute or two the ear-splitting WHAP of rifle and carbine fire cut through the air. The racket was deafening. The vibration of surging vehicles was felt eagerly by the mounted entourage. But then, after moving only about four hundred yards, the column stopped. It was all over. Word came to dismount. They had failed.

A Night Never to be Forgotten

Darkness was settling; it was after 2100. As the men were dismounting from the trucks, a corporal offered the Lieutenant a pistol. He said it was left on one of the truck beds, and no one had claimed it. The Lieutenant then field-stripped his own, clogged with dried mud, and threw the parts away. He spotted a white phosphorus grenade on another truck bed. He put the grenade in his pocket, bulky as it was. It might come in handy at a later time.

Thus armed, he walked to the head of the column. He soon learned that the lead tank commander had spotted abandoned vehicles further down the road, indicating either another roadblock or something more serious.[1] Since, if this last column was going to continue moving, those abandoned vehicles would have to be shunted by hand, and a pursuing NK patrol or patrols might reach the group in the process, causing numerous casualties, quick decisions would have to be made.

In this moment of need and confusion, two men seemed to "take over."[2] Few in the group knew who they were, as faces were becoming too shadowy for clear recognition. But authority rang from the voices, and the men willingly obeyed.

Soon other officers from the infantry cluster began assisting these two, a sense of duty and order rising from the frankly chaotic atmosphere. Both Coles and the Lieutenant stood by, understanding that authority had been assumed and that what was needed now was cooperation, not more authority. Five officers, it appeared, took charge. The remainder, officers and enlisted together, fused into a mass of cooperative strength. This is the way it should have been, and this is the way it was.

After a short conference, it was decided that the group should leave the road and move by mountain trail in the direction of Taejon. Several ROK interpreters were with the column assigned as liaisons, and these were charged to guide.

Next, all stretchers with wounded were removed from the medical jeeps and trucks and laid along the left of the road. Once this was done, the order went out to push all vehicles into the ditch on the right and overturn them if possible. Men strained to follow this order. Left in the vehicles, on order, was all manner of personal and unnecessary military equipment. Men could carry only arms and ammunition. Expensive cameras were not to be brought out. No vehicles would be set afire, as this action would alert the NK to the group's position.

A number of men labored to destroy vital parts of the vehicles and howitzers. Breech blocks were carried into watery paddies. Firing pins were pocketed.

All infantry with rifles were now ordered forward, placed under the command of a lieutenant, and told to stand fast.

The organizational struggle was now reduced to the last and most pressing problem, care of the wounded. These wounded, on stretchers, were brought forward and laid in the middle of the road. There were twenty-five stretchers.[3] Then all remaining soldiers, those without rifles and including artillery with or without carbines, were lined up in two columns. The count-off was by groups of four; each group of four assigned to a stretcher; two carrying while two rested. The charge given to the rifle-carrying group was to provide escort for the stretcher-bearing body.

Organization of the group was now complete. Heavy darkness had settled. In the process of assigning men their duties, there had been delays. Several officers walked the line warning everyone that an NK patrol was due. "If we don't hurry," they admonished, "an enemy patrol will cut us to ribbons." Then, when all was in readiness, and with the infantry guard leading, the group moved off the road and up a narrow, cultivated hillside.

The Lieutenant was assigned to one of the stretcher units. Carrying became difficult, almost impossible. Men had to walk on slender, dirt paddy walls, and sometimes a man would slip. The result was a curse or a sob from the carried stretcher.

The wounded had been warned that loud outcries might alert the enemy. There were several halts. One halt was made when it was apparent that a man had died. After a brief word by a chaplain who was with the group, the stretcher was laid off the trail, and the others, following, gazed at the remains of an American soldier whose temporary place of repose was on this lonely, dried-up Korean grain field.

Every ear of every man was attuned to the rear during this trek. The NK probably knew by now that the men from the vehicle column couldn't or didn't get far. The questions for the NK were simple. How strong was the American group, and how fiercely would it fight if trapped?

Just after the group left the road with the stretchers, the tank commander set fire to his tank. Everyone cast a fearful glance at the blaze. The group was about halfway up the hillside when a mortar shell exploded near the tank. The NK had seen the fire and were zeroing in. Several more rounds came in, but as long as the mortar was being aimed at the light, the stretcher men were safe.

Finally, despite earlier protestations to the contrary, the burden of carrying became too difficult. The strength of even the strongest was ebbing, having been dangerously drained during the melees of the morning and the hazardous moments during the afternoon. Moreover, the paddy banks were becoming too treacherous to continue much farther. A small plateau was reached and the stretchers laid on the ground, the bearers gathering about.

Suddenly, carbine shots came from the direction of the ditched vehicles on the road. These were enemy test shots, it turned out, designed to draw fire. At the same time, the men became aware of a loud noise coming from a small mound, a short distance down and away from where the group was huddling. The noise was repeated at even intervals and seemed, at first, to be that of a wild animal, perhaps a pig.

Then, discernibly, the men began to recognize the voice as human and the noise that of a man screaming "Help me!" The men listened, but did not move. They had experienced too much that day to become unnerved by the frantic screaming. The obviously incapacitated soldier continued screaming for close to a half-hour before hoarseness set in and the sound faded. The atmosphere there on the hillside plateau was torturous.

With an enemy patrol probably down among the abandoned vehicles, it was decided to send several patrols out to scout the area. These returned within the hour, reporting that the NK were looting the vehicles and that there were some enemy on the hill mass just to the rear of where the group was sitting. It was time to leave.

Someone said aloud that the wounded would have to be left. There was silence for a moment. Then an answering voice, a voice fully poignant, was heard from one of the stretchers: "Put yourself in our place."

Men just turned away. Nothing further could be done. The choice was clear. Either sacrifice a hundred and twenty or so men in an attempt to save the stretcher cases, many of the former without weapons, or relinquish the latter to the whims of the NK and hope for the best. Meanwhile, the remaining able-bodied would chance a return to friendly lines to fight again.

The infantry guard had disappeared by this time. No one knew the circumstances, but it was thought that that group, expecting the stretcher bearers to keep up and continue on, kept going. The men who remained with the wounded that early morning of July 17 were mainly artillery, medical, and infantry without arms. Ironically, the wounded were nearly all infantry.

A chaplain made the final decision. The group would leave without the stretchers. An order was given to all wounded who could to get up and prepare to walk. Several did. About seventeen or eighteen could not. Two officers were seen bending over these men, talking and ministering. A medical lieutenant was said to have volunteered to remain, as did an enlisted corpsman.[4]

It was about 0130 on the morning of the seventeenth. Only the rustle of feet on dry grass marked the departure of the healthy and the walking wounded. As the moving line of men passed the stretchers, every face was averted except for one man who looked down and said, "My God, I feel like hell."

There was continued silence for a moment, and then in a clear, unwavering voice, one of the men on a stretcher replied, "How do you think we feel?"

Few looked back to where the remaining wounded lay. It was enough that this abandonment aroused guilt in the minds of every man walking. Still, there was common recognition that the decision to abandon was a necessary by-product of momentary circumstances, a simple military black and white. For the men on the stretchers, the Conflict was over. For the group on foot, the Conflict was continuing. It was now single file forward, each man straining to keep the man in front in sight. A grim fate could meet those who lagged or strayed.

As the men moved along, they could see, on occasions, the main road and small fires burning. What lay on the road no one knew or cared to discover. Several halts were made to firm direction and watch for NK activity. Each time the group halted the men sat and remained silent. There was never a word above a whisper, and no one lit a cigarette.

A soldier who had been on a stretcher previously now scampered along without shoes or socks. Walking on the hard and sharp, stony ground was dreadfully painful for him. But he told the Lieutenant he would walk until his legs became stumps, if he had to. Other wounded continued moving and were helped over steep ground rises.

First light began to trace through the sky when the group reached a high hill. It was at this point that the valley below widened and lower hills ringed each side. On this last precipice two GIs were discovered. They had been with the 11th Field and had been on the point all night. This general area, a juncture of a small creek and the larger stream that flowed down the valley toward the Kum, had been where both the 11th and 13th Field Artillery Battalions had gone into position. A concrete bridge crossed the water here.

Now down the side of the precipice the group went, half stumbling and half sliding in the soft dirt. Many paused at a little hillside rivulet at the bottom and gulped water. It was the clearest, coldest water most had tasted in several days. Dysentery was furthest from the mind. Quenching of thirst was the priority at this stage.

After tarrying a few moments, the group moved off into the valley, still in single file. The men kept to a path along the base of one of the hills paralleling the road. Wary eyes riveted on hills on both sides of the road for signs of NK movement. The walking wounded were being hurried constantly. One soldier with a bleeding wound in a buttock, having received the wound while crossing the open space at the roadblock on one of the jeep trailers, periodically needed a new compress. He was growing weaker, and several medics were walking close to him.

Another soldier had suffered a bullet wound in the chest area. He was small and wiry, but breathing with some difficulty. He spoke to the Lieutenant once to ask if the latter was formerly at Camp Younghans. The fellow had been with the 49th Field there and had been sent down to the 52nd as a replacement. Neither the Lieutenant nor the wounded man remained far apart throughout the rest of the journey to Taejon.

Suddenly, as the day broke clearer, with the sun shining for the first time over a low-lying hill, a shout was heard. From a bend on the main road there emerged what looked like the head of another foot column. South Korean police led this file. The group with the Lieutenant shrank against the side of the footpath for a long moment in fear that this new group was NK. But soon GIs began appearing, carrying rifles, and there was relief all around.

With the appearance of this new group, the Lieutenant's group began crossing intervening paddies to effect a merger on the main road. It was soon learned that the men in the new group had been in the stalled vehicle column that prevented use of the road by the last motor convoy. There had been a skirmish and casualties. The survivors had waited in the surrounding hills until about an hour before daylight and then began walking out.

Still apprehensive, but sure the worst was over, the men began talking again. Some even nervously began to laugh, the strain receding rapidly. And in a while, the heretofore disciplined files began disintegrating into groups without noticeable leaders. None tried to reimpose discipline. It was better to permit each to relax in his own fashion for the time being.

Several hails were heard from a distance. Individual soldiers could be seen moving along the low-bordering hills and waving. They, too, had waited out the night, cut off, and now, seeing the crowd on the road, were on their way to join it.

Hunger was spreading. Where, during earlier moments of crisis, few thought of eating, those thoughts were now present. The Lieutenant had noticed an unopened can of ham and eggs on the hood of a jeep just before it was ditched the previous night and decided to take it, just in case. He was glad he had so decided because now he would be able to replenish his sagging strength.

He opened the can and, again, using a flat stone, began consuming the contents. Almost immediately he noticed a soldier walking near him, his skin tightly stretched and exhibiting first traces of shock. The man was watching the Lieutenant eat. Without words, the Lieutenant offered the soldier what remained in the can. The fellow barely stuttered his thanks at first, but shortly began to smile a bit and talk to himself. He was obviously feeling better.

Then, that for which everyone had been waiting was glimpsed—an artillery L-5 spotter plane. A speck in the distance at first, but flying closer, the pilot and observer had not as yet seen the men on the ground. But in a minute the plane dove, and the engine roared. Up the valley the plane flew and began circling above the road. Men waved. They had been seen. Their predicament was almost over.

And so, with the arrival of the spotter plane, feelings of security spread throughout the walking groups. The psychological result, as always under these sorts of circumstances, was that the men became greatly solicitous of each other. The slightest wound or difficulty exhibited by one or another was immediately attended to. A number closed around a tall, lanky soldier who was hobbling on a game leg. The boy without shoes was being carried. The hard, graveled road was proving too much for his endurance. A dozen or so men grouped around to spell the carrier.

Medical corpsmen had organized and were with the walking wounded. This group had been sorted out and moving separately. No one would fail or fall out these last few miles. Two self-appointed scouts set off at a fast walk to carry word of the approaching group so that transportation would be available at an established pickup point.

The village of Yusong was reached. Yusong was about two miles from the Taejon airfield. The group with the Lieutenant had been about nine miles in the hills or on the road since leaving the battle line the day before. The regimental supply depot had been at Yusong, and a number of unopened C-ration boxes lay scattered about. Several of the group began rummaging through the boxes, and a few stopped to eat, they were so hungry. But the majority hurried on.

Now the first American was encountered with his jeep. He was 1st Lt. Jerome Christine, an engineer officer. He had blown a bridge the night previous and had driven out to the crossing to inspect the result. He had already radioed 3rd Engineer headquarters about the withdrawing men and told someone near the Lieutenant that the pickup location was along the road another half-mile. He took several soldiers, wounded or near exhaustion, with him, including the man without shoes, and drove back to Taejon.

At the pickup point, finally, the men sat down to rest. Many, including the Lieutenant, were so weary that they ached all over. The Lieutenant walked over to a store building, in front of which was a thick bamboo mat. He lay down on the mat and almost fell asleep in the next instance. But he heard familiar voices and raised up. There, sitting but a few feet away, were several artillery section chiefs who had formerly been with the 48th Field in Japan. They were Sgts. Newton V. Grantham and James A. Fosdick. M/Sgt. Pianca, a former 48th Field operations chief, was sitting nearby. The three had been in the group with the Lieutenant, all three now assigned to the 52nd Field. Pianca asked the Lieutenant if he was the one who nearly brought fire on his own position the morning of the sixteenth. He said he heard the entire conversation with Lt. Col. Stratton and Capt. Simpson on another wire line. No one spoke after that, each lost in his own thoughts.

Trucks began arriving. The Lieutenant decided to leave with the second truck and so climbed aboard. He must have been an odd sight, pistol in one hand and the WP grenade in the other. But most everyone coming out that morning were strange sights, so no one mentioned anything.

During the ride, one of the soldiers spoke the word "Chaplain." The Lieutenant looked up and saw, seated on the truck bed across from him, a man with an earnest, youngish-looking face. He wore an officer's insignia under his collar.[5]

The soldier spoke, "What happened to the other one?"

The answer by the chaplain: "We tossed a coin, and he stayed."

The Lieutenant remembered, now. The two men bending over the wounded on the little plateau were chaplains. There were two in the group rather than the one about whom the Lieutenant had been aware. When the time came to leave, the two had to decide how to divide their ministering, so they simply tossed a coin. The other one remained,[6] while this one came out. Both were accomplishing their missions; both serving God.

The truck's vibration made the Lieutenant sleepy, so he dozed. Then the truck stopped at the division artillery CP, a factory compound. Col. James Beynon met the artillerymen as they dismounted and herded them into battalion groupings. The Lieutenant was the only one from the 13th. The agent from the 13th was summoned and instructed to take the Lieutenant to that CP.

In a few minutes, the agent's jeep pulled into the courtyard of another factory compound, wherein had been gathered the entire 13th battalion. Howitzers were hooked onto trucks. Men in the immediate area stopped to stare at the Lieutenant as he climbed from the jeep. He was mud and grime from head to foot and still carried his pistol and WP grenade. Someone poured a cup of very cold water for him, and then he was guided to the CP where the battalion officers had gathered for a briefing.

Maj. Kron caught sight of the Lieutenant as the latter walked through the CP door and rushed to greet him. After a few welcoming remarks, the major informed him that he had been temporarily listed as missing in action. However, the adjutant, Capt. George Mayer, would correct the Morning Report.

He was asked about the other three men in his section. He replied only that they had not accompanied him out and should therefore be presumed to be missing. He further reported that Cpl. Thacker had suffered a serious wound and that it was unlikely saving medical assistance was available for him.

Lt. Col. Stratton was missing, the Lieutenant now learned. He had been in the vicinity of the 19th regimental CP at the time of NK attacks in the headquarters area. There bad been no word from him since.

Coles had returned to the 13th earlier that morning. He had not been assigned to a stretcher team the previous night so had joined the infantry escort, remaining with that group as it continued on without the stretcher bearers. One man from his section was still missing. "Tex" Fullen was missing. His recon chief, Cpl. Cletus Fitzgerald, had reported that "Tex" had been wounded in the stomach at one of the roadblocks and had been left because no one could carry him out.

Capt. Prescott, the Lieutenant was told, had been on the hill with the machine gun section above Taep'yong-ni on orders from Col. Meloy. Prescott, too, was missing.[7] First Lt. Pate looked tired and begrimed, a picture of dejection. He and his section had been trapped at a roadblock, forcing those with him to walk out during the night. Two of his section were still missing.

No one smiled or laughed during the short Officers' Call. Maj. Kron announced that the battalion would leave Taejon immediately and go into position about five miles further east. While all the other officers stood during the briefing, the Lieutenant sat on one of the few steel chairs in the room. The briefing passed him by. He was too tired to care.

Hushed tones and weary movements marked the exodus of the 13th Field from Taejon. On the way out of the city and toward the new position, the Lieutenant learned something of the drama played out the day previous as affecting the 13th. An NK roadblock had been established during the late morning about a half-mile beyond the artillery. For a time, the artillerymen observed regimental vehicles coming hell-bent down the road after escaping the roadblock.

Then, about 1300 hours, the NK snipers began peppering the artillery area, forcing many to take cover. This action was followed by intermittent mortar fire. The 13th suffered its first combat death as the result of the mortaring. A young private, despite being warned to remain in a defiladed position, broke cover and went to a battery latrine trench. He was killed by a mortar shell that exploded near the trench.

At the height of the sniper and mortar fire, a Chaffee tank lumbered down the road approaching the artillery position. An apprehensive howitzer section chief ordered his crew to fire at the oncoming tank. After the round was fired, the dumbfounded tank commander retaliated by cutting loose with a burst of machine gun fire, sending the howitzer crew tumbling.

That was all for the 13th. As Lt. Col. Stratton, the CO, was still forward near regimental headquarters, the remaining authority ordered a withdrawal to new positions.

A number of vehicles were on the road back by this time, this following the last failed attack by the NK at Taep'yong-ni. About 1400 hours there began a scramble of both infantry and artillery vehicles and men on foot heading to the rear. Part of the 52nd Field made it out. The other part, the group with the Lieutenant, had been a few minutes too late. NK roadblocks choked off all vehicle withdrawals shortly after 1400.

The Lieutenant was further informed that the Second Battalion had been given orders to break the roadblocks and relieve pressure on the beleaguered First Battalion, then trying to withdraw in organized fashion. Col. Meloy, although wounded, had gotten through and was able to give orders for the relief operation. Maj. Gen. Dean, also, arrived at the scene to lend support.

However, instead of the entire battalion being committed, only one company, G Company, actually went into battle formation, and this company, spreading out, advanced but a short distance before returning. The attempt to break the NK strong points was apparently half-hearted. After a few hours, the battalion withdrew, leaving the First Battalion remnants and artillery battery survivors to their respective fates.

Earlier, when the plight of the First Battalion was becoming recognized as desperate, Lt. Col. Stratton volunteered "five hundred carbines on the line," should these be needed in a rescue operation. The offer, of course, was rejected. The Lieutenant was told also that the two 13th firing batteries had withdrawn so quickly that they left ammunition around the howitzer pits.

As the 13th began to wind its way out of Taejon, civilians were noticed packing their goods in preparation for their own departures. There were no smiles or waves. Their glances at the Americans were impassive.

The Lieutenant fell asleep soon after the column left Taejon and woke only when the jeep turned into the new battalion area. Here, alongside the road, a deep, clear stream was flowing. Shade trees were in evidence. The new position was an ideal camping spot, if one were so imaginative as to consider such an activity at this stage of affairs.

Dismounting wearily and without giving much thought to anything else, the Lieutenant stripped off his clothes and plunged into the stream for his first refreshing soaking since leaving Taegu. Later, having rid his body of accumulated grime and after rinsing his clothes and shaving, he lay down to sleep under one of the shade trees. He opened his eyes as light faded, having missed supper. After scrounging several C-ration biscuits, which were filling, he dozed again.

He awakened one more time to strange sounds coming from the roadway fronting the battalion position. A clamor of voices could be heard amidst a general welter of other noises. Then a jeep passed with headlights on. He saw immediately what was happening. The population of Taejon was on the move, those civilians who had remained and were in that city as the 13th artillerymen were leaving. The people must have begun walking in late evening, with the sun down, and now, in the darkness, were passing by on their way south.

The Lieutenant sat up and watched for a minute or two. Then, carefully, he again lay down. The buzz of human confusion rose and fell as the refugees walked on. Mosquitoes swarmed about his head, but he was too tired to swat. Consciously, his lips moved with the prayer that had become so much a part of him these past several days: "Have mercy on us."

He dozed finally, and the night slipped on.

TAEJON[1]

LT. COL. STRATTON RETURNED TO THE 13TH CP ABOUT 1600 HOURS ON THE AFTERNOON of the seventeenth, while the Lieutenant was sleeping. Stratton had been trapped near the 19th CP during the morning of the sixteenth. Realizing that he might not be able to break out by jeep, both he and his Japanese houseboy, Ging, who had accompanied the colonel to Korea, went into nearby hills.

Stratton was over forty-five years of age and the physical exertion of being on foot in hill terrain was almost too much for him. As a result, at nightfall Ging took the colonel on his back at intervals, and together in that fashion they reached Taejon. This truly was one of the more unique experiences endured by a higher rank during the early Korean fighting.

The morning of the eighteenth saw an unusual display of power and confidence on the part of the NK. Six Soviet-built YAK biplanes flew down the valley, along which the artillery was situated. They appeared over the American positions in two groups of three planes each. Their mission, ostensibly, was to awe the Americans with this display of swagger.

But there was a collateral mission as well. The main rail line from Pusan ran beside the road fronting the position. A steady stream of supplies had been brought up by rail the past several days, as it became increasingly evident that the Taejon airstrip might not remain viable much longer. A major objective by both NK guerrilla squads and air units was the severing of this rail line.

The YAKs approached just as breakfast was being served to units in position below. No aircraft warning had been passed along as no aircraft warning radio net was operating at that time. Most of the Americans stood astonished at the sight of the oncoming planes.

Once over the town of Sinch'on, just south of the artillery, the planes circled and began retracing their flight path. Suddenly, just as the circling was completed, an explosion rent the air. One of the planes had dropped a bomb on the rail line a short distance from where the headquarters battery of the 13th was located, damaging one of the two rail lines.

The explosion jarred the artillerymen. Many began scurrying about for shelter, although it was becoming obvious that the planes were reconnaissance types rather than fighters. One plane did dip slightly to strafe one of the howitzer battery positions, but at such a high angle that nothing was damaged nor anyone hurt.

The appearance of the planes and subsequent bombing went unanswered. No antiaircraft vehicles were with the artillery batteries at this stage of combat. These were either with the infantry or at major CPs. The only antiaircraft protection in battery positions were .50-caliber pieces, and most batteries had only two ground mounts and one ring mount on the single maintenance truck.

As the Americans continued to watch, a mass of white was seen to flutter down from several of the planes. It looked suspiciously like a leaflet drop but was too far away for correct identification of same.

Word reached most later in the day that leaflets had indeed been dropped, that the message printed on each leaflet dropped called upon Americans to surrender, promising "good treatment" for those who did so. The entreaty was allegedly signed by an American officer, Capt. Ambrose H. Nugent, S-2 (intelligence) of the 52nd Field, captured somewhere near the town of Ch'onan earlier.

Few if any felt that Nugent had signed this plea for surrender willingly.[2] Knowledge of NK treatment of American prisoners at that time was such that many were resigned to having to act similarly if and when captured. The leaflet drop was purely a propaganda stunt, nothing else. No minds changed. In fact, most felt sorry for Nugent and his fellow prisoners because of the torture and possible death awaiting them, such NK treatment then being circulated by word of mouth. On this note of NK arrogance, the battle of Taejon commenced.

The city of Taejon in 1950 was a major rail and highway center in south central South Korea, it being the terminus of a difficult rail trek through the mountains northwest from Pusan. The terrain eases gradually as it stretches away from Taejon north toward Seoul. Food processing plants were established here as well as some cotton spinning firms and a tannery. There was an estimated prewar population of 70,000, and its downtown district gave the appearance of considerable western influence.

The Japanese had built an airstrip just outside the city to the north and the ensuing American Occupation saw the strip enlarged. In the early stages of the Korean Conflict, the field was of such strategic importance, particularly relevant to the airlift of ammunition, that it is permissible to assume, had it not existed, American units might have faced significant disintegration through lack of necessary supply.

Now with the natural barrier posed by the Kum River in enemy hands, the airfield was in mortal danger. The Taegu field was still being enlarged and would be ready shortly for full operation. The scuttlebutt had it that Eighth Army was asking that Taejon be held at least two more days. Military strategy was apparently being organized to carry out this request.

The city itself was far from ideal as a defense posture. The best defensive positions lay outside the city to the east, where the main highway to Pusan begins its winding way through the mountains. But the airfield was to the north, at the edge of a flat valley leading to the Kum, and so the defense had to expand from there.

Ranges of hills, small to medium, surrounded the city. Roads led out in every direction. Several of the more important roads were the main road north, along which the bulk of the NK were advancing; one to the south toward Kumsan, one to the west toward Nonsan, and then the major artery east, important as the key withdrawal route.

The primary defense line was ranged to the north beyond the airfield, astride the valley leading to the Kum and tied to hills paralleling the valley.

The 34th Regiment was given the challenge of defending both the airfield and the city. That regiment was in the best fighting condition, its losses at Kongju having been negligible when compared to those suffered by the supporting artillery. The main line of resistance (MLR) was based on a protective dike north of the airfield and near Yusong. The 21st Regiment, assuming the role of supporting force, dug in about one mile east of Taejon astride rail and road tunnels. Its mission was to keep those arteries open should the developing military situation dictate another withdrawal.

The first hero of high rank during the early days of fighting was Col. Robert R. Martin, replacement commander of the 34th Regiment. He had been killed assisting with a 2.36 launcher team against a T-34 enemy tank. Now, as his replacement, came the former commander of the 32nd Regiment, Col. Charles E. Beauchamp. The Lieutenant overheard remarks from other artillery officers that Beauchamp was an aggressive fighter, aiming to transform the 34th. Wherever enemy was sighted he dispatched a company on the theory that where there is smoke there is fire. Some of the more optimistic voiced the hope that perhaps the Conflict was reaching a turning point.

By late evening of the eighteenth, booming from the city's environs indicated that NK artillery was beginning to find the range and that artillery duels would commence soon. Whatever the outcome of this new battle, the end would not be long in coming.

The morning of the eighteenth saw the Second Battalion, 19th Regiment, ordered into Taejon to assist the 34th. So, too, was a battery of the 26th AAA AW battalion, a unit that operated with half-tracks on which were mounted quad .50-caliber machine guns. The mission of the 26th was to provide close support for the infantry, as close to the front as possible.

Following the Second Battalion into Taejon was its direct support artillery, B Battery, 13th Field, commanded by 1st Lt. Thomas B. Monsour. This battery joined the 34th Regiment's support, B Battery, 63rd Field, commanded by Capt. Anthony F. Stahelski. General support artillery was provided by A Battery, 11th Field, commanded by Capt. John B. Heard. In addition, one 105-mm howitzer and crew, all that remained of A Battery, 63rd Field, after the NK overrun at Kongju, was brought up, the crew commanded by 1st Lt. Arthur P. Lombardi. A complete three-battalion regiment now faced the oncoming NK, supported by a normal complement of twelve light and six medium howitzers, plus one.

All available tanks were ordered into Taejon. That morning, a flatcar train of Chaffee tanks, elements attached to the First Cavalry Division, passed the 13th Field area. These had been ferried to Pusan when it was recognized that the number of tanks assigned to the 24th Division was insufficient. Few cheered as the train chugged by, but all stopped work to watch and hope.

When B Battery went into Taejon, Cody, Coomer, and Nattras accompanied as observers. These had been with the 21st Regiment at the holding position outside the city. Now replacement observers were needed. As the 52nd Field was away to the east supporting ROK troops, three officers from the 13th were summoned. So the Lieutenant, Dewey Coles, and young 2nd Lt. Samuel E. Hoover, a staff assistant, were ordered up with the 21st.

After securing his gear, the Lieutenant called down to A Battery for an observer party and jeep. He waited awhile, but none arrived. Then Lt. Col. Stratton called. He was informed that no one had volunteered. The shock of Thacker's probable death and the disappearance of both Wallace and Payne had quelled whatever initial enthusiasm there had been for living dangerously. Stratton then ordered a section to report immediately to his CP. Not five minutes later a jeep was seen leaving the A Battery area and shortly the Lieutenant was looking at his new observer party.

Two men arrived with the jeep. The driver was a husky man with native Indian background. His name: Pfc. Gardener Van Fleet. The other man, a diminutive, extremely soft-spoken individual, was Pfc. Charles W. Dear.

Pfc. Dear had found himself in some difficulty while the battalion was yet quartered in Taegu, a situation not altogether his fault. With several others, some Korean whiskey was secured. After some imbibing, several members of the group went temporarily berserk, indiscriminately firing their carbines. When the battery commander was nearly hit, the group was apprehended and held for courts-martial. However, due to the exigencies of the moment, trial was postponed and area confinement imposed. Now, in this emergency, each member of that group was informed that punishment would be overlooked if one or the other joined the Lieutenant's observer section. Pfc. Dear volunteered.

Lt. Col. Charles B. Smith, 21st Regiment, commander of the first infantry battalion flown into Korea, was a quiet, seemingly unassuming man with curly hair and fair complexion. Not tall, yet well-proportioned, he seemed the prototype of whom one might encounter behind a chief of personnel management desk. He was, at that moment, commanding seven infantry companies, the sole battalion commander of record within the regiment.

Smith was sitting under a makeshift, Arab-style tent when the observer parties arrived, and he appeared preoccupied as if grasping for a solution to a serious problem. He welcomed each observer with a firm and sincere handclasp and then proceeded to detail instructions. All he asked was that the observers fire when necessary and not be afraid of bringing fire in close, if such was in the best interests of all concerned. Then, with a frustrated grimace, he told the observers that his positions were unusually hot. Men had been "dropping like flies" all morning from the heat, he said. Be careful, he warned, and good luck.

The Lieutenant went out to D Company, the weapons unit. The men were dug in on a hill overlooking the main road leading to Taejon and the junction of a side road, leading due north and just east of the city. It was expected that if the

NK chose to organize a major roadblock, this would be the likely spot. A village lay just off the side road and in front of the position. Now deserted, it would soon be fired to prevent it from becoming a haven for snipers.

The men on the hill were tense. They talked in low tones. Many were survivors from the initial action at Osan. First Lt. Delbert Gates, the commander, was cheerful but not optimistic. He had managed to survive the actions to the moment. He felt that somewhere in these hills the whole division might be cut off. None questioned this prescient remark.

The booming from Taejon became louder as the day wore on, but tapered off toward dusk. Van Fleet was sent back with the jeep. Vehicles had to be saved at all cost. There just weren't replacements at this stage. If the situation demanded, Dear and the Lieutenant would walk out with their equipment. Night fell on an uneasy calm.

The operation known as the Battle of Taejon was fought on July 20, 1950. Actually, there were two days of preliminary skirmishing, so one might rightly consider all three days as constituting the battle. Whichever, the tactics and maneuvering that decided the contest came to fruition on the twentieth, so it is this date that is generally accepted as fateful.

Several accounts of this battle have been published. Most accounts follow the multiple-narrative pattern, a number of individuals narrating or reporting a particular experience or a series of same.

Each published account has one element in common with the other: the NK tactical attack pattern. There was, from July eighteenth on, a continuous infiltration of the city by NK guerrillas. This infiltration was followed by a series of frontal assaults against defending infantry. Breakthroughs by NK tanks occurred at intervals. Finally, under pressure and in danger of being fatally flanked, the infantry gave way. Withdrawal from the city was impeded both within the city by myriad sniping activity and on the escape roads by the now-familiar roadblock stratagems. Losses on both sides of men and materiel, particularly American, were considerable.

Four artillery officers and one enlisted individual in Taejon during crucial stages have related something of the overall tactical picture and the parts played by some of the smaller units. Then-2nd Lt. Ellsworth Nelsen, executive officer of B Battery, 13th Field; then-2nd Lt. Raymond J. Cody, observer with B Battery; then-1st Lt. Arthur P. Lombardi, executive officer of A Battery, 63rd Field; then-2nd Lt. Ernest P. Terrell, executive officer of A Battery, 11th Field; and then-Pvt. Bernard W. Robinson, cannoneer, assigned to B Battery, 13th Field, have contributed to the following account.

On July 17 and 18, flushed with victory and booty that fell into their hands along the Kum, both at Kongju and Taep'yong-ni, the NK hurriedly organized a plan of attack on Taejon. Their engineers presumably completed the underwater bridge across the Kum at Taep'yong-ni the night of the seventeenth, making the river fordable for their tanks, gun carriages, and towed artillery. The eighteenth saw this equipment in place around Taejon.

While the NK regulars were thus engaged, guerrillas, many dressed in civilian garb, began making their way into the city. These were relatively unhampered by the Americans, who were yet not fully cognizant of the danger of permitting so-called refugee groups to pass through their lines without a thorough inspection of belongings carried.

These guerrillas began to occupy key positions for sniping purposes, the objective being to panic the Americans into making a sound defense of the city impossible.

When the call for additional friendly artillery came, both B Battery, 13th Field, and A Battery, 11th Field, moved forward and underwent night occupations of position. Both batteries located near the extreme north edge of the Taejon airfield, along with howitzers from the 63rd Field. The three batteries were primed to provide viable close-in support for the infantry manning a line near the town of Yusong.

With dawn of the nineteenth, the reason for the night move became clear. Without cover or concealment, B Battery particularly, to use an expression, stood bare-assed in full view from enemy-held terrain. Not unexpectedly, the NK began to shell B Battery's position, forcing most cannoneers to ground cover except during fire missions, and preventing observers from going forward. One 11th Field howitzer was disabled by an NK shell burst.

During this phase of the battle, B Battery, 13th Field, received fire missions through a centralized division artillery net. This interposition resulted in fewer support missions being fired and zero missions when wire communications failed at intervals, to the detriment of the supported 34th Regiment.

About the middle of the morning of the nineteenth, after some infantry began drifting back from the forward dike MLR, it was becoming clear that the MLR and the airfield could not be defended much longer. First Lt. Monsour left on a reconnaissance mission to select a new artillery position inside the city. During this time, NK counterbattery fire disabled two prime mover trucks and six or so men were injured. Although several NK shells exploded between howitzer trails and a fire broke out behind one howitzer in the ready ammo pit, no one was killed.

Disastrous to the battery's support efforts, obviously, was the severing of wire lines to the fire direction center at division artillery headquarters. Ground communication to supported infantry also was interrupted. Of considerable immediate concern to the artillerymen was a fire that began at or near an infantry ammunition storage hut bordering the airfield. Within a short time after the fire started, rifle and mortar ammunition began exploding, sending troops in the vicinity to cover.

NK firing ceased temporarily at dusk or about 2100 hours, so the battery withdrew (march-ordered) while it could. One howitzer at a time was pulled out of position and taken into Taejon. The maneuver was designed to deceive the NK into assuming that the battery was remaining in place. One or another of the howitzers fired harassing rounds, contributing to the deception effort.

B Battery left its forward position at a fortuitously charmed moment. Within an hour after the last howitzer was moved, several NK tanks appeared, bent on a destruction mission. The arrival of the tanks was probably tied to the earlier cessation of NK firing, the cessation permitting the battery to withdraw without damage.

The 11th Field's A Battery also withdrew, their new position being at the western edge of Taejon. As the 13th Field's B Battery had done, the 11th Field withdrew one howitzer at a time until finally the fifth and last howitzer was operable in the new position just prior to daybreak on the twentieth.

Then, shortly after the last 155-mm howitzer was in place and integrated, several NK tanks approached. With one of the new 3.5 bazookas or launchers, issued to the battery the previous day, 2nd Lt. Ernest Terrell and Cpl. Walker, as a launcher team, fired two rockets at the tanks, one over and one short. Although not damaged, the NK tank crews halted, reversed track, and left to pursue other mission objectives.

At some point during the night of the nineteenth/twentieth, trigger-happy guards at both division and division artillery headquarters compounds began mistakenly to fire at each other, the two CPs being quite close. A regular "battle" developed until an unknown hero managed to bring about a cease fire.

The NK attack against the city began in earnest several hours or so before dawn on July 20. The bulk of the 34th Regiment had been positioned along a defensive dike north of the airfield. Elements of the 19th Regiment covered flank and rear approaches.

First Lt. Lombardi had been positioned with his lone 105-mm howitzer in a direct-fire stance behind the 34th defenders. That line broke shortly after 0300, forcing him to abandon the position and tow his piece into Taejon and to a new location close to division headquarters. Encountering a division staff officer, Lombardi spelled out the battle predicament as he saw it, but was informed that the 34th still held the dike line.

By about 0430, however, a report was received that NK tanks were advancing along the main road behind the American defense line and toward Taejon. With this report, no one doubted that a general withdrawal by American forces had begun.

By the middle of the morning, about 1000 hours, no firm defensive line existed. Infantry and artillery were mingling at Taejon's outskirts. Some point-blank firing by the artillery was begun, but it was soon apparent that such action was wasted.

Amid all this confusion, some infantry glimpsed several NK tanks that appeared to have been mired in a watery rice paddy. An infantry staff officer arrived at the B Battery CP with this information and prevailed upon 1st Lt. Monsour to send two howitzers forward and onto a small ridgeline, from which line-of-sight firing with antitank shells might destroy or at the very least damage the tanks. That the artillery was called upon in this instance indicated either a state of great ignorance concerning the whereabouts and tactical commitments of the American Chaffees, which were supposed to be present in abundance in and around the city, or the fact that the infantry no longer trusted these light tanks for antitank action.

As it turned out, only one howitzer was able to be maneuvered into a firing position. Then, before the crew could fire a first round, the supposedly mired NK vehicles began counterbattery action. This, combined with enemy small arms and machine gun firing, forced the artillery crews to temporarily abandon both pieces. Returning within a short time, the men were able to rehook the howitzers to prime movers and beat a hasty retreat. Mercifully, only one casualty was suffered by the American group: 2nd Lt. Nelsen took a fragment in one leg and his bayonet scabbard was severed.

Maj. Gen. Dean, meanwhile, came upon the lone howitzer brought back by 1st Lt. Lombardi and which was parked near division headquarters. The general ordered the piece emplaced at a point near the center of the city and prepared for direct-fire missions. Lombardi later recollected that the position selected by Dean was a poor one, but recognizing the extreme duress the general was under, he accepted the order without question.[3]

By noon of the twentieth, panic reigned in Taejon. NK infiltrators, many white-robed, began a heavy, continuous sniping fire on passing vehicles, causing many casualties. The Americans, in response, literally began to shoot at anyone and anything as they moved from one objective to another. Also by noon, NK tanks were reported operating within the city limits, and these were soon positioned at strategic points, acting as streetblocks. Taejon's defenses were cracking wide open.

A train stood at the railroad station where the medical facility was located, waiting to evacuate the wounded. Medical personnel from both the infantry and artillery were there. Sometime in the early afternoon, as guerrilla activities intensified, the area around the station began to burn.

The train's engineer, becoming extremely apprehensive and fearing that another moment might be too late, tied down his whistle and pulled on the throttle. Amid a hail of bullets, he succeeded in breaking through the closing ring with the last complete train to leave Taejon. In that melee, one of the surgeons was seriously wounded and died shortly afterward. His death was a serious blow to the division's medical services at this stage.

About this time the 34th Regiment was given orders, wherever chains of command existed, to fall back and withdraw from the city. So disorganized was that regiment that small groups formed under the direction of any present officer or NCO, and these groups began shooting it out with guerrillas wherever withdrawal was hampered.

Many from the 19th Regiment's Second Battalion began grouping about Monsour's B Battery, not only to give that unit additional protection, but hoping to ride out of the city on battery vehicles. Theirs was not hoping in vain. At about 1400 hours, Maj. Gen. Dean ordered B Battery, mounting infantry from the 19th, to clear a vehicular passage out of the city along the east road. The word to march-order was given and, within minutes, that unit was on its way.

Within this march column were vehicles, howitzers, and men from B Battery, 13th Field; vehicles and men from the 24th Quartermaster Company; vehicles and men from the division artillery headquarters; and a scattering assortment of men and vehicles from other division units.

A second column already was forming consisting of the 11th Field battery, the 63rd Field battery and, again, assorted division vehicles.

Finally, all infantry who could clambered aboard any truck or jeep with room, welcome additions to the forming convoys. More rifles and BARs firing meant lessened apprehension over NK snipers and potential roadblock activity.

And so, the many vehicles comprising the columns began moving, in line and slowly at first, infantry and artillerymen crouching together, balancing, standing atop full loads of equipment and ammunition boxes, caught up in a euphoria of security as each adjusted to the deep-pitched engine noises welling up, the vibrations and general road clatter welcome changes from the horrific combat experiences of the previous days and nights.

When the B Battery-led column began its withdrawal, little NK sniping was noticed. However, when the column swung onto a narrow street lined with buildings two stories or higher, sniping and other types of harassing fire poured onto the passing vehicles. Every man on board the trucks and jeeps returned fire. The riding infantry suffered many casualties. Several were killed by a grenade thrown onto the bed of a truck.

And just when everyone felt the worst was over, another road turn brought the column into a very narrow street where the NK had pushed telephone and electric utility poles to form low vehicle-impeding angles. Men in the column had to push poles away and brush wires aside in order to keep moving, all the while drawing NK fire.

An NK machine gun had been positioned inside a fairly substantial white stone building along this street, and its devastating effect forced the column to pause briefly. Then one soldier, who had been carrying one of the new 3.5 bazookas, hopped off a three-quarter-ton truck and quickly but carefully aimed a high explosive rocket at the building. His aim was perfect. A portion of the building collapsed and the NK gun crew presumably disabled as firing from the building ceased.

As the eastern edge of the city was reached, the column encountered a final, formidable series of roadblocks organized on the sides of hills paralleling the road. It was here that much damage was done. The vehicles and the men riding in them were completely exposed to NK rifle, machine gun, and mortar fire.

The column hit this final series of roadblocks at full speed. Straight into the teeth of enemy fire the column roared until mountain turns were reached and then safety within the lines of the 21st Regiment, the latter standing mercifully to receive the battered withdrawing elements. It was something of a miracle that only two 13th Field trucks and one howitzer were disabled and abandoned during the run past the final roadblocks. Although several in the artillery were wounded, only one suffered a fatal injury.[4]

Back in Taejon, meanwhile, guerrilla activity heightened with the movement of withdrawing troops and vehicle convoys. Men still on foot struggled from corner to corner. Burning buildings and stalled vehicle groupings drove many frantic as they jockeyed for an edge that might see them safely away.

The 11th Field's A Battery, in its new position close to the city, spent much of the morning and early afternoon of the twentieth firing missions called to the battery from air observers. At least five T-34 tanks were reported disabled as the direct result of firing from the 155-mm howitzers. But increasingly that battery came under small arms and machine gun firing from a ridge along the position's left flank. It was becoming evident that its position would have to be abandoned, so Capt. Heard left to reconnoiter for a new position.

About 1600 hours, 2nd Lt. Terrell received a message from division artillery headquarters to load battery personnel on wheeled vehicles and immediately abandon the battery's position in preparation to leave Taejon. The howitzers and prime movers were to be left. Somewhat perplexed by this order, Terrell protested that although the march-order exercise might be a bit slow, he desired to do everything possible to salvage both the howitzers and the tracks.

The DivArty officer refused Terrell's response and gave him a direct order to evacuate only battery personnel. Terrell accepted the order, loaded his men on all available wheeled conveyances, and left the position.

Maj. Gen. Dean must have received word almost immediately of the order affecting the withdrawal of the general support battery personnel. He sent his Aide, 1st Lt. Arthur M. Clarke, in search of the wheeled artillery convoy. Fortunately, the convoy had been caught up in a traffic jam while still within the city's limits, enabling Clarke to overtake it and speak with 2nd Lt. Terrell. Clarke asked Terrell to leave the convoy temporarily and report to Gen. Dean. The convoy vehicles should remain parked along the street until, he, Terrell, returned.

At the 24th Division headquarters, and after relating, again, the order received from division artillery headquarters, Terrell was asked by the general if he could retrieve both howitzers and prime movers, as well as any other equipment left, and do so if an infantry platoon was provided for covering support? Terrell replied that he could. An arrangement was then made for the infantry unit to meet the artillerymen at the howitzer position.

Returning to the parked convoy, Terrell selected twelve men to assist in the retrieval effort, then ordered the remainder of the battery to continue withdrawing by joining the main vehicle column that had just begun moving, if very slowly.

The promised infantry platoon was in place when Terrell and his detail arrived at the position. Each of the operable howitzers and their prime movers were moved quickly from their firing locations and onto the nearby road in withdrawal order. The covering infantry did its job so well that none of the artillerymen were killed or wounded during the retrieval undertaking.[5] *The five tracks with howitzers, including Terrell's vehicle, formed a small convoy that moved to join the larger, second column endeavoring to leave Taejon, the one that had jammed up earlier.*

This second column, one comprising a multitude of vehicles from different divisional units, and including Capt. Stahelski's 63rd Field battery, 1st Lt. Lombardi's lone howitzer, and retrieved howitzers and tracks from A Battery, 11th Field, met disaster. Led by a higher-echelon staff officer, the column made a wrong turn in the city and found itself in a section overrun by NK. In the process of reversing direction, a number of men, vehicles, and battery equipment were lost. Then, after the correct road exit was reached, additional casualties and vehicle losses were suffered running the same guerrilla gauntlet endured by the 13th Field battery.

The 11th Field battery emerged, finally, with only a few trucks, prime movers, and one howitzer. Losses incurred by Capt. Stahelsky's battery were such as to raise questions later concerning the continued viability of the 63rd Field as a support unit within the division.

Smaller groupings of vehicles continued to form, maneuvering past guerrilla harassing points and following along streets leading to the city's eastern exit. These groupings included service, antiaircraft, and medical vehicles, the latter carrying wounded. Dismounted men were observed hurrying across open areas or crawling in ditches to escape the more accurate of the NK riflemen. And occasionally a vehicle would slow, allowing a dismounted soldier or two to fling themselves aboard.

One of the last vehicle columns streaming out of Taejon that day was Service Battery, 63rd Field, commanded by Capt. Maurice S. Slay. The battery's trucks were loaded with ammunition and other military essentials. Losing contact with his headquarters, Slay decided to withdraw along the west road leading to Yuch'on.

After traveling a short distance, the battery encountered an impenetrable roadblock, several trucks and Chaffee tanks having been trapped there. Not hesitating a moment, Slay ordered the column to reverse there on the road, the road being just wide enough for the passage of a truck and a jeep, and head east. Slay's order rendered all trailers, including the kitchen trailer, expendable.

Taking a deep breath, the column tore east through Taejon without stopping and reached friendly lines with the loss of only two trucks. Despite his quick thinking and acting, which decisions secured the safety of a complete battery of men as well as valuable supplies, Capt. Slay never got over the fact that his footlocker, with all his personal possessions, was left behind in one of the trailers. Such are the casualties and heartbreaks of war.

Second Lt. Terrell, meanwhile, leading his battery track convoy, although realizing that he, too, had missed the street leading to the east exit road, continued on the south road that led to Kumsan. Only two tractors followed him, the remaining tractors halting to attempt a turnaround with the other convoy vehicles. NK rifle fire disabled Terrell's vehicle, forcing him to climb onto the side of one of the two following tractors and hanging in that position until safety in the countryside was reached. While clinging, he suffered wounds from mortar fragments, wounds that were not serious.

Unknown to 2nd Lt. Terrell at this time, Maj. Gen. Dean, accompanied by 1st Lt. Clarke, his Aide, had already driven out of Taejon, past the very heavy NK presence at the city's outskirts and down the south road toward Kumsan. A few miles outside of Taejon, Terrell, now with only one track vehicle, came upon Gen. Dean's wrecked vehicle, the general lying beside it. He did not seem to be wounded or injured. His Aide, along with five or six American soldiers, was resting alongside a nearby house.

Terrell endeavored to convince the general to climb aboard the remaining track and continue on to friendly lines in this fashion. But Dean refused, noting that the track already was crowded with wounded. He felt that the vehicle ought to continue without him. Terrell, then, had no choice but to order the track driver to continue. He, Terrell, would remain with the general.

By the time darkness fell, there were twenty or so soldiers gathered. This group, to include Gen. Dean, began to walk along a ridge paralleling the road. It was hoped that pathways atop the ridge might lead to the new American combat position.

Reaching the top of the ridge, the men began a steady pace, but soon Gen. Dean decided to leave the group and descend to the valley floor in search of water. At this, the group ceased walking and sat until near dawn in the expectation that the general would rejoin them. He did not return and so, after changing direction and walking a bit farther, the group again stopped to wait out the day (July 21), continuing on after dark.[6]

Sometime on the twenty-second, Terrell formed a smaller group. This group left the hill trails and began walking toward one of the small hamlets that dotted the Kumsan road. At one of the hamlets they secured food and some native clothing. Thus attired, this smaller group began mixing with refugees along the way. Finally, on July 23, Terrell's group reached the line organized by the First Cavalry Division's 8th Regiment.

From his OP location within the 21st Regiment's line, the Lieutenant looked out over the main road and saw vehicles of the withdrawing forces approach. For several hours they appeared, some after long intervals, most in groups of four or more. Some vehicles were undamaged, the men in them unhurt. A few overloaded trucks, engines pushed to the limit, stalled just inside the 21st outposts. Most every vehicle carried at least one wounded soldier. Many vehicles doubling as medical conveyances carried casualties resulting from roadblock actions. Then, there were no more.

Yet the drama continued. About 2000 that evening, a whistle was heard on the rail line beyond the outpost stations. An engine was seen to come down the tracks, steam escaping from cracks in the boiler, but still moving. The whistle was tied down. The engine disappeared through a tunnel and emerged on the other side, stopping somewhat north of the 13th Field position.

Several dismounted soldiers had located the engine somewhere within Taejon, it holding enough steam for operation, commandeered it, and brought it and themselves to safety. It was a deed of both ingenuity and heroism.

The road out of Taejon became quiet. It was time for the 21st Regiment to withdraw. Stragglers were still coming down the road, walking, and individuals would continue to do so throughout the night and perhaps into the next day.

There was now no relief regiment. The 19th was being reorganized with new regimental and new battalion commanders. The 34th had disintegrated for the moment. What constituted strategy now no one knew. All that mattered at this late hour was the destruction of both the road and rail tunnels and protection for the remaining operable artillery.

The pullback began about 2300 hours. It was pitch black at first. D Company, furthest up, was the first out, the remaining companies following. When everyone was clear, the rail tunnel was blown. The road tunnel would be destroyed in another hour.

As the Lieutenant stood by his jeep awaiting further movement, an 11th Field track appeared out of the darkness. By some miracle, the track and the men in it had traveled the entire distance from Taejon without being fired on. The track driver said that the last roadblock had been abandoned and that stragglers were at that moment walking on the road. He asked directions to the nearest aid station, as he had several wounded men in his track. The Lieutenant pointed to a small shack about two hundred yards further on. The driver politely thanked the Lieutenant, then drove off.

A peculiar light began to illuminate the sky about this time. Looking up, the Lieutenant saw, reflected on a low-hanging ceiling, a strange and eerie coloring with red tinge. None needed to be told what was happening. The city of Taejon was burning. The light from the fires bent low over the infantry walking along the road, and the Lieutenant was reminded of WWI battle descriptions that detailed burning towns and villages in France.

D Company had been given the assignment of protecting the two firing batteries and the headquarters battery of the 13th Field. The remainder of the 21st went into a roadblock stance a short distance beyond on the main road and near the blown tunnels.

After some stop-and-go driving among groups of the 21st, as the latter waited or walked about on the road, the D Company column reached the 13th Field area. First Lt. Donald L. Seem, Headquarters Battery commander, guided the jeeps with trailers off the road and into the battery areas.

It was late; nothing to do now but sleep. No one thought of the morrow. Weariness had come to everyone. There seemed little hope. When will all this cease?

The Lieutenant acted to shut out these thoughts by curling up on the hood of his jeep and falling asleep.

Relief

Another pullback took place at 0900 the next morning. As the 21st Regiment remained the only viable combat unit within the division, and there being numerous opportunities for the victors of the moment to slip down side roads and through mountain passes out of Taejon, it was decided to establish the next major defense line some fifteen miles to the south in and about the communications center of Yongdong. Some excellent hill positions just north and west of the town dominated a terrain that could be used to good advantage in further delaying the NK march.

As to artillery support, the 52nd Field had been moved somewhere to the east behind ROK forces, and no one knew the status of the 63rd Field. On July 21, two batteries of the 13th Field and one battery of the 11th Field constituted supporting artillery for American troops in Korea.

Both Dear and the Lieutenant had been sitting on the top of a narrow, wooded ridge opposite the headquarters battery, observing a road that led west toward Taejon. News of the pullback came first over the infantry radio, and the Lieutenant became aware of what was happening when, shortly, they found themselves alone.

Both quickly strapped their SCR-610 radio onto packboards and then stumbled down a path to the main road. They reached the road berm just as the Headquarters Battery column began turning out onto the road. Not knowing where his other section member was, the Lieutenant decided not to take chances by waiting, so stepped into the line of traffic, causing a three-quarter-ton to stop. The two climbed aboard and crouched on the truck bed the entire jolting journey south.

A hospital train was standing in the Yongdong rail station as the 13th column entered the town. The vehicles halted next to the train while Maj. Kron reconnoitered for positions. Glancing at the faces framed by the passenger coach windows, the artillerymen were not above voicing feelings. These were the "lucky ones," the wounded and the sick. They were going back to where it was safe, where civilization began again.

More than once, the utterance, "You lucky bastards," was heard along the column. These were not angry outbursts. Rather, they were voiced combinations of pity and chagrin, the latter a touch of feeling sorry for oneself. For those who may not fully comprehend the coarse language of the ranks, the phrase "lucky bastards" may properly be equated with "You are, indeed, the most fortunate of men, and I am envious of you to no end." There were a number in both the 21st Regiment and the 13th Field who fancied a ride to Pusan in a hospital train or in any other conveyance, for that matter.

Maj. Kron returned shortly and the column, making a U-turn in the depot lot, headed wearily toward the next planned battle area and into position. At the northern outskirts of the populated community, the howitzers once again pointed north.

Col. Richard Stephens, indeed, had chosen formidable defense positions. The hills were high, and observation from them was excellent. However, most positions were bare of significant vegetation, making camouflage difficult. An overstrength battalion of the 21st went on the line. The Lieutenant occupied an OP that was the highest in the area, it being termed King Mountain. Ray Cody and Sam Hoover went up with companies on the left side of the road and forward by several hundred yards of the Lieutenant's OP. The Lieutenant was alone, without supporting infantry.

It had begun to rain that afternoon, the first precipitation since July 15. This was one of those slow, drizzly rains that usually usher in periods of cooler weather. In contrast to the blazing heat of the past several days, the weather change now settling in was chilling. There was absolutely no shelter where the Lieutenant sat, high up by himself on King Mountain. A grave mound offered only a back rest.[1]

Later, when it was almost dark, and wrapped in his poncho, the Lieutenant began experimenting with various curled positions so that he might keep most of his body and his shoes dry as he dozed. He lay with steel helmet on, twisting it in such a way as to shelter his face. Soon he was satisfied. Water still dripped on his chin, and he could feel some damp from the ground through his poncho, but he would remain fairly dry through the night.

The rain ceased falling by morning, but the sky continued heavily overcast. The Lieutenant spent about ten minutes moving his arms and legs so that circulation might resume normally and aching muscles find relief. He had spent most of the night curled in one position. He now faced another tension-filled day. An officer from D Company was telling people the day before that both the 25th and the First Cavalry Divisions had been alerted, and that some 25th Division units already were in Korea. Another officer had staked his reputation on the assertion that a Marine unit was on its way from the States.

None of the line troops in Korea were officially aware of any new manpower developments. The unofficial service newspaper, *Stars and Stripes,* was as yet unavailable for frontline distribution and, of course, there were no civilian radios about. Yet rumors of relief seemed reasonable, and every American soldier within the division continued to hope that relief or assistance was just around the bend in the road.

"Those sons-of-bitches had better get here soon," someone warned in shivery tones, "or there'll be none of us left to be relieved." Similar voiced declarations were heard throughout the 24th Division ranks the morning of July 22.

Some unusual activity was spotted about 0930 ahead of the line and near a concrete bridge, now blown, marking the edge or boundary of the defense plain. Men were observed walking along the road toward the blown bridge. The Lieutenant was too far back to observe clearly, but Sam Hoover, on the hill closest to the bridge, began to transmit that stragglers from the 34th Regiment were approaching and that vehicles should be sent forward to pick them up.

Within minutes, vehicles, including ambulance jeeps, sped up the road. The approaching men, perhaps fifty in number, began crossing the stream by the bridge. Few had equipment of any kind, and only one or two had helmets. Several were walking wounded. They had been on the road or in the hills since the evening of July 20. None appeared to show any emotion as they struggled up the stream bank to where transportation waited. They merely climbed aboard the waiting trucks and sat down, totally exhausted, wanting little more than a hot meal and opportunity for unbroken rest.

And then it happened. Unknown to the Lieutenant and the other observers, liaison officers from the First Cavalry Division arrived at the 21st Regiment CP about the time the stragglers from Taejon were first spotted. Shortly, though, perceiving uncommon activity on the main road to his rear, the Lieutenant switched on his radio and then listened as both Cody and Coles were exulting their happiness to each other over the arrival of a relieving cavalry. But it was Sam Hoover who then came on to voice the sentiment of all by suggesting, "We should get down on our knees and thank God."

Second Lt. Delorimier, the liaison with the observers, broke in on the transmissions to warn the observers not to leave their positions until officially relieved, meaning a battery of cavalry artillery in place and a base point fired. He would let everyone know, he said.

About 1300, a pushed coach train started to edge up the valley from Yongdong. There was considerable speculation at first about this movement. Always able to procure the best in Japan, most thought that the cavalry was managing to ride the rails right up to the front line. This was a new one all right.

But the coaches were empty. The 21st, when relieved, would mount up and ride back. This was more like it. The train ride was a fitting gesture to a regiment that had been the first to fight in Korea and had lost so much. The train continued backing and then stopped. Everyone waited, just waited.

They arrived an hour later, crammed full in trucks. There was no shouting or waving this time. The wet and tired remnants of the 24th Division just sat and looked. Like starving eyes on a tray loaded with food, they watched the cavalry dismount, form troops, and then begin the long climb to the hill positions.

It took so long for them to negotiate the pathways. Officers still wore the pale faces of garrison duty. The men were immaculate in clean fatigues and were clean-shaven. Their weapons were spotless, and they carried the regulation pack. Even the steel helmets shone in the dull light. They were ready for a parade around the Plaza in Tokyo.

They came up now, C Troop, 8th Cavalry Regiment.[2] Most of the officers were second lieutenants. They looked nervous, even after the Lieutenant tried to tell them it might be another day before the NK appeared. They merely shrugged and looked wan. There must have been some horror stories circulating about earlier engagements.

The relief observer came up. He was 1st Lt. Emerson L. Reffner, with A Battery, 99th Field. He had just been assigned to that unit after holding a desk job somewhere in Tokyo. He told the Lieutenant that Eighth Army was "cleaning out" headquarters units to find combat fillers and replacements.

Reffner also reported that the cavalry had just completed an amphibious landing at P'ohang-dong on the east coast. He chuckled a bit when he related this because, he said, although it was a combat operation for which the division would receive an *arrowhead* insignia, Eighth Army brass watched the landing from the shore.[3] (The Lieutenant recalled that the cavalry had been the first Occupation division to complete amphibious training at Camp McGill, Japan.)

DeLorimier called the observers. The cavalry artillery was in position and the 13th Field now officially relieved. The Lieutenant and Dear saddled their radio onto packboards and moved away. The Lieutenant waved to Reffner, but the latter was too preoccupied to respond. He was now alone, as the Lieutenant had been a week previous. The men of the 21st Regiment continued to file into the rail coaches, a pitifully few compared to the cavalry troops.

It had begun raining again as the two reached the road and climbed into a waiting vehicle. They headed for the town of Yongdong, where the artillery was gathering for a rearward trip.

On reaching the outskirts of Yongdong, the Lieutenant's jeep joined the main 13th motor column as it entered the main road. On the right, the 99th Field was in position. And as the 13th column straightened and began leaving the Yongdong area, the remaining cavalry artillery battalions approached. These were the 61st, the 77th, and 82nd Fields. The cavalrymen were standing up in the trucks gazing at the men of the 13th sprawled in theirs. (Someone wrote about the relief operation as follows: "As (General Gay's) men moved to the front, they met the gaunt, bone tired GIs of the 24th Division, some barefooted, some almost naked, all staggering from exhaustion."[4]

This was a highly imaginative and mostly inaccurate description of the relief operation. The 21st, at that moment, was the most rested of the three regiments. Although a number may have appeared to be or given the impression of being near prostration, the actual case was a highly exaggerated sense of deliverance. Whatever the troops looked like, and it was true that they were not unsoiled specimens, the appearance of the cavalry was a restorative. The Americans in the 24th Infantry Division were more relaxed on that afternoon than at any time previously in Korea.)

Rain continued and heavy this time, a bad omen. Rain and overcast skies helped the NK in that friendly air support was hampered. The NK were probably on their way out of Taejon that very moment and moving toward Yongdong. If this weather continued, the cavalry would be fighting very soon.

The cavalry artillery was behind them now, and the road was becoming a mess of mud and ruts. Slowly as a result, and then a bit faster, the 13th Field continued its lonely march to the rear and rest.

No Rest for the Weary

The 13th Field motored down the main road to the town of Waegwan, just south of the Naktong River, and then turned northeast along that river to a comparatively level, rocky, almost dry streambed. There, without going into position but establishing an informal motor park with howitzers still hitched to trucks, the men dismounted and sat down. They remained sitting until supper, sat while they ate, and later, when darkness fell, merely pulled on ponchos or unrolled blankets and lay down.

Despite the need for alertness, only a minimum guard was posted for the night, allowing most an unbroken slumber. In this way, as Lt. Col. Stratton put it, the men would be restored more quickly and rise the following morning to carry on in former fashion.

Stratton was wiser than many thought. Now that all were together again, observers, gunners, and headquarters, the Lieutenant took a closer look at his "old man." Although both had been at Camp McGill before the Conflict broke out, the Lieutenant had heard about Stratton only through Bill Gibbons. Garrison life being somewhat different than battle, the real evaluation had to wait until now.

The colonel, typically, was a man of action. He was West Point trained. Somewhat short and paunchy, he had graying sandy hair and blue eyes that pierced when angry. He had stern features, a Roman nose, and a red face, darker when exposed to the sun, lighter when indoors awhile.

When in battle dress, his irrepressible hustle was so disheveling that any press or distinction to his uniform vanished almost from the moment he donned it. Further, he was never able to make his helmet liner and steel cover fit snugly on his head. More often than not, as he faced one way, his helmet faced obliquely another direction or was perched comically on the rearward side of his crown.

Yet these personal oddities or flaws aside, Stratton was in his element in a battle situation, constantly thinking ahead and shuttling continuously between his CP and forward units. He had created quite a favorable stir among the supported infantry as one who would never abandon the foot soldier, no matter the circumstances.

His proposal to volunteer his men to help rescue the 19th Regiment's beleaguered First Battalion, north of Taejon, regardless of the inexpediency of the offer, endeared him to the infantry leadership. Also the fact that, along with other infantry, he had been trapped behind roadblocks south of the Kum and eventually found his way back without suffering harm, added to his reputation.

The plain result was that the colonel's presence forged a strong rapport between infantry and artillery, and such that the mere mention that the 13th Field was firing the howitzers instilled maximum confidence to all facing the NK across the narrow valleys.

Stratton also had a rather unorthodox way of saluting and responding to salutes that were sources of amusement yet comfort to his men. When departing on one of his frequent jaunts, he would invariably give last-minute instructions to a subordinate, and then, when the latter would salute his understanding, he would respond with a wide sweeping motion of the right hand to the side of his helmet, affirm his own acknowledgement with a well-mouthed "Good-o," motion to his driver, and be off in a cloud of dust. More than once, in extremely tense situations, this drama would elicit smiles all around. Lt. Col. Charles W. Stratton was a soldier's soldier.

The morning of the twenty-third found the battalion tending to those simple chores of personal sanitation and cleanliness. Bodies were bathed, faces shaved, clothes washed, and haircuts given. Attention then shifted to the cleaning and lubrication of vehicles and howitzers. Radios were attended to and wire rewound. No supervision here. The men were automatic in their application to essential unit needs. Later in the morning mail was delivered, and all work ceased for a short while as messages from home and Japan were read.

About 1300 that afternoon, Stratton called the battalion together. Standing on the hood of a jeep, he first complimented everyone on the fine job accomplished so far in the course of battle. He regretted the casualties, becoming somewhat emotional at this point, but he hurried on to express his hope that this would be a long rest while the 19th reorganized.

Secondly, he announced that the Department of the Army had imposed a one-year freeze on enlistments and on officer categories. This meant that those in the ranks, whose enlistments would expire shortly and normally would be able to return to the States, would have to remain in Korea in the units to which assigned. This order affected some key NCOs immediately and, of course, a significant number of enlistees as the weeks and months wore on. The order affected officers as well, particularly those whose commissions were Category Two (two years active duty) and who already had served more than a year in the Occupation.

(The officers understood and accepted. Many affected enlisted men were quite bitter at first. However, as the campaign continued, there was grudging acceptance, aided by commanders moving to place "short timers" in less dangerous positions after replacements began arriving more steadily.)

Then, Stratton told the men officially what some had heard unofficially, that Maj. Gen. Dean was missing in action, and that Brig. Gen. (soon to be Maj. Gen.) John Huston Church, Gen. MacArthur's personal advisor and head of the

American Mission in Korea (AMIK), had assumed command of the division.[1] Stratton would have spoken longer had not two F-51 planes chose that moment to fly overhead. Not sure of the ID on the planes, Stratton hesitated, then yelled "Scatter!" The men did and that ended the speech making.

This being Sunday, one week after the Kum River battle, two chaplains arrived in mid-afternoon. The Lieutenant had seen both earlier, but had not learned their names. He was told that these were division artillery chaplains, 1st Lt. James W. Helt (Protestant) and Capt. Paul D. Roche (Roman Catholic). Both carried sidearms, an unusual precaution, but understandable in light of the newly held perception of the NK as cruelly contemptuous of the wounded, those aiding the wounded, and those who were the army's religious mentors.

It was the Lieutenant's understanding that *everyone* attended one or the other religious service that afternoon, everyone except guards on duty and a few kitchen personnel, and these were given opportunity later to speak with a chaplain. None, including the few whose persuasions were not Christian, permitted this opportunity to communicate with God to pass. The experiences of recent days had shocked the men into accepting religion as a necessary ingredient of human existence. Both Lt. Helt and Capt. Roche spoke at length with many in the battalion that day.

The early morning of the twenty-fifth brought a sudden change of plans. A messenger from division artillery headquarters arrived and, shortly, Stratton ordered an Officers' Call. The general battle situation was too serious at the moment to permit the 24th Division to remain inactive, he said. Therefore, the 34th Regiment, now strengthened with replacements, was to be trucked to the vicinity of Kun-wi, east of Kumch'on, to bolster the 8th ROK Division, struggling to contain an advancing column aimed at the main east-west road between Taegu and P'ohang, a port on the east coast. If that road was cut, the Taegu-Pusan road would remain the only viable supply route for the Americans fighting north of Kumch'on. And already some were talking about a last-stand ring about the port of Pusan, preliminary to a mass evacuation.

Meanwhile, a new infantry regiment from Okinawa, the 29th Regiment, had been brought into Korea. The regiment had no integral support artillery. The mission given it was to counter any NK advance to the west and south of the main cavalry line so as to prevent a successful flanking maneuver, a maneuver that had the potential to threaten the port of Pusan. That port had to be held at all cost. Artillery support was necessary for the 29th to carry out its mission successfully.

The 13th Field, then, was to be split. Accompanying the 34th Regiment would be A Battery. Headquarters, Service, and B Batteries would motor south and join the 29th Regiment.

Jittery apprehension returned as the command to march-order rang out. Several replacement vehicles had been driven in during the Officers' Call, and the Lieutenant was given one of them. He noted the bumper markings: 63FA, Hq 1. He had been given the jeep assigned to the 63rd Headquarters Battery Commander. Had the 63rd finally disintegrated without hope of reorganization? No one knew.

Van Fleet and Dear were waiting. Equipment was loaded. Then, with 2nd Lt. Edwin L. Mattes, A Battery XO (executive officer), leading the howitzer prime movers, the battery pulled out. Men waved to each other. It was separation time, into the unknown. The familiar, choking dust cloud began to rise, and all settled down quietly for a long trip.

Kun-wi was reached in the middle of the afternoon. The battery entered the town seeking a bivouac area. A victory arch had been erected at the entrance to the town, and freshly cut tree greens decorated it. A sign had been made and attached to the top of the arch. It read: WELCOME UN SOLDIERS. The populace cheered madly as the trucks went by. But when it was discovered that the best bivouac was located just south of the town, the column reversed, leaving the townspeople standing there, puzzled. It was decided to remain in the bivouac that night and attempt to contact the KMAG unit with the 8th Division the following day.

With both Stratton and Maj. Kron gone south, the commander of the A Battery task force was Maj. Leon B. Cheek Jr. Cheek was a tall, bronzed Floridian with a deep, deliberate voice which he never raised unless extremely angry. He was the S-3 or operations officer for the battalion, and now, with A Battery, he would be responsible for both maneuver and fire control. His presence commanded respect, and his unhurried manner inspired considerable confidence. He was assisted by Sgt. Francis W. Slaughter.

The men were quick to note Cheek's demonstrated concern for proper military decorum. He noticed immediately that the two observers, Coles and the Lieutenant, were without insignia, these having disappeared during the difficult hours preceding the Kum River affair. His first order to the observers: "Have insignia on your shirts by supper."

The Lieutenant was at a loss. How could he acquire insignia? Coles, fortunately, had an extra pair, leaving the Lieutenant to look about for a solution. Wandering over to the mess truck, he became aware of several coffee cans, the metal of which was gold in appearance. Receiving permission to use one of the cans, he borrowed a pair of plain scissors and proceeded to cut out an artillery crossed cannon emblem and a second lieutenant's bar. At the ends of the cuttings, he pointed the metal. When finished, he bent the pointed ends, placed the emblem and bar properly on his jacket collar, pushed the pointed ends through the fabric, and then bent them back underneath. All this done, he reported to Maj. Cheek. Cheek stared a full ten seconds and then broke out laughing. Men in the immediate area, aware of the major's request, joined in. The ice was broken.

The following morning, both Maj. Cheek and 1st Lt. Pate traveled to the 8th ROK Division CP. They were gone quite a while when a cloud of dust heralded their return. Instead of supporting the ROKs, the 34th Regiment had been ordered immediately to the left flank of the cavalry. There had been a serious NK breakthrough in the Yongdong vicinity, and the NK were now to be prevented from making a flanking movement from the west toward Kumch'on and the cavalry rear. Both the cavalry and the NK were fighting each other in extremely mountainous terrain. Only the main north-south road was open for cavalry communications and supply. The Lieutenant wondered how the men in C Troop, 8th Regiment, were doing and particularly the status of 1st Lt. Reffner.

The battery march-ordered and pointed south toward Waegwan, passing the massed 34th Regiment waiting to mount in trucks. Col. Beauchamp was standing alongside the road carrying his swagger stick, an item that set him apart from most commanders. It was another hot day, and some of the men became sickened by the dust. The Lieutenant was suffering from a severe headache that eventually was alleviated by some healthy vomiting.

The column turned at Waegwan and started north again toward Kumch'on. How the Lieutenant knew this road. But this time, unlike before, the road teemed with refugees. The same familiar family groupings; the women with children, all carrying bags of belongings, the size of the bags dependent on the size of the carriers; the ever-present ox-drawn carts groaning harshly, the carts filled to overflowing.

When the Americans first entered Korea, they were intrigued at the style of cloaks worn mainly by rural women. The upper tunic had tabs that lifted up, permitting the women to breastfeed their babies. Now, with the extremely hot weather, the tabs were open, not for babies but for comfort. Hardened veterans of Korean life, the men scarcely glanced except when a baby was being fed, and then sympathetically.

Reaching Kumch'on, and as the column prepared to turn onto the west road, two things caught the eyes of the Americans. On a railroad bridge over the road stood a hospital train. Looking down from the bridge was a nurse, the first the men had seen in Korea. She waved and the men enthusiastically returned her wave.

More important was the appearance of the sky to the north of the town. A huge pall of smoke hung ominously, and it was apparent that if the smoke was resultant of battle action, the cavalry was really in trouble, lending urgency to the mission of the 34th and its support.

As the column moved along the west road out of Kumch'on, evening began to set in. Realizing that the objective, the town of Koch'ang, could not be reached before darkness, the battery halted near the town of Chir-ye, setting up machine gun and howitzer roadblocks at each end of the halted column.

Some firing was heard during the night, but none could determine its source. An NK recon plane flew over the area, probably fitted for machine gun harassment. It was deduced thus because an American officer in a jeep headed for Kumch'on stopped briefly at the battery bivouac about 2200 hours. It was a very short while after he left that the NK plane flew over and machine gun firing was heard from the direction the officer took.

The battery continued on its way the next morning, and the town of Koch'ang was reached by early afternoon.

Koch'ang in 1950 was a fair-sized, typical, ramshackle Korean town located about thirty-five miles due south of Yongdong and about thirty miles southwest of Kumch'on. Distances in Korea were often measured as the crows fly. It was not easy to map-read accurate mileage as existing maps, based on older Japanese surveys, were not always precise. Correct procedure dictated that commanders build in at least two additional hours of ground travel over long distances to account for twists and turns in the roads and state for the record the actual distance traveled only after such travel took place.

Koch'ang was primarily a communications center. A major road from the western city of Chonju leading through a mountain valley to the Naktong River and into Taegu intersected in Koch'ang with both the Yongdong road and the northeast road to Kumch'on. Control of this area of South Korea quite obviously lay in the hands of the side that controlled the Koch'ang hub.

Meanwhile, the Lieutenant learned that NK units of considerably more than company strength were filtering down the road and trail systems west of the main Taejon-Pusan road. The 19th Regiment earlier had entered the town of Annui, west of Koch'ang, and encountered NK probing strikes. That regiment then moved further south along the Annui-Chinju road to block expected action in the vicinity of Chinju. The 34th Regiment was now engaged in filling the gap left by the 19th, concentrating a defense at Koch'ang. It was also learned officially that the 25th Infantry Division had entered the fighting as east flank protector for the cavalry, a defense focusing in and around the Kun-wi sector.

At a point just south of Koch'ang, A Battery pulled off the road. Shade trees and light, rippling grass were in abundance, presenting an atmosphere of contentment and relaxation to the men as they flopped onto the ground to rest. Normal vehicle dispersion was enforced by the battery first sergeant, William K. Knott, as he walked from vehicle to vehicle with words of encouragement. Maj. Cheek had gone forward with the battery commander to reconnoiter positions.

No one knew what to expect here. The NK were undoubtedly near, but out of sight. Shortly, a convoy of heavy trucks approached. This was D Company, 3rd Engineer Battalion, division engineers. The regimental combat team was now complete.

The men were dozing. It was difficult not to doze, given the hot sun of a Korean summer. One conserved strength by resting in this fashion.

Suddenly, the battery agent's jeep was seen to approach the temporary bivouac at a high rate of speed. When the vehicle entered the bivouac, the driver called out in a high-pitched voice, "They're coming down the road!" Panicked, the men jumped up and climbed into their vehicles. Ed Mattes circled with his truck to form a column. The Lieutenant ordered Pfc. Dear, now the section's permanent driver, to move out immediately behind the agent without waiting for the battery to follow. He would go into Koch'ang.

Once on the road, he recognized 1st Lt. Pate approaching in his jeep. The latter stopped, turned about, and signaled the Lieutenant to follow. The Conflict had begun again.

Back to the Naktong[1]

Dear gunned the jeep as fast as he could toward Koch'ang. The urgency of the moment was all too apparent. The Lieutenant's face was a frozen mask as he squinted into the dust raised ahead by Pate's jeep. Both jeeps sped through town and out on a side road east.

Then, over a rise in the road, they came upon Maj. Cheek standing by the road, conversing with a South Korean policeman. A large, open field was close by. Cheek looked up in surprise as the bouncing jeeps hove into view. Smiling, he waved them to a halt. It was a false alarm. There was no danger yet.

The main battery group arrived a few minutes later, the men standing up in the trucks with carbines on hips for immediate action, should that prove necessary. They were noticeably relieved when told that the earlier message was highly exaggerated. Nevertheless, they wasted little time going into position and digging trenches for individual protection. Cheek then instructed both Pate and the Lieutenant to scout for an OP west of the town. Coles would remain with the battery as a spare observer.

A new operator had joined the section that morning, a lad by the name of Pfc. Lynn E. Duckworth. He was from California, he said. He had volunteered his services, the first one in the battery to do so since the Kum River battle.

Dear, meanwhile, had found himself something of a hero, being an observer section driver. He was up where the action and danger were and, although few in the battery had any desire to accompany, they respected him. He had become one of the more conscientious soldiers in the outfit.

Just to the west of Koch'ang on the road to Annui, a high, bare earth mound was situated. At the foot of this mound the road branched, one fork stretching west to Annui while the other trailed north into hill country. The earth mound was a perfect OP for the time being as it commanded a 180° field of observation. Pate instructed the Lieutenant to prepare data for immediate firing, but there would be no prior registration, as this would alert enemy in the vicinity. The 34th Regiment was not yet ready for a combat operation. Pate then departed, leaving Duckworth and the Lieutenant to consolidate and improve the OP.

South Korean police were observed standing about the road junction near a sentry box. The townspeople were mostly gone, either to the south or into nearby hills, apparently alerted to NK activity at Annui.

The infantry arrived about 1900 hours. Two companies walked slowly toward the road junction. The Lieutenant noted pitifully small groups of men plodding forward. It was obvious that the regiment had received fewer replacements than anticipated. Replacement priority, most probably, had been given to both the cavalry and the 25th Division for full strength build-up. What the Lieutenant observed were mostly the tired remnants from Taejon. One company, walking haltingly on the north road, numbered only about sixty-seven men, close to half strength.

About this time, a large touring or command car approached the road junction from the direction of Koch'ang. The vehicle was a former Japanese staff car, now South Korean and flying a South Korean flag. Seven men were in the car, all ROK army men, and obviously officers.

The vehicle stopped at the foot of the OP. One of the number approached an American officer standing near the junction. The ROKs were on the way to Annui with a high-ranking officer of their army. Would the American please share whatever information was available concerning NK movements along the road?

The American officer informed them that NK were known to be in the vicinity of Annui, but just how far along the road was not known. The ROKs held a brief conference and then decided to risk passage. They disappeared in a whirlwind of dust.

They were back within several hours and in sad shape. They had encountered a roadblock, and most of the group suffered wounds, with two or three dead, including the officer of high rank. The command car had been riddled. Although tragic, the incident carried some comfort in that it was clear that the NK were not yet advancing toward Koch'ang.

About 2200 hours, as darkness settled over the isolated forces, the Lieutenant was startled to see a lone officer of the regiment appear at the top of the OP hill. He was 2nd Lt. Norman A. Jensen of L Company and a former Marine. His movements were slow but deliberate. Youngish in face and with a ready if wry smile, he sat and talked a brief while with the Lieutenant.

He was in charge of a roving patrol down on the road and although the men were calm now, they had been so tense he feared they would fire at the slightest sound. He had climbed the OP hill to check it out and relieve his patrol's anxieties. Jensen was about to leave when he offered a judgment that seemed to express the feelings of every American in Korea.

"It's a dirty, filthy war," he said.

With a smile and a wave, he slipped down the hill to his waiting patrol. The Lieutenant never saw him again.

Nothing happened that night. The following morning, Col. Beauchamp decided to pull the companies back from roadblocks and into the town. The Third Battalion would remain in the town and engage if necessary. The First Battalion would go into position along the southeast road, a road that led to a bridge and then disappeared into a range of hills. There was a long open area from the edge of Koch'ang to the bridge, and the roadway was lined with trees, reminding the Lieutenant of some French country roads. The line of withdrawal for the

Third Battalion would be along this road, so the First Battalion was charged with keeping the road clear. Already one company was dispersed beneath the trees, waiting.

With the change in tactics, A Battery left its initial position and moved to an area beyond the bridge, an area edged by low-lying hills. To the moment of the move, the battery had not been forced to betray the infantry locations by firing, but after a report from natives that the NK had been sighted definitely advancing, not only from Annui, but along the road from Kumch'on, the need for security passed.

Nevertheless, Maj. Cheek waited until dark before permitting artillery action, and Pate initiated by firing a concentration into a small streambed. Once the exploding rounds were seen, both he and the Lieutenant began compiling data for ensuing adjustments to relevant targets within Koch'ang.

At the last moment, Maj. David Rosen, Third Battalion commander, decided that no observer would be sent out with the companies, but would remain at his CP for further instructions. Both Pate and the Lieutenant then went to the CP, organized inside a small abandoned store near the center of the town, to wait out the night.

There, in the Third Battalion CP, with shelter-halves over the doors and windows to prevent light from a small Coleman lantern from betraying the location, was gathered the staff. There was Maj. Rosen, Maj. Curtis Cooper, the S-3; and young, loquacious 1st Lt. Jim C. Little. Little was the S-2. His job at the moment was *not* to set up a battle map on a tripod. No time for that. He was the runner to the companies. Sleeves rolled up and carrying a rifle, Little was the picture of self-assurance as he went about his duties. Others of the staff grouping sat or lay quietly on the floor.

The night had an eerie quality to it. The heat was stifling, and the mosquitoes were very bad. The Lieutenant could hardly contain a feeling of being trapped. This is not the way it should be. A force installed defensively in a town or built-up area was an easy mark for encirclement; not so easy out in the open. However, the men were comforted somewhat by the thought that the First Battalion was holding the so-called bug-out route, which would be taken when prudent.

A few mortar rounds came in about 2300, apparently to test range. These betrayed the NK as being fairly close and would probably attack in the morning. The Lieutenant lay on the wooden floor, half under a table. Maj. Rosen dozed in a chair, as did Maj. Cooper.

Suddenly, about 0500, the stillness was broken by the ringing of a bell.[2] There was a shout and Rosen jerked to his feet. Outside there were sounds of men running. Then the shots began, few at first, but more frequent as the seconds passed. The NK had begun an infiltrating movement within Koch'ang. The attack had started.

Both Pate and the Lieutenant jumped up and dashed outside. The enlisted observer parties were already up and by the jeeps, ready to leave. The Lieutenant switched on his radio. It had hardly warmed when the voice of 2nd Lt. Coles was heard. His high-pitched tone stressed urgency. In short, punctuated

English, he reported that the artillery position had been fired on by guerrillas and that the battery was on the road, heading to the rear. He told the observers to get out of town.

Maj. Rosen had just stepped from the door of the CP as Coles was completing his report. Pate conveyed the situation as heard on the radio. Rosen turned to his S-3 for counsel, but as he did rifle fire began crackling across the main street that led to the open space and the bridge. An ambulance parked just down from the CP took several bullets, and the driver dashed for cover.

At the height of this drama a K Company machine gunner, evidently aiming at a suspected sniper's nest to his rear, fired a burst down the main street, right by the CP and into another ambulance. That was enough for Rosen. Without artillery support, resistance was useless. Not waiting another second, he yelled at the observers, "Scram!" and then ordered 1st Lt. Little to contact the companies to prepare for a quick withdrawal.

Pate's driver, Pfc. John L. Hurst, had already started the jeep's engine, and Dear was only a few seconds late in his diligence. With Pate leading the way, the two jeeps moved at top speed, all of thirty-five miles per hour, toward the open space. When they reached that area, no troops were to be seen. Where were they? Would Rosen's men be trapped?

The two teams continued on, the men instinctively crouching low. And then the bridge was crossed. It was after the crossing that the First Battalion outposts were encountered. That battalion had withdrawn across the stream and was holding the bridge. The companies would have been sitting ducks in the open and the Lieutenant now realized that.

Hurst slowed his jeep now that friendly forces were about. The end of a truck column was reached in a few moments, a column composed mainly of engineer units. The line had halted for a reason unknown to the observer parties.

The men in the two jeeps were just beginning to relax a bit when a mortar shell exploded in a low rice paddy about forty yards to the right of the road. The observer parties exited their jeeps in seconds and dashed into a small nearby ravine. Dear was the first out as his short legs demonstrated the proper coordination required at the moment. The two groups remained in the ravine until the motor column began moving again and then, waiting until the last moment, piled into the jeeps and gunned over a little hill, out of sight of Koch'ang and, they hoped, the NK.

Once over the hill, the observers learned that a small NK roadblock had just been obliterated. The harassment began with the killing by an enemy sniper of the engineer jeep driver leading the motor column. There he was, sprawled back in his seat, blood seeping from a wound in the forehead.

Nearly opposite this tragic scene had been the A Battery howitzer position. The Lieutenant noticed in a quick glance that an aiming stake was still in place, although the howitzers were gone.

The A Battery maintenance truck was parked on the berm of the road, its ring-mount .50- caliber machine gun being fired at the suspected sniper's location by one of the maintenance mechanics, Cpl. James A. Carter.

All the men in passing vehicles were asked to aim their weapons at the suspected spot and fire until beyond it.

About a mile further on the column halted again, and the Lieutenant saw artillery truck prime movers, which had been at or near the head of the motor column, being waved off the road and into an open field preparatory for temporary emplacement. The observers, reaching this new position, pulled to the side of the road to wait. While sitting, the two learned something of the circumstances leading to the battery's earlier withdrawal.

About 0500 that morning, the time the infantry in Koch'ang first began receiving enemy fire, some shots were fired on the battery position by NK. As the men in the battery already were tense and expecting an attack at any time, there was growing unease. Men began crowding about the battery vehicles, but no one left.

Then someone yelled, "Get out of here!" No one knew who yelled this, but few took time to investigate. Vehicles began moving and a number left their assigned posts to jump aboard. A few trotted off down the road. The battery commander appeared to have lost control.

Minutes later, however, the prime mover drivers returned to the position with their trucks and, one by one, aided by other returning personnel and by Maj. Cheek, the howitzers were hooked up and sent off to a new rendezvous. One three-quarter-ton, towed almost from July sixth, was left, as were, unforgivably, several aiming stakes.

Now at the new position, Maj. Cheek was in terrible temper. Pacing back and forth, he spoke harshly to those whom he considered responsible for the chaotic withdrawal. At the height of this state of agitation, he relieved the battery commander, an action taken with the full battery looking on.

Pate decided that this was not the time to report, so, motioning to the Lieutenant to follow, he turned about and drove back to a small bridge and farmhouse, beside which Col. Beauchamp had been seen standing as the motor column hurtled by a half-hour previous. Reaching this temporary regimental CP and parking their jeeps in a nearby courtyard, the two officers sat down on some logs to await further developments. It had been a hectic morning.

The Lieutenant began to eat some noodles from a C-ration can, looking about as he did so. He noticed another officer sitting nearby, so he introduced himself. The other man turned out to be a chaplain, 1st Lt. Carrol G. Chaphe, chaplain for the 34th Regiment. Chaphe had been with the regiment since its arrival in Korea, and he had survived the Taejon battle by walking out under fire.

Chaphe was tall and rather slender, and he spoke in a well-educated and quiet manner. He was Episcopalian. Both sat together on the logs, eating from C-ration cans and chatting about developments of the morning.

Within half an hour, the Third Battalion arrived at the CP center, riding on trucks. The men dismounted and began lounging in ditches and along the road, waiting for the First Battalion. The latter unit arrived after a space of an hour or so, walking. Their trucks and other vehicle conveyances had been sent into Koch'ang to speed the departure of the Third Battalion.

Koch'ang had been given up without a struggle, due to the plight of the supporting artillery. And yet, a prolonged defense of the town might have been suicidal, leaving fewer men to continue the delaying action. Now the commanders of the 34th were gathering for a conference.

Meanwhile, the relieved commander of A Battery arrived at the CP and sought out Col. Beauchamp. Greatly disturbed and somewhat disheveled, he related his side of the dispute that had occurred earlier with Maj. Cheek. Col. Beauchamp listened impassively. Then the artillery officer offered to join the infantry at whatever assignment the colonel might proffer. At this, Beauchamp, quietly and almost paternally, suggested that the officer ought to report back to his own commanding officer. When the relieved officer persisted, Beauchamp turned away. Nothing further would be said. The former then left, presumably to act as Beauchamp suggested.

Already present for the strategy conference was the regimental executive officer. Frowning and caustic, he had been through the entire gamut of withdrawals and was becoming resigned to continued retrograde movements.

Maj. Rosen walked up. He was still a bit nervous after the experience of the morning but looked calmer. Rosen was a tactical opportunist, tending to make instantaneous decisions. In this Conflict and at this time, this approach was a recognized asset.

Another commander arrived, a man whom the Lieutenant did not recognize, but whom Pate referred to as Ayres. This was Lt. Col. Harold B. Ayres, sandy-haired with a smooth complexion and ready smile. He constantly exuded patience and the calm demeanor of one who is seldom perturbed.

Ayres, too, was a veteran of the early actions and seemed now to accept the inevitability of continuing withdrawals. Nevertheless, there was an element of tenaciousness in his character that prompted aggressive resistance whenever possible within his command structure.

They gathered, these commanders of a worn-out, subdued regiment, to consider the next plan of maneuver. Beauchamp wanted to go into position right there. He warned that the regiment could not constantly withdraw without making a major stand in the area. The executive countered by pointing out both the condition of the men and the fact that the terrain above and about the command post did not lend itself to a hard defensive stance, the hills paralleling both valley and road.

Some map work followed, and the command group finally decided to organize a defensive position further on at a place named Kwanbin-ni where, for several hundred yards, the main road split around a small hill and narrow valleys led off in perpendicular fashion.

A Company would be positioned on the high hill just above this temporary CP to make contact with the NK when the latter approached and then withdraw in the direction of the now-determined MLR (Main Line of Resistance.) It was hoped that this tactic would serve to delay the NK advance, making these think that the regiment was positioned in strength. An artillery observer would remain with the company so that both artillery and small arms could be brought to bear at initial contact.

The conference broke up. Col. Beauchamp drove off, as did the others, including the chaplain. Only Pate and the Lieutenant remained, waiting until A Company arrived to undertake the delaying mission.

While waiting, the two became aware of quickening activity by the inhabitants of the farmhouse, the yard of which had been the temporary CP. Preparations for flight by these Koreans was obvious. The women were gathering clothing and kitchen utensils and making packs. The men gathered equipment and began readying a cart.

One young man had caught a small pig and had cut its throat, draining the blood into a pan which he held. For what purpose one wanted pig's blood the Lieutenant couldn't figure. The squeals of the pig were such that Pate got up and walked away, although the Korean boy continued smiling and motioning that all was well. About this time, A Company marched up.

Both artillery officers watched as that unit began climbing the craggy hill. Although the height was only a little over six hundred feet, it was a full half-hour before everyone reached the top. The men literally dragged their feet.

Down on the road, meanwhile, a platoon of D Company with machine guns had been ordered to assist in the delaying action. These men had already arrived, but instead of mounting their weapons and seeing to other equipment, they were stretched out on the ground or merely sitting staring at nothing in particular. The lieutenant in charge made little effort to effectively organize this group.

It was time for the Lieutenant to go up and join A Company. Pate just looked. His face was expressive, even if there were no words. This delaying tactic might be fatal for everyone. A wrong move or the failure to withdraw in time, either one, and the company might be encircled fatally.

For the first time since the Conflict began, the Lieutenant felt emotion rising. In the short minute prior to his climb upward, he cursed sobbingly at the world and the bad luck he was encountering. He was falling into the trap of feeling sorry for himself, the first step on the way to an emotional breakdown.

During the weary climb, however, he began to feel better, and soon all traces of his emotional outburst vanished. He finally reached the highest level of the hill, there encountering the First Platoon of A Company, 34th Regiment. There were two platoons in the company and only two officers. The commander, a deliberate man named Adolph Damish, led the first platoon, while an officer unknown to the Lieutenant led the other. The second platoon had taken a position beyond the first and along a narrow saddle, out of sight of the Lieutenant.

There they were, the first platoon, sitting or lying along the edges of a narrow, circular perimeter, a leveled area created some years previous for the purpose of erecting a grave mound. Most were resting, and those who weren't were conversing in low tones.

Several had no helmets. Also, several wore khaki uniforms. One boy, who seemed to be doing quite a bit of talking, had no teeth. A medical corpsman, whom the group addressed as "Doc," moved about the perimeter, asking how each felt and dispensing pills. First Lt. Damish was sleeping.

The Lieutenant was not surprised at the hushed atmosphere. A few of the company had turned to look at him as he picked his way through the edge of the perimeter, but now that he had arrived these looked away, resuscitating inner soliloquies. These men knew the score. They understood their predicament. Doom was on their minds, and they were quietly preparing themselves for the inevitable.

Duckworth came up with the radio, and he and the Lieutenant got it ready for transmissions. Part of the strategy, of course, was to bring artillery fire as well as small arms on the advancing NK. The SCR-610 radio seemed to be sending, but there was yet no reception. Most probably, no one was standing near the battery's SCR-608 at the howitzer position. Both men sat down to wait.

Few of the company slept much that night. It was a waiting game. The machine gunners nodded by their machine guns. All others dozed fitfully, their hands on rifle stocks.

Then, about 0415, still dark, the NK appeared. Many carried little pencil-type lights which they flashed about, reminding one of a horde of fireflies. They came on and converged both at the little farmhouse at the bottom of the hill and in the field across the road.

Where was the machine gun platoon? That unit must have withdrawn during the night. A Company was alone.

It was time to call on the artillery. The Lieutenant warmed up the radio and called. There was no answer. He called again; still no answer. Frantic, he opened the battery case. The new batteries put in the previous day were damp. There was not enough power for transmission to the battery location.

This turn of events left the matter wholly up to the company. Damish gave the order and the machine guns cut loose. For the first few seconds, as the bullets tore into groups of NK, there was no response. Then there was running and shouting. The guns continued a deadly chatter. Screams were heard as human targets fell. But the red tracers also targeted the American position. All realized this.

After about four minutes of firing, Damish sent word to the second platoon to quit its position and join him. That group readied itself, and their heads began appearing over the edge of the perimeter; still no NK counteraction.

Then, a mortar shell exploded on the hillside just below the perimeter. It was time to leave. Damish gave the order. It was cease fire and disassembly for packing. When all was ready, Damish gave the signal to move, but as he did, a mortar shell exploded on the escape trail just ahead.

Everyone sat down. Each began a personal, deliberate countdown to the seemingly inevitable face-to-face meeting with the NK.

Several more shells exploded on or near the trail, and then the Lieutenant saw a familiar glare, a lighted A-frame at the bottom of the hill. This could mean an impending NK attack. He communicated his suspicions. The company had to make the break now.

Damish led the way and the two platoons followed. The men walked at good intervals. Mortar shells still fell, but off the trail. There was no point in running. It was walk only in steady fashion.

Shouts were heard. NK officers were urging their men up the hill, no doubt. Still, the company did not panic. Damish kept a steady pace forward along the trail, just below the ridgeline. Legs cried to go faster, but the brain counseled a steady state, and the brain proved smarter.

Within ten minutes the hill was far behind, and no further NK activity was heard. The light of day began easing down between the tree branches.

There was yet one more hurdle to surmount, the approach to and passage through friendly lines. With nervousness of the regiment already well substantiated, every sense was attuned to the reception the company would receive once it was spotted by outposts.

Under ordinary circumstances it wouldn't be too difficult for Americans to pass through their own lines. But incidents were already on record where NK had donned American cloth uniforms and helmets, so that confusion over identification had resulted in American casualties being inflicted by their own. The men of the 34th, aware of instances of NK trickery, might not hesitate to shoot first and ask questions later, hence mounting apprehension now that A Company had successfully disengaged from its delaying action.

July thirtieth dawned gray and overcast. Some raindrops were already falling when, up ahead, shots were heard. These were single shots at delayed intervals, probably the result of sniper activity. The men became noticeably tense and turned to their officers. Damish was equal to the occasion. He called out, "Third squad, second platoon." This squad would reconnoiter and show itself.

It went forward, this squad, slowly but deliberately. The remainder of the company squatted or stood. Then, shortly, the order was passed to move out. The squad had accomplished its mission. There would be no trouble.

The company main body emerged from the shelter of the trees to face the new main line of resistance. The men edged down into a narrow valley fronting several small, wooded hills. B and C Companies were up there among the trees and bushes, dug in. Already some NK had been sighted, scouting for their main body, the latter no doubt the group fired on earlier by A Company. Had A Company not been positioned on the hill above the farmhouse, an attack by the NK might already have begun. As it was, fighting was delayed several hours.

The withdrawing company broke into the open in full view of the new line and walked quickly toward the main road. A jeep was parked along the road in front of the line. An officer was speaking to someone seated in the jeep. As the withdrawing company passed, the Lieutenant recognized the seated officer as Jerome Christine, the same engineer officer who stood at the blown bridge below the Kum River welcoming approaching remnants of the 19th Regiment the morning of July 17. Christine was smiling and waving to the men as they passed. Here was one officer who never seemed to be bothered by danger.

Col. Beauchamp and his staff had chosen well this new MLR. The narrow valleys fronting the dug-in defensive force provided excellent fields of fire. And unless the NK would decide to circle through the adjoining hills in a flanking maneuver, he would have to show himself here at Kwanbin-ni.

Since the skies were overcast and rain falling at intervals, it seemed certain that the NK would mount a frontal assault. Fighter planes usually didn't come over the front on days like this, so the NK had learned to take full advantage.

The First Battalion had gone on the line. The Third Battalion was in reserve. B and C Companies were already in dug-in positions. A Company would be permitted an hour's rest and then be moved up.

The Lieutenant reported to Pate. The latter now had the only operable radio. He would go out on the hill, he said, leaving the Lieutenant at the battalion CP to be used in an emergency.

The First Battalion CP was located in a small house and courtyard facing the rear of B Company's hill position. Lt. Col. Ayers moved about the premises constantly, checking on details of all sorts and maintaining radio and wire contact with his commanders on the hills. First Lt. Charles E. Payne, the adjutant, was there attempting to assemble records and reports. He was being assisted by Capt. Leroy Osburn, the Headquarters Company CO. Other officers and enlisted men shuffled about in their duties. The Lieutenant stood apart, careful not to interfere with the course of business being transacted prior to a battle all knew would soon commence.

About 1000, before any noticeable action had begun, several trucks pulled up to the CP. The trucks were carrying replacements. Everyone in the CP rushed out to look. Sure enough, here were about seventy-five officers and enlisted men, complete with duffel bags.

Ayers could hardly contain himself as he ordered the enlisted men lined up and counted, each line company receiving more or less an equal number of men. This done, the trucks turned about and departed, duffel bags strewn along the roadside.

Within ten minutes the new men were marched to their assigned companies and the replacement officers, after a briefing by Ayers, distributed as needed. First Lt. Payne had secured the service records of the men as they stood in company replacement groups and began marking assignments. Mail had come up with the trucks and a new sergeant, assigned to headquarters because of previous supply experience, began the job of sorting it out.

In the midst of this heightened activity, an explosion was heard. Men stopped whatever they were doing and looked at each other. The noise was similar to that of a mine being detonated. What vehicle would now be out in front of the line? Then realization struck home. First Lt. Christine had been out there in his jeep. The jeep was presumably loaded with explosives.

The telephone rang. After a minute of conversation, an enlisted man turned to the waiting staff and reported that a jeep had been blown up and the two men in it probably were dead. An NK sniper bullet or a propelled grenade detonated the explosives carried in the vehicle, causing the destruction of both the men and the vehicle. The point of the tragedy was too far out to permit recovery of the bodies. A rescue team was certain to come under NK fire.

The CP was quiet for a moment. Lt. Christine had been well known and liked. He had been a good soldier. Later, several engineer officers came up and inquired about the incident. After being assured that nothing could be done, they left.

Pate, meanwhile, had gone up on the hill above the CP where C Company was dug in. His projected OP would overlook the road junction a hundred yards or so beyond. On his way up, he spotted a high rock near the top of the hill and indicated to the soldier accompanying him that that would make an excellent OP. He was assured that the rock was in friendly hands.

But just as the two edged in that direction, a whine forced them to flatten on the ground. The rifleman with Pate was bewildered. "We're friendly," he called out. His declaration was answered by another shot. An NK sniper had infiltrated the line and was, at that moment, ensconced behind the rock, threatening the two Americans.

Then it was noticed that several C Company men were moving about on a high point above the rock. Pate shouted to them, describing his situation. The group promptly descended toward the rock and, in a minute, killed the lone NK who had infiltrated. The NK earlier had killed an American corporal guarding the rock area and now, in turn, was himself killed.

As it turned out, there was a great deal more significance attached to the killing of this particular NK than the immediate securing of the position for observation purposes. The infantrymen who were instrumental in bringing about the demise of the NK, upon searching the rock area, discovered that the weapon used by the NK was a new automatic carbine type with perforated metal covering and flash guard. Further, the weapon was of Soviet make, and the date of manufacture was 1950.

Now the Soviets had been denying that they were supplying the NK Army with weapons and materiel of recent origin. That nation had stated repeatedly that the NK were utilizing obsolete Soviet and captured Japanese equipment. The United Nations had even been asked to look into the matter.

The capture of this weapon seemed to refute completely the Soviet assertion. The find was deemed so important that a ranking officer from regiment was sent up to secure the weapon and convey it back to Eighth Army.

(A short time later the Lieutenant learned that a similar weapon had been displayed to the United Nations membership as proof of recent materiel support by the Soviets to the NK. It may always be in question that the weapon displayed was the same as captured at Kwanbin-ni. However, if it was, the United Nations might pay its respects to 1st Lt. William A. Pate—later Capt. Pate—now deceased, and his often stubborn temperament, for this prize obtained at a crucial stage in the conduct of the Conflict.)

The main body of the enemy now began its advance to the attack.[3] Pate spotted approaching columns and began bringing artillery to bear. He estimated at least two battalions of NK, with more in reserve.

Listening at the First Battalion CP, the Lieutenant recognized artillery firing, and there were moments when the intervals between volleys were so close that both he and the infantry there with him thought two batteries were involved. The cannoneers in A Battery were working as hard as they could to assist the 34th in making this stand a memorable one.

A Company began moving up the hill on the right, where B Company was already in position. Damish did not accompany the unit this time. He had been a relief commander. The assigned commander, 1st Lt. Albert A. Alfonso, now led the men forward.

The Lieutenant watched as the men began climbing the hill opposite the CP. There was Doc, and there was the fellow with no teeth, still talking. One of the newly assigned officers to the regiment was with them.

The company went into position along the ridge of the hill, just in front of B Company. But before the former could thoroughly and protectively dig in, the NK launched their main attack.

The men in the CP now heard clearly the small arms firing. At the rear of the CP was a high stone retaining wall, built against a sloping hill mound. Headquarters men began eyeing the wall and Capt. Osburn placed several large stones at the foot of the wall, just in case.

It was about 1400 hours. The NK had begun showing themselves around noon. Pate was continuing to do an outstanding job disrupting their attack plans. Over 150 artillery rounds had been fired from a meager ammunition supply, but Maj. Cheek had ruled that, if necessary, the battery would fire until the supply gave out. This was one battle that had to be fought well.

Alfonso soon called the CP to report that his unit had suffered many casualties. He requested consideration to moving B Company forward to replace his group on the line. Ayres agreed and gave the order. The movement was termed Plan A.

The Lieutenant looked out and saw the first of the A Company wounded leaving the hill. Some were walking alone, but several were being helped. Ayres, seeing them, started to walk across the road. But as he did, firing intensified. The NK, sensing the American units changing position, attacked furiously.

B Company had no sooner completed its position move than the NK reached the forward edge of the hill. The suddenness of the NK attack unnerved the defenders, who had not been able to undertake a complete organization of position. Resistance began fading.

The American companies began withdrawing the moment the NK reached the hill's forward edge. NK riflemen, as a result, were able to reach the rearward side of the hill and begin firing on the walking A Company wounded. The battalion CP also came under fire.

Lt. Col. Ayres, now across the road and helping to guide some wounded to safety, yelled at the driver of a three-quarter-ton truck that was parked along the road to remain and ready the truck for wounded evacuation. Chaplain Chaphe also ran across the road to assist Ayres. Both men began pointing the walking wounded toward the waiting truck.

Meanwhile, several CP personnel charged the rear retaining wall of the compound. Like squirrels, they were up and over, stumbling up the side of the low hill toward the top and safety. And out on the paddy field, separating the CP from the hill on which the battle was taking place, more men were now observed, some running, part of the American force that was now in a state of complete withdrawal. One of these, a wounded man being helped, tripped. The man's buddies did not hesitate and, taking hold of his feet, began dragging him through the watery field on his belly.

NK firing became worse. A machine gun was heard, an American .30-caliber, but this time turned against the defenders. This meant that the NK had begun occupying a major segment of the former American position. It was time to leave. The sergeant who had been sorting the mail, the new one, ran toward the wall. He was quite stout. He might not make it.

A bullet smacked into a wall near the Lieutenant, prompting him to make his move. He had already sent Duckworth back, as well as Pate's driver. Now, looking along the road, he saw 1st Lt. Damish begin to walk up a slight draw next to the CP. Damish's movement was fiercely steady and deliberate. He was showing by example that this was not the time to panic. The Lieutenant started in Damish's direction.

Upon reaching the hilltop behind the First Battalion CP, the Lieutenant encountered M Company, the heavy weapons company, in reserve. The men were observing the battle action, but were not firing their machine guns. The Lieutenant was told that no one could fire unless an order was given, this to conserve ammunition.

The right front of the First Battalion had completely collapsed by this time leaving C Company endangered on the left. The Lieutenant looked in the direction of that company. As he stood there looking, Pate strode into view. He was smiling. When the NK began charging the OP hill, he had fired one last mission and had withdrawn just in time.

Both now stopped at the Third Battalion CP, where they heard Maj. Rosen on the phone to regiment, trying to explain what was happening. When he saw the Lieutenant he paused and then said, "Here's an FO. He knows what's going on."

Taking the phone, the Lieutenant began speaking with the regiment's S-2 (intelligence), explaining the attack, the movement of the companies as he had observed them and, finally, the NK charge that took the hill, forcing evacuation of the First Battalion CP.

Regiment wanted to know if artillery had been firing, and the Lieutenant replied that it had. This ended the conversation.

Pate and the Lieutenant continued walking toward the artillery position. After a brisk walk of several minutes or so, with rain now pelting, the two saw Maj. Cheek standing along the road ahead, the battery lined up in readiness to leave. The appearance of the two officers was the signal for departure, because Ed Mattes took one look and waved the battery forward.

Exhausted, the Lieutenant climbed into his jeep. Duckworth was already seated, wet and shivering. Pate was bemoaning the loss of his jeep trailer, left behind at the battalion CP. No one volunteered to go back for it, however. So, with a roar of motors, A Battery once more pointed to the rear.

Two miles later the battery went into position. It was darkening earlier than usual what with the cloudy skies and the rain. Both Pate and the Lieutenant were soaking wet from the waist down. The two crowded as close as possible to one of the fires under a washing can near the kitchen to dry.

While thus engaged, the Lieutenant learned more about the artillery withdrawal the morning before. Leading the scramble out of the position were the kitchen and supply sections, and these vehicles reached the Naktong River, miles to the rear, before stopping. Coles had been dispatched to bring them back.

About 1700, a group of about eight infantrymen came down the road, walking. They were from A Company. Each asked for some coffee. The Lieutenant asked Sfc. Antonio Lucero, the mess steward, to do what he could for these men. Several were shaking. Within a short while, after thanking the mess personnel for the coffee given then, they left to return to their company's location.

A three-quarter-ton passed by the new artillery position about this time. It was the same vehicle that had been parked near the First Battalion CP. The vehicle was carrying battalion wounded. Chaplain Chaphe was sitting on the front seat next to the driver. He, too, had been wounded. From the infantry still standing along the road drinking coffee, the Lieutenant learned that the heavy sergeant in the headquarters section, newly assigned as a replacement that morning, did not make it out.

After supper that evening, Maj. Cheek left for the regimental headquarters to check plans. Returning shortly, he told the observers to get ready. The regiment had gone into position just at the eastern edge of Kwanbin-ni, where two high hills overlooked the village and were connected by a concave ridge, bisected by the main road. Both battalions had been placed on the line, the First Battalion occupying the hill mass to the right while the Third Battalion took a position on the connecting saddle.

A third unit now occupied the left hill mass, the 17th ROK Regiment, that unit having arrived just that afternoon to assist the Americans in the defense of the valley. The 17th Regiment was considered the best ROK unit operating at the moment, and the news that they were here cheered the artillerymen.

It was dark when the observer parties went up. Both Coles and the Lieutenant would be used this time. But a firefight involving both American battalions was in progress as the observer parties arrived. No one knew the reason for the firing or whether the NK were involved, but the shooting lasted over an hour and precious ammunition was being consumed.

Desultory firing continued until about midnight when most realized that Americans were firing at each other and at the newly posted ROKs. Then firing ceased. Nevertheless, it was decided not to send observers up to the line until the morning.

Soon after daybreak, after the Lieutenant had eaten the cold contents of a ham and egg C-can, an NK prisoner was brought down by several ROK soldiers, the first prisoner the Lieutenant had seen thus far in the fighting. POWs had been extremely rare for the UN side, and although the ROKs had captured a number, they usually did away with them by firing squad or a convenient pistol before Americans could question them at length.

Now cowering in a dirty brown uniform, this young NK was anticipating the same "no quarter" his own comrades had meted out to ROK prisoners and some Americans as well. However, Lt. Col. Ayers, alerted to the find, came running from his CP across the road and ordered that this POW be saved. Then, despite looks of disgust on the ROK faces, Ayres and his interpreters began to question the prisoner. He would wind up eventually in a POW enclosure.

With the line now totally quiet, the Lieutenant, having been assigned to the Third Battalion, began his ascent to the saddle ridgeline. He had Duckworth with him again, and a new man, Marvin C. Nezvensky. A Polish blond, Pfc. Marvin C. Nezvensky had volunteered for the observation assignment just the previous evening.

On their way up to the line, the observer party came upon a particularly gruesome sight. The Lieutenant recoiled. There in a narrow draw or gully lay a group of perhaps twenty or so men, women, and children, dead, their hands tied and bodies thrown in a pile like so many scarecrows. What he was seeing was an execution atrocity committed by the South Koreans. Heretofore atrocities had been reported as relating only to the NK. Not so, now.

The Lieutenant recalled that a number of soldiers who had served in the Korean Occupation had characterized the Koreans as an extremely cruel people in their methods and modes of punishment. Life meant little in the long run to these people. When the father in a family was found guilty of some capital crime, such as treason, his entire family often suffered punishment with him. This, no doubt, was the case with these dead lying in this rough gully outside Kwanbin-ni. Later, when the Lieutenant asked a local policeman about the bodies, the reply was, laughingly, "Communists."

Visibility was partially limited on this particular morning due to the rain the previous day. However, the Lieutenant spotted some NK activity. Several enemy groups were moving about in the town and in the vicinity of yesterday's battle-ground. He took these groups under fire, effectively scattering them. While he was so engaged, a pair of F-51s flew over and proceeded to strafe and rocket, causing several fires.

About noon, several NK were observed crawling along a dry streambed toward the saddle. Maj. Rosen, sitting with I Company just along the forward edge of the saddle, ordered riflemen there to shoot at the NK in as accurate manner as possible.

Five men, expert riflemen, took the patrol under fire. The men sat or lay along the forward slope, carefully aiming. Others in the company watched, voicing encouragement and cheering silently when one or another of the NK was hit. The Major joined in the acclamations, his encouragement bolstering the shooters.

Meanwhile, on the right, where the First Battalion was in position, an NK attack began. For the first time in the Conflict, the Lieutenant heard bugles and accompanying shouts as the NK officers urged their men forward. This action broke up the "crow shoot," and Third Battalion companies returned to their positions in anticipation of NK assaults their way.

Just after the Third Battalion settled into position, several mortar shells exploded below and on the road behind the position. At that moment, the Lieutenant spotted a group of NK edging up a sunken path that branched off the dry streambed leading to the saddle. This group carried a machine gun.

The Lieutenant called the artillery, intending to send a fire mission, but could not raise the battery. Moments later, rifle shots began to spray onto the battalion position from a small rise on the left, higher than the saddle positions occupied by the Americans. "Where are the ROKs?" someone shouted.

When this rifle fire began, K Company officers began urging and bullying their men over to the left flank to defend it. The officers were trying if their men were not.

Then it happened. No one knew who started first, but all Third Battalion companies began to withdraw hastily down from the saddle and onto the road behind.

The Lieutenant had been crawling about trying to determine the cause of the radio's failure to function and had removed both radio sections from the packboard for closer examination. Suddenly he realized he had been left alone there on the saddle, almost as if a breeze had quietly lifted everyone away. The company officers apparently were unable to forge a stand, and for all he knew in that instant the NK were right behind.

He shouted at both Duckworth and Nezvensky to leave and then, unable to drag the radio sections and packboard further, opened up the crystal case and smashed the crystals, rendering the set useless.

He continued crawling to the rearward edge of the saddle. Seeing no one around him, he concluded that he was probably the last man left on this part of the former defense line. But then he noticed he was crawling over a defense hole dug the previous night, in which were two Americans. One boy was crouched almost to the ground, while the other, too, was crouching, but in such a position as to be shielding the other. The latter looked up as the Lieutenant passed overhead, but said nothing. The two were not wounded, but appeared paralyzed with fear. Whether the two finally mustered the courage to leave that defense hole or not, the Lieutenant never learned.

Upon reaching the saddle's downside and then the edge of the road, the Lieutenant encountered a number of men walking rapidly. He was informed that the First Battalion companies had already withdrawn from their positions and that the Third Battalion had been on the line alone for many minutes with a wide-open right flank. It was this predicament that precipitated the quick withdrawal by the Third Battalion.

At the moment the Lieutenant joined the men walking along the road, an ROK officer ran up looking very bewildered. He made wild motions with his arms indicating that the Americans ought to go back up to their former positions. He was ignored. The men continued on. It was a rout.

A jeep was seen approaching at a fast clip. Dear was the driver. He was hunched over the steering wheel and looking anxiously at the saddle hill. He soon saw the Lieutenant and turned the jeep about to wait.

A wounded man was being helped along the road, and the Lieutenant motioned for him to get into his jeep. Then as many infantry as could crowded into and onto the vehicle. The jeep was a veritable mass of legs and arms as it moved slowly east and away from Kwanbin-ni.

The 34th Medical Detachment had been located about a half-mile down the road from the saddle. The medics were gathered outside a small Korean hut that served as the clearing station, watching the withdrawing infantry, and not a little dumbfounded. But they recovered quickly and within minutes had loaded their wounded and their gear onto trucks and jeeps, departing to establish a new station. For a few short minutes that day, the medical point was the front line for the UN troops in this valley of misery and death.

Col. Beauchamp stood in the middle of the road just beyond the medical station. As the withdrawing regiment approached, he called out that the companies could not go back any further. He ordered officers to file the men into the hills on both sides of the road. All would have to remain and fight, he declared. He waved his swagger stick to punctuate the order. The withdrawing men merely looked and then turned away, but they were seen shortly to leave the road and go into position along the ridges paralleling the valley.

The Lieutenant continued on to the new battery position and reported to Maj. Cheek. After relating the situation, to include the loss of the radio, he went off by himself and slept.

At supper that evening, Cheek introduced a new battery CO. His name was Capt. Edgar E. Still. He had arrived earlier that afternoon from the 13th Battalion headquarters which, at that moment, was operating in the Chinju area further south.

Still had been a filler from the 25th Infantry Division and, after Capt. Prescott was declared missing, had been assigned the battalion intelligence or S-2 post. He was an Oklahoman, extremely soft-spoken, with a rich sense of humor. Not being an excitable type, his presence was reassuring, as the battery needed a strong and steady leader at this stage of the Conflict.

The Lieutenant felt much better after his rest. Cheek then told him that the 21st Infantry Regiment had replaced the 34th on the line and that the battery would now be in support of the former. The battery wire crew had strung a phone line to one of the companies and that he, the Lieutenant, would go up immediately and occupy a position in the relative vicinity of the wire location.

It was dark when the Lieutenant reached the front. Both Duckworth and he dismounted at the point where the phone wire led into underbrush and up a hillside. They were to follow the line up. So, taking a telephone unit, they began a climb to the supported company area.

No sooner had his jeep turned about and headed back to the battery than a sudden "Halt" turned both observers' stomachs upside down. Both stood rooted. Two soldiers popped up from a bush and spoke the interrogative portion of the password. The Lieutenant blurted out the countersign, hoping he sounded convincing as well as correct. Then, after a moment of silence, one of the infantry began laughing. The Lieutenant had been identified earlier. The two soldiers were only testing his reaction—some fun. Only silence from the NK that night.

In the morning, August 1, the Lieutenant learned that he was with B Company, 21st Regiment. The CO's name was 1st Lt. John J. Doody. The 34th had passed through the 21st's lines the previous afternoon and had been trucked to the rear.

While the two officers were talking, a whispered warning from several of the men focused attention on the side of a hill across the valley. A five-man NK patrol had emerged from a ravine and now stood, grouped, reading a map. This was real drama in that it was obvious the NK were not aware of the new defense line and perhaps of the new regiment facing them.

Then, as the Americans continued to watch, one of the NK dropped his pants and squatted in full view over a ledge, relieving the pressure on his large intestine. As the man quite obviously was suffering from a touch of diarrhea, one GI sighed softly in commiseration, "The poor bastard." Quiet laughter met this apt analysis.

Two of the NK group then detached themselves from the patrol and, crossing a small stream in the valley, began walking down the road in front of the American line. The men in B Company fairly quivered with excitement. The NK sauntered to a point directly below the infantry without becoming suspicious.

The two then entered a small hut located at the foot of the American-held hill, remaining there for several minutes. They soon emerged and began walking rapidly away from the line. Something or someone must have warned them concerning the American proximity. The B Company men now reacted.

The forward squad of the company opened fire, and one NK, most likely an officer, was shot down. The other dashed back into the little hut. A patrol was dispatched, and the second NK and a young man who had inhabited the hut were taken prisoner. They were taken immediately to the rear. The firing of rifles alerted the NK, of course, and mortar shells soon began exploding on the hill across from B Company. The battle had resumed.

What ensued was not a big nor important action in the defense of this valley, as it led from Koch'ang back to the Naktong River, but the stand, such as it was, was conducted in a surer manner than had been the case with the 34th Regiment. A and C Companies were across the road, and the 17th ROK Regiment was positioned on a hill mass farther on the left.

The NK attacked the ROK position about 1000 hours and were repulsed. Dewey Coles was the observer with the ROK regiment, and he brought a considerable amount of artillery into play, including white phosphorus. The shouts and screams of the NK resulting from the artillery shelling could be heard throughout the American-held positions.

Redeploying, an enemy platoon trotted down a cut into a streambed in full view of the Lieutenant. He fired on this group, causing some casualties. All NK activity ceased about 1400. The line of the 21st Regiment and the 17th ROK Regiment remained intact.

In early evening, it was learned that the regiment would abandon these positions which, from a tactical standpoint, were untenable. The UN force would pull back to a major road junction, one spur leading to Taegu, and the other, more southerly then easterly to the towns of Ch'ogye and Changnyong. If the 21st had chosen to remain on the present line, the NK most likely would infiltrate and seize control of that junction, forcing the Americans into a roadblock entrapment. This possibility could be disastrous. Word came that the withdrawal would take place at 2300 hours.

With only a few hours to go before withdrawing, NK mortar shells began falling behind the American line, mostly along the road. One NK weapon, a fieldpiece, was aimed at the B Company position, but the rounds came in too high and harmless. Nevertheless, there was constant tension over the possibility that a short round could result in a tree burst with resultant casualties. Withdrawal time couldn't come too quickly this particular night.

The hour finally arrived. As the men started to move, four mortar rounds landed across the road and on the position defended by A Company. This happened just as that company began emerging from their holes. A boy began screaming. He continued screaming for about a minute until a sudden silence led everyone to believe that he had either been knocked out by a fist or given a shot by a medic.

Down on the road now, and the companies began lining up. Vehicles were to be pushed the first quarter mile before being started. The pullback was to take place in complete quiet.

A Company was the last down, and someone asked who had been hurt. An answer came out of the darkness, "It was Rummy. He's okay, now." That was all that was said. Word passed. "It was Rummy. Rummy got it." The men filed off down the road.

Dear was waiting with the jeep just a short distance along, as was Pate and his driver. Men began pushing vehicles. The Lieutenant pushed with the rest. NK mortars fell on the abandoned positions, but no one cared. A small bridge was reached. Motors revved. The column would continue two miles more.

Several small villages were passed, and lights shone in the window ports of many of the huts. These were 17th ROK Regiment CPs and supply points. Here were housed native carriers and the rice that was the Korean staple food. ROK soldiers stood guard. They wore impassive looks as the Americans drove by.

The new artillery position was soon reached. Howitzers already were in firing positions, the crews standing alongside each weapon. The Lieutenant guided his jeep to a far corner of the field. In short minutes all was quiet.

For whatever reason, the following morning found the men in better spirits. Perhaps it was the change in infantry that caused it. At any rate, there was more unconstrained activity and joking throughout than during days previous. Maj. Cheek even was in good humor as the officers gathered about the little mess table for breakfast.

Maj. Cheek announced that the same pattern of preparation would prevail as had been arranged the day before. A wire line would be strung again, the OP operating with telephone. The Lieutenant was assigned the telephone line, as before. A Battery of the 11th Field was expected later that morning to provide additional fire support. The major seemed somewhat worried about the possibility of an NK flanking maneuver, but he didn't express his feelings on the subject at length.

The Lieutenant went forward within the hour and took a position with C Company, 21st Regiment.

The ROKs had been busy that morning gathering supplies from the little villages in the area. Their trucks, all older Japanese and American types, were being loaded fully with bags of rice and other edibles. They had been ordered to scavenge what they could for the future of both their and other ROK army units. Once, a forage group began working too far in front of the line, and the Lieutenant almost brought fire on them. Their uniforms, a light greenish brown, often were indistinguishable from the dirty brown of the NK.

While on the line that morning, August 2, the Lieutenant learned that the Eighth Army commander, Lt. Gen. Walton Walker, had issued a "Stand or Die" order. The order had been issued on July 29. The Lieutenant remembered Col. Beauchamp calling to his men that they couldn't withdraw any more. He now understood Beauchamp's imploration.

The men on the line also said that, although most in the regiment knew of Walker's order, their "Old Man," Lt. Col. Charles B. Smith, hadn't come right out and passed down the order officially. The First Battalion had been through so much since initial commitment at Osan that to tell the men now that they had only to look forward to possible death involved too much for such a fine soldier as Smith.[4]

As the hours passed, the battalion just sat in position along the ridgeline. Little was said. What conversation there was concerned relief. One sergeant remarked that he had been looking back down the road since arriving in Korea and the only time he saw anything or anybody was at Yongdong when the cavalry arrived.

Another, a replacement, reported seeing Marines two days previous at Taegu, just before he joined the 21st. His information had been passed quickly along the line. If only the Marines would come. One private promised he would "kiss every Marine (he saw) on the butt once a day and three times on Sunday" if they arrived to help out in this mess. The often-repeated rumor of the 82nd airborne Division being alerted for Korean duty was voiced by several. The men continued to sit, rumormongering and hoping.

About 1300 that afternoon word came *not* to dig in. The men reacted instantly. "Walker can go to hell. We're going back again." They were indeed. About 2000 hours, the regiment would pull back leaving only the 17th ROK force in position.

When the time came and the men started down the hillsides, Maj. Cheek rang and asked the Lieutenant to wait and fire a base point registration. The registration fired, Cheek told him to close station and return to the battery. At this moment, a ROK officer sprinted up to ask the meaning of the withdrawal. The Lieutenant couldn't answer. The Korean officer then walked away, puzzled.

Once away from the line, the Lieutenant learned that the 17th had asked to make one more attack before withdrawing. He learned, also, that this particular withdrawal, a strategic one, would be the last. The next line was slated to be a permanent one.

Dear arrived with the jeep, and both the Lieutenant and Duckworth climbed aboard. At the battery position, vehicles and howitzers were already lined up. With the appearance of the Lieutenant's jeep, the battery began moving. The road march would be made using blackout lights.

Two miles or so along, lights were seen along the side of a rather high hill to the front. Other units were behind them, the Lieutenant mused. Then, with a turn in the road, he saw that the lights emanated from activity taking place along the road as it wound its way up the hill. Soon, as the column drew closer, division engineer troops were identified as conducting preliminary detonation operations, stretching daisy chains and mining the upper portions of the hillside. After the last units passed, the ROKs in this case, the engineers would blow the road at this strategic point. The Lieutenant noticed that every fourth engineer stood guard with a rifle.

The column moved on and soon a bridge was crossed. The vehicles and men of the 13th Field had reached the Naktong River, one of the few remaining natural obstacles to the NK advance.

A right turn was made after the bridge crossing and then the column slowed. A new position was reached. It was now pitch black. The howitzers were guided to placement by sighting sticks. First Sgt. William Knott led the remaining vehicles to the motor park.

The Lieutenant left his jeep and looked about. More vehicles were coming down the road. This might be a general withdrawal, not just a local, tactical maneuver, he speculated.

He was tired now. Dear and Duckworth had already found spots for sleeping. As the battery quieted, he lay down, his head resting on his dispatch case, a familiar pillow. Only the buzzing of mosquitoes broke the silence of a dozing soldiery. It was as if the Conflict was nonexistent. In a short while he, too, slept.

Manning the Perimeter

The Eighth United States Army mostly disengaged itself from NK forces on August 3, 1950. To avoid imminent and potentially mortal flank thrusts from the west, the effect of which would be the severing of critical supply routes, an increasingly grave problem along the southwestern front, the Army withdrew behind the general configuration of the Naktong River. The resulting contracted defense line was such that, for the first time in the Conflict, a contiguous front was attainable, enhancing United Nations chances for survival on this bloody peninsula.

The Naktong, gathering width from numerous tributaries in the north, reached acceptable proportions for defense about the town of Naksong-dong, about fifteen miles north of Waegwan. From Waegwan, the river continues a southward course, offering ample defensive positions until, south of Yongsan, the river veers sharply to the east and then finally flows into the ocean just west of Pusan. Units positioned south of Yongsan hewed to a mythical Naktong line, tactical considerations excepted. Some of the bloodiest encounters of the summer fighting took place along that mythical line.

The town of Indong lies about ten miles north of Waegwan. The UN defense line pivoted east from Indong toward Uihung, T'osong-dong, and out to the coastal village of Chongha, north of the vital harbor P'ohang-dong. P'ohang-dong was to be held at all costs, and American naval units had been ordered to provide every assistance to ROK forces fighting in that vicinity.

This new defense line became widely known as the Pusan Perimeter, so named because it was around this port, the vital key to the defense buildup, that the Eighth Army repositioned itself. (Interestingly, within the perimeter outline was the capital of one of Korea's ancient kingdoms, the city of Kyongju, capital of the Kingdom of Silla. It is doubtful if many of the soldiers along the perimeter that summer were aware of this historical fact.)

Spread along the perimeter initially were the 25th Division and attached units to the south, the 24th Division from Yongsan north to Hyonp'ung, the 17th ROK Regiment around Hyonp'ung, the First Cavalry Division in the Waegwan-Indong region and, as the line veered eastward, ROK divisions to the coast.

More important to the morale of A Battery was the news that Marine elements were now in Korea and assigned to the southwest sector near Chinju, protecting the flank of the newly assigned 25th Division. The Marines were only a brigade strong and at the moment were committing but one battalion to the fighting.

Aside from all this, the men were eager to learn the outcome of B Battery's experience with the 29th Regiment. Although fragmentary at first, something approximating the whole episode was soon voiced. The following officers provided some of the essential details of the action: B Battery executive officer, then-2nd Lt. Ellsworth Nelsen; then-2nd Lt. Ray Cody; and CO of Company C, 19th Regiment, then-2nd Lt. Charles T. Bailey.[1]

Shortly after Lt. Col. Stratton received word at the rest area near Waegwan to split the battalion, B Battery was ordered to Chinju, a large town about fifty miles west of Pusan—straight map distance—and a few miles north of the East China Sea coast. In simple fact, Chinju was the gateway from the west to the port of Pusan. It was also a portal of defense, surrounded by a group of particularly rugged mountains that offered much in the way of deterrence. The site would be highly dangerous if held by the NK.

Advancing NK patrols had been reported west of Chinju, so it was logical that the newly arrived Okinawa-based 29th Regiment would be ordered to the vicinity as a precautionary measure. The regiment having arrived in Korea without supporting artillery, one battery of light 105-mm howitzers and one battery of medium 155-mm howitzers were sent in support.

Second Lt. Coomer was designated as the liaison officer with the 29th and he was sent ahead to make contact and the necessary arrangements for close support. He arrived in Chinju ahead of the artillery, but assured the infantry that the howitzers were on the way. The 29th however, anxious to begin battle, informed him that if the batteries were not present and in position by the time prescribed for the "jump-off," the infantry would go it alone.

This is exactly what happened. Minor vehicle difficulties and poor road conditions slowed the artillery column so that when it finally reached Chinju the infantry had indeed begun its forward movement.

With 1st Lt. Monsour, B Battery commander, out ahead to scout positions, 2nd Lt. Nelsen led the battery motor column through Chinju to the west and to a point where the road led through a narrow pass up an extremely high hill. After what seemed to Nelsen like an eternity, the worn-out trucks reached the top of the pass and began descending.

Meanwhile, further along the road near Hadong, the Third Battalion, 29th Regiment, made contact with a sizeable NK force, encountering small arms fire from hills overlooking the road. This being their first combat commitment and totally unused to mountain warfare, the 29th continued moving through the narrows with the result that the platoons began suffering casualties.

Finally, battalion officers, learning quickly in the heat of battle, attempted to form their companies for an assault against the NK hill positions, but it was too late. Without artillery to neutralize NK infantry, indecision began to spread. Within just a short time the battalion "broke." The committed companies, I and L, and the reserve K Company began streaming back.

Vehicles were commandeered for both the able-bodied and the wounded. A general withdrawal began.

A rout was avoided through heroic efforts by some key officers and NCOs, who established a fire line a mile or so behind the point of initial contact. The battalion escaped being trapped and cut to pieces as a result of these efforts. It was this streaming mixture of vehicles with wounded and apprehensive riflemen on foot that greeted Monsour, causing him to end his search for positions and turn about to warn his motor column of danger.

The artillery column had just reached the forward base of the high hill when Monsour's jeep approached in a cloud of dust. Monsour yelled at Nelsen to turn the column about and return to Chinju. He then continued on to select a firing position in the city itself.

The road being quite narrow, Nelsen chose to continue on another mile or so. In doing so, he encountered the main body of withdrawing soldiery. Not wasting another minute, he stopped the column and ordered the vehicles turned. To comply, men had to unhook the howitzers and manhandle them to a reverse position. Trucks jumped back and forth in turning movements. One M-10 ammunition trailer slipped into a ditch and had to be abandoned. All the while, groups of infantry appeared, shouting about the close proximity of the NK and causing the artillerymen to sweat and suffer agonies of apprehension. It was a scene of the most panicky confusion.

Finally, with the column facing the rear, Nelsen led the battery back up the steep hill, but this time two trucks failed. The boiling heat plus heavy loads affected the engine oil so that motors froze. Both trucks and one howitzer had to be abandoned. A friendly air strike later rendered the equipment useless to the NK.

First Lt. Monsour, meanwhile, had located a position inside Chinju, and the battery, now with only five howitzers, spread trails and awaited the worst. The 29th, however, managed to effect a line stabilization just west of the city and, with both Ray Cody and Joe Coomer as observers, and now with artillery support, maintained a relatively successful defense.

The 19th Regiment arrived at Chinju that same evening, as did A Battery, 11th Field. Upon learning of the NK attack and the reaction of the 29th Regiment, the 19th assumed complete command of the sector. The remaining intact battalion of the 29th was relegated to flank-guard responsibilities.

NK pressure against the city of Chinju mounted during the next several days, forcing the 19th to withdraw into the city. On July 29, the NK mounted a furious offensive, threatening for a time to push the battle line a considerable distance toward Pusan. However, with strong artillery support, sometimes effecting continuous fire and occasionally mistakenly dropping rounds in the midst of friendly troops, the attack was blunted.

One day later, the 19th withdrew from the Chinju area eastward to a location known as Haman Pass, where the NK earlier had attempted to emplace roadblocks for the purpose of curtailing communication and the movement of supplies to Chinju. Almost immediately after going into position at the pass, the First Battalion of the 19th was hit hard by a slashing, frontal NK assault. The battalion held.

Hoping to catch the NK around Haman off-balance after their failed attack, the remaining companies of the 29th were ordered to pursue. These men started out from the MLR in trucks and jeeps, but were ambushed only a short distance beyond. Many of this group became casualties before being able to dismount from the vehicles, and the mission proved a failure. This was the last organized action by the ill-fated 29th in South Korea, the date being July 31, 1950.[2]

As to the final disposition of the men in that regiment, many were absorbed by the 19th Regiment and later, officially, the companies were parceled to other surrounding units.[3]

The NK strength in the Chinju-Haman sector prompted the dispatch of another regimental combat team, the 27th "Wolfhound" Regiment from the 25th Division, commanded by Col. John H. Michaelis. The regiment with its direct support, the 8th Field Artillery, arrived on August 1. It mounted its first attack on August 2. Although unsuccessful, the attack infused additional strength along the American line in that sector.

It was late on that date that Ray Cody was wounded, one of the few 13th Field observers to sustain injuries during the early days. The wound was not serious, and he returned to duty within a day.[4]

Back at Hyonp'ung now, on the morning of August 3, it was learned that both the Headquarters Battery and B Battery had disengaged from the Chinju sector and were in position near the town of Yongsan, about twenty miles south of Hyon'pung. B Battery was supporting the 34th Regiment, in position several miles west of Yongsan on a group of hills bordering the Naktong River. Several units of the 19th Regiment were occupying hills just to the north of the 34th as were several companies from the 21st Regiment.

Since the 17th ROK regiment had been with the Americans in Death Valley, as the valley east from Koch'ang was being increasingly called, it was logical that this unit be assigned a sector along the Naktong River to include the point where the withdrawal route from Koch'ang ended. This indeed is what transpired. Theirs was to be the defense of Hyonp'ung and direct artillery support would be provided by A Battery, 13th Field. So about 1030 on the morning of August 3, Maj. Cheek ordered the observer parties readied, to report to the 17th Regimental CP before noon.

The 17th ROK Regiment, an organic unit of the ROK Capital Division, had been in position north and west of Seoul when the NK invasion began on June 25. Under its commander, Col. Paik in Yup, the regiment had been one of the few ROK army units to mount a counterattack against the NK. In doing so, it inflicted numerous casualties among the invaders, but the overall result was failure to materially delay the NK advance. Nevertheless, in appreciation of the heroism demonstrated, each surviving member of the regiment received a promotion. The men wore their chevrons and decorations proudly, and their morale, collectively, was higher than might be expected at the moment within the ROK army. The commander of the regiment currently was Col. Kim Hi Chun.

There was considerable observed activity outside the regimental CP, a converted schoolhouse in Hyonp'ung, as the observer parties arrived. Even though the unit had arrived only the previous evening, it had already begun recruiting replacements, outfitting and training them there in the schoolyard. Mortar drill occupied much of the training space in the yard, while inside the building, in the enlisted quarters, classes concerning the care and cleaning of both rifle and carbine were being held.

Stepping into the building, the Lieutenant noted an active business-like atmosphere. ROK officers were hurrying about their duties and much conference activity was noticeable, not a few grouped at several maps spread about the room. The Lieutenant took note of one young officer who wandered into the so-called map room, sat down at a convenient desk, and merely surveyed the bustle. He thought this strange, but did not inquire as to the identity of this stupid one. That officer's head would surely roll when Col. Kim walked in.

The Lieutenant was musing thus when a shot was heard from the direction of the rifle class. Some running and shouting were audible, and then all was quiet. First Lt. Pate asked one of the ROK officers what had happened. He was told that a trainee's rifle discharged accidentally, killing the man next to him. What happened to the offender? "We are taking him out to be shot," came the response. Oriental military justice is quick, if sometimes intemperate.

The regiment had been assigned a sector stretching about ten miles as the river turned. An ROK soldier was stationed, theoretically, about every twelve yards. However, the defense was organized around a series of outposts and strongpoints, so that there were stretches, sometimes up to a mile, where no soldiers were posted.

Artillery observation for the battalions would be furnished by A Battery. And, contrary to previous policy, the observers would remain on the line with the ROKs both day and night. Before, American observers usually left a hill late at night when assigned to ROK units and then returned the following morning. Lack of confidence in ROK staying power prompted American commanders to play it safe with their observers.

The NK were not expected to mount a major offensive in this particular sector. Although a bridgehead existed about a mile or so north of Hyonp'ung, where the units from "Death Valley" had crossed the Naktong, the main NK objective was expected at the bridgehead leading to Waegwan, further north. It was there that the main road to Taegu was located. No major road artery existed east of Hyonp'ung that would attract NK activity. Therefore, although the Naktong River could be crossed quite easily here—the river paralleling the road for about two-thirds of a mile—the strategic advantage of attacking in this sector was not sufficiently rewarding to justify the effort and potential casualties.

The Lieutenant was assigned an observation sector just north of Hyonp'ung, where the Naktong parallels the road. First Lt. Pate, discarding his role as liaison temporarily, went out on an OP quite a distance from the main road, where the Naktong makes a wide bend westward and then veers south. Coles also went out in the same vicinity, his OP facing southwest while Pate's faced northwest.

The Lieutenant's OP was halfway up the side of a high hill overlooking the road and river and a good distance beyond. Both he and Pfc. Duckworth, again his operator, sat on a pile of rocks a day-and-a-half watching. There was absolutely no activity anywhere excepting, of course, the movements of the ROK troops on the road below. Several little farm hamlets across the river had been completely evacuated. Not even a caretaker was in evidence, contrary to practices in villages further north.

On the fifth, Syngman Rhee, the president of South Korea, visited Taegu, and within hours after his arrival, the 17th Regiment was ordered from its Naktong position to a sector north and closer to that city. Rhee was the nominal commander of his country's armed forces, and he had forcefully indicated his desire that this regiment be moved to a more strategic (at least from his point of view) location.

A short time before the ROKs were scheduled to leave, the Lieutenant moved his OP across the road and onto a low hill bordering the river as it began a long westward turn. Before manning it, however, he asked a Korean soldier to guide him to the nearest ROK officer so that the latter and presumably also the regiment be informed of the new OP location.

Off they went and after a brisk walk along the riverbank the two arrived at a small village compound, inside which an ROK officer was addressing a group of native civilians. The guide called out. There were answering voices. Then the gate was opened. There, in front of the group, stood the young officer from the ROK CP, the one whom the Lieutenant feared would be sacked for inactivity. The guide barked admiringly, "Col. Kim."

Well, the Lieutenant stood open-mouthed for a few seconds, but quickly recovered. Remembering his best military manners, he saluted and then offered the colonel a cigarette, the standard gambit. The colonel, in turn, offered one of his own. The Lieutenant lit both.

Then, talking and signaling, the Lieutenant informed Kim of the change in OPs. The effort at conversing took several minutes, and then the Lieutenant, saluting again, took his leave. Col. Kim treated the Lieutenant respectfully, but in the proper military context given the difference in rank. He was the colonel, and the Lieutenant was the subordinate. Yet there was nothing in Kim's manner to suggest haughtiness. No wonder his men fought hard for him.

Upon leaving the compound, the Lieutenant realized that his guide and he had, for whatever reason, traversed a miniature "great circle route" to visit Col. Kim, for the new OP position proved only a short distance from the compound. A tiny farm village nestled just below the new OP hill, and as the Lieutenant and his guide made their way along a winding path that was the main thoroughfare of the village, he heard rising voices and calls to neighbors through the stone walls of the individual family dwellings.

He was a little puzzled at all this noise until he spotted a gathering of village men at a spot seemingly reserved for village council meetings.[5] The grouped men were watching the Lieutenant approach and began calling to the Korean soldier acting as a guide. When the soldier finally responded, the men became agitated and talked loudly to each other. An agreement was seemingly reached for the men began stamping their feet and voicing the Korean equivalent of "Yes." With this, the meeting ended.

Meanwhile, as it was now late evening and growing dark, the Lieutenant decided not to go up on the OP, but wait until morning. The battery wire crew had not left enough wire for OP use, so a night spent on the hill without communication would be a useless exercise. Maj. Cheek was notified of the circumstances, and he agreed with the Lieutenant's decision.

The three in the observer party (Pfc. Nezvensky had rejoined) organized a guard on the pathway leading from the village to the main road. Each took a three-hour stint, the Lieutenant taking the final three hours.

About 0430, as signs of approaching dawn appeared, activity began buzzing within the village. By 0500, movement was apparent. Shortly, families began gathering outside the huts. Not a baby cried or child whimpered during all of this. At about 0520, as daylight broke, the village populace began moving down the narrow thoroughfare, passing in front of the Lieutenant. The women carried utensils, babies, and large, cloth-wrapped bundles. Children carried smaller loads and, as necessary, younger brothers and sisters. Younger men mounted A-frames on which were tied heavier items. Finally, older men guided oxen, on which large packs had been placed.

The group moved slowly, but determinedly. None looked back. Several smiled at the Lieutenant as he stood there watching. These were sad smiles, smiles of frustration. But most were stony-faced and looked straight ahead. This was the decision reached at the village council meeting the evening before, the decision to evacuate and walk south, away from an expected NK appearance. It was a decision to join the thousands of their countrymen who had gone before, abandoning the known for the unknown, away from the horror of NK subjection.

The Lieutenant watched them until there was nothing more than a blur of white on the road south. Then, turning toward the now-empty village, he began cursing the humanity whose folly brought the nation of South Korea to such a pass. For a brief moment, he felt, as have other extremists, that liberal doses of the atomic bomb should be dropped on all communist nations in retaliation and punishment for all the hardship and suffering imposed by their political and military theories. The unleashed anger passed quickly, but not before he had spoken aloud, and the force of his voice woke the others.

The ROKs were gone. The Lieutenant and his group were now alone. He had learned the day before that the 3rd Engineer Battalion would arrive soon and take positions for defensive purposes, albeit listening posts only along the river. The Lieutenant's observer group, at this moment in time, represented the front line for the Eighth Army there near Hyonp'ung on August 6, 1950, and A Battery, 13th Field, was in direct support.

The additional wire needed was delivered shortly after 0800. With great difficulty, the three men began pulling the line to the summit of the new OP hill. To move the line the last thirty yards or so, the Lieutenant tied the line about himself and then, with the other two pulling, struggled to the top, all with the aid of a liberal touch of appropriate expletives.

Once at the top and with communication set, the Lieutenant registered on a village across the river, the first round exploding at the exact center of the cluster of houses, destroying the headman's or magistrate's abode. He chuckled as the building collapsed, not so much at the damage done, but at the thought that he probably was the only observer in Korea who had hit the exact center of a town or village with a first shot and undoubtedly would be the last.

That afternoon, the three held a practice withdrawal or bug-out. The group reasoned that there was real danger of NK infiltration, so that it was prudent to prepare for the worst while there was still time. Several withdrawal routes were plotted along the ridgeline, and the men talked about what they would do individually should the NK suddenly appear. All agreed not to show themselves on the ridgeline, and the Lieutenant cautioned against resting or sleeping next to the telephone, as infiltrators would tend to follow a wire line. The group was not able to see the fruits of their planning because that evening the Lieutenant was relieved by 1st Lt. P.F. Judson of the 11th Field.

It was almost dark when the Lieutenant's group left the OP hill. As their return route led through a number of open fields, the Lieutenant felt it best to wait until daybreak to continue. The ever-present danger of NK patrol action, plus possible misidentification by nervous, friendly guards, placed overland night travel at risk. Guard arrangements were made, and the group spent a rather uncomfortable night in an area that seemed to be the social center of the local mosquito population. Better temporary discomfort than permanent oblivion, and the group was unanimous in agreement. With daylight, the group continued on, the battery position reached about 0545.

August 7, 1950, was the first day of complete relaxation for the Lieutenant since the short rest around Waegwan. Finding a spot near the kitchen truck, he sat down to read his mail and back issues of the *Stars and Stripes*. Mail was arriving regularly now, and some had received piles of it.

He read thoroughly the *Stars and Stripes* issues that had come up. He had glanced at issues earlier, particularly during the last few days in "Death Valley," but not thoroughly enough to gain a clear picture of the fighting. Now the sequence unfolded without a gap.

The woman he had seen at Taep'yong-ni was a reporter named Marguerite Higgins. Maj. Gen. Dean's disappearance was chronicled, with the speculation that he had been betrayed at the last moment. He read about the cavalry withdrawals and fighting in the streets of Yongdong. There was a headline of Lt. Gen. Walker's "Stand or Die" order. This, even now, was past history.

Activity around Masan occupied much space. The Marines were fighting there in the finest tradition. Help had indeed come up the road, and the men who had been in Korea the longest no longer felt alone.

A fire-mission began while he was reading. Both Pate and Coles had spotted some NK infiltration and were doing splendidly in keeping them off balance.

Nevertheless, as the Lieutenant looked about, he noted that morale was not high. The seclusion of the artillery position and the general feeling of helplessness should the NK decide to attack across the river contributed to a level of apprehension that was not healthy. None could resist looking back at the next ridgeline as if mentally preparing for another quick withdrawal, an every-man-for-himself type of withdrawal. This was just the way it was.

His reading finished, the Lieutenant went off by himself to bathe and wash clothes. Afterward, feeling better but tired, he lay down near a clump of bushes and slept soundly until noon.

Into the Jaws, Again

Maj. Cheek informed the officers on the early afternoon of the seventh that he had just received word of a major NK river crossing west of the town of Yongsan. The 34th Regiment was defending in that hill area and had been hit hard. Several companies, according to Cheek, had been isolated. The remaining companies, together with the 19th Regiment, which had been grouped near Yongsan after having been pulled back from the Haman sector, were struggling to keep the penetration from becoming a major threat.

Of greater significance to Cheek was the fact that B Battery had been attacked in the initial melee, and the major was frank in admitting he did not know if that unit was able to continue in full support of infantry. Now, with both the 19th and 34th regiments committed to battle and only three artillery batteries available for direct and general support (one battery of the 13th and two batteries of the 11th), Cheek voiced the opinion that A Battery might be needed there soon, if not at once. He asked the Lieutenant to drive to the Yongsan area, find the location of the 13th battery, speak with Lt. Col. Stratton, and bring back all pertinent information concerning impending operations by the battalion.

The Lieutenant was elated over being able to travel through the so-called rear areas again. After so many days with infantry, it was refreshing to be out on the road and see how other troops were living and operating. So with Pfc. Dear driving and Pfc. Duckworth accompanying, he started down the river road toward Yongsan.

The town of Ch'angnyong was reached where some division headquarters units were located, but little activity was noted anywhere throughout. The few soldiers who stood alongside the road stared laconically at the jeep and its occupants, more curious, perhaps, because the bumper marking still read "63 FA," and the 63rd Field had not been operative within the division since the battle of Taejon.

Then, nearing Yongsan, the Lieutenant jerked upright. A jeep had pulled out from a side road, a vehicle with different bumper markings. Instead of the familiar "24," where the divisional marking should be, the number "2" was seen.

The Lieutenant ordered Dear to speed up. Inside of thirty seconds, they were close enough to read clearly the complete marking: "2D, 15FA, B2." The three began laughing and shouting to each other. The 2nd Infantry Division, complete or in part, was in position somewhere near Yongsan. Things couldn't be bad much longer. They could only become better.

The 13th Field CP was soon located, just off the road and beside a dry streambed. It was eerily quiet as the jeep halted near the S-3 tent. The Lieutenant stepped out of the jeep and looked around. He thought for a moment he was in the wrong place. Then he heard murmuring voices and the low, insistent hum of a radio. He walked to the tent entrance and opened the flap.

Inside this standard Army operations tent, Arabic-style in appearance, it being slightly askew, was gathered the key staff of the 13th. 1st Lt. Donald M. Dexter, the assistant operations officer, was involved in a fire-mission. First Lt. Robert B. Ball, the communications officer, stood near the tent entrance and looking for all the world as if an enemy sniper was lurking on a nearby treetop. Maj. Kron was there, too, and occasionally he would step outside and look up and down the adjoining road. It was clear, even without a word being spoken, that the Lieutenant had arrived in the middle of a precarious situation.

Moments after reporting to Maj. Kron, the Lieutenant was being briefed. Things were indeed bad. The 34th Regiment was on the verge of complete collapse. If this happened, a huge gap in the defense line would occur and the artillery endangered. It was this latter dreaded prospect that caused the operations section and other headquarters officers to wear tired and apprehensive looks.

Information about B Battery was soon volunteered. Located about two miles behind the main line of resistance, the battery had been in the direct path of the NK in the latter's attempt to encircle companies of the 34th Regiment. It was early on the morning of August 6 that both 1st Lt. Monsour and 2nd Lt. Nelsen spotted NK on the hills to the battery's left front. The two were so surprised that they initially assumed the soldiers to be ROKs in different uniforms.

Soon additional troops, similarly dressed, appeared on a hill to the right of the position. Then, about 0930, a machine gun began spraying bullets into the battery position, forcing cannoneers away from their howitzers. There was no question now as to the identity of the men facing Americans. A hurried call to headquarters brought the response that a reserve company from the 34th would be dispatched immediately to protect the battery.

Meanwhile, as that regiment's heavy mortar (4.2) company was but a short distance on the right, NK ground activity was directed at that unit first. Then, about 1030, the mortar company having been overrun, the NK returned to the artillery. With brown-suited figures sighted to the rear of the battery, permission was received to march-order.

The B Battery motor park had been organized in a bamboo thicket in front of the howitzers. A call to the drivers stationed there went unanswered. Drivers and mechanics in the park had been scattered by an earlier NK thrust. This misfortune left the battery with a half-track mounting a 37-mm gun without an aiming sight, the kitchen truck, two jeeps, a three-quarter-ton, and an ammunition carrier. The situation became desperate.

When word came to march-order, Sam Hoover, the operations officer with the battery, began to tear down the fire direction center. He had almost completed the job when an enemy mortar shell exploded close by, wounding him severely and killing his operations chief, Sgt. David J. White. Sam would have died right there had not a private in the battery, Marvin Koppelman, chose that moment to drive into the battery position in an ambulance he had discovered empty in the now-vacated infantry mortar area. Koppelman loaded Hoover and several other wounded into the ambulance under intense fire and then drove them to safety.[1]

The battery cannoneers, realizing that the prime mover trucks were not coming, began scrambling up the side of a hill at the rear of the battery position. The men withdrew in small groups, most to come out safely, but a few to become wounded or die along the way. 2nd Lt. Nelsen walked and trotted about a half-mile with twenty men or so before reaching safety. Altogether, perhaps twenty-five men of the ninety-plus men in the battery were scattered that day. All vehicles were lost except those mentioned above and, of course, all usable howitzers.[2]

Now, resupplied with equipment taken from the 63rd Field, then in bivouac near the town of Miryang, about five miles east of Yongsan, the battery was in position and handling fire missions normally.

Lt. Col. Stratton arrived in his jeep about this time, and the Lieutenant reported to him, stating his mission. After a few personal remarks, Stratton mentioned that by looking off to the left front, one could see a rather high hill, at that moment in enemy hands. This was Hill 311. The entire bulge, including the CP beside which the Lieutenant stood, was under NK observation.

As if to emphasize the danger posed by the NK at that very moment, Stratton said that the road leading east to Miryang, the only direct escape route for the men fighting in this bulge, had been cut that morning, and all road communication to division headquarters and supply points at Miryang had ceased. The colonel wasn't nervous, at least so far as the Lieutenant could tell, but the extreme urgency of the crisis had marked his usually smiling countenance with frowns and an unaccustomed sternness.

Stratton then took the Lieutenant on a terrain ride, pointing out possible locations for A Battery. The colonel had not, to this point, said definitely that the battery should join the battalion at Yongsan, but his manner of selecting positions left little doubt as to his final decision.

Then abruptly, after indicating two position possibilities, he turned to the Lieutenant and asked, "How soon can you get the battery down here?"

"By 2100 this evening, Sir."

"Good-o," the colonel acknowledged, and with his familiar salute wave, he departed on another errand-mission.

The Lieutenant smiled. It was good to be back. The 13th Field might eventually disappear beneath a mighty wave of enemy, but not before everyone, led by Lt. Col. Charles W. Stratton, gave a full accounting.

Before leaving the Yongsan area, the Lieutenant learned that only one combat team from the 2nd Infantry Division was in Korea. This was the 9th Regiment supported by the 15th Field Artillery Battalion. The remaining two sister regiments were due soon. The 9th had gone on line to the right of the 34th Regiment and was under command of Maj. Gen. Church.

Back at Hyonp'ung once more, the Lieutenant reported to Maj. Cheek that the battery was to move immediately to Yongsan. Capt. Still then issued orders for the men to prepare for imminent movement. The Lieutenant would take an advance party of section chiefs and the remainder of the unit would follow later, executing a night occupation of position.

How does one go about preparing an artillery position for occupation, part of which may be under enemy observation? Well, Fort Sill doctrine mandates that howitzers be placed so that firing will not stir dust that would immediately signal the enemy. Muzzle blasts should be shielded as well. But in Korea that summer, it was practically impossible to emplace artillery in grassy areas or heavy dirt. Most so-called grassy areas were rice paddies, often so waterlogged that prime movers were apt to become mired. The only acceptable alternative was to position the howitzers so the muzzle blasts, at least, would not be seen directly and hope that rising dust and smoke would be carried away quickly by the wind so as to delude enemy spotters.

Fortunately, a very small, pimply hill mass, similar in general outline to an elongated WWI American steel helmet, stood out in front of one of the two possible positions suggested by Stratton. A relatively level but narrow rim, wide enough for two vehicles, bordered the rear of the slight hill mass, disappearing into a group of low, eroded earth mounds. At the rear edge of the rim there was a sharp drop of six feet to a paddy field, a field quite muddy but waterlogged only in spots. This was the nature of the position finally selected by the Lieutenant.

The Lieutenant decided to position the howitzers along the rim above the paddy. The motor park would be further along the rim, beyond the howitzers, and edging the eroded mounds. In the occupation of position, the trucks would move along the rim in single file, drop the howitzers, move to the motor park, turn around, and prepare to return along the rim in the event of a withdrawal emergency. Both howitzers and the prime movers were afforded some defilade from all but direct hits from enemy mortars and artillery.

The Lieutenant had noticed earlier that afternoon that both batteries of the 11th Field, firing 155-mm howitzers, were located to the right rear of A Battery's new position. And although these units were emplaced behind fairly pronounced hill masses, the firing raised tremendous dust clouds, drawing occasional counterbattery fire from the NK. He hoped that the clumps of grass along the edges of the small hill mounds fronting A Battery would limit considerably dust raised there.

The battery fire direction center or exec post would be located just behind the howitzers, down on the paddy field. Ed Mattes might not be able to see every cannoneer, but his voice would be heard clearly, and his group would remain fairly secure from enemy counterbattery action. The kitchen and battery CP were sited across the road, somewhat more in the open. Having thus outlined the new position, the section chiefs began work on position entrances, site and aiming stake locations, and wire lines.

The battery arrived just at dark, using blackout lights. As the first jeep approached bearing Capt. Still, word to dismount was given, and all the men climbed down onto the road. Walking thusly and led by members of the advance party, the men accompanied their vehicles and howitzers into the area and into position. It was a perfect night occupation, better than any the Lieutenant had witnessed or been part of in Europe during WWII, and executed by men who were, presumptively, battle-weary and extremely fatigued. The unit had great reserve, the Lieutenant opined.

The officers stood aside on the road where the occupation activity could command attention and watched. Not a promptive order had to be issued. By 2145, all was ready. Section guards were organized and perimeter security posted. Soon the battery lay quiet, waiting.

By the side of the road where he had stood during the occupation activity, the Lieutenant finally lay down. Somehow more excited and enthused than he had been for days, he anticipated a tense but not hopeless situation. He was smack in the middle of one of the most crucial battles of the Conflict. It would be something to remember, all right, if he lived long enough to remember. He wondered how soon he would have to "go up." Sleep caught him as he was speculating.

THE FIRST BATTLE OF THE NAKTONG POCKET[1]

THE NK FORCED THEIR FIRST SERIOUS THRUST ACROSS THE NAKTONG RIVER IN THE Yongsan sector on August 6. Already assuming a successful drive to Pusan from Chinju, the NK hoped to drive a secondary wedge into the UN lines at a point between Pusan and Taegu. This thrust would necessitate the commitment of available UN reserves in two sectors, further weakening the defensive perimeter.

The site of this secondary thrust, a few miles west of Yongsan, was strategic in that a road led directly from the river to Yongsan and then east to Miryang, the latter on the main road and rail line from Pusan to Taegu. The distance between Yongsan and Miryang was only about fifteen miles. If the NK could force the Americans back to or near Yongsan, and then cut the road between Yongsan and Miryang, and further cut the road and rail line both north and south of Miryang, not only would the 24th Division units be in jeopardy, but so would the cavalry sector and numbers of ROK units as well. NK success with this strategy could well result in a calculated withdrawal from Taegu with attendant political as well as military problems for the UN forces.

Understandably aware of the seriousness of the situation as it was unfolding, Eighth Army directed that the NK be held back at any cost. So on this note, the First Battle of the Naktong Pocket, or the battle of the Ch'angnyong Pocket as the encounter is sometimes called, commenced.

After a rather wide western swing away from the town of Hyonp'ung, the Naktong River meanders gradually eastward. However, at the minuscule paddy village of Ohang, about six miles west of Yongsan, the river begins another wide bend, this time around a large hill mass called Kugin-San (Hill 311). Numerous smaller, eroded hills, gullies, treeless ridges, and dry streambeds abound in this terrain bulge, making for what many Americans who fought there term the landscape (among other unprintable descriptions) "Hell on the half-shell." The rocks, dust, bugs, mosquitoes, and cement-like earth made every defensive step a battle against a part of the world that God must have dismissed as completely uninhabitable.

The 34th Regiment had been given defense responsibility for this area. The Third Battalion was on the line, the companies extremely spread. The defense test was not long in coming.

Showing once more a mastery of guerrilla strategy, elements of the NK 4th Division slipped across the Naktong during early hours of August 6, both at Ohang and at a nearby ferry landing called Paekchin. The immediate objective was a draw or narrow valley that led south from Ohang, behind one of the 34th Regiment's defensive positions, to the village of Ch'iryonni, also on the Naktong as it winds westward. Control of this little valley would have the effect of severing part of the American defense line and securing access to the road leading from Paekchin east to Yongsan. Once secured, the NK could enlarge the attack, using tanks and other attack vehicles.

Daylight on the sixth saw both sides locked in battle. The forward, finger-like ridges leading out to the river were overrun by the NK, as was Kugin-San (Hill 311). Several companies of the 34th had been isolated by the NK advance, and these were being mortared and sniped at constantly. As at Taejon and later, in the "Valley of Death," the 34th Regiment was taking the brunt of relentless NK assaults.

Now that the NK strategy was clarified, both battalions of the 19th Regiment were ordered into an attack in the Ohang vicinity, the attack designed to bolster the right flank of the 34th. The First Battalion of the 34th, also, moved up to meet this new threat. And then, as the tired and gaunt remnants of the 24th Division once more faced up to their duties, help in the form of a new contingent from the States arrived.

Rumors that the 2nd Infantry Division, stationed at Fort Lewis, Washington, had been alerted for Korea had been rampant since Taejon. But they were rumors only. Now, suddenly, in the midst of the heat and fury of the developing Naktong battle, the 9th Regimental Combat Team, 2nd Infantry Division, appeared and was thrust into the defense line between the 19th and 34th Regiments. For a brief interval, the 9th became a fourth tactical regiment within the 24th Division.

Immediately upon being committed, the 9th went into an attack which, although competent, failed. Yet the companies did not withdraw, so that its position on the line represented a stability sorely needed at the moment. This, then, was the general situation the evening of A Battery's arrival from Hyonp'ung.

There was no call for fire that first night, so everyone rested. The quiet dawn of the eighth was soon broken by the roar of several four-motor passenger planes circling. Everyone jumped up to look. Perplexed at first, the men soon learned that the planes, DCs from military air transport, were engaged in a mission to resupply troops of the trapped companies of the 34th Regiment. The pilots were waiting for a propitious moment to drop food, water, and ammunition.

The pilots continued circling for about an hour when one plane was seen to level off and dip sharply to the left side, all the while descending slightly. As the men in the battery watched, they saw objects fall from the plane's left compartment door and then small parachutes open, floating the objects to the ground. Once this maneuver was completed, the plane revved and disappeared from the combat zone. The second plane went through the same maneuver shortly afterward, although at a slightly different location along the defense line.

Later that day, an infantry sergeant stopped at the artillery position. He volunteered the information that only about half the supplies being dropped were gathered up by the encircled soldiers. The NK would hold fire until the drops began. Then they would fire to keep the Americans from securing the needed supplies, especially water. He did say, however, that the drops would continue. Sure enough, the planes flew over again that evening and the next several days until the encirclement was broken.[2]

There was considerable tension within the artillery position that first full day. The NK engaged in intermittent shelling and mortaring a roadway about three hundred yards to the rear of the battery. Also, as firing by the 11th Field stirred up a great deal of dust, some of the NK firing was directed at that battalion.

Even with the few rounds of intermittent NK firing, accuracy of enemy data was shocking. More than once the men looked about and beyond the position to discover if NK observers were nearby. There being a rather high hill to the left rear of the 11th Field position, with several huts scattered on the face, suspicion rose that NK observer agents might be operating from one or the other of the huts.

Around noon, Lt. Col. Stratton ordered the antiaircraft half-track, the vehicle without an aiming sight, brought to a point near the 11th Field's position. Once situated, the vehicle's 40-mm gun was trained, in succession, on each of the huts on the hillside. The fact that the gun was minus a sight did not hamper the gun crew's efforts.

The gun was aimed with reasonable accuracy by sighting down the barrel, and several direct hits were scored on the structures. One white-robed civilian was killed as he ran, obviously panic-stricken, from one of the huts. The operation turned out to be a useless expenditure of energy and ammunition as NK shelling continued unabated and with the same effect.

During the antiaircraft shelling on the rear hillside, someone at the 9th Regiment's supply dump, located just ahead and across the road from A Battery, discharged an M-1 rifle. This noise had the effect of triggering razor-sharp nervousness on the part of the artillerymen. Several raced over to the service unit and demanded, in no uncertain terms, that there be no firing of individual weapons except at close-in targets. The risk of injury or death from indiscriminate firing was too great here, and the men of the 13th had been in Korea too long to now become victims when there was no call for same. That was the end of the rifle firing from the infantry service area.

The battery, as were other units, had been warned against the threat of NK infiltration efforts, and those who had been issued binoculars kept them trained on the hillsides, particularly the hill just southeast of Yongsan. On the morning of the tenth, the Lieutenant spotted a brown-suited figure standing on the ridgeline of that hill. The man was soon joined by others and, shortly, the hill appeared to be crawling with them.

As if his observation was being witnessed by higher headquarters, several vehicles from the Heavy Mortar Company, 21st Regiment, raced by, followed by infantry in trucks. Second Lt. Delormier also swept by with his observer section.

The Lieutenant called Capt. Still and together they discussed the sighting, plus the possibility that the NK might block the main road and then move to confront the firing batteries of both the 11th and 13th battalions. The captain began to contemplate a position move away from this new enemy threat.

That evening the Lieutenant, as did everyone else in the battery, crouched in ditches or slit trenches during an unusually prolonged NK artillery barrage aimed at the rear areas. A battery of four guns was being fired, the millimeter equivalent perhaps of the American 57-mm gun. The barrage lasted about thirty-five minutes, the volleys in rapid succession and with good accuracy.

Working quickly while no American planes were overhead, the NK artillerymen swept the terrain between Yongsan and the infantry CPs. The men in A Battery could hear the initial firing detonations and then, seconds later, the high-pitched whine of the projectiles passing above the position or close by. None landed in the battery area, although several exploded on a mound to the front and on rises to the rear. The 11th Field batteries sustained some shelling, but there was no word concerning casualties.

The next day about noon, after some unusually heavy shelling of Yongsan by the NK, a fire began. The men in A Battery watched as black smoke billowed straight up into the sky. Then explosions were heard. The whiny zings of mortar shells being set off were met with apprehensive silence. The 19th Regiment's ammunition dump had been fired. There was no question now. It was time for the battery to move.

Leaving 2nd Lt. Mattes in charge, Capt. Still and the Lieutenant went on reconnaissance. Up the road and past the 13th CP they drove until they spotted an area that, on the right, dipped slightly to form a small, dry valley with ample defilade on three sides, and on the left reached into a narrow gully of small terraced but dry paddies. The valley part of the position offered space for the six howitzers, while the service sections of the battery would fit nicely within the gully pattern. Capt. Still immediately pointed out the howitzer locations to the platoon sergeant, Sfc. James A. Davis. The Lieutenant staked out the various locations for service and communications groups.

While thus engaged, a movement from down the road caught the eye. There were only barely discernible noises at first indicating movement. Then, shortly, a long file of native civilians came rapidly into view. It was a panic-stricken lot, herded by South Korean police, and there were unmistakable sounds of sobbing and wailing within the crowd. Most clutched a bundle or two and several were herding livestock. But most had little but the clothing on their backs, and it was these who were bemoaning their fate.

The little group of Americans stopped working and watched. The civilians being hurried along seemed to be all that remained of the population of Yongsan. They had earlier gathered in a dry streambed just south of the town with all their belongings on carts to wait out the military action. However, the infiltrating NK had fired on them, causing casualties and forcing them to scatter. The group seemed to have had very little time to gather up their baggage, many driven off without anything.

They first of all had run back into the town of Yongsan, only to be met by the exploding ammunition dump. Now they were here on the road north and moving into the unknown. It was a pitiful scene and sobering for the watching Americans. But the latter could not stop long to sympathize. They forced themselves to resume working, although none laughed or joked for some time afterward.

Capt. Still soon left to march-order the battery and lead it to the new position. The column arrived within an hour, prime movers with howitzers leading the march. These turned off the road and went into positions quickly. The kitchen truck was led to one of the terraced paddies on the left, as was the maintenance truck.

A perimeter defense was established and a BC Scope was mounted on the hill mass fronting the unit, to be manned continuously for signs of NK guerrilla activity. This was the real fear among artillery units here. A sudden attack, breaching friendly lines, could place batteries in extreme jeopardy. UN forces could not risk the loss of artillery support at this critical juncture in the fighting.

Word came late that afternoon that the supply road between Yongsan and Miryang, the railhead for supplies and reinforcements, had again been cut. The remaining supply route led north along the road that passed through the A Battery position to Ch'angnyong, from which town a road led east to Chongdo and Taegu. With the blocking of the Miryang road, division headquarters would be placed temporarily at Ch'angnyong.

Now, if the NK could establish a roadblock north beyond A Battery, 24th Division units in the pocket would have a difficult time continuing high-level military operations. The 21st Regiment, heretofore only nominally a part of the Yongsan defense, was alerted to careful watchfulness along the river line north.

Medical jeeps and ambulances from all three committed regiments traveled back and forth along the road past the battery during the remainder of the day, carrying both dead and wounded to a newly established clearing station somewhere to the north. The men in A Battery watched and said little. Unit morale was ebbing.

About 0100 the following morning, after an evening punctuated by a few raindrops, several men came walking up the road, calling out. One was a captain. This man strode into the battery area asking for the battery commander. The Lieutenant jumped up and directed him to the spot on the hillside where Capt. Still was rousing himself. The captain informed Still that the NK had broken through the 34th Regimental line with tanks and were, at that moment, moving north from Yongsan on the road leading to the battery position. He said there had been a complete breakthrough.

The men were stunned. This may be *it*. If someone had shouted "March-order," a mad dash of trucks and howitzers north toward Ch'angnyong could not have been headed. But Still refused to be panicked and risk another rout, as had occurred east of Koch'ang. Instead, every man was awakened and given a duty. All available weapons went on the perimeter. Two howitzers were turned so that they faced the road as antitank weapons. The Lieutenant took charge of the small hill fronting the battery position on the south. He had with him cooks and drivers. If the NK did come up the road, they would meet the Lieutenant and his group first.

Nothing happened. The furor and warning were based on faulty information. When daybreak came, it was learned that there had indeed been an NK attack, but the attack had been contained after a short, tactical withdrawal. The men were somewhat shaky, but still determined as Sfc. Lucero readied a huge vat of hot coffee. The coffee steadied everyone, and most soon relaxed enough to laugh about the affair and josh the kitchen personnel about their "combat experience."

The short respite for the Lieutenant came to an end on the 14th. Even before the battery telephone stopped ringing, he knew the message. He had been ordered up again. He experienced the usual tight stomach feeling and facial tautness. As before, he found himself reacting a bit more sharply to questions. Yet it would be different this time. There was a combat line now, and company fronts were more compressed. It was much more difficult for the NK to launch flanking operations and endanger whole platoons and even companies.

Although the fourteenth was a Monday, the Protestant chaplain, Chaplain Helt, had driven into the battery area and was preparing to hold services. His arrival had been delayed due to roadblock activity by the NK east of Yongsan. While Dear drove to the battalion communications center for a radio check, the Lieutenant went to services. It may be the last time, he thought.

All was soon in readiness. As before, Charles Dear was the section's driver. However, a new man arrived to accompany the Lieutenant to the line. He was Cpl. Cletus Fitzgerald, a seasoned, calm NCO, who had previously been with "Tex" Fullen and later with 1st Lt. Pate. He would be a good companion on this upcoming mission.

When a new artillery observer, or one who had not worked with a regiment for some time, goes up, certain amenities are performed. He reports first to regimental headquarters, then to battalion, and finally arrives on the line with his assigned company. This day, August 14, what with new commanders on both regimental and battalion levels, correct protocol was followed.

With Capt. Homer Owsley, Jr., the liaison, the Lieutenant arrived at the 19th Regiment's headquarters. After being ushered into the command tent, the sides rolled up completely for air conditioning, he was introduced to a slightly stocky, somewhat diminutive man wearing a spotless white T-shirt and easing nonchalantly on a steel army-issue chair, watching and listening to members of the assembled staff as they worked. This was Col. Ned D. Moore.

By way of returning Moore's courtesy, the Lieutenant casually mentioned that he had served previously with the 19th, with C Company at the Kum River. Instantly, all work ceased in the tent as eyes turned to him. Did he know that only thirty-seven men and two officers were known to have survived from that company in the aftermath of the Kum battle? He was besieged with questions as to what actually happened. What were the circumstances surrounding the disappearance of 1st Lt. MacGill?

The Lieutenant related all that he knew. He was shocked to learn that 2nd Lt. Stavrakes was listed as missing. He led the platoon that had been sent out to cover the company withdrawal, and he had been with the Lieutenant when the group began mingling with A Company in the withdrawal from the river. Stavrakes must have remained too long in or around Taep'yong-ni, rounding up stragglers or waiting for more escapees from the C Company position. That would be like him, solicitous always of his men.

As to the surviving officers, one was George Lowe, injured during the early hours of the fighting and removed to a forward medical station without incident. The other was Augustus Orr. The Lieutenant recalled having seen Orr amid the swirl of men in Taep'yong-ni prior to the organized withdrawal. For a brief time the present faded as the Kum River affair once more jabbed at the memories of those in the CP tent who remembered. Then it was time to leave.

The First Battalion was commanded at this time by a tall, bouncy major named Robert M. Miller. Miller had been acting CO since the Kum battle. At first sight, where Owsley said the CP was located, only a few huts and a large well were in evidence. But after a loud "Halloo," up popped the major from his post, a large dugout against the side of a hill, sheltered ingeniously by a camouflaged tent-covering.

Miller welcomed the Lieutenant in a pleasant, rangy voice, trying hard to minimize the danger. Fitzgerald and the Lieutenant would go up on what Maj. Miller called "Bailey's Hill," reporting to the commander of B Company, whose name christened that bit of friendly real estate. B Company, according to the major, had been the one company in the battalion that had not given way to NK pressure since initial commitment there in support of the 34th Regiment. Two men from that company were at the moment by the large well, drawing water for canteens. The observer party would accompany them up to the line.

Sounds of shelling were heard plainly now. Mortars particularly were exploding with regularity. Fitzgerald and the Lieutenant kept looking at each other, but neither said anything. One of the B Company men at the well was Daniel D. Maderas. He had been with the company since it arrived in Korea. It was the "best damned company in the regiment." Every company in every regiment was, of course. But more importantly, the Lieutenant was going to meet the "best damned CO around." His name: 2nd Lt. Charles T. Bailey.

Bailey and his company occupied a bald ridgeline just north of a position controlled by a unit of the 9th Regiment, a position termed Cloverleaf Hill. The left portion of the ridgeline held by B Company dropped off into a deep gully while the right flank wound slightly back and into holes and trenches defended by A Company. NK mortars and direct fire artillery had made Bailey's Hill a constant target. Several night thrusts had been made by the NK without success. Approximately seven men per day had been wounded or killed during the previous week, the hill receiving the sobriquet "Purple Heart Hill."

As the four began their slow climb to the hill position, they met several wounded being helped down the trail, wounds in both arms and legs, casualties from NK mortar firing. One man, half carried by two medics, pleaded with the Lieutenant for water. Between swallows, he said water was so scarce it was rationed to the platoons under an officer's supervision. For an instant, the

Lieutenant thought the man would quaff the entire canteenful. But the injured man had shaken the canteen a bit before beginning to drink, as if to measure the contents, and only drank a quarter before returning it. He smiled wanly as the Lieutenant turned to go. "Good luck up there, buddy," he said. He was on his way back. The Lieutenant was on his way up.

Near the top of the trail, just before reaching the company position, several rifle belts were discovered. These were not strewn about, but were folded neatly and placed under small bushes. Maderas remarked in an offhand manner: "Bug-outs."

Men had left the line here, allegedly deserting their comrades. True or not, they were either on their way back toward Pusan or wandering aimlessly along a rear echelon roadway, with little thought of voluntarily returning just yet. The military police had too many other chores to perform to check on these men, but the fact that they were away from the line was treasonous in view of the momentary critical situation.

Then, rounding a slight bend in the trail, the group came upon B Company in position. On the backside of a dusty, hard-earth baked ridgeline, with little other than a small bush or two to break the skyline, a company of perhaps eighty-two strong sprawled or sat, waiting. The area was littered with personal equipment, discarded ammunition containers, and empty C-ration cans. About halfway down from the ridgeline, several shelter-halves had been propped up to provide some shade from a boiling afternoon sun.

This was no practice bivouac. However tired or listless the men appeared, they were in dead earnest. They were resting and recuperating from previous bouts with the NK and preparing for God knows how many more. Here was a group of thoroughly combat-tested men, men who had seen over forty of their number wounded or "get it" during the past several days on this hill, and were now endeavoring to shut out of their minds the possibility that more would be wounded or "get it" tonight or tomorrow. This was a terribly understrength infantry company along the Naktong River line. This was B Company, 19th Infantry Regiment, 24th Infantry Division, on the late afternoon of August 14, 1950.

No one greeted the relieving observer party as it strode into view. The two company men and their water cans were more important at the moment. The tinkle of empty canteens was heard as platoon sergeants gathered them up and dispatched platoon members to the CP for regular rationing procedures.

The Lieutenant now noticed two soldiers stationed near the center of the line, gazing intently at him. A packboard lay next to one of the men, on which was mounted an SCR-610 radio. This must be the observer team to be relieved, the Lieutenant reasoned. He walked over to the two men, struggling a bit to keep his footing as the hill sloped rather sharply, making walking difficult.

One of the two men turned out to be the observer, a lieutenant whose name sounded like Hallahan. The officer looked quite pleased that he was to be relieved. The Lieutenant asked him if NK activity had been strong. "Are you kidding?" came the reply. The man's recon sergeant had already gathered up their equipment and was ready to depart, notwithstanding the fact that the Lieutenant had been standing there only about fifty-five seconds.

With a motion, Hallahan waved the Lieutenant onto the forward side of the hill and there pointed out several check and concentration points he had used. The Lieutenant wrote down the numbers and memorized the locations. Hallahan reminded the Lieutenant to keep his head down above all else. Then, with a smiling "Good luck," the twosome set off on a fast walk to the rear.

The Lieutenant took stock of his new location. The hill was mostly hard earth and rock, soft earth having eroded badly over the centuries. Most of the company men had labored long to carve holes deep enough to protect against all but direct mortar hits. Forward lookouts had dug shallow scoopouts and then camouflaged them with greens. These posts were easily spotted, of course. No forward lookout could be constructed well enough on these bare hills to avoid detection by the NK.

The most urgent problem for all, as the Lieutenant gathered on his approach to the hill, was the water supply. There was absolutely no water available here or in the immediate vicinity. The nearest usable well was at the Battalion CP, a good five-minute walk down and a ten-minute walk back. Water details were constantly coming and going.

Yet *in toto*, the men seemed in good spirits, even despite the casualties suffered, which was more than could be said at the moment for some rear echelon units, and morale seemed better than anticipated.

While the Lieutenant was pondering thus and discussing matters with Cpl. Fitzgerald, a large figure loomed. The Lieutenant looked up and into the round face and Southern smile of the slightly rotund leader of men on the hill, "Bill" Bailey himself. Several of the company NCOs were with him. They had walked over to introduce themselves and take the measure of the new observer.

After the initial round of handshakes, the Lieutenant promised he would do the best he could, and Bailey replied that that was all anyone asked. When apprised that the Lieutenant had been at the Kum, Bailey got chummier. He had been there himself, he said, and was one of the several company grade officers still untouched by wounds. The NCOs stood around, saying nothing.

Finally the Lieutenant mentioned he would like to go to one of the lookouts and begin surveying NK-held area fronting the company. Immediately one of the NCOs offered to accompany and point out suspected trouble spots. The Lieutenant sighed. He had been accepted.

The sun had set when the Lieutenant finally stretched out in his slit trench as best he could to secure a few winks preparatory to being aroused should an NK attack begin.

About 2200 he was sharply shaken by one of the infantry sergeants, who informed him that a battery of NK mortars was firing into American lines, the firing spotted from the left observation post. With Fitzgerald bringing the SCR-300 radio, the Lieutenant went out to the point. A small group of infantry had gathered there, the point or OP being just above the gully or notch separating the company from the 9th Regiment's position. The area of the enemy target was identified and, within a minute, sure enough, four small streaks of blue flame shot upward from what appeared to be a battery of four small field pieces.

Fitzgerald radioed the fire-mission, and the Lieutenant asked for a probing round, from which an adjustment could be made. After two probing rounds, he asked for a battery volley of mixed high explosive and white phosphorus rounds. The volley came, three rounds each of HE and WP, the latter balls of flame down the side of a small hill that had provided some defilade for the NK battery. Following another adjustment, he requested another volley of the same. This time, the HE exploded just about where the guns were located, but the WP, although closer, were still landing on the hillside.

The Lieutenant called for a suspension of fire after the second volley. If the NK firing continued, he would resume the mission. If the guns remained silent, the assumption would have to be that there had been damage, injured enemy personnel, or a reluctance to continue firing and risk total loss of the weapons. Nothing further was sighted or heard from the NK position the remainder of the night.

The NK began mortaring Bailey's Hill in earnest beginning about 0900 the following morning. The NK may have figured that the artillery observer who fired the mission the previous night was on this hill, as nothing had been heard from the 9th Regiment's artillery support.

The rounds came in, three or four a minute. Only one mortar was used, par for such an enemy mission. The men lay prone or crouched in their holes. Casualties mounted. Second Lt. John H. English, the executive officer, was injured in the ankle when a round exploded near the company CP. This left Bailey as the only infantry officer on the hill. Another man, a colored corporal, the first the Lieutenant had seen with white troops, was wounded at the same location. His injuries were more serious. Altogether, five men had to leave the hill for treatment from the shelling, further depleting company strength.

The Lieutenant had been at the left OP point when the mortaring began. Both Fitzgerald and he stood in a hole dug laboriously several days previous by Sfc. Clifford D. Hamric. When the Lieutenant asked Hamric earlier that morning if he could use the spot as an OP, the sergeant leaped out with a "Help yourself." The Lieutenant now fully understood the reason for the sergeant's quick cooperation.

Bailey's Hill didn't offer much of a target. The hill rose sharply on the front and dropped off almost as sharply. Only about three to five yards of comparatively level ground topped the hill, with men dug in just off the edge of the rearward slope. Most of the incoming mortar shells landed on the lower slope of the hill. But one of the last rounds fired seemed aimed deliberately at the little OP manned by the Lieutenant. The round hissed angrily as it passed overhead in the last split second before exploding about ten yards or so straight down behind the OP hole. Fitzgerald leaned back weakly, and the Lieutenant took his helmet off in nervous anxiety. That had been close. Another few feet or so short and there would have been little left but unidentifiable strings of anatomy.

In retaliation, the Lieutenant began firing at every likely trouble spot. This burst of firing wrote *finis* to the NK mortaring, and the men spent the remainder of the day in quiet anticipation.

It was during this retaliatory firing that the Lieutenant had occasion to use the proximity or variable time (VT) fuze for the first time. He had been briefed prior to going on the line that the fuze was now available, but he had hesitated to use it earlier because the hilly terrain make premature bursts a real concern.

The fuze, developed during WWII, contained a radio device that, upon activation, as the round began its propelled circular motion through the howitzer barrel, caused a burst approximately twenty-five yards from a solid mass or object. These fuzes were ideal replacements for the older mechanical fuzes that had to be hand-adjusted relative to an observer's or a fire direction center's considered judgment and therefore not always accurate. Some in B Company gathered to watch the effect of the VT-fuze-fired artillery on the ridge of the slope opposite the company's position. Noting the dust kicked up by the bits of flying shrapnel, the general reaction was, "Thank God the gooks don't have the same."

Sundown ushered in one of those nights, the kind that makes nocturnal animals more cautious and humans edgy and fretful. There was no moon. The older hands predicted an attack. There hadn't been one for several days. The stillness made one feel like shouting just to break the spell. It was like this quite often in Korea. During these kinds of nights, one would almost cry from fear, anger, or homesickness.

Bailey asked for a flare about 2300 hours. The Lieutenant responded quickly, and a flare shell from the 11th Field sailed over, bursting just beyond the position and lighting not only the B Company field of fire, but that of the 9th Regiment company as well. Not a stick or a stone was out of place, nor any mysterious shadow seen. The men felt better and a settling was sensed in all quarters.

Then, about 0300, the usual time for an NK attack, sounds were heard from the left across the notch, words and high-pitched babble. The NK had chosen the 9th Regiment-held ground as the object this time, the men dug in on Cloverleaf Hill.

The battalion of that regiment held positions stretching several hundred yards to a point where the hills intersected with a road leading from the Naktong River and the Paekchin Ferry crossing. Both the 9th and the 19th Regiments were in a salient that was extremely vulnerable to attack from the direction of the ferry road. However, the NK apparently thought that the hill occupied by the First Battalion, 9th Regiment, was of more strategic value because it was higher than others in the immediate vicinity. Control of this bit of terrain might force flank units to withdraw without a struggle.

Several NK companies carried the attack, and they were successful at first. Shouts and screams came from the left. The Lieutenant heard one loud voice calling, "They're on the hill; they're on the hill!" And then, "Help me! Help...!" The scream was cut off. Small arms firing became intense.

Then the artillery came, not onto the hill but into the valley beyond, where enemy reinforcements might be gathering. Volley after volley whistled in from the 15th Field.

The Lieutenant, noting approaching dawn, called for several volleys from the 13th, placing them in the valley in front of B Company, just in case the NK thought of shifting the attack. The rounds came quickly, but were not needed.

The NK operations ceased at dawn. The entire area was thick with smoke and the acrid fumes of burned cordite. The buzz of a pair of F-51s broke the tension and brought smiles of relief to many. The pilots couldn't bore in until the smoke and fog lifted, but a clearing of the air was only a matter of short time.

Peering over, the men in B Company saw native stretcher-bearers edging their way up the rear trails, a sign that the fight had ended. Men began eating breakfast chow, soon to stretch out for a rest denied them those several hours of the attack. The American line of defense remained intact.

That afternoon, the afternoon of the sixteenth, rumors began circulating that a major UN attack was imminent. Second Lt. Bailey received word that the 34th Regiment, having been squeezed out in the south by a lengthening of the 9th Regiment's lines and a widening of the 25th Division sector, would occupy his position. B Company would then withdraw, circle about, and then pass through A Company to spearhead an attack on some high ground to the right. This attack would signal a major push forward by all units, the river's edge being the objective.

The men were now extremely relaxed after the enemy failure of the morning. They were confident that they could hold a line here indefinitely and soon be strong enough to counterattack into NK-held territory.

The 34th failed to rendezvous that evening as expected, leaving the men on Bailey's Hill to face another night. Not unexpectedly, the NK made an appearance, this time engaging in harassing fire, using a machine gun. The "chit-chit" of the gun continued crisply for a number of minutes when the field phone rang and instruction was given the Lieutenant that the regimental CO, Col. Moore, wanted the gun silenced at any cost. Apparently the 34th was still anticipated, although darkness was about to envelop the entire battlefield.

The Lieutenant dragged his SCR-300 to the top of the hill and, with the aid of the forward lookout, Pfc. Herbert C. Carlson, determined the gunner's approximate location. Fortunately, the 11th Field had fired a concentration nearby so, without waiting to adjust, the Lieutenant asked for a two-howitzer volley on the concentration, one howitzer loading a high explosive round and the other, white phosphorus. He needed only one further adjustment for Carlson to pronounce that the target had been hit, or very close to being hit. Pausing, it was clear that the NK gunner had ceased his efforts. Ending the mission, the Lieutenant mused that the NK had either become a casualty or the fear of WP was too much to stomach.

The 34th Regiment arrived about 0700 the following morning. It was August 17. The Third Battalion led, and the Lieutenant recognized many in the group. Maj. Rosen scurried about raising communications. First Lt. Little began holding conferences with several company officers.

Charles Delorimier was the liaison with the battalion. He looked tired. As the Lieutenant waved, Chuck responded cursorily, his expression showing pain. He had been with the 34th ten straight days, and he was worn out.

The moment the 34th was spotted trudging up the rear trail, B Company was given the word to saddle up. There were mixed feelings as the men began filing off the hill. It had been quite a position, this one. Good men had died here, and a number of others saw their last battle action in Korea defending this ridge, memories to be played out in hospital beds in Pusan or back in the States. There had been no withdrawal, and each NK attack had been beaten off with vigor. Most took a last look just as the turn in the trail led them below a knoll and well beyond the men now ensconced on the hard earth pile.

Down the trail they went, and then they swung onto a wider path leading to the ferry road. The strategy called for B Company to circle behind the main battle line and then veer back toward the river. The company would link up with other regimental companies, now massing at a point east of a terrain location known as Ohang Hill. A jump-off against Ohang Hill would take place late that afternoon. The 19th and 34th regiments would then launch a coordinated attack the following morning as part of a major UN attempt to push the NK back across the Naktong. Rumors of Marines coming up from Masan to assist in the push had been passed along, but nothing definite had been heard or seen.

As the company strode along the path, they glimpsed the ferry road for the first time. Soon they were puzzled to see a long file of men marching toward them along the ferry road, a file which destination seemed to be a hilly area to the left of the 9th regiment, a file of men going into an attack.

Those at the head of the B Company column strained to identify these troops when, surprisingly, everyone began to notice that the approaching men wore leggings rather than regulation combat boots. Shouts of "They're Marines!" "The Marines are here!" were raised and passed back. "Those sons-of-bitches look good, don't they?" And so it went. Then, as the path joined the ferry road, a map speck with the most improbable name of Sangnigok, B Company began filing back on its side of the road while the Marines pressed forward on the other.

They looked tall, these Marines, and appeared every inch the men they claimed to be. The Lieutenant glanced back on the Army company file. These remnants of the early days, with some recent additions, were certainly what could be described only as a conglomeration. Some were tall, others short or small. Still others were medium but slender, like the Lieutenant. A few wore glasses, and one or two squinted because their glasses had been lost or damaged.

The stink of sweat from days on dusty and sun-bleached hills swept over the road. Many faces were unshaven and grimy, the whites of eyes showing in strange contrast. And several wore pants out of boots because of tears in either the cloth or the leather. Almost all carried personal gear and food in bulging pockets, combat packs a rarity.

This was B Company, 19th Infantry Regiment, on its way back and toward a new challenge, passing a fresh Marine contingent stepping forward, immaculate in clean fatigues, combat packs properly positioned, and no items of equipment missing or hanging awkwardly. The Second Battalion, 5th Marine Regiment, was entering battle in Korea for the first time.

Few words were spoken as the two files passed. Eyes told the story. The Lieutenant noted the Marines hardly daring to look at the Army men on the opposite side of the road. Yet their eyes were full of respect for these combat-weary veterans, and their faces grew taut as they anticipated their own baptism.

B Company, a proud company, riveted forever together by superlative battlefield accomplishment and by remembering those whose sacrifices had contributed to the successes of recent days, was coming out. The Marines were going in. The two files passed until their passing was no more, and only sounds of battle could be heard from the hills behind as the Marines, too, began to bleed and die in this Korean holocaust.

Someone goofed that day. Instead of using a shorter bypass, the company was forced to march about three miles in a circuitous route to the attack rendezvous. Several men collapsed as they walked under a blazing sun. The days on the hill prevented most from engaging in proper exercise. Heat exhaustion took its toll. Men begged for water from each other and from anyone passing in vehicles. Two medics, enforcing water discipline with their own canteens, were cursed occasionally for their soldierly approach.

Fortunately, Dear, with his jeep, met the company on the road and picked up the most weakened, shuttling them to a previously designated rest location with shade trees and a small running stream. A temporary aid station had been established at this location, and salt tablets were dispensed to those needing same. By mid-afternoon, the regiment was reunited, and the B Company men were all feeling better and steadier.

With the arrival of B Company, a new battalion commander called key officers and artillery observers together for a pre-battle conference that included a look at the immediate objective, Ohang Hill. The CO was Lt. Col. Morris J. Naudts (pronounced "Nots"). Naudts had arrived in the division only that day and was sent down to the 19th without delay, replacing Maj. Miller, who had been wounded by an exploding mortar shell a day or so previous.

Ohang Hill had been a prime objective of the Second Battalion, 19th Regiment, for the past several days. Several attacks had been made on the hill, the battalion losing men and key officers in the process. The hill was a rather small, toad-shaped mass, fronting another, larger group of hills. A circular grove of trees crowned the top, surrounding a prominent grave mound. The hill had been defended with vigor by the NK and presumably was still occupied by them, although, when the First Battalion began looking in that direction in preparation for an assault, no sign of NK activity was observed.

Naudts told the group that the Marines were at that moment attacking to the front of the former 34th Regimental sector and that the 9th Regiment would stand fast until bypassed. The 19th would attack on the right to clear hills nearest the north portion of the bulge. The 34th Regiment, now in position on Bailey's Hill, would move onto the hill mass directly to its front in the morning and eventually link up with the Marines. Hill 311, the highest elevation in the Naktong Pocket, was the ultimate Marine objective.

Now, B Company would attack Ohang hill, A and C Companies following. The Lieutenant went forward to determine data for support once the companies moved out. He would remain on the hill behind to observe the infantry's progress. Then, once the objective was secured, he would move to Ohang and organize his OP there.

All was in readiness. It was about 1800 hours. The sun was setting behind the hills there in the pocket. The men, refreshed, were eager to get this job done. Dewey Coles, up with A Company, fired the artillery preparation, a mixture of high explosive and phosphorus. Mortars joined in the barrage.

Second Lt. Bailey gave the signal and a platoon, led by Sfc. Hamric, filed into view. Bailey was still the company's only officer, but his platoon sergeants were officer caliber. The rest of the company now began circling out from behind a small grove and swung into a skirmish line at the foot of Ohang. It was impossible to edge up Indian fashion. The hill, as were most in the area, was bare except at the top.

The men started up. There was as yet no resistance. When the company reached the halfway point, Coles lifted the artillery. Mortar fire ceased. Then an NK machine gun chattered and the men flattened. Bailey called for a squad to move around the base of the hill to the right, near the river. The squad might be able to flank the hill from that direction.

The squad moved forward. A tall Negro led these men. They continued with caution. Then the machine gun fired again, and two men crumpled. The remainder of the squad broke into a run and disappeared from view along the far side of the hill's base.

The distraction of the running men proved to be the turning point of the attack. Sfc. Hamric's platoon, on the left, had been working its way slowly up the hill, crawling ever so painfully, or so it appeared. But after the divertive action by the squad on the right, Hamric stood up and led his men in a rush to the crest, a number firing their rifles as they pressed forward.

The rest of the company, seeing the rush by Hamric's platoon, straightened and moved quickly to the hilltop. A flurry of running and firing completed this final phase of the attack and then silence. The hill was won. The NK, numbering perhaps two squads, had withdrawn. Several NK had fled down the hill to the right and were now trapped in a small gully. A squad from A Company was dispatched to that location and soon reported the NK as either killed or running toward the river. Following this last burst of attack activity, the Lieutenant and Cpl. Fitzgerald moved to join B Company on Ohang.

A gruesome sight greeted the men on Ohang. Scattered about under the tree grove were bodies of NK defenders. Several were clothed in the familiar dirt-brown uniforms, but two had been outfitted in GI fatigues and helmet liners. These latter were officers or NCOs. One or two NK were not dead, but gravely injured, so one man informed the Lieutenant.

At the rear edge of the hill, in a shallow slit trench, two NK were charred black, the result, no doubt, of WP fire. Their faces were drawn up in such a manner as to lead one to infer that they died screaming. The warm evening air was already hurrying decay, and the resulting pungent odor was beginning to sicken some few whose stomachs had not yet become accustomed to certain battlefield realities.

Sgt. Alfred Amacker, the platoon sergeant, had located the machine gun that earlier had held up the company advance. It was a Soviet-type weapon with wheels for mountain maneuver. The weapon had been abandoned with the cartridge belt still in position for firing. Amacker turned the gun toward the enemy side and fired a few test rounds. The gun appeared to be in good working order. Then he and another man set the weapon as a defense point should it be needed in an emergency. He turned away from it, finally, to join others who were resting and waiting.

The sergeant had just started to move from the forward edge of the hill when someone shouted. In the next instant, what appeared as a blinding light and subsequent explosion burst on the now-forward edge of Ohang. A dark cloud rose and, with this, one of the men started to run back.

The Lieutenant had just taken his M-2 compass out of its case, preparatory to firing a defensive concentration, when the explosion, probably a concussion-type grenade, took place. He looked up to see a mass of arms and legs moving as a number of men, unnerved by the suddenness of the noise and the sight of one man running, hurried off the hill's crest and over the rearward edge. Finding himself alone and not understanding what had happened, he too ran to the rear edge and flung himself down to roll lengthwise a number of times.

In this confused state, with many of the company hesitant and looking apprehensively toward the hilltop, the Lieutenant heard the voice of the company commander, "Bill" Bailey. There he was, upright, and walking slowly up the side of the hill, calling encouragement. "Come on," he cried, "let's go back up." The sight of that solid figure waving and calling, not threatening, heartened everyone within hearing. The men now moved swiftly and determinedly to regain the crest.

Not everyone had left the hill. Three men remained near the forward edge, the three led by Sgt. Joseph P. Guzniczak. Several NK had crept back to a point just below the hill's crest, unnoticed initially as the B Company men were relaxing, and it was from that point that a concussion grenade was thrown. Guzniczak and the two men with him saw what had happened and, resisting the urge to escape this counteraction, began firing their rifles at the NK attack party, forcing that squad to retreat.

Guzniczak's group was quickly joined by Sgt. Amacker, who began firing the Soviet machine gun in the direction of the retreating NK. With the return now of the bulk of the company, there was no lounging about.

With the hill secured once more, holes were dug. A Company filed across a ravine and took up positions along a short saddle on the left. C Company remained in reserve. The Lieutenant adjusted defensive fires and once brought a two-howitzer concentration so close that the rounds sailed just over the ring of trees above the grave mound. Bailey jumped but was not angry. The NK might attack the hill again that night, so a close-in artillery concentration might prove useful in the defense.

The Lieutenant finally sat down on the forward edge of Ohang to rest. He was sitting next to the fetid remains of a dead NK. The air reeked with the odorousness of decaying flesh, not only NK but American as well, for the company was now in the area where the NK had carried their initial attack. Bodies of Americans were presumably still lying about, to be discovered in due course and removed for burial. Yet despite the discomfort, which was the worst of his experience in this battle thus far, he managed to doze a bit and so prepare himself for the final attack operation scheduled for the following morning.

The general push forward began on the morning of August 18. The Marines had continued to move on the left. The men on Ohang could hear their mortars and machine guns. Someone had reported that their casualties were heavy. The F-51 Mustangs flew early over the line and the hills in front of both the 19th and 34th Regiments were heavily rocketed and strafed.

It was on this morning also that the Marine airmen flew over the line for the first time, teaming with the Air Force to blast NK-held positions. The ground troops paused, enjoying the show. Most observed that the Marine flyers, in their F4U Corsairs, dove lower than did their Air Force counterparts. Their planes seemed slower by comparison, with the result that their strafing was probably more effective. The Marine pilots seemed to brush the bush and treetops in every strafing run.

The First Battalion staff was on Ohang by 0800. Naudts called the Lieutenant over for a briefing. He wanted plenty of artillery preparation on the objective before the companies moved out. The Lieutenant then turned to prepare his data.

While working, he noticed that the 34th had already jumped off on the left. K Company was leading, and several squads were moving slowly up the hill mass fronting Bailey's Hill, Hill 240. As the men on Ohang watched, the lead infantry line neared the top. A small knoll capped the hill, directly in the middle, and this knoll appeared to be the specific company objective. A footpath swung around it to the rear and downside.

Suddenly, the lead soldier of the group approaching the knoll was seen to duck. He jumped back, fired several times, and then turned and started to run back down the hill. The others in his group, watching, followed him down. Two NK then appeared from behind the knoll and were seen to fire on the running Americans. The man who had led the group and had panicked, was hit and fell to the ground. His companions grabbed him and half-dragged, half-carried him to a point where they were out of sight of the NK. The attack had failed.

The Lieutenant then switched on his radio and attempted to contact any observer working with the 34th. A lieutenant named Campbell answered. The Lieutenant asked Campbell if he could see the action as it was evolving. The latter replied in the negative.

Meanwhile, having overheard the transmission between the two observers, the artillery liaison with the 34th, 1st Lt. David H. Guier, radioed the Lieutenant asking for information. Guier, presumably, was with the regimental CO, Col. Beauchamp. The Lieutenant responded by reporting details of the attack failure, but in as few words as were necessary. He then volunteered to bring fire on the objective if permission could be granted. Guier radioed an immediate "Okay," and a subsequent transmission from the 13th operations radio operator told the Lieutenant he was clear to fire.

The Lieutenant set to work quickly. Data was transmitted and, shortly, two rounds came over, exploding just below the knoll. With the next adjustment, he could fire for effect. He asked for VT, one volley, battery left.

The rounds came, the number six howitzer firing first. Five VT air bursts were observed, in perfect pattern along the ridgeline. One round apparently had a fuze failure. The Lieutenant asked for one more volley. Again, a perfect pattern, six bursts twenty yards or so above the ground.

Not able to observe clearly the results of his firing but assuming the explosions were effective, the Lieutenant asked that a spotter plane be requested as a final check on the presence or lack of same of NK on the hill. A plane arrived within minutes, and mortar shells were seen exploding on or around the knoll shortly afterward. Meanwhile, K Company was observed regrouping halfway up the hill. They would begin a second advance soon.

Zero hour for the 19th arrived, and the Lieutenant requested his own preparation. Both batteries of the 13th fired volleys onto the hillside and ridgeline opposite Ohang Hill, Hill 223. C Company was tapped to lead out with A Company following. B Company remained in reserve this morning. Once the objective was reached, the Second Battalion would pass through and move out to the last hill mass bordering the Naktong River.

Looking down from his OP, the Lieutenant saw 1st Lt. Louis B. Rockwerk lead C Company down a trail and out into the open below the first objective. This was the first time he had seen C Company in action since the Kum River. There were all new officers, of course, and a mostly new complement of enlisted men.

A Company followed, and then both companies fanned out in attack formations. Artillery continued firing as the two companies began moving up, small red aircraft identification panels pulled along marking the lines of advance.[3]

Then the Lieutenant saw trouble. At the summit of the immediate objective, in a cluster of small trees and bushes, a group of five NK appeared, one carrying a machine gun. Within a minute, Rockwerk radioed that he was receiving enemy small arms fire and casualties occurring as a result. Naudts, observing the predicament, ordered a squad from A Company to crawl up to near the front of the nest and attempt to silence the gun. The squad was seen moving up, reaching a point fifteen yards of so below the NK nest. There the men stopped. It seemed impossible for grenades to be thrown accurately, at least that's how it seemed to those watching. Artillery now was looked to as a final resort.

The Lieutenant called the 13th Field operations and spoke with Maj. Cheek, explaining the situation. He was granted permission to adjust one howitzer in the manner of a base point registration, using a howitzer crew that could be trusted. A *short* round could mean death for some members of the infantry squad lying just below the nest. An *over* round would land either just behind the nest on the ridge of the objective or uselessly in the valley behind.

The firing began. Several rounds exploded within the clump or cluster, but just behind the target machine gun crew. None exploded on the gun or target itself. The infantry squad was seen to cover their ears and burrow their heads when the rounds whistled in. They were praying, certainly. Lives were at stake. Still, the enemy gun continued firing and Rockwerk continued to report casualties. It was an awkward situation, one machine gun holding up two companies. But, in mountain warfare, such a defense is possible.

Finally, the Lieutenant called for a suspension of fire, a pause to give him time to confer with Lt. Col. Naudts as to the application of another option to the NK gun problem. Then, in the first few moments of the suspension, three NK were observed rising and turning to the rear, carrying the gun. It appeared that the strong point was being abandoned. Word was radioed to 1st Lt. Rockwerk, who immediately sent up a patrol. The A Company squad began crawling ahead, also. The NK had indeed withdrawn from the hill. The objective was taken.

It was now time to move off the OP and onto the newly won ridgeline, and the Lieutenant was glad to be able to move ahead rather than back, as he had done so many times before. This was his first forward movement, and he felt enthused that he had contributed to the success of the First Battalion companies. He noted, as he started forward, that the men from the 34th Regiment had gained their objective, several already edging to the right to link up with squads from the 19th. The Lieutenant felt good about contributing to their success.

As both Fitzgerald and the Lieutenant moved together through a draw, following elements of the Second Battalion that already were in the process of moving beyond Hill 223 in preparation for their own, final attack on the remaining hill masses, they passed two American dead sprawled along the footpath, their features hardly recognizable after days of lying under a hot summer sun. The two most likely had been with L Company of the 34th Regiment, the unit holding the line in this particular area when the NK first attacked. By their body positions, each had probably been caught either in attempting to escape entrapment or in an attempt to locate the company's main body after being cut off.

Pausing on the little trail with the two observers, an infantry sergeant volunteered the possibility that the two Americans had been off the line the night of the initial NK attack, securing water. As he put it, many men from all companies along the river line were coming and going constantly for water. He stated further that it was believed the NK were able to effect a breakthrough because many of the able in the American companies were on water detail, weakening the regiment's defensive posture. Nothing further was said, and the observers and the sergeant parted.

At the top of the objective, Hill 223, the Lieutenant looked about. He saw where his adjusted rounds had scuffed the ground and chipped the trees and bushes in the clump. Two of the machine gun crew lay there, literally torn apart, their bodies appearing like enlarged rag dolls.

Men from C Company were sitting or standing around. The Lieutenant did not recognize anyone, so he motioned to Fitzgerald to continue on. Then, as he moved to follow his recon corporal, someone called to him. From a group of soldiers sitting in a circle, a boy got up and approached, stretching out his hand. The Lieutenant stopped, puzzled.

Then the boy spoke, not only to the Lieutenant, but also to the others around him. "This officer saved my life."

There was a moment of silence as even the Lieutenant did not comprehend.

The boy spoke again. "Don't you remember? I was one of the two who followed you across the rice paddies to the dike at the Kum River."

There were tears in the Lieutenant's eyes as hands clasped. "Of course," was all he could say in response. They looked at each other.

The boy recalled further, "I was right behind you. My buddy, over there, was the one who got it in the shoulder."

The Lieutenant glanced in that direction and saw another soldier sitting with the others, waving.

As the two stood there, facing, reminiscing silently, a call came from a ridgeline beyond for an observer. The Lieutenant tightened. He spoke quietly, "Take it easy. We'll get together, again."

The boy smiled. "Don't worry," he responded. "I'm going to make it all the way."

The boy turned back to his friends; the Lieutenant to his duty; each with a lighter step on the occasion of this brief, poignant remembrance of the early afternoon of July 16, one month and two days preceding.[4]

As he hurried in the direction of the call, the Lieutenant suddenly realized that he was the only observer with the regiment. Coles had returned to the battery CP, and the Lieutenant, instead of waiting with the First Battalion, had, without orders or direction, moved onto the newly won ridge and toward a new OP. He would be with the Second Battalion now and so informed the 13th fire direction center (FDC).[5]

An infantry officer was motioning wildly, causing the Lieutenant to hasten his steps. Now on the OP, he reported to the battalion commander, Lt. Col. Tom McGrail. Then, with the assembled Second Battalion staff, he witnessed a thrilling scene. In sight was the curving Naktong River and the Paekchin Ferry point. But more importantly, he saw dozens of swimming figures. NK, in panic, were swimming the Naktong to escape the combined Marine and Army attack. It was the fear that the Americans would sweep right to the water's edge that drove the NK to take such a chance in broad daylight.

The Marines who, meanwhile, had taken their final objective, Hill 311, had already begun firing on the swimming figures, using both high explosive and phosphorus. Quickly, the Lieutenant called for a mission using VT fuzes and, after describing the target, the 13th responded just as quickly. With the Marines concentrating on a large NK group directly fronting Hill 311, the Lieutenant began raking that part of the river bend in front of Ohang. Volleys soon began bursting over the heads of NK as they struggled in the water. The men in the 19th gathered on the OP knoll to watch the slaughter.

Then Marine Corsairs appeared and the artillery had to cease firing, although the Lieutenant was reluctant. There was an exchange between the Lieutenant and the 13th FDC resulting in a firm order to him not to continue the mission under any circumstances. He accepted the order and signed off.

It is often difficult to watch a plane dive on helpless men, enemy notwithstanding. As the group on the hill continued to watch, they riveted on three NK swimming desperately away from their compatriots, hoping to gain the far side of the river without becoming targets. But a Corsair pilot on his way down the river after a first pass spotted the three and bore in.

The men in the water saw the plane and, in helpless gestures, raised their hands above the water. Their efforts were futile. A spray of .50s caught them, the men bobbing with shock. They half-turned, crimson streaks appearing, and sank, faces down. It was a lonely, agonizing end for these three, far from home in the communist north.

The NK who did reach the opposite shore were seen to scurry through underbrush and copses, visible to the men on the American side. One Corsair began to strafe these fleeing men, but only halfheartedly, it seemed. Soon the enemy side was devoid of any observable activity and no surviving figures in the river. The planes soon flew off, and silence once more enveloped the battle area.

It was about 1600 hours. Men began pulling out C-ration cans and canteens. All noted that the water supply for the battalion, despite several ongoing water details, had reached a danger level.

A four-engine transport plane now appeared over one of the ridgelines, flying low. The plane made one pass and then, returning, dipped to one side. An open side cabin door was observed, and out of this doorway boxes of rations and five-gallon water cans were kicked, all with little red parachutes attached. Regiment had asked for a food and water drop to the companies upon completion of the afternoon attack.

The men watched the boxes and cans fall, and there was a general amount of cursing as the water cans burst open upon contact with the ground. The plane had settled too low and the parachutes hadn't fully opened to break the fall of the cans. There was more than enough food. Water continued in short supply.

After a minute of observing the supply drop, Lt. Col. McGrail called to the Lieutenant and asked him to fire a preparation on a ridgeline leading up to Hill 311, then occupied by the Marines. Two small peaks jutted up, much like castle turrets, and the rest of the ridge presented the appearance of a saddle as it led to the Marine-held high ground. Several of the battalion HQ grouping reported observing NK hunched about the two peaks, and one sergeant stated categorically that the area was "crawling with gooks."

The Lieutenant requested a mission. After a first lost round, the second came in well for further adjustment. He requested VT fuzes should NK really be on the peaks. Both peaks were soon showered with shrapnel.

The Lieutenant then learned that both the 19th and 34th Regiments would make a coordinated night attack, the first by either regiment since the onset of Korean fighting. The saddle and the twin peaks were the objectives.

From his vantage point, the Lieutenant could observe the companies of the 34th organizing for attack. He radioed Dave Guier, the regimental liaison, and told him he was in a position to observe the attack and could provide covering fire. After some minutes, Guier radioed an "Okay." A Battery then began firing volleys and the First Battalion, 34th Regiment, began its movement.

The attack began just prior to darkness, so the Lieutenant could spot the red aircraft ID panel being dragged by the lead elements. Firing continued until a short round burst too close to the lead squad and a cease-fire was ordered. The 34th gained its objective without any NK response.[6]

Meanwhile, E Company of the 19th had moved out into a narrow valley separating the OP hill from the twin peaks ridge. Nothing but silence greeted the climbing company. Several officers had been uneasy about the operation and the Lieutenant had asked Maj. Cheek for covering fire. This had been refused as too dangerous. Within half an hour the company commander radioed that he had reached the objective without opposition and that a perimeter guard had been posted.

The remainder of the battalion sat down on the OP hill and prepared to spend the night. The day had been extraordinarily trying. Tempers had been short, among other matters, and both officers and enlisted personnel had engaged in tongue-lashings that would not have occurred under ordinary circumstances. Even Cpl. Fitzgerald, normally even-tempered, lost it when a request came from the 13th operation center for a body count vis-à-vis the number of rounds expended.

"Goddamn it!" he yelled into the radio mike. "I'm not going over on the next hill and count dead gooks."

Hearing this outburst, the Lieutenant knew he would be called to account, and he was. The field phone rang, and Maj. Cheek came on the line to criticize him for Fitzgerald's intemperance. Patiently but firmly, he informed the Lieutenant that such information is routinely requested by higher headquarters, so that it is absolutely necessary that these requests be in compliance.[7]

The Lieutenant agreed that his observer group would do everything to comply, and then he reported the number of enemy bodies seen that most probably were the result of artillery fire. He also related the fact that artillery fire definitely had contributed materially to infantry success thus far and to a feeling of security all around. So ended the conversation. Later, both the Lieutenant and Fitzgerald agreed together to be more careful when verbalizing to the 13th operations.

It had been just too miserably hot. As some of the men had been without water since morning, several eased down to the river's edge and filled their canteens with questionable water. The Lieutenant had refused to drink river water that had been brought up, although earlier, he had filled his canteen from a "snake hole" in a rice paddy on his way to Ohang Hill. The water may have been worse than river water, but he had dropped six halizone tablets in the canteen just in case.

The men were just becoming comfortable when, about 2300, an artillery round from the American side burst along the river's edge, just below the dozing battalion. About ten minutes later another round burst at the same spot. The men moved restlessly on their backs. What was needed now was rest, not friendly harassing fire.

The Lieutenant sat up and waited for the next round. He saw what looked like a flash in the distance upriver and heard another round coming. A battery several miles north was firing this harassing and interdictory (H & I) mission, not knowing, of course, that friendly troops were spread out along the hillside above the target. The rounds probably were being fired by a battery of the 52nd Field.

The Lieutenant radioed the 13th FDC and Lt. Col. Stratton came on the air. He promised to locate the battery and silence the mission. Harassing rounds still kept coming. Finally the Lieutenant radioed again, giving the approximate weapon location in code. Firing ceased shortly thereafter. The men in the battalion sighed with relief and dozed the remainder of the night in peace.

Awake the following morning, the observer group moved immediately to the E Company position on the castle peaks. There, munching on C-ration breakfast, the Lieutenant noted several newly killed NK, shrapnel wounds about the heads, probably those observed the afternoon previous by several infantry. The deadly function of the VT fuze was displayed for all to see. But there was little time for sightseeing. The rest of the Second Battalion began arriving, setting about preparing to attack the remaining finger ridges leading out to the river fronting Hill 311.

The Lieutenant called for a preparation. With B Battery, 13th Field, firing, air bursts from VT fuzes were perfect along the ridgelines. F Company started forward, followed by G Company. He maintained contact with the lead elements simply by changing channels on his SCR-300.

In a short while, he radioed that he would leave his OP and move closer to the new objective, there being no sign yet of an NK presence. But as he was talking, he noticed movement in a large underbrush growth to the left of the ridge objective and on the downside of a small hill, in direct line of the advancing companies. He called a warning to the infantry.

Lt. Campbell, still with a company from the 34th Regiment and on a saddle overlooking the movement by the 19th, overheard the warning transmission and broke in to say that he, too, had seen NK movement in the brush area and would call in a fire mission, if the Lieutenant would permit him. It was his way of repaying the favor of the day before. The Lieutenant gladly assented.

Only one registering round was fired. An estimated platoon of NK had hunkered down in the underbrush area. Their mission was anybody's guess, but they probably were waiting until the Americans organized a new defense line along the river and then launch harassing attacks preparatory to a new offensive action in the bulge.

At the instant, however, the NK platoon, receiving the one registering burst, panicked at the prospect of artillery being brought to bear, particularly air bursts from VT fuzes. Up they popped and ran the short distance to the ridgetop, disappearing down the other side.

The advancing companies met one more resisting group. As F Company cautiously proceeded, four NK rose from slit trenches and fired at the Americans. The lead squad stopped. For a second or two the Lieutenant thought the men would turn and run back, as happened with the 34th the day before. But the squad leader held his ground and returned fire, whereupon the four NK turned and began running along the ridgeline, away from the squad. The other squad members fired after them. One NK was shot down immediately, while another, after running about twenty yards or so, was seen to plunge forward as if hit by an enormous sledge hammer. The other two escaped. That was it.

Turning around, his radio now on his back, the Lieutenant saw an older, slightly graying man squatting, field glasses trained on the ridgeline ahead. Hailing the man and speaking in a companionable voice—there being no strangers among these first Americans in Korea—the Lieutenant said, "Come on over with us. It looks like everything is okay now."

The man looked up as if startled, then smiled, getting up as he did. "Sure thing," he replied. "Let's go."

Together, they walked down a path and up and onto the newly won objective, the Lieutenant talking somewhat aimlessly about the heat and lack of water.

As they approached a group of officers gathered near the center of the finger ridge that was the objective, one walked over and asked the man with the Lieutenant, "How did you like the show, Colonel?"

The Lieutenant stiffened in surprise. There was no insignia on the man's collar, or was there? Looking closer he saw, unmistakably, the pin that fastened the insignia. The insignia was under the collar, of course, out of sight.

The Lieutenant then turned and looked the man in the face, seeing the latter grin at his, the Lieutenant's, perplexity. "I'm taking over the battalion this morning, lieutenant," said Lt. Col. Oliver G. Kinney, "and if the artillery is as good as I saw it this morning, we (infantry-artillery) are going to get along just fine."

Everyone on the little knoll was smiling. Conversation all around was cheerful. The battle of the Ch'angyong/Naktong River Pocket was over.

Rest, at Last

THE REMAINDER OF THE MORNING WAS SPENT CONSOLIDATING THE NEWLY WON POSITIONS. Patrols were dispatched into the little hamlets nestled in the several finger-like valleys and gullies near the river. Although some shots were exchanged with NK snipers from across the river, the atmosphere, on the whole, was quiet.

Inspection of several lookout points that had been established by the 34th Regiment prior to the first NK attack revealed remains of men who had been caught during that first night attack and shot or bayoneted as they sat, probably asleep. One of these gruesome finds was remarkable for the state of preservation. The Lieutenant stood quietly in front of this lookout point, heavily covered with brush. The dead soldier inside seemed almost alive in a sitting posture, head erect, arms hanging carelessly and mouth slightly open as if in normal slumber.

The tactical carelessness that often plagued American defense planning and maneuver was evident by the construction of these lookouts. They were, first of all, in plain sight of the enemy. An NK intelligence officer did not have to resort to patrol action to determine the defensive state of an objective. He had merely to peer from a reasonable distance and form his judgment.

And secondly, with the heavily overlaid foliage as protection, both for camouflage and against the elements, these lookouts stood out like castles in the sky. As castles fall through stealth and siege, so were these lookouts exterminated and defeat of the main body soon followed.

On Hill 311, Marines began flushing out several NK who had been hiding among the brush and rocks just below the crest of the hill. The Lieutenant and several from G Company watched as the prisoners were disrobed in typical fashion and led to the hilltop, the prisoners trembling noticeably. At the same time, a helicopter was seen to hover over the hill and finally settle down, for what purpose none in the 19th knew. This was the first helicopter that Army men had seen in Korea.

The heat was stifling. All were suffering from lack of water. Fitzgerald had gone back with a water detail and had returned with a steel helmet full. When two men appeared with five-gallon water bags, the others were ordered to sit in rows as officers doled out the liquid. The Lieutenant sat with the rest and received his ration.

Word came in early afternoon to move out. It developed that the battalion had been ordered to evacuate the forward hill position and occupy a higher, more defensible site. Some of the men became upset. To pull back after fighting so hard to gain was heresy to the ranks. The fierce heat and water shortage aggravated the situation. Nevertheless, they rose, saddled their gear, and slowly filed off the bare slopes.

Sweating and cursing they returned to the saddle peaks, the jump-off point of the morning. But instead of withdrawing farther, the column angled to the right and in the direction of Hill 311. The men filed past the 34th Regiment companies, sitting or sprawled among the short pines along a thin saddle, and then walked slowly up a winding path and onto the large hill mass in front. Every man was quiet. All now realized they would be relieving the Marine contingent.

The Lieutenant was near the lead squad of the battalion, and when that squad broke into the open, he saw, for the first time, a Marine group in normal battle deployment. However, he perhaps expected too much. Like most Americans, he had read accounts of the Pacific battles of WWII, featuring the grim, almost super-human strength of the individual Marine, subdued, but fiercely competent and always hovering over his weapon or engaged in some similar activity of military importance.

But these Marines were young men, too, just like in the Army, and they were joking and laughing or merely being friendly. They were lounging at or around their battle stations waiting for something to happen, or so it seemed. They were men who had just completed a hellish job in good fashion and, for the few moments allotted them, were deporting themselves in as effortless a manner as were their individual natures.

As the two fighting forces began mingling, the Lieutenant walked toward a small bush near the forward side of the hill, where a small Marine group with a radio had gathered. He inquired as to the whereabouts of the Marine forward observer. A mustachioed man stood up. "You look good," he said. "Step over here and I'll show you around." He was 2nd Lt. Jerry D. Fly.

Army and Marine artillery observer teams shook hands and became acquainted, exchanging news and data. The Marine group looked relaxed now that the fighting had ended. 2nd Lt. Fly said he thought the Marines would be going back to rest and then take a boat ride. The Lieutenant missed the significance of the prediction until Fly added, "You know, an amphibious ride." It clicked. The Marines might spearhead an amphibious attack somewhere behind NK lines to break the stranglehold along the perimeter.

The Marines didn't remain long. The changeover took only about ten minutes and then the last of them disappeared down the hill. The Lieutenant waved to Fly and then turned to his new responsibility.

The first item was a registration, which was accomplished in short order. There was an interruption of a few minutes as several NK artillery shells exploded near the crest of the hill, forcing everyone in the vicinity to lie prone for a bit. These were harassing rounds, and the NK could be expected to pursue a war of nerves for the time being while they gathered courage and strength for another try across the river. The battle map showed a populated valley beyond the ferry point on the NK side. Enemy forces were probably regrouping already in that area.

The Second Battalion, meanwhile, was completing its occupation of Hill 311. Lt. Col. Kinney inspected the perimeter and then began drawing plans for a defense. No one knew what the next division move would be, but one thing was certain. Something other than NK operations was in the wind. The men could talk of little else but relief. Their hopes were buoyed now that the bulge had been cleared. When not engaged along the crest of the hill searching for stray NK, they sat on the rearward slope, looking back as if expecting an entire relief division, with flags flying, to appear suddenly over the nearest rise.[1]

The Lieutenant was just as hopeful. There had been kind of a desperate humor throughout the recent battle action. The men were confident they would be relieved sooner or later, but there was constant apprehension over becoming a casualty before that happened. So there was a morbid quality to the talking and joking about relief. Now, with the front quiet, a general relaxing of tension was evident and a return of normal combat equilibrium.

Looking with the others on the rearward side of Hill 311, the topographical panorama stretching out in complete form, the Lieutenant at once realized how the NK had been so accurate with artillery fire, albeit in limited quantity. Possession of this hill provided an observer with an almost perfect visual access to any segment of the Naktong Pocket. He could see where A Battery, 13th Field had been in position. He noted the area where the 11th Field was currently emplaced.

Looking more closely, he could see men standing up on the ridgelines, probably on hills or rises in front of new mortar and artillery positions. Really, all one had to do was aim at the standing soldiers and trust that over-target rounds would explode on units emplaced behind. This was allegedly the NK artillery tactic in some instances. The Lieutenant concluded that the perimeter sentry system, as practiced by many American units, acted at times more in the enemy's favor than to his disadvantage.

Hill 311 had been a major NK battle strongpoint. Some underground works had been fortified OPs. American close support aircraft flew many sorties against NK command structures on the hill, using both rockets and napalm. All that remained from the days of battle and air strikes were craters, mounds of loose dirt, and scatted papers and pamphlets. Among the latter were several technical manuals printed in the Russian language. The Lieutenant noticed one manual describing the nomenclature and function of the 122-mm mortar, a type used by the NK. He asked that this manual be sent back to the 13th CP for perusal by higher headquarters.

Early the following morning, a call from the foot of the hill informed the Lieutenant that several NK artillery pieces had been located in camouflaged positions along the river. They were undoubtedly ones used so effectively against American artillery and other rear area sites. He watched as a short time later the pieces were brought out in tow. Several were Soviet makes of small caliber, but two were American-built 105-mm howitzers, possibly ones captured from B Battery, 13th Field.

The afternoon of the 21st brought a call from regiment directing the Lieutenant to contact the artillery liaison officer there if supporting fire was needed. This was unusual in that it heralded a break in direct communication with the 13th. The obvious conclusion was that a change in mission was in the making.

The Lieutenant suggested to Kinney that the directive could only mean imminent relief, that new artillery moving into an area usually presaged new infantry. The suggestion set off a chain reaction of rumors. Men clustered about and talked excitedly. They began scanning the roads leading to Hill 311 more intensely. In fact, most were not on the hill mentally, but were somewhere, anywhere, away from the battle line.

And then, early on the following morning, three men struggled up the rearward slope of Hill 311 and into view. They were an observer section from the 503rd Field, 2nd Infantry Division. It was all eyes as the group reported to the Lieutenant and introduced themselves. The 503rd was relieving the 13th Field that very moment. The main infantry body would be up the next day. The 24th Division would then go back.

No one shouted. Excitement was suppressed. The only visible sign of emotion was a sudden preoccupation with equipment. Rifles were stripped and machine guns dismantled, cleaned and oiled. Personal gear was attended to. From experience, the only way to make time fly was to engage in something. The men of the Second Battalion, 19th Regiment, were trying to make time pass as rapidly as their individual capabilities would allow.

No officer came up with the observer group. He would be up later. The new men looked apprehensive. They had heard all the stories. This was their first combat assignment. While others gathered to watch, a registration was fired, the sergeant-observer lying prone with field glasses. The men of the 19th just stood about on the skyline.

With the registration completed, the Lieutenant was told to close stations. It took exactly thirty seconds to carry out that order. A full minute or so was spent speaking with the battalion staff.

On the way down, Fitzgerald and the Lieutenant walked through the narrow draw into which the latter had poured rounds that first night on Bailey's Hill. They looked for damage done and saw the seared hillside, the shrapnel cuts along the ground, and the cleared area where the NK artillery had been emplaced.

Then, as they walked along a bend in the trail, they came upon the target, four small caliber field guns, lined up and positioned under a small grove of trees. The guns seemed not to have been damaged, but it was obvious that firing by the Lieutenant had forced the crews into a less advantageous emplacement.

Dear was waiting with the jeep as the two finally reached the ferry road. Climbing into the jeep, both the Lieutenant and Cpl. Fitzgerald felt human for the first time in over a week. Neither had bathed or wet any part of the body. The Lieutenant had removed his socks once and noted that his feet were in good condition, that the cloth had acted as a sop to draw sweat from the skin. His feet were clean, the dirt having been drawn off.

Back down the road they traveled, toward the 13th CP. Just north of the position lately occupied by A Battery, from which the Lieutenant left to take part in the Naktong push, they noted many vehicles belonging to the 2nd Division. Lined up were new full-track M42 antiaircraft machines with twin 40-mm guns. Other full-track personnel carriers, also new, were present. Even the standard two-and-a-half-ton trucks used by that division looked new, although on closer inspection they were the same WWII models the Occupation forces brought with them from Japan.

On they drove and then up a narrow gully where the 13th CP was located. The Lieutenant stepped out of the jeep and walked to the operations tent. A majority of the staff had gathered there, relaxing.

Tempers had been short occasionally during the final two days of the attack. Firing had been suspended several times because of conflict over infantry boundary lines. The Lieutenant had been particularly sharp with 1st Lt. Donald Dexter, the assistant S-3, over a firing suspension during the drama of the NK swimming in the Naktong River. Another instance had been the unfortunate exchange concerning a request for a body count. Maj. Cheek had reprimanded the Lieutenant over that incident.

Now the Lieutenant took the initiative and apologized to the assembled staff for intemperate remarks made. He took full responsibility and spoke very personally to 1st Lt. Dexter regarding his feelings. It was well understood that the 13th had been as much under pressure for accuracy and consideration of other units as the Lieutenant had been to get fire out there. Everyone had been tired and worn, even behind the lines. The end of the battle proved balm to the contentious personalities, however, and Lt. Col. Stratton, after reminding the Lieutenant, using hard-bitten vocabulary, that he must **ALWAYS** defer to battalion fire direction authority, told the Lieutenant, a smile breaking out on his face, to "Get the hell out of here and find a stream to soak in a couple of hours." The Lieutenant saluted, turned heel, and departed.

Shortly, Dear turned the jeep into the A Battery position. The men lounging about looked up. The battery had fired hundreds of rounds during the final attack, a great portion for the Lieutenant. Now the men on the howitzers turned to watch the return of the group partly responsible for the firing.

Lt. Col. Stratton issued an Officers' Call for that evening at the CP. Promotions were announced. A number moved up to 0-3 (captain), among whom were Pate, Ball, Dexter, Monsour, Seem, and Guier. All second lieutenants were promoted one grade. Few had appropriate bars or tracks to wear. Guier gave the Lieutenant one of his silver bars, now no longer needed.

A new officer was present, a lieutenant colonel. Someone said his name was Langlois, newly assigned to the battalion. A rumor had it that Lt. Col. Stratton was going to division artillery as the new executive officer.

After the Call, Stratton approached the Lieutenant and asked him if he would consider becoming an air observer. A vacancy had occurred in the air section and the 13th was asked to fill it. Air observers had a much better time of it than ground observers. Their missions were of shorter duration, and their living quarters were sumptuous when compared to general combat field conditions. However, the Lieutenant had always been wary of flight experiences, having survived several close ones while in the air with student pilots at an airport where he occasionally worked while in high school. He politely turned down the offer. He heard later that Ed Mattes, A Battery executive officer, had accepted.

It began to rain near the close of the Call. The rain turned out to be one of the most severe of the summer. As the officers were returning to their respective units, they encountered a battery of 2nd Division artillery pulling out onto the road. Their position had been flooded, the position having been a dry stream bed. The bed was dry no longer. Thank God, thought the Lieutenant, that he was not on the line tonight.

Earlier that afternoon, Capt. Still and the Lieutenant had reconnoitered a route that seemed to lead through an extremely mountainous area to a jointure with the main Ch'angyong-Taegu road. It was a passable route so, when the order came the following morning to close stations and march-order, the battalion followed this route.

What was not anticipated was a point where the route intersected with a very wide but shallow stream. Beyond a bend in the stream unseen by the two officers the day before were hundreds of civilians, perhaps several thousand or so, gathered along the stream.

Here were massed many of the refugees from Taejon and Kumch'on, as well as from "Death Valley," Koch'ang, and east to the Naktong. They were waiting out the course of the Conflict. The elderly were the keepers. Younger women cooked and handled the necessary chores. Many waved at the passing Americans, an almost automatic gesture now. Up or down, back or across, there was hope as long as the Americans stayed.

The column joined the Taegu road and executed a left turn toward that city, traveling but a short distance. At a narrow crossing, the column turned right and moved down a well-worn cart trail toward a river, the Kumho River. There, along a sandy beach, where apple orchards stretched almost to the river's edge, the column halted. The 13th Field would bivouac in the orchard area and swim in the river.

Dismounting, the men were in the river in minutes, vehicles still more or less in column formation. Little else mattered now. The war was behind them for the time being. Tension dissolved. The men of the 13th began to feel human once again. The hoped-for, longed-for rest period had begun.

Reflections While at Rest

Are there still some who remember? Perhaps fewer than a handful today of the thousands who set foot on that troubled Land of the Morning Calm during early July, 1950, may recall the one thing or mood if you will, that thematically served to convey an imaginative foreboding that the easygoing, self-indulgent years of the Japanese Occupation might end tragically for many hundreds of the military stationed in that recently conquered land. It was a mood induced from the haunting strains of Maurice Ravel's *Pavone pour une Infante defunte (Death of a Pagan Princess)*, also known as a semipopular contemporary song, *The Lamp Is Low*.

Each workday evening during 1949 and early 1950, following the 2300 hour news, the Armed Forces Radio Network presented a program titled Words and Music. This fifteen-minute offering, heard in Northern Honshu via the Sendai station, and usually the final program preceding the National Anthem and sign-off, embodied an announcer solemnly reading passages of verse or prose of serious contemplative nature, the reading interspersed with impressionistic organ tones. Ravel's *Pavone* was always the musical theme of this program and it, coupled with the reader's reverential intonations and with appropriate harmonic background accompaniment, seldom failed to provoke deep introspection on the part of the listeners in that quiet, far corner of the world.

Many were the late evenings when the Lieutenant, as an example, would lie awake in one of the several bachelor officers' quarters at Camp Younghans listening to the *Pavone*, then the reader's somber voice, and ponder his own life and the lives of those about him as well. Certainly, the apathy and monotony inherent in a military occupation chore offered little to those whose ambitions ran counter to a routine steeped in a daily sameness existence. On the other hand, the economic security and a forced social coalescence, always enticements so far as a military is concerned, beckoned many, the strong as well as the weak.

It is not too extreme to suggest that a fair percentage of the American Occupation garrison, lying scattered about three of the four main Japanese islands in June 1950, had mostly, passively, contracted to exchange an existence grounded on self-sufficiency for a guaranteed state of being, a tendering by the military of all necessities and predetermined daily task schedules in return for a duteousness that demanded little in the manner of particularized ingenuity.

In consequence, the American Occupation force in Japan remained not much other than a collection of uniforms, the particular determined by the army, corps, or divisional patches worn; the collective straining to merely achieve passing individual and group efficiency criteria. It was a military marking time and additionally, coping, sometimes well but sometimes badly, with the ever-present distraction of an alluring sensuousness proffered by a willing female cluster among the conquered.

So even today, approaching a half-century beyond, whenever the dirge of the *Pavone* is heard, the tones venerative and funereal, the mood recurs and memory relives, once again, the tranquil Occupation years; then the shattering climax occurring that Sunday morning of June 25, 1950, a calamity that struck without warning, shredding once and for all the complacency that had long infected the Occupation force.

That calamity shortly would doom many in that underprepared Occupation Army on hot, bare hillsides, in rice gullies, at impenetrable roadblocks, wired together after capture, and later, in one or another of the several prison stations or camps.

And for more than a few, death would come while lying wounded and alone in a trench, in a paddy field, or along a barely discernible cart trail or footpath, hours after those who remained able stole away to escape a "no quarter" advance and to fight another day.

Kilroy Junior

There is an old adage that goes something like this: Every war is different, yet every war is resemblant. Succeeding wars unveil new and different weapons, tactics, and adversaries, but the individual soldier—his likes and dislikes, his problems, his wants, and his environment—remains ever similar.

The driver who led Sennacharib's Fifth Chariot Squad; the lead scout for the Third Legion of Marcus Claudius; the assistant loader (cannon) with the First Firing Section at the battle of Crecy; each fought and slept in fields, looted and foraged in the villages, trembled at first sight of the enemy, and then later, after a victorious clash and emerging unscathed, laughed and strutted. A piece of cake? Yeah.

These men did their duty as trained; cursed their officers guardedly or silently; gambled their pay; coveted women; damned the weather; prayed to God or idol when all seemed lost; and generally said or did things they wouldn't have said or done had they remained constrained in the villages or towns of their births. Kilroy, 1941–1945, you say? The same.

The United States Army from 1941–1945 was a robust, charging, foul-mouthed crew that battered the portals of the world, leaving as its mark a scowled "Nuts!" It thought tough, trained tough, and fought tough. What else? Total victory was its legacy to the postwar or "new army," and then these veterans of the "good war" settled into the rest of their lives confident that junior would carry on in the same seasoned fashion, if and when.

Well, junior had to graduate the hard way. Whereas his *combat-oriented* predecessor began basic training at 0515 hours with a "Get the hell out of those bunks and on your feet!" voiced by SSgt. Gorilla, blankets jerked in the process. Kilroy Junior's *career-oriented* experience was less blustery and, consequently, at least to many observers, less effective and certainly less bonding. As it was, whatever the mixture, to include the experience beyond of unit training, it all came apart at the seams the morning the first North Korean People's Army squad charged into view and up a hill toward American foxholes. For the first contingents in Korea, the shock of facing strong, well-disciplined, combat-oriented troops on a one-to-one basis never completely wore off.

And perhaps it is true that the average American soldier entering Korea in July 1950, for whatever reason or reasons, did not measure up to a nation's expectations of what ought to be accomplished on a field of battle. A generalization embodying this alleged deficiency has evolved over the years, an assertion of condemnation that may never be completely erased, no matter proofs to the contrary. Yet for whatever it is worth, Kilroy Junior's combat behavior during the early days of the Korean Conflict ought to be understood within the contexts of the following rationales:

First: Most combatants would not, in all respects, accept the fact that they were being required to sacrifice themselves without reassurance that such sacrifices would lead to both immediate and ultimate success. There was, as well, a disinclination to advance a cause about which many understood little.

Second: As there were lacking, generally, extended lateral battle lines, contrary to experiences throughout much of WWII, and the Korean topography being what it is, line units during the early action regularly anticipated and encountered NK flanking attacks. Initial battle action by the Americans often proceeded smoothly enough, but concern for both unit cohesion and the well-being of the individual soldier-participant in the face of these NK flanking maneuvers led commanders ultimately to execute retrograde planning as an every-other-day-or-so occurrence.

Unfortunately, a number of ill-managed and out-of-control withdrawal strategies led military observers looking for scapegoats to settle on the "weak-kneed" and "flabby" within the ranks as the responsible villains. From such scapegoating was born the generalization that America's battle warriors were somehow less than adequate, a generalization tarring the ranks, but not the officers who led them. It is a generalization that is mostly unfair.

Third: Pullbacks or retrograde maneuvers, often occurring quickly, carried the risk of wounded being left to the whims of a barbarous enemy. This risk occasioned serious morale problems and an accompanying hesitation to take chances or, in the extreme, stand fast against attackers.

Fourth: It was learned very early in the combat action that there was a limited future being a prisoner of war, a fact that motivated many combatants to think more about escape routes than attack routes.

Is it any wonder then, given the actualities of the above, that there was an observed lack of confidence on the part of the average line soldier in himself and, by extension, in his perceived leaders, unfortunately translated by an anxious and irritated home front as youth incompetent?

Yet after August 3 there was a discerned change. When men knew there were friendly and courageous units on hills to their flanks, confidence in themselves and their arms was renewed. The Pusan Perimeter became not merely another battle position. It became the turning point in this hell of sweat, blood, and tears, in that order. There would be serious battles to come, but the outcome of the fighting would now never be in question. It was no longer *whether*. It was *when*.

In the space of four bruising weeks, Kilroy Junior had matured. Like his vet elder, he had begun cursing heartily and hating in the best military tradition, with the result that, in step with the WWII style of doing things, that gook son-of-a-bitch on the hill over there had better either raise his hands to the sky or run like hell, because he'll be got to sooner or later. And that's the way it was.

"No Salute, Buddy!"

It was common knowledge that, very early on, officers were singled out by NK snipers and combat squads or destined for harsh treatment as POWs. Further, since artillery had caused more grief within enemy front areas than had other weapons, including air, artillery forward observers and their parties could look forward, according to whispered reports, to summary course of conduct upon capture, but only if identified, of course.

Before the regimental motor march to the Kum River position, 1st Lt. Pate warned the Lieutenant to fasten his gold bar beneath the fatigue jacket collar with only the pin remaining visible. He should dispose of the crossed-cannon insignia, Pate suggested. The Lieutenant complied.

But on July 15, with combat approaching, he removed the bar and buried it. He noticed that the infantry officers had done the same. The Lieutenant's ID would be the red cloth on his pistol belt.

After the Kum River battle, the Lieutenant didn't worry about the lack of insignia until Maj. Cheek ordered a resumption of display. By that time, conforming to a widely used practice, he affixed a strip of white adhesive tape vertically to the back of his helmet. NCOs placed a horizontal strip on their helmets.

During all the time at the front throughout the summer of 1950, the Lieutenant never saw a combat-wise officer or enlisted man display insignia and rank openly, rest periods or rest areas excluded. The men who counted knew who you were, anyway.

A Living Hell

This subtitle might seem more appropriate in describing a battle rather than an ordinary day. As it was, the American soldier fought two battles during the first weeks; one against the NK and the other against the weather. The fact was, the summer of 1950 in Korea was one of the hottest on record. The heat at midday on one of those crumbling, bald mounds of dirt and rock was almost beyond endurance.

The men had been yanked abruptly from the relatively comfortable countryside's of Japan. They had not undergone hours of march conditioning and full field pack maneuvers prior to the outbreak of fighting. Legs were rubbery and lungs weak. From July 5 through late August, only one word can fully describe the physical battle for survival: *hell.*

One who has never visited South Korea and observed the bare, desolate hillsides of central and west central sections cannot really appreciate the significance of this human struggle. From ages past Koreans had stripped the hills of timber so thoroughly that resulting erosion lowered and rounded the higher elevations, leaving high mounds of hard clay and rock.

The Japanese had made some effort to reforest these hills during their long stay and, as one traveled the roads, root lines could be seen near the crests of hills where rows of trees had been planted. However, whether through obstinacy or something indefinable, these experiments had not been continued after 1945 and the hills were already being denuded.

So when Kilroy Jr. began scouting the tops of these hills, he found that camouflage and normal shade from the beating sun, which trees and underbrush usually provided, were both in very short supply. There were trees in the valleys and within protected areas on hillsides, but these served nicely as CPs and did not benefit the rifleman.

The result was obvious. With strength being drained by the constant movement up and down hills, sweat streaming and drawing out precious body salt, a number of men simply collapsed.

Lt. Col. Charles B. Smith, commander of the First Battalion, 21st Regiment, remarked to the Lieutenant and other observers at his CP outside Taejon, that many of his men were dropping like flies. Besides the limited tree and bush shelter available, many of the American contingent had not accustomed themselves to water discipline or the habit of swallowing salt tablets at required intervals. Smith's statement was an admission that many Americans, at that moment, were unwilling to practice military reasonableness during these terribly adverse circumstances, hurting the UN effort by becoming needless casualties at a crucial moment in the fighting.

Later, during the First Naktong Pocket Battle, men literally crawled up hills during attacks. Water details were constantly coming and going. Water was seemingly more valuable on the line than cartridges.

The general exertion required to maintain a combat stance induced many to rest and nap often. One was up and about in early morning, but by 1000, when the sun really began to beat down, a nap was in order. After a noon snack or meal, another nap was called for. Night rest, more regular off the line than on it, usually began about 2230. Little was detrimental about these rest periods. In fact, until the men could accustom themselves to the climatic conditions, rest was medicinal.

By the middle to late August, of course, the survivors from the early weeks reached maximum physical conditioning and, although few double-timed in carrying out myriad duties, all were prepared for most eventualities.

Nevertheless, the heat, the road dust, the bugs, and the general discomfort of those rivers of sweat streaming down face, neck, and body engendered more profanity aimed at the Republic of Korea and its unfortunate geographic circumstance than any other focus of complaint.

"Ouch"

If any one statistic happens to be voiced today by those who prowled the hills and valleys of Korea that summer of 1950, it would probably be in reference to that country's mosquito population. In the thinking of the average GI that summer, the number of mosquitoes buzzing about seemed to be double that in any other spot worldwide. At night, all low-lying areas were home to mosquito swarms looking to breed as well as filch meals from those ever-present, tasty American soldiers. The convenient human manure-fertilized paddies offered the best mosquito marriage beds ever encountered.

Mosquitoes pose problems for all armies. Not only is there the annoyance factor, serving to irritate and tire, limiting military efficiency. Mosquitoes are also prime carriers of malaria, and malaria, as most know, can rob an army of much of its fighting capacity in a short space of time.

Little was done at first to prevent these insects from annoying and biting. Some were lucky enough to have come through early disasters with full nettings. Some of these few cut their nettings into smaller pieces, large enough to be draped around head and neck, selling the pieces for whatever to their unluckier comrades. Many infantry carried makeshift face and neck protectors.

Also, as soon as the Americans realized that their collective safety was partially dependent on their holding hill rather than valley positions, they also learned that the higher the hill the fewer mosquitoes, and many comfortable nights were spent by infantry on higher terrain levels.

The Lieutenant carried a full netting onto the line at the Kum River, wrapping himself in it at intervals. The netting became a casualty of the battle there. Forced to find a solution quickly, he rummaged through the A Battery supply pile. His search brought success in the form of insect repellent bottles. Units had been issued a number of such bottles, but few took advantage or knew of their existence.

Taking a bottle with him when he went up with the 21st Regiment outside Taejon, he applied the liquid the first night. The mosquitoes were very bad there. He rubbed his face, neck, and hands with the stuff, but not his lips. He was careful to keep his jacket sleeves down and collar buttoned. You guessed it. He greeted the dawn of the 20th with swollen lips.

Yet the repellent was a success. The real value of the liquid lay in warding off the bastards until one could doze. The Lieutenant was to hear countless swarming mosquitoes in the months he served in Korea, and never once during the season was he without a bottle of repellent, which application became almost as much ritual as the late evening trek to the battery or company latrine trench.

Chow

Well, it's too much to relate that the typical American soldier, on the line and in the rear that summer of 1950, became chow-hound first-class. It was a self-promotion. Food, on hand and anticipated, occupied a major portion of the soldier's thoughts wherever he was or whatever his duty or requirement.

So what, you say. Isn't this like every other war? Yes, in many respects that is true. Feeding an army and feeding it well is a task that ranks high on a commander's list of supervisory responsibilities, and disaster can be expected when that task fails or is not accomplished properly.

Psychologists mostly generalize that frustrated persons often tend to eat more than those who are relatively well-adjusted. The former seemed certainly the case early on in Korea. The days and weeks of diminishing hopefulness; the fear that becoming a casualty was the only future for those in a combat stance, these seemed to direct the mind to search for compensatory diversions.

The most immediate source of such amelioration was the chow line. Here, both within the immediate combat zones and in the support areas, troops mingled, if only briefly. Where the remainder of a day or night might be spent on a lonely perimeter point or at a switchboard or on a forward lookout, mealtime offered a return to a more normal stream of living.

Considerable attention during the interim between the end of WWII and the outbreak in Korea had been given to alleged shortcomings within the military mess system as revealed from WWII experiences. Prodded by the Army Chief of Staff, Dwight Eisenhower, improvement in both dietary planning and unit level preparation resulted.

The Occupation forces in Japan were the beneficiaries of a generally excellent quality of food preparation, as the food service personnel responsible for the preparation experienced a much more comprehensive level of training than had been given their WWII predecessors.

Unfortunately, the course of early combat in Korea precluded many from being served hot meals, sometimes for days at a time. But when the opportunity came for hot meals to be carried forward, the men were eager in anticipation, anticipation well rewarded. No one, at least within the hearing of the Lieutenant, denigrated the prepared hot meals in comparison with C-ration offerings even when the latter could be distributed warm.

And yet, in all fairness, the cold C-ration wasn't all that bad. The K-ration set had been phased out even before WWII ended, replaced by the new cold food series, the C-ration can. This ration consisted of prepared food in a can, ready to be consumed cold or heated (in the can), and an accompanying can filled with biscuits, condiments, cigarettes, toilet paper, etc. The first troop elements in Korea carried the WWII C-series, loose cans in large cardboard boxes.

Shortly, however, a modification of the C-series became available. Packed in handy, smaller cardboard boxes, a ration set that could be stretched into a sufficiently satisfying daily repast—to include a fruit can—was distributed to each frontline soldier. An equal ration was thus guaranteed, an improvement over previously haphazardly random disbursements from the larger boxes. The new boxes were compact enough to be carried by hand or tied and slung over the shoulder or on a cartridge belt.

One problem with the new ration cans was noted immediately. Can units began arriving in the Korean combat theatre sporting shiny, virgin tin. This fact, combined with offhand carelessness on the part of numerous GIs, provided an observer with instant knowledge of where American troops had been and, unfortunately, where they were currently in position.

The Lieutenant, peering through the BC Scope emplaced on a rise fronting A Battery's position near Yongsan, noted at once where the combat lines had been by the reflected sun's rays on discarded C-cans. Had the NK been able to muster the most limited use of aircraft during the Naktong battle, it would been a simple matter for an enemy pilot to spot the American MLR and attack same.

As to chow behind the line of resistance, in artillery batteries, engineer companies, medical stations, etc., perhaps the following might be representative.

Wherever he is today, Sfc. Antonio E. Lucero, mess steward of A Battery, 13th Field, can take special pride in the knowledge that his general supervision and work in the preparation of food for the battery during July and August 1950 is well remembered by the men in the battery assigned during those months.

The Lieutenant, as were many of the other battery personnel, was, by August 5, tired and bordering on the listless. Morale, in other words, was not very high despite the daily canned reports to the contrary to higher headquarters.

The units were receiving B-rations—canned foods, butter, powdered milk and eggs, dehydrated vegetables, etc. Canned beef and gravy was a daily noon staple, adequate but hated, as every GI knew that beef and gravy can be next to garbage if not prepared properly or not kept away from the hot sun during the few minutes before serving. More cases of diarrhea result from improper handling of this beef than from many other food sources.

So it was that one of the first things Lucero did, once the line was stabilized behind the Naktong River, was to go out into the countryside and barter some of the issue canned beef and unused egg powder for fresh vegetables. This was contrary to regulations, of course, because garden fertilization in the Orient was such that worms might result from consuming such items. Nevertheless, regulations or no, he gathered the best he could find—radishes, onions, and others — and used these to supplement and flavor daily menus.

Change in the men's spirits was instantaneous. They began looking forward to meals that included fresh delicacies. And all became aware that the mess section was working its hardest to make this important element of Army life a satisfying one.

Later, during the Kyongsan bivouac, when the battery was in place ten full days, Lucero and his staff worked overtime to provide hot rolls at least once during each of those days. And the Lieutenant, as well as most others in the battery, remained continually astonished at the number of visiting officers and officer VIPs who just happened—just happened, mind you—to drop by and visit about mealtime, and yes, be invited to masticate one of Sfc. Lucero's master meals.

Without being too strong about it, it seems pertinent to suggest that the conduct of a unit's mess facility is a major key to gauging that organization's morale, especially under combat conditions, and that unit that manages well-prepared and sufficiently diverse menus in most instances, even when experiencing unaccommodating circumstances, is usually a successful unit in every respect.

Again, for the improvement in food service training after WWII, one can thank Gen. Dwight Eisenhower.[1] But in the immediate, for the sustenance of morale in Korea during the hot summer of 1950, among other contributing factors, one can thank the mess stewards and mess personnel of the combat organizations. An opinion shared by many was that more serious problems might have occurred after initial NK military successes had the "second line" contributed in less than first-rate order. The "second line" was the mess line, and the mess stewards and cooks standing behind it were damn fine soldiers.

Summer Styles

If the North Korean Army did one thing that proved a Godsend to the American Army, it was in the matter of uniform color selection. The NK attacked in uniforms of rich oak brown. This color precluded the use by Americans of olive drab wool, which had been the uniform in North African and European theatres during WWII, and which would have been suffocatingly uncomfortable under the hot Asiatic sun.

The Americans rode into combat wearing the conventional herringbone twill uniforms (fatigues). These were as comfortable a summer combat uniform as could be imagined outside of the dress khakis. The line troops wore their one fatigue set without change or until time was afforded during infrequent rest periods for rinsing out the worst of accumulated grime and body sweat.

During the first several weeks of combat, replacement clothing items were in very short supply, forcing supply personnel in some units to knife open stored duffel bags for useable wear. This practice was short-lived as replacement items soon crowded the pipeline. But for a brief period early on, it was not unusual to see combat infantry wearing a khaki item or two, but never, ever, any wool ODs.

Some pictures of troops, distributed early by the media, showed men with open fatigue shirts hanging out and down, the inference partly being that the subjects were careless and probably poorly disciplined. To the contrary. These men, finally unable to stand their own stench from the sweat and other elements absorbed into their clothing, were engaged merely in airing both themselves and their clothing. Cool uniform or not, the American Army in Korea during the summer of 1950 was probably one of the smelliest armies ever gathered together.

The first troops in Korea carried all the normally issued clothing and equipment necessary for combat usage. The infantry carried complete packs, the artillery their bedrolls and musette bags, and the other units such wear and piece as was customary. A number of officers, expecting short stays or perhaps a bit of Occupation duty and taking advantage of vehicle trailer space, took footlockers filled with necessaries and others.

The latter was discouraged, of course. The Lieutenant was told the morning he reported to the 24th Division Artillery duty officer at Camp Hakata to store his footlocker with the 11th Field supply, and that he might take only what he could carry. Other officer replacements, arriving later at Camp Drake, the first stop in Japan by stateside personnel destined for the war zone, were ordered to store every item of personal gear and take only those items that might be conveniently carried in infantry packs or small handbags.

The Lieutenant carried a musette bag packed with personal articles and a poncho. He also carried an Air Force-type V-pack with fatigue changes, a suit of khakis, and extra combat boots. While still at Camp Kokura, he prepared a bedroll consisting of two blankets and a full mosquito net. This, too, he carried. As he eventually expected to place these packs in a truck or jeep trailer, he did not mind the extra discomfort of lugging them about on foot.

When the shooting started, however, packs, bags, and rolls lost significance. As vehicle columns were ambushed and trucks and jeeps destroyed or abandoned, many a line officer and enlisted man lost all but clothing worn and equipment carried.

The 13th Field had established a temporary storage depot in the town of Okch'on, about seven miles east of Taejon. After the Taejon debacle, the withdrawal to Yongdong was accomplished so rapidly that the duffel bags and packs stored were abandoned. By July 21, an infantry soldier carrying full field pack was a rarity.

The steel helmet, pot, or whatever name seemed to fit, has always been a necessary nuisance: necessary, obviously, because of the protection afforded from glancing shrapnel and bullets, but a nuisance when the wearer has to move quickly and engage in enemy and terrain-inspired contortionist responses. When the Lieutenant first arrived at Taep'yong-ni and encountered withdrawing 21st Regiment personnel, he noticed immediately that many were not wearing helmets. "They got in the way," volunteered one soldier.

The Lieutenant was reminded at that moment of a policy dictated by Lt. Gen. George Patton when commanding the Third Army prior to the D-Day invasion: "Steel helmets will be worn on duty at all times," Patton ordered, "even by mechanics under trucks." And later, in 1944 and 1945, not wearing the pot anywhere within the combat boundaries of the Third Army could get the offender a court-martial.

Well, after the pullback to Yongdong, steel helmets became style once more, and by the First Battle of the Naktong Pocket, early to middle August, no one questioned the need to wear same.

"Whad'ya Need?"

Unit property accountability ceased the moment the 24th Division boarded planes or LSTs for the trip to Korea. The same held true, largely, for the remaining Occupation combat divisions. More than one supply sergeant boasted later that the first order of business, the moment his LST cleared the Japanese coast, was to dangle the unit property book loosely over a rail as a buddy began tickling his ribs. For a harassed company or battery commander with some long-standing shortages of organizational equipment, the outbreak of the Korean Conflict was a miracle from Heaven.

Units were supplied on order during the first months of the Conflict. Little effort was made to account for property, as men weren't going to take more than they could carry. Besides, there was no black market on the firing line nor in the immediate support areas. Losses of most every type of equipment were heavy at first due to ambush, accidents, and just plain hard usage. No one questioned lost equipment. The point was, get more of the same.

The two most critical items of supply, beside ammunition, were vehicles and radios. There were plenty of rifles and sidearms. Artillery ordnance, although not ample in numbers, were normally replaceable almost immediately, one reason being that few of those weapons were lost. But vehicles, always critical regarding parts, and workable radios were the major casualties. Roadblocks took their toll of jeeps and trucks. Radios, bulky and heavy, were left or destroyed when men were struggling to escape ambush or encirclement. And some radios, particularly the SCR-610, the WWII workhorse used early by artillery observers, often failed to work properly or there were problems with the battery packs.

All units, in the main, were driving WWII-manufactured vehicles, many having been driven hard under combat conditions and then either left in Japan or ferried there after the using units were demobilized. Many were and remained over time in various states of disrepair.[2]

Once, at Camp Younghans, during an ordnance inspection, a jeep was discovered to have a cracked frame. The vehicle was sent to Sendai Ordnance Depot for major repair. It was returned within two weeks. Ordnance authorities dictated that there would be no major repair done on any vehicle until one broke down completely. In other words, vehicles must be driven until they could no longer function.

A number of 24th Division vehicles broke down early in the fighting due to mechanical defects. The Lieutenant underwent the experience of a jeep halting in front of an NK machine gunner at a roadblock south of Taep'yong-ni, the jeep's engine failing at a critical moment.

The plain fact was, the Occupation divisions had not been supported well by higher headquarters respecting maintenance echelons of vehicles.[3] And there was no question but that casualties occurred in Korea as the result of vehicle failures during crucial circumstances.

Ammunition, critical during the first week or so of the Conflict, soon became plentiful. Depending on rail or truck transport availability, there was no curtailment of requests as presented at ammunition supply points (ASPs), including requests from ROK forces. Artillery ammunition was regarded as such an absolute necessity in the supply pipeline that a major task outlined for drivers assigned to the first truck company to reach Korea was to make regular trips to the fighting areas with as many ammunition boxes or containers as could be conveyed safely.

These road trips were essential because, as early combat lines were very fluid, ASPs were constantly shifted, making it difficult for individual battalions to maintain contact with the point. Also, as individual artillery batteries often operated separately in direct support operations, there were insufficient firing battery trucks available for continuous ammunition supply runs. Thus the Negro drivers of that first truck company to arrive in Korea, who often drove out alone to find artillery locations during those early days, were heroes in every sense of the word.

In sum, no one was really concerned or tuned to the finer nuances of supply procedure early on other than (1) getting all necessary and relevant gear and materiel to Korea in the first place and then (2) hurrying same to the front. If the

7th Cavalry Regiment needed twenty SCR- 300 radios, they were placed on the next truck going forward. If the 24th Regiment needed five 81-mm mortars, they were sent out immediately, no questions asked. The defense of South Korea and the immediate well-being of each American soldier during those early days were deemed far more important than fine-line property accountability and by-the-book supply regulations and directives.

"Dear John,"

When Korea became a battle zone, mail clerks still demanded the same six-cent airmail rate per letter that had been in effect in Japan. But not only did many of the men not have the money, the clerks soon exhausted their supply of stamps, and there was no immediate resupply of same. Finally, Capt. George E. Mayer, the 13th Field adjutant, directed that mail be sent with the statement *Postage Unavailable* on the upper right-hand corner of the envelope's face. This proved to be a temporary solution. *Free Mail* was established by Congress on July 11 for all combat zone troops.

Writing materials were scarce at first. Although most had carried paper, envelopes, pen, or pencil to Korea, much was lost during and the result of early actions. Personnel sections soon secured writing materials from local sources. The Lieutenant often wrote on paper that was dirty and water-stained. Envelopes supplied were mostly Korean-manufactured from thin, plain wrapping paper.

Censorship was imposed early with every officer delegated the power to censor mail written by men in his section or platoon. This order was soon rescinded and censorship imposed on a spot basis at Army level. There was very little security need, even early on, as the combat area was limited to a small peninsula. Furthermore, press correspondents had been granted considerable license in their reporting. The stories of defeat and withdrawal soon became well known in the States, anyway.

As many of the men had Japanese girl friends and some native wives and, of course, civilian dependents sat waiting in camp quarters, mail from Kyushu was heavy at first. The same, probably, was true for Honshu, home of the cavalry and the 25th divisions. Each written line received was read many times over as love and devotion were expressed in words and phrases peculiar to the vocabulary of lovers, understood the world over.

Yet after several months, letters from Japanese lovers and friends were fewer and fewer, the result often of the girl acquiring a new GI boyfriend or, finally, a Japanese husband. Then, too, many of the men were coming to realize, some for the first time, that home and the stabilizing concept of the "girl next door" were more vital in life's scheme of things.

Some, obviously, were not able to handle well these changing Japanese-American GI relationships. More than a few rumors swirled about concerning men who left line units to somehow return to Pusan and then back to Japan to confront an alleged errant friend or wife.

Well, as in all wars, letters received were carried in pockets, sacks, bags, dispatch cases, and helmet liners. They were read and reread until moisture and other elements rendered the ink or pencil virtually unreadable. Each Betty, Connie, or Mary Sue was raised to Goddess First-Class just because "her" letters were composed in alluring feminine script and sprinkled liberally with "her" choice of sweet-smelling GI-killer. Most paused in the rereading of letters to sniff hopefully, even after all traces of the original aroma had succumbed to the earthy odoriferousness of the Korean countryside.

To the average soldier in Korea that summer of 1950, a letter in hand represented what was important in life, meaning a comprehension that his very being was significant and of value to others, and that his terribly draining combatant efforts were not being overlooked.

"Remember Them Chelsies?"

The new breed never knew. It took the "old soldiers" among the troops to jar memories of WWII cigarette supplies.

Perhaps the most striking recollection was that of a preponderance of a cigarette brand named "Chelsea," packed in many of the early K-ration boxes. The men in A Battery, 912th Field, were known to wax choleric over not being able to receive Luckies or Camels anymore. The Chelsea brand came to symbolize, more than any other particular to the far-flung forces of democracy, the sacrifices each was being called to make, even in combat, to ensure ultimate victory and the return of the so-called name brands.

Then, sometime after VJ-Day, a story appeared in a magazine somewhere that stilled forever the frustrated cries over having to smoke Chelseas. It seemed that early in the war, when the government was ready to unveil the new K-ration, quartermaster officials asked several large tobacco companies to cooperate by manufacturing a cigarette and accompanying package slightly shorter than normal. The package would hold four cigarettes and fit neatly within the size specifications of the K-ration box. Since this was a new development, and the major companies were already producing at full capacity, they hedged on a commitment. However, the company manufacturing the Chelsea brand volunteered to comply with the specifications, with the result that many of the first ration boxes contained Chelsea cigarettes.

Actually, Chelseas didn't taste that bad. Most complaints stemmed from imagination and the fact that the taste was dulled somewhat by the cigarettes being packaged with food in watertight containers.

But the GI has a long memory. The Chelsea Company had to go out of business sometime after the war, so great was the antipathy against the brand as translated into buyer resistance, a sad commentary on industrial patriotism and its effect, immediate and far-reaching, concerning a little known facet of the war effort.

For soldiers in the Korean fighting, the cigarette name brands were included in the C-ration B-cans, in little waterproof bags. In addition, five regular-sized packs per man came up each week, included in the so-called PX ration. Many were the instances, during fighting lulls, when the first sergeant of a line company could be seen edging up a hill with the "chigees," the Korean bearers, bringing the weekly ration of smokes, candy, and gum. Toilet articles and the like, also part of the ration, were held for distribution during rest periods.

Many took every cigarette pack allotted. These were carried about in Band-Aid boxes or similar containers brought from Japan. Chewing tobacco was popular, with more plug found in the ration distribution than had been the case during WWII. There was no cause for griping about cigarettes among Americans in Korea, and the Lieutenant heard none.

In truth, however, the men smoked too much. The Lieutenant noticed that many men tired quickly after smoking. As one who was not an abstainer, he became aware that he tired more when smoking on hot days than when he abstained. It was harder to climb a hill after several smokes.

Nevertheless, smoking had a quieting effect on the men's nerves. When a crisis arose, a quick smoke helped settle the mind. And of all the bonding agents available to a discomfited military, huddling close to despair during those days and nights in July 1950, the offering of a cigarette, particularly to a newcomer, spelled acceptance into a band of gritty survivors, trusting that the new man will readily shoulder his fraction of the burden in the struggle to endure the maelstrom of blood and sweat that was Korea in 1950.

Unit Security

A number of units within the 24th Division, during the first weeks of fighting, had been careful to sustain a certain secrecy regarding their presence in the combat area. This was particularly evident respecting vehicle markings. It was simply commonsensical to withhold information from potential NK agents lurking within territory controlled by the South Korean government, and the simplest and perhaps most effective method of censorship was the elimination of normal divisional and unit digital markings on vehicles. The adopted method of deception was the use of a code letter or configuration in place of the normal digital identification markings on vehicle bumpers, both front and rear.

The 52nd Field, for example, adopted the Greek letter *delta* as the battalion identification configuration. Delta, incidentally, was also that battalion's code designation. The 3rd Engineer Battalion used the letter H for identification purposes, probably after the first letter of the commander's surname, which was Hyzer. (That battalion later adopted the sobriquet phrase "Hyzer's Tigers," the expression appearing on most of that unit's vehicles through the ensuing winter and into the 1951 spring.)

The 11th Field adopted the code letter C, continuing with it during the first several months of the conflict.

The code letter for the 13th Field was Q, and even after the Naktong fighting, when most other divisional units replaced code letters or configurations with numerical identities, the 13th Field retained its letter. And then, at the Kyongsan Bivouac, battery sign painters added the word "CLAN" to the Q code, making the appellation "Q CLAN."

Most were a bit bewildered at seeing this extended identification, although by itself, a definition of the word *clan* was not a problem. Knowing that the word represented a certain air of togetherness in a superior sense was enough. Besides, the letter and word together was a different sort of identification, and individuals cater to being different, even in war.

What was not common knowledge but became so gradually was the fact that the word "CLAN," with respect to the 13th Field, is a throwback to pre-WWII days when the battalion (then regiment) was stationed at Schofield Barracks, Hawaii, but not yet a part of the Hawaiian (later 24th) Division. The 13th Artillery was known among soldiers stationed there as a very clannish outfit due, probably in part, to the extra pride in belonging to a unit to which was affixed the number 13. And it was also known and respected that members of the 13th often reacted with an "excess of enthusiasm" when challenged, individually or *en masse*.[4]

Now, as the record of the 13th thus far in the Conflict was little less than excellent, there was the decision to heighten an already high *esprit* by proudly exhibiting this new ID code: Q CLAN, that symbolically represented the "best damn artillery battalion in the Eighth United States Army."

(The 13th Field became known in Korea as the Q CLAN outfit until April 1951, when a picayunish artillery colonel assumed command of the 24th DivArty, a man who didn't give a hoot in hell about hard-won traditions within the four battalions comprising his command. His order restoring all numerical designations wiped out a bit of color as well as history in a fight that, to that moment, had been all too bare of color.

Wars are led by the elite; fought by the common. The former must always leave space for the latter to exhibit pride and sense of accomplishment. Not to do so or not to do so much forges a military structure more closely aligned to the mechanistic than the opportunistic, with narrowed achievement inevitably in consequence.)

"We're the Yew En Army Now."

It was about 1430 hours on the afternoon of July 20, 1950. A battle was being fought in and about the city of Taejon, just a few miles from where the Lieutenant was sitting, manning an OP within the perimeter of D Company, 21st Infantry Regiment. Smoke was rising up ahead, and F-51 planes were both heard and seen buzzing about and diving on targets, some, it seemed, just over the next hill.

Already, stray vehicles were approaching, descending a hilly road at high rates of speed and into the welcoming line of the 21st, looks of relief on the faces of those riding.

Aware of the struggle taking place beyond and hearing voices and other noise from the road, the Lieutenant slipped down from his OP to where a group of men sat, clustered about a machine gun covering a road junction through which vehicles were passing. There were about five in the group, including a young officer whose name sounded something like Spivak.

Joining them, the Lieutenant heard two of the men, both drawling Southerners, discussing the state in which the American Army was finding itself.

"We're gonna get pushed right on down to Pusan," one said, perhaps somewhat facetiously, "and they're gonna have to have all them LSTs waiting, because if they ain't there, there's gonna be an awful lot of boys learning to swim real fast."

Some laughter ensued, and then the other one, a man from somewhere in the Middle Belt, dark, deliberate, and manly, replied, "Well, this ain't the Yew Es Army anymore. This is the Yew En Army. Lots of other countries are going to send troops in here. They ain't going to let us go back too much more. Them communists will take over the world if we lose here."

No one said much after these remarks. The Lieutenant was so struck by the simple, direct, perceptively expressed insight of the man that he stood a full half-minute staring at him. Then he turned and climbed back to his OP.

Lots of units are termed "best damn." As he sat down again to watch the road, the Lieutenant reflected on the conversation that took place moments before and concluded that D Company, 21st Infantry Regiment, 24th Infantry Division, had earned the right to be called, at that instant in time at least, the best damn company there is in this goddamn, stinking asshole of the world.

The Kyongsan Bivouac

During the final American counterattacks along the Naktong, resulting in the NK being pushed back across the river, the 13th Field Artillery Battalion literally became the center for artillery operations. The 13th provided direct support for both the 19th and 34th Regiments, somewhat remarkable in that that battalion still had only two firing batteries. The 11th Field, in general support, fired missions as called for by the 13th. The 52nd Field, whose supported infantry, the 21st regiment, was engaged in blocking and mopping-up operations, tied in with the 13th in a reinforcement role, and after the 9th Regiment was squeezed out by Marine units, its support, the 15th Field, took on a reinforcement function with the 13th. The 63rd Field, still reorganizing at Miryang, was not used at all.

The Marine artillery supported its own, but there were instances when, with their observers becoming casualties, the Marine commander offered to fire missions as directed by the 13th. Their observer casualties probably resulted from the tactic of placing observers with the lead squads.[1] The Army, in contrast, places observers within company ranks and perimeters so that artillery support can continue well into a battle action. It may be a tired truism to reiterate that Army tactics may rely too heavily on accurate artillery support, but it is nevertheless fair to state that heavy use of artillery tends to lower the friendly casualty rate, with men more confident as to a battle outcome.

Artillery support during the recently completed battle consisted solely of divisional and Marine brigade component batteries. During the last day or so of the battle, 90-mm guns of the newly arrived 6th Tank Battalion provided harassing and interdictory fire on targets well beyond the river. There were no Army or corps-level general support artillery battalions of light or heavier caliber present.

Obviously complimentary regarding his leadership role in the fighting thus far, Lt. Col. Stratton, also the ranking artillery commander within the 24th Division, was tapped for promotion and a boost up to the position of division artillery executive officer when that slot fell vacant upon the conclusion of the Naktong fighting. His promotion took effect two days after the 13th arrived at Kyongsan.

Stratton's successor was Lt. Col. Silas R. Langlois, a native of Massachusetts and a former National Guard officer. He had arrived only nine days previous. Langlois had been the regimental liaison who had informed the Lieutenant about the change in artillery support while the latter was still on Hill 311.

Now, with a new "old man," the men glanced frequently in the direction of the CP, trying to "size him up," the general morale of the battalion and of the officers, particularly, depending greatly on the caliber and personality of their new commander. Stratton's was a hard act to follow. Most adopted a "wait and see" attitude as a matter of course.

Everyone plunged into a series of commonplace chores such as cleaning equipment, washing clothes and selves, and writing letters. The men also found time to swim, explore, and otherwise laze about.

On one such comfortable afternoon, the Lieutenant looked up to see an old friend walk down the sandy beach toward the bivouac. He was 1st Lt. Richard M. Hager, formerly with the 49th Field at Camp Younghans, Japan, and one of the members of the first SABAOC group at Fort Sill. Both Richard and the Lieutenant had been ordered to Korea originally but, with the change of orders, were finally assigned to the 7th Infantry Division.

The Lieutenant whooped happily and was, in turn, greeted by a wide, toothily handsome Tennessee smile. Both stood for a moment in cheerful unembarrassed silence. The renewal of friendship ties under circumstances such as were occurring is always profound, if sometimes emotional.

Hager was serving with the 8th Field, the supporting element of the 27th Regiment, 25th Infantry Division, known as the Wolfhound Regiment. The unit had just emerged from the line in an area north of Taegu bisected by the Taegu-Kunwi road, where a major NK attack had been thwarted. As the NK had used tanks in considerable number, the defenders had nicknamed the road the "Bowling Alley." The battle had been a nightmarish experience. Now, however, with the NK push slackening, the regiment had been withdrawn and placed in reserve in Taegu, to be used if another such emergency arose.

The Lieutenant was delighted to hear that other former 7th DivArty officers were also with the 8th Field. He immediately asked Capt. Still for permission to drive into Taegu and visit briefly with these men.

In Taegu, the Lieutenant saw and renewed acquaintance with Lts. Ralph Edwards, former Camp Younghans club officer, Hal Godwin; Bill Plummer, Charles Howard; as well as several others he had known. The group sat and chatted about the future; nothing very intellectual was voiced. The major topic was the question when the UN forces would become strong enough to begin pushing the NK back. As both mortar and artillery fire from the cavalry sector could be heard plainly where the group was sitting, the extent of this speculation was curtailed.

The Lieutenant mentioned his being with the group that walked out from the Kum River battle, and there was some discussion about that. The officers in the 8th Field had heard about the battle and about wounded being left. A rumor was strong that all the wounded left behind had been killed soon after the able-bodied had withdrawn. A medical officer had escaped after seeing the massacre take place, so someone said.

In a short while, the Lieutenant said "Goodbye" to each and left. They would meet again, they all said, in Seoul.

On the way back to Kyongsan that afternoon, the Lieutenant encountered a curious convoy approaching Taegu. As the vehicles in the convoy drew near, he recognized Land Rovers and lorries swaying along the dusty, uneven road. Then he saw the Union Jacks tied to radio antennae. The British had arrived, the first UN ground combat force to assist the ROKs and the Americans in the struggle.

The *Stars and Stripes* had heralded this arrival for several days, this brigade from Hong Kong, and here they were. Both Dear and the Lieutenant waved as the advance vehicle party passed, and the British waved in return. No one felt embarrassed during this early period in extending a welcome to new troops. All were friends in this bloodbath, and the snobbishness often displayed to newcomers in normal battle circumstances was nonexistent at this stage.

The Lieutenant was interested in the insignia of the brigade. He noticed what looked like a rooster, painted yellow, on the side of one of the vehicles. If that was the insignia, it was certainly unique.

(The Lieutenant was to learn later these vehicles constituted the advance party of the First Battalion, Argyll and Sutherland Highlanders, and the First Battalion, Middlesex Regiment. A battalion from Australia, scheduled to arrive later, would complete the brigade. Their commander was Brigadier Basil Coad.

Each brigade battalion could boast of belonging to a regiment with a long military history. This was particularly true of the Highlanders. This regiment was famed during WWI as the "Ladies from Hell" regiment, the German Army providing the sobriquet.)

Just after supper chow that same evening, the Lieutenant looked up to see another old buddy kicking sand and gravel along the beach as he made his way to the 13th CP. The smiling countenance of 1st Lt. Kenneth E. Ankrom burst onto the scene, and the Lieutenant was engaged in recounting old times once more.

Ken also was a SABAOC graduate, the same class as Hager and the Lieutenant. At the conclusion of the Ft. Sill sojourn, Ken elected to return to Columbus, Ohio, for a last visit with his folks. To swing the trip, he borrowed $100 from the Lieutenant. When he turned up at Camp Stoneman, the port of embarkation, he announced his marriage. What a razzing he took from Hager, Pete Golden, and others, but he bore up. The ceremony was a rush/rush affair, and he was the happiest second lieutenant in the camp. Jean Ankrom had been at Camp Hakata the night the Lieutenant passed through, but the two did not meet.

The Lieutenant learned about Ned Books, the young cavalry officer who had been part of the pipeline group from Tokyo to Pusan. Ken Ankrom was with A Battery, 52nd Field, and Books joined that battery late on July 9.

The following morning, the infantry was hit by an NK attack. Both Ankrom and Books were on hills across the road from each other and were in constant radio communication. When the time came to withdraw, Ankrom's company went one way while the company with Books traveled another path. Fate decreed that the latter group would take the "wrong" trail for, shortly, these men encountered an enemy force that captured a number from the group, including Books. His fate at the moment was unknown, but it was assumed he was being held, with several hundred other American prisoners, in Seoul.[2]

On the fourth day of rest, the Lieutenant was ordered to the division artillery headquarters along with Joe Coomer, Ray Cody, and Charles Delorimier. A number of key enlisted men also were included. All would be attached to DivArty temporarily for a special assignment. Each wondered what assignment as they drove to a secluded, wooded spot across a narrow stream to the CP. They were not to wonder long.

Immediately upon the group's arrival at DivArty's rendezvous site, a division staff officer began an orientation session. The division, under orders from Eighth Army, was to experiment with integrating South Korean trainees within American complements, the Koreans to perform as ammunition carriers and alternate skirmishers within infantry companies, and as defense guards for the artillery.

A continuing shortage of trained enlisted men still plagued the American divisions. The introduction of Koreans into the filler pipeline, it was reasoned, albeit in limited fashion, might act to relieve the shortage, at least temporarily; thus the move to experiment in training the Koreans in American Army methods and techniques, with a hoped-for successful integration resulting.

A three-day indoctrination and basic training course would be implemented, the shortest training period for a comparable group anywhere. The assembled representative artillerymen would conduct the training. Supervision would be provided by a staff group commanded by Lt. Col. Robert H. Dawson, CO of the 63rd Field.

The men in the assembled group began looking at each other. How could they conduct training when none could speak the Korean language? As if reading their thoughts, the briefing officer went on to explain that a cluster of South Korean police would accompany the trainees, not only acting as interpreters, but as security agents in the event that some of the trainees proved untrustworthy or politically unreliable. There was noticeable relaxation after this statement.

Nevertheless, there was some apprehension. Delorimier lowered his head and sighed, "For Christ's sake." Others nodded sympathetically. Most foresaw hours of confusion, with language the biggest hurdle. It might take two days alone to fully orient the trainees and who knows how long to get on with the instruction. However, each American present resolved to give the project a good try, as all units needed additional manpower.

They arrived, these Koreans, jam-packed in trucks. Instructor personnel stoically stood waiting. The policemen detrucked first. Necessary orders were given, and soon there was a mass scrambling off the trucks and into what passed for a general formation. Each Korean came completely equipped and carried a carbine. Each wore new fatigues, boots, and every last tent peg was packed into the musette bag. Instructor officers looked over their new commands and sighed. This was it?

The Lieutenant was luckier than many of his colleagues, as it turned out. The gendarme assigned to his group had had some Japanese Army experience, and he was eager to demonstrate his military skills. So after a few introductory remarks, which the policeman translated—or at least the Lieutenant hoped was translated, and correctly—the first order was given.

The three days passed quickly. Under better-than-average instruction assistance provided by the policemen, with American supervision, the KATUSAs (Korean Augmentation to the United State Army) learned to field-strip and fire the carbine, the M-2 rifle, and both machine gun calibers. They hiked and learned infantry squad formations. They set up perimeter defenses and absorbed a bit of military courtesy and drill.

A highlight of this training, at least for the Lieutenant's company, was a gimmick thought up on the spur to kill a few moments at the end of a short hike on the first training day. The Koreans were to imagine themselves facing a line of NK, the latter with their backs to the small stream bordering the camp. Fixing bayonets, they would charge toward the stream, simulating the act of forcing the enemy into the water.

This exercise became the last operation on each day, and it was prudent that no one be in the way. The KATUSAs charged at a dead run, clicking triggers and screaming at the tops of their lungs. A ranking division officer came upon the charge on the last training day and was so startled that he stood open-mouthed for a long moment. He was observed walking away wearing a broad smile. They would be all right, these KATUSAs.

For many of the Korean boys, the heavy combat boots were the first real shoes worn in their lives. This caused some difficulty with leg and foot muscles. Several times, in the dead of night, the call for a medic was heard, and a boy was carried to the aid station in the throes of painful foot or leg cramps. Some Americans could never understand these occurrences, but then, there were those who never really tried.

One had to be careful to defer to the accompanying police. These were the real leaders of the KATUSAs, the buffer between what was American and what was Korean. Cigarettes proffered publicly at the right time and place; permitting them the privilege of presenting and dismissing assembled squads; including them in policy conferences, all part of the ritual of delegated authority. This deferent policy conveyed to the KATUSAs the feeling that, after all, they were retaining their own integrity as a national group, the Americans only assisting and training them. This show of deference was a major key to the success of the brief training period.

On the final day of training, the KATUSAs were assembled and complimented by the division artillery commander, Brig. Gen. H.J.D. Meyer. An American civilian was observed standing near the general, an object of curiosity in that he wore khakis, but no insignia. He was an elderly, friendly looking man who smiled broadly.

When the general finished speaking, he introduced his companion as the Rev. William E. Shaw, formerly associated with the Methodist Theological Seminary in Seoul, now an advisor to Eighth Army. Whereas all assembled braced themselves for another onslaught of English, followed by the words of an interpreter standing by, the Rev. Shaw surprised everyone by speaking the Korean language. The KATUSAs seemed to approve his spoken thoughts because their smiling "Hahs" were audible and continued such until the minister finished. The Rev. Shaw made a hit that day, and the KATUSAs looked happier.

This ended the training. The trainees were parceled out to the batteries, each receiving about twenty men. American Army units were now more integrated than at any time in past history what with the recently begun indiscriminate assignment of Negroes to previously all-white units and now the KATUSAs. All three races were thus afforded opportunity to mingle and learn more about each other, thereby effecting greater cooperation in anticipation of difficult times lying ahead.

One of the more eagerly awaited rituals observed by many of the men there on the sandy beach at Kyongsan was the gathering at 2130 hours each evening, usually at headquarters batteries, to listen to Radio Seoul broadcasting an English language news program, directed particularly at the men in the UN army. The transmission was received on a new type of radio, the ANGRC-9, issued to headquarters-level units only, the radio often referred to colloquially as the "ANGRY-9."

The voice of the newscaster was that of a woman, an elderly woman, so many concluded, because the tone was none too steady and somewhat thin, like that often projected by older individuals. The men nicknamed her "Seoul City Sue," although in reality she never played the part of temptress after the fashion of the Axis Sallys or Tokyo Rose of WWII.

The woman began broadcasting punctually each evening. Her program, a half-hour in length, dealt mainly with NK "victories" and the "vast economic gains" made in the South Korean provinces occupied by the NK forces.

Toward the end of each program, she always made a pitch in the manner of attempting to generate discontent among American troops. She tried to explain the futility of continuing the war; that the soldiers were in fact fighting for "capitalist war-mongers," and that, in the final accounting, should the war continue, the UN Army would be unable to counter the "victorious armies of the Democratic Peoples' Republic of Korea."

To punctuate the latter prediction, the woman never failed to announce names of those Americans who, according to NK records, died during recent engagements. Most of the men whose names were announced had heretofore been listed only as "missing in action." The NK broadcast appeared to confirm, unofficially, their ultimate fate.

The listening men who crowded about the radio sets were there primarily for the names. Every so often a familiar name was announced and soft cursing would be heard from those who had known the man. The announced casualties on these evenings were usually from one of three battle areas: Kongju, where the 63rd Field was overrun; "twelve miles north of Taejon", the Kum River battle, and Taejon. Cavalry names were reported occasionally as were casualties from the 29th Regiment.

Throughout all of this, the lady announcer very often referred to the traitor, Rhee Syngman, and many were puzzled over the name. Then it was explained that Koreans place the surname first, and that the West knew the man as Syngman Rhee, current president of the Republic of Korea.

The men knew propaganda when they heard it. Victories and casualties reported by the NK were grossly exaggerated at this stage, they knew well. Few remarks were made during the course of any broadcast. Only when the transmissions were terminated were voices heard and then only some "goddamns" and the probability that the woman was being forced to talk, her voice breaking noticeably on occasions.

(Speculation concerning the true identity of the woman announcer and commentator continued even after hostilities in Korea ceased. A Chinese news dispatch in early September 1950, and picked up by the *Army Times*, Sept. 9, 1950, p. 12, reported the name of the woman in question to be a Mrs. Sou, American wife of a Korean.[3] Her program ceased a few days prior to the recapture of Seoul in September 1950, possibly as early as September 15, and she was never heard from or about since.

In his book, *Enter the Dragon*, a narration about Chinese involvement in the war, Russell Spurr describes a train departure from Seoul on the night of September 15, 1950, the date of the American landing at Inch'on, the train carrying many NK civilian officials and their families including, no doubt, South Koreans who had sympathized with NK policies. En route to P'yongyang, the train was attacked and bombed just as it reached the Kaesong station, resulting in close to 300 dead. It may be assumed that Mrs. Sou and her husband perished aboard the train in question [pp. 97–101].)

On one of his walks through and about the rest area, the Lieutenant was hailed by what sounded like a familiar voice. Turning, he saw the smiling countenance of John A. Anderson, now Capt. John A. Anderson, late of Camp Hakata where he had been the post motor officer. He was now motor officer for the 24th Division Artillery Headquarters. Both sat for a few minutes recapturing old times.

The Lieutenant was curious about the reaction of dependents at Hakata to the receipt of casualty notices and asked Anderson about it. John replied that he had had the duty of occasionally aiding in the delivery of telegram notices to wives whose husbands had been killed. He shook his head as he related instances of shocked disbelief and near hysteria.

In the silence following this recollection, the Lieutenant remembered those brightly lit dependent quarters that last night he spent at Hakata. For one military dependent to lose a husband while others living near still had theirs was perhaps more than could be borne. The atmosphere at the many dependent areas in Japan was certainly not quite that in the States where tragic news of this nature can be cushioned by the constant pulsation of a heterogeneous environment.

One afternoon, the battalions were informed that all Japanese KPs (kitchen police), who had accompanied units into Korea, were to be returned immediately to Japan. These Japanese nationals, most in the sixteen to twenty-two age group, had worked in unit kitchens in the training camps and then had volunteered to accompany the forces to Korea. Not only did these young men or "boy-sans" look forward to some adventurous times, but they also desired to continue being paid by their American employers.

If the experience of the 13th Field with these KPs paralleled that of other division units, the Americans simply dressed their KP boy-sans in regulation fatigues, gave each a carbine, placed them aboard the kitchen trucks, and transported them to Korea. It was all illegal, of course, in that Japan was officially neutral regarding the Korean dispute.

Then, soon after the first battle engagements, the NK government began charging that the Americans were using Japanese as fighters in the ranks. The charge was serious and denied, of course. Yet there probably was a kernel of truth to the allegation. Obviously, if the Japanese KPs found themselves in untenable situations along with their American friends and employers, they, too, might resort to force of arms to save themselves. This, apparently, is what may have happened within batteries early committed in the war, several having been overrun.

It was the Lieutenant's understanding at this time that no Japanese KP who may have been captured was known to have survived, lending credence to the conclusion that the individual was shot immediately or shortly afterward, so great was the animosity between most Koreans and the Japanese people at the time.[4]

Now, Eighth Army flatly ordered the return to Japan of all its remaining worker nationals. There were no ifs or ands about the matter. Most of the boy-sans were downcast at the thought of leaving their friends, but there was mutual understanding of why the order was issued. Then, too, the Americans had discovered already that Korean civilians would work just as hard for limited wages and the opportunity to eat well. Most units acquired Korean help by September 1950, a practice that would continue to the mutual satisfaction of all concerned.

This was a time of reward for outstanding services rendered, particularly affecting enlisted personnel. Recommendations for battlefield commissions had been made prior to the rest period, and now these recommendations had been approved.

M/Sgt. Robert A. Totty, chief of operations of the 13th Field, received his promotion to second lieutenant and was assigned to A Battery. M/Sgt. Traver R. Farmer, also with operations, was commissioned a second lieutenant and assigned also to A Battery.

Headquarters Battery JWO Joseph S. Tucker was promoted to second lieutenant and became that battery's executive officer. And Daniel P. Sullivan, the battalion communications chief, was promoted to second lieutenant and assigned battalion assistant communications officer.

There were promotions within the several batteries of enlisted personnel who had been performing jobs in the next highest grade. Among these was Cletus Fitzgerald, promoted to E-5 (sergeant) grade. All privates E-2 were promoted to E-3 (privates first-class), and privates E-1 to E-2.

Morale-wise, the 13th Field was now in tip-top shape and the feeling was not limited to the 13th. Both infantry and artillery and other division units bounced back nicely to the eager and keen levels of preparedness commanders look for when gauging troop readiness for combat.

There was growing enthusiasm to get on with the job. The days of rest at Kyongsan and wherever the division infantry was based were highly medicinal. But now, with promotions effected and the men provided with the best rations available, which mess stewards and their assistants prepared so assiduously, and what with renewed confidence, both personal and collective, restlessness was noticeable.

This was a healthy sign. Sense of duty was prevailing over desire for continued inactivity. The men knew that other divisions were still on the line, and that these had not been accorded the rest opportunity provided the 24th. Besides, after comparing notes, events could have turned out far worse for the 19th RCT during July and early August. A growing ebullience pervaded each unit's rest area allotment, funneling a sense of certainty that, however difficult resumed combat challenges might become, the division would endure in good order until this bloody mess, as the Conflict was being described, ended.

Near the end of the first full week in rest bivouac, a serious NK breakthrough occurred near the town of Kyongju, an old imperial site. The breakthrough, if true, threatened the main east-west road between the coastal port of P'ohang and Taegu. The ROKs were on the line in that vicinity and were not able to completely contain the strong NK drive.

At the same time, the cavalry, facing the NK northwest of Taegu, was feeling very heavy pressure, and the bivouacking 24th Division could hear artillery shells exploding in the outer environs of that city. Clearly this last week of August was becoming a crucial test of the Perimeter.

The 21st Regiment had not suffered as much as the other two division regiments during the Naktong action, so it seemed logical that this regiment would be the first called should additional forces be needed to strengthen weak spots along the perimeter. And the call came. The regiment pulled out one morning en route to Kyongju, and the remainder of the division knew that rest time was coming to an end.

Then news came on September 1 that the 34th Regimental Combat Team was being dismantled. Its infantry and supporting artillery would be distributed to the 19th and 21st regiments and to the 13th and 52nd Field Artillery battalions, rounding out full combat teams of both men and equipment and retrieving what was lost by the one-third reduction order of 1949. Perhaps, had the 63rd Field not been hit so hard at Kongju on July 14, the 34th combat team might have continued to give a good account of itself. But then later, the 34th Regiment was virtually torn apart at Taejon and never completely recovered.

Several officers who seemed to be authoritative about the regiment felt that both the 34th and the 63rd would be reconstituted in Japan as a training regimental combat team and perhaps rejoin the 24th Division at some future date.[5]

As to distribution, the First Battalion, with Lt. Col. Ayers still commanding, became the Third Battalion, 19th Regiment, while the 34th's Third Battalion went to the 21st Regiment. A Battery, 63rd Field, with Capt. Loren W. Sullivan commanding, came to the 13th as its C Battery. B Battery, 63rd Field, went to the 52nd Field. The 11th Field, meanwhile, at last received enough equipment and men to form a C Battery. All units of the division now were at full triangular strength. But what of a third regiment?

The last regimental combat team to leave the Korean Occupation in early 1949 was the 5th Regiment supported by the 555th Field. The team was reassigned to Hawaii. Now, with immediate need for combat units in Korea, the 5th had returned, having arrived in early August to replace the ill-fated 29th Regiment. As the 5th was the only separate regiment in Korea, it was ordered attached to the 24th Division temporarily. Continuing to face NK pressure on the Masan front, where it had been fighting since its arrival, the regiment was unable to effect a jointure immediately, but would at a propitious time.

The new C Battery arrived at the 13th's bivouac area the afternoon of September 2. Capt. Sullivan reported to Lt. Col. Langlois. With Sullivan were 1st Lts. Arthur P. Lombardi, Kenneth R Maxson, William Mabry, and Arnold R. Yates.

Moments after the arrival of the new battery, Langlois ordered Close-stations, March-order. The 13th would prepare for a night motor march. Something had broken again at Yongsan. The Marines had been recalled. A massive attack had upended the 2nd Division units in the area of the former Naktong Pocket, the penetration reaching almost to the outskirts of Yongsan. The men became tight-lipped. Back to that hellhole?

The column pulled out of the bivouac at 2000 hours. Col. Stratton stood alongside the road waving to his old command. The men yelled and waved in return, but they quickly quieted. They were veterans, now. Veterans don't shout or wave much anymore.

Darkness fell quickly. A rain was brewing, a long one this time. Climatic conditions dictated that the time of year was right for a continental weather change that brings prolonged precipitation. The Lieutenant shivered as he thought about the wet and colder days to come.

The road dust began to rise more thickly, and the Lieutenant burrowed his face deep in his field jacket. After ten days of rest, the 19th RCT was moving back into the fray.

Eighth Army Firemen

During the first months of fighting in Korea, four combat groups merited being referred to as "Eighth Army Firemen." The first was the Marine brigade, along the Masan front with the 25th Division and, later, twice in the Naktong Pocket. Then the 27th Regiment Combat Team was pulled from the south to straddle the road leading from Kunwi to Taegu, the road known as the "Bowling Alley." And the 21st RCT also was called upon at intervals.

The last was the 19th Regiment and its support, the 13th Field. The 19th was now completely battle-wise and rested, filled with both American replacements and KATUSAs, and ready for any job handed to it. On September 2, it was the only uncommitted regiment within the Perimeter.

Now, into the night the column ground, south to Miryang and then west to a point about halfway between Miryang and Yongsan. There, the vehicles and men were waved off the road and into fields of high, wet, green rice to wait and rest until daylight.

It was shortly after breakfast that morning that news of what was transpiring filtered through the units. The 2nd Division had been pushed back severely. Major fighting was taking place just outside the town of Yongsan itself. The Marines had been hurriedly recalled, and the Second Battalion of the brigade had begun a counterattack just west of the town. It was a Marine/Army coordinated drive. Casualties were mounting, but the attack seemed to be more successful than not. The 19th would not be committed unless the drive faltered. Everyone relaxed and settled down to wait.

Church Call for the artillery came down about 1100, and the road was soon crowded with vehicles from the 13th batteries heading to the CP where both Catholic and Protestant services would be held. Chaplains Roche and Helt were punctual, as always. The men were grateful for this brief opportunity to meditate.

The observer teams went up to the infantry early that afternoon. Capt. Pate, together with officers from A Battery, reported to Lt. Col. Naudts and the assembled First Battalion staff. The new officer, Totty, was introduced and made welcome. Both Coles and the Lieutenant knew most of the staff. Naudts assigned Totty to A Company, Coles to C Company, and the Lieutenant went back to B Company and the newly promoted 1st Lt. "Bill" Bailey.

As the observers surveyed the company areas, they became aware of changes that had taken place during the rest interim. Men literally swarmed about the areas, were clean-shaven, dressed in clean uniforms, and smiling. They moved about in quick-step, with an air of grave responsibility. Clinging, accepted, but not yet proven, were both replacements and KATUSAs. But these had caught the spirit and were preparing to distinguish themselves in the manner of their comrades, veterans of the recent Naktong victory.

Bailey greeted the Lieutenant in his usually courteous fashion, accepting congratulations on his promotion. First Sgt. Bobby J. Hunt then appeared and the three briefly discussed their rest activities. They were soon joined by several of the sergeants: Clifford D. Hamric, Ken H. Smith, Patrick J. Stowell, and Alfred Amacker.

The Lieutenant noticed several new officers in the company. There was a young graduate of West Point, Class of 1950, smooth-faced with reddish complexion. He was Ray M. Dowe Jr. Ray had married immediately following graduation, and his honeymoon was a trip across the country to Camp Stoneman, where he embarked for Korea. He was a bit bewildered by all the rush and dispirited over leaving his wife so soon. He mentioned that his uncle had once commanded the 19th Regiment. Clearly, Ray had tradition behind him and would do a good job under fire.

Another officer stepped forward. The Lieutenant noticed his armor branch insignia. "Hell, yes," the officer replied. "They found an infantry platoon leader's MOS in my Form 66, and I was yanked into the infantry." Other armor officer replacements had evidently been similarly assigned. First Lt. James Mattson was given the weapons platoon spot in B Company.

The Lieutenant nodded at and waved to others in the company remembered from Bailey's Hill: Sgt. Robert L. Hartley, Cpl. Ray S. Boggs, Sfc. Leo Lupton, Cpl. Elmer D. Jennings, Cpl. Melvin C. Lile, Pfc. Herbert Carlson, Cpl. Larry Holder, Cpl. Cliff H. Smith, Sgt. Bernard Witherspoon and, of course, "Doc" Caldwell. Seeing these men made him feel good inside. He felt he would never again be with a bunch quite like this one.

In a short while, the Lieutenant walked the perimeter of B Company's area and discovered that C Company was bivouacked just across a small brook. He crossed over and there encountered 1st Lt. Augustus Orr. Both saw the other at the same time, and there were smiles of recognition. Orr mentioned that he, too, had crawled in the paddies south of Taep'yong-ni and was with the infantry group during the night escape toward Taejon. He had been evacuated for hospitalization, rejoining the regiment at the rest area.

While speaking with Orr, the Lieutenant noticed another familiar figure nearby. He was former Sfc. Chester W. Van Orman. Van Orman had been tendered a battlefield commission to the rank of second lieutenant. The Lieutenant heartily congratulated him. The three spoke for a few minutes and then parted to carry out necessary chores and duties.

A very heavy downpour hit the bivouac that night. The Lieutenant, bedded down in the B Company CP, a makeshift arrangement of several shelter-halves, awoke to a rushing stream coming through the CP just beyond his feet. Everyone got up and, after a few minutes of vigorous work with entrenching tools, diverted the stream. The Lieutenant shuddered in thought about the men along the combat line west of Yongsan.

A Marine helicopter flew low up the valley the following morning, and by this time the men were aware of the missions flown by this aircraft. Fastened on the sides of the copter were two oblong boxes or nacelles. Each could hold a stretcher and one wounded soldier. The wounded individual or individuals would then be whisked to an evacuation hospital within minutes, while a half-hour jeep movement might be fatal. The men grew reticent as they watched the copter wing its way toward the front.

Maj. Gen. Church drove through the bivouac that morning. The men who saw him waved and saluted. Church was not a young man as generals go. He had been about due for retirement. But after Maj. Gen. Dean's disappearance, Church, the only ranking general officer on the scene who was acquainted with the military situation, was given the division.

The fact that the 24th remained operative through the recently fought Naktong struggle was a credit to Church and the inspiration he engendered. The men gave their respect willingly and gladly to this elderly, fatherly officer who was their undoubted leader.

A story was making the rounds of the division by this time, apocryphal perhaps, but given credence by a surprising number. The setting was Kumch'on, or thereabouts, the 24th Division headquarters, as the First Cavalry Division was advancing to relieve on the line that had been established northwest of Yongdong. Both Church and Maj. Gen. Hobart Gay, the cavalry commander, and key division officers, were scheduled to meet with Eighth Army Commander, Lt. Gen. Walton Walker, for a briefing prior to the cavalry commitment.

The 24th Division officers were waiting with Lt. Gen. Walker when the cavalry group arrived. There followed the usual polite greeting from all concerned and then a cavalry officer, who forever remains anonymous, announced, "Well, the retreating is over. The First Team is here."

At the arrogance expressed, Maj. Gen. Church took a step forward as if to physically remonstrate, but was stopped by Walker. The remainder of the meeting understandably took place in an atmosphere of the coldest of courtesy.

True or not, the sequel to the story, and again, widely recounted by the men of the 24th, was that the cavalry withdrew further and faster after their baptism at the battle of Yongdong than had any 24th Division unit previously.

The jaundice directed at the cavalry, begun in Japan, continued even in Korea. Having led themselves and the other Occupation divisions into believing that theirs was the best all-around division, it was quite a come-down to realize that their initial showing could only be described as a bust. To be plainly frank about the matter, the cavalry was disdained during the early months, with little sympathy expressed, even as that division was hard-pressed in the Waegwan area, as was occurring at that very moment.

Shortly after the noon meal, word came down to march-order and be quick about it. A mad scramble followed as tents were struck and equipment packed. The Lieutenant, bewildered, sought out Pate. He was told that the NK had launched a strong drive along the east coast, this time to a point just north of Kyongju. If that important road and rail junction fell, the Pusan Perimeter would be threatened. The cavalry was still holding about seven miles north and west of Taegu, but the pressure there was tremendous. So, too, was the situation at Yongsan, and at Masan, where the 25th Division was waging a struggling defense. Monday, September 4, was a dark day for the United Nations forces.

Lt. Col. Naudts walked out of his CP tent the moment before it was struck and announced that the battalion had been given a "march objective"—a movement until enemy is sighted. Tanks then appeared in the bivouac, elements of the 6th Tank Battalion that had been landed at Pusan during the closing phase of the Naktong battle. The battalion had modified Shermans and M-26 Pershings. When all was ready, the infantry climbed aboard the tanks. With B Company leading out, the column began moving, following several minutes behind the I & R Platoon led by 1st Lt. William A. Patch, grandson of the famous WWII general.

As the column passed the site of the artillery bivouac, the cannoneers were out on the road preparing to load up. Good-natured jeering was immediately directed at the enlisted members of the observer parties, the latter giving as good as received. The exchange reflected a state of high morale within the combat team.

The task force passed through Miryang and then turned south toward Pusan. At Chinyong-nit, however, the force turned east, crossing the Naktong River delta just north of Pusan. Then, as if fate was guiding, the force turned north onto Route 1, the same coastal road the regimental advance party and artillery traveled on the initial movement north on July 7.

Although now late in the afternoon and with rain clouds threatening, not at all like the weather on that hot, humid July day, many of the old-timers in the task force were quiet as they recognized towns, villages, and landmarks passed. What went though their minds is not recorded, but the Lieutenant's thoughts turned again to the missing men of his first observer section: Thacker, Wallace, and Payne, and whether he would be able to return to the Taep'yong-ni area at least once more.

About halfway up Route 1 toward Kyongju, the heavens opened up and rain pelted the column. Hunched and tired, the men resigned themselves to this added discomfort. Better rain than live ammunition directed at them.

Then, about 1900, the column halted. The task force was at a point a short distance south of Kyongju. Members of KMAG met the column commanders. After a short command conference, the First Battalion moved up and onto a nearby hill. The Second Battalion remained in the valley adjacent to the roadway.

The next day, what with combat probabilities still uncertain, the observers remained near the road readying their equipment. While the Lieutenant and his section were still engaged in early afternoon, the weather still gray and overcast, a messenger from the First Battalion CP approached and asked 1st Sgt. Hunt to locate and escort four platoon sergeants from B Company to the CP. Hunt wore the trace of a smile as he started up the hill. The Lieutenant remained unaware of what was transpiring.

A few minutes later, the five appeared on the trail, 1st Sgt. Hunt leading. Following him were Joseph Guzniczak, Clifford D. Hamric, Kenneth H. Smith, and Patrick J. Stowell. Standing by his jeep, the Lieutenant watched impassively as they walked by.

The group returned within an hour and a half. And then the Lieutenant saw what had occurred. On the shoulders of each of the four sergeants, pinned to clean field jackets, clean because of absent combat conditions, were shiny new second lieutenant bars. The Lieutenant jumped up and, with a broad grin, saluted the newly commissioned. The four were a bit embarrassed, and only Hamric had the presence of mind to return the salute. But this was no place for formality.

The six stood there a brief moment while the event was recounted. Several other sergeants also were commissioned. The ceremony took place in the division CP tent. A Signal Corps photographer was present and took pictures. Maj. Gen. Church pinned the bars. That was all.

That was all? The Lieutenant remained standing for a short while after the four new officers left to wind their way up the hill and to the B Company position. It was more than just a ceremony. The event was a culmination of heroism and devotion to duty, devotion to the company and to the regiment, and abiding by the highest standards of military conduct under fire.

Alone with only Bailey and 2nd Lt. English and later, only Bailey, these four were key to holding the company together as a fighting unit, bringing credit not only upon themselves as leaders but upon the company and the battalion. B Company was one of the few units to hold fast during the spate of NK attacks and counterattacks within the Naktong Pocket. Bailey didn't manage this achievement single-handedly. It was a collective effort, inspired in large part by the calm and decisive leadership of Bailey as passed through the ranks by Guzniczak, Hamric, Smith, and Stowell.

"Up from the ranks"—that's what the military calls this form of commissioning. Some will say it is impossible to be a good officer once the mark of an enlisted rank has been fixed. There is too much leniency in the enlisted character, and leniency does not make for impartial discipline.

On the other hand, others will say that it is impossible to be a good officer until one experiences personally the conditions peculiar to enlisted service, both in garrison and in the field.

Each with his own opinion, of course, but the expressive "officer and gentleman" has, over the centuries, described men from all classes and walks of life, including men from the common ranks, and the United States Army, a practicing example, has remained strong throughout.

The specificity of offering battlefield commissions has never been without its critics. The Lieutenant overheard one battalion staff officer remark that enlisted personnel should not be commissioned until opportunity exists to observe prospective candidates in garrison life. He meant: after the Conflict ends and the battalion returns to Beppu, Japan, those under consideration for commissioning can be evaluated and, if all remains well, given their reward.

Needless to say, the officer was criticized by most other colleagues and his opinion disregarded. The Battle of Beppu would not be renewed. The Conflict in Korea was yet to be won, and what was needed sorely in the immediate was leadership from ranks currently engaged, not promissorily.

Within a short while, the Lieutenant and his party moved up to the line. The position of the 19th was determined as tactical. He went out to Stowell's platoon and organized an OP. The OP overlooked the road extending from Kyongju east to the ocean.

The Lieutenant was not destined to remain long with the company. Battalion called the following morning and directed him to report immediately to that CP. Upon arrival, he learned that both he and Ray Cody would go up with the 17th ROK Regiment. The 13th had been ordered to support that regiment's position within the overall containment strategy to prevent the NK from reaching Kyongju. The 19th's Third Battalion had already been committed. Under the command of Lt. Col. Ayers, that battalion was already attacking in an area that had been infiltrated by the NK.

Both observer parties, along with Capt. Pate, drove north from Kyongju. On the way to the ROK CP the group observed evidence of the struggle that had taken place several days previous. Burned-out three-quarter-ton trucks and damaged artillery pieces were at angles along the road. Personal equipment was seen scattered, too. Yet despite damaging personnel loss suffered by the regiment, the 17th had fought well and had managed to recover much lost ground. Nevertheless, the NK were still strong and capable of continued offensive action.

The ROKs never had much effective artillery of their own. However, recently, they had been given a number of 57 and 75-mm guns and howitzers. The 17th Regiment positioned a battery of 57-mm guns echeloned in depth along the edge of the main road, gun crews standing by. A battery of 75-mm pack howitzers, dug in a valley to the left, were firing volleys at regular intervals.

The regimental CP was off the road to the right, against the side of a hill and within a cluster of huts. The CP was the center structure, the so-called headman's residence. Jeeps and trucks were parked nearby along the road.

The Lieutenant noticed an odd situation. All the ROK vehicles were parked one way, facing south. He asked an interpreter about this and was informed that when circumstances are precarious drivers react by lining up vehicles in the direction projected for withdrawal. No one gives orders for this reaction. It just happens.

The interpreter then warned that the entire valley was under enemy observation, the NK controlling a very high hill some distance beyond. All should be wary of NK mortar and artillery fire. As the sky was still heavily overcast, with intermittent drizzle, friendly planes were not flying supporting missions. An NK weapons barrage and accompanying attack could be expected.

The observer parties arrived at the CP and there, again, the Lieutenant saw Col. Kim Hi Chun. The colonel welcomed the group. With him was the KMAG advisor, Maj. Robert B. Holt. Holt, too, was glad to see the observers. He had barely escaped with his life a day or so ago, but was now smiling about the adventure. He announced that an ROK attack was slated for later that afternoon, but that meanwhile the observers would remain at the CP.

The Lieutenant had a new section chief this trip, Cpl. Robert T. Walsh. Fitzgerald had asked for a rest, and he well deserved one. Nezvensky was up again, and Dear continued as the driver. Now the men were becoming acquainted with some of the ROKs, exchanging cigarettes and other items. Such mingling was good for both armies.

During the day, the Lieutenant noted the meals received by the ROKs. At noon, the men were served a rice ball wrapped in paper that appeared to be a news sheet. Korean characters were printed on the paper, and the men read as they ate. The evening meal, he was told, was much the same except that some meat was included, as well as some vegetables.

Most of the Koreans in and around the CP wore American-style uniforms. Enlisted men wore caps while the officers wore helmet-liners with rank painted on the front. Recruits wore greenish-brown hand-made uniforms. They wore canvas or rubberized shoes. Col. Kim lounged informally without a fatigue shirt, exposing always a clean white undershirt. He was continuously busy, holding conferences with staff members and the occasional visitor.

Preliminary to the attack that Maj. Holt said was being prepared, the three battalion commanders arrived for a final briefing. These men were youngish-looking and seemed hardly the commander type. Nevertheless, Maj. Holt declared that these three were among the best in the ROK army.

One battalion commander was a recent replacement, his predecessor having been shot for disobeying orders. The order had been to stay on the line with his men at all times. However, one night, during a particularly tense situation, the commander's mortar section became edgy and unstable. The commander descended from his hill position and waited the night with the mortar group to steady them. Despite the reasonableness of his action, he was shot.

The movement to the attack began in late afternoon. A battalion of the 17th was given orders to sweep across a rice paddy valley to the foot of Hill 285, the hill from which the NK could observe the road leading south to Kyongju, and mount an attack on the hill itself. The observers and their parties would not accompany the attackers but would remain in the valley, watching the advance, and fire on call. A preparation would precede the operation.

Ray Cody fired the missions. The Lieutenant stood by as an extra, if needed. As the ROKs passed the observer parties on their way forward, they smiled at the Americans and patted their rifles. Some of the ROKs had entered the regiment as replacements only that morning. This would be their first, and for a few, perhaps their last combat action.

The two artillerymen stood together as the attack began. An ROK intelligence officer stood close with an SCR-300 radio, maintaining contact with the lead elements. Cody began firing the preparation. A Battery, 13th Field's howitzers responded.

Up the ROKs climbed until they were out of sight in a low overhead cloud. The NK began defensive fire from the heights. The small arms exchange couldn't be heard by the observer group, but radio reports revealed mounting casualties. Then silence.

In a few moments, another voice came on the air. The original operator with the attackers had just been killed. He had been a pleasant, smiling chap whom the observers remembered from Hyonp'ung. The little group there in the valley was momentarily saddened. Cody now placed fire on the extreme top portion of the hill. The explosions reflected a dull red with the cloud formations ringing the hill.

Then a yell came from the ROK officer manning the radio near the observers that the summit had been reached and the NK were running down the other side. The officer was all smiles, but soon turned pensive when he learned of the deaths of two officer friends.

With the job done, Cody and the Lieutenant, with their parties, walked back to the 17th CP. The sky was darkening early. As the front was yet unstable, the observer sections would return to their home batteries for the night.

On the way back, a sudden flash and a deafening sound nearly panicked the two parties. The jeep drivers stopped their vehicles and the men made ready to fling themselves into nearby ditches. After peering through the gloom, however, the source of the flash and sound was discovered. A heavy tank platoon from the 6th Tank Battalion was firing at NK targets using indirect firing procedures. Their 90-mm guns made heart-stopping roars with each firing.

The next day, an attack by elements of the 19th Regiment's Third Battalion took place on a high hill directly opposite the 17th CP. The group in the CP watched as an American platoon emerged into an open area about thirty yards or so from the top of the hill, the point of departure being a tree and bush entanglement. Halfway between the departure point and the hill's crest was a small copse of high bushes and a lone tree.

Bobbing heads of NK defenders were now noticeable along the hill's summit, and although it was probable that the American attackers could not observe the NK line, hesitation by the Americans brought the forward movement almost to a standstill. A squad only continued on to the copse.

Up on the crest, meanwhile, a crest or ridge that was bald, an energetic NK figure was moving about, gesticulating as he moved, and occasionally peering over the peak edge of the crest at the advancing Americans. At the moment the American squad reached the copse, the gesturing and hurried movements of the NK leader conveyed the image of a man shouting and kicking. In the instant, about seven NK left the crest and charged down toward the copse.

Pressed by this counterattack, the American squad withdrew from the copse and loped back to the tree and bush line where the bulk of the platoon had remained. Two Americans didn't make it, shot as they withdrew. They were seen to pitch forward and roll for a short space before lying still. Firing from the platoon forced the NK to leave the copse area and return to their crest position, seemingly without casualties.

While the observer parties at the 17th CP watched this drama, debating whether to break in and interfere with the unfolding action without clear authorization, a jeep was seen to come up the road quite rapidly. Soon, 1st Lt. Delorimier was recognized as he began searching for a point along the road that offered clear observation of the action taking place on the hill.

Locating such a point just below the group of huts comprising the 17th Regiment's CP, Delorimier began gathering firing data and, shortly, artillery shells began exploding on the NK position along the hill's crest. After a solid artillery pounding, the platoon in the entanglement began once more to move out into the open and toward the crest of the hill. This time the attackers went all the way. And, as it happened many, many times previously, artillery fire provided the cover and assist for the Americans in the face of determined NK opposition. Danger had not yet completely passed, but for the time being a threat to the flank of the 17th ROK Regiment had been blunted.

The 12th NK Division, the enemy unit facing UN troops at Kyongju, was now contained north of the city, but a threat yet remained along the coast, at P'ohang-dong. ROK units had stemmed an enemy drive in that region, just short of the port facility, but were unable to advance due to NK-held high ground both north and immediately south of the port town.

The high ground to the south led to a chain of extremely high mountains stretching to the town of An'gang-ni, a key population center on the road north from Kyongju. If UN forces could gain a foothold in these mountains, pressure on the NK might force their withdrawal from the Kyongju salient, relieving the stress on the 17th ROK Regiment and enabling it to attack north and link up with the P'ohang-dong defenders.

It was decided that the NK positions to the south of P'ohang-dong were the more serious threats to UN efforts. So the 19th Regiment, less the Third Battalion, was ordered to mount an attack there. Commander of the proposed operation was Brig. Gen. Garrison Davidson, assistant commander of the 24th Division.

Thusly, on trucks and tanks, the remaining infantry of the 19th Regiment, along with their artillery support, headed for P'ohang-dong and the second phase of their fireman's mission. Just south of the port, near the town of Togu-dong, the men detrucked and bivouacked. The plan of attack called for the First Battalion to jump off and take a group of low-lying hills below the main objective. The Second Battalion would then pass through the First and attack the high ground and final objective, Hill 482.

The burned-out port of P'ohang-dong nestled between hills and the ocean, to the right of the American force. The town lay at the entrance to a valley that stretched west. Nearby hills and mountains were relatively steep but crumbling, the result of centuries of erosion. Patches of light brown dirt stood out, giving the terrain a lifeless appearance. The hills north of P'ohang-dong were in NK hands.

The American cruiser, *St. Paul*, was standing offshore, firing its guns in support of ROK forces manning dikes just west of the town. White phosphorus shells were fired occasionally, the explosions spewing fireballs with burning particles showering every which way.

Once, splashes in the water close to the cruiser denoted NK counterbattery fire. This brought a quick response from the ship. A smoke screen was hurriedly manufactured, and the ship's position was altered a bit to confuse the range for NK gunners.

The Second Battalion jumped off about 1700 that afternoon, but E Company, leading out, advanced only about 100 yards before the men were pinned down by the firing of an NK machine gun. Several well-camouflaged NK positions on the high hillside had eluded earlier observation efforts. Concluding it to be useless to continue an evening attack, the battalion remained in place, allowing the hillside to be raked by harassing artillery fire through the night. At dawn, several prone, lifeless NK were seen, presumably some of the NK who had held up the advance the previous evening.

An air strike was on the agenda, scheduled to begin prior to the renewal of the ground attack. Promptly at 0900, four F-51 Mustangs flew over. After circling a bit to get their bearings, the pilots peeled and hit the hillside with napalm and .50-caliber bullets. The area was too large for pinpoint raiding by the pilots, but their attacks were morale-building.

The ground push was then resumed, and this time there was no resistance. The NK had bolted. Warm rice was found at the top of the hill, evidence that the NK had intended, at first, to make a stand. The size of the American force, plus the appearance of the planes, probably changed their minds.

The success of this clearing operation paved the way for area occupation by ROK units. Their troops began moving in immediately, men from the 22nd ROK Regiment. This regiment would soon spearhead an attack across to An'gang-ni to relieve pressure on the 17th ROK Regiment, north of Kyongju. The American 19th Regiment now began withdrawing, leaving only one casualty, an E Company sergeant killed the evening before.

The two 19th battalions remained in the vicinity that night, and for the first time since arriving in Korea, because the weather was still damp and chilly, Ray Cody and the Lieutenant, with their enlisted parties, bedded down in a Korean farmhouse. One of the men made a fire in the stove in the kitchen portion of the house, the stove being slightly below ground level. The heat thus generated began flowing under the floor of the doll-like sleeping quarters—the raised portion of the house—making everyone feel comfortable.

However, the generated heat also began to force out the little mites burrowed in the dried mud floor. Where else could they find pleasure but on the bodies of the sleeping Americans? About 0300, the Lieutenant had reached his itching limit and moved outside, dampness notwithstanding. His departure was not popular with nature's littlest creatures for they left him quickly to seek diversion elsewhere, permitting unbroken slumber until dawn.

The new day broke warm and clear, and the combat team began retracing the road to Kyongju. The Lieutenant's jeep, by this time, still the castoff from the 63rd Field, was almost completely worn out, and it chugged to a halt about three-quarters of the way up a long last hill. The driver of a truck following, loaded with infantry, eased behind the jeep and, shifting gears appropriately, began pushing it to the crest where the motor was restarted. Dear promised, for the twenty-seventh time, to look into the possibility of securing a replacement jeep.

Firemen days were over for the 19th Regimental Combat Team. Bivouac was the order of the day while the ROKs continued to reorganize and consolidate their positions. The forward observers were recalled to their respective batteries and spent the next several days resting, attending to hygiene and generally preparing for the next call to duty.

Maj. Holt had hinted several days previous that something big was about to break. In fact, he had stated that he had orders in his pocket that he couldn't disclose, but that it wouldn't be long until he could reach for them and read them aloud. His statement prompted the Lieutenant to recall Jerry Fly's comment about the Marines getting ready for a big movement.

Meanwhile, the Americans continued readying their equipment, securing shelter from the continuing coolish weather and hoping that whatever was going to happen would happen. "Let's get this damn war over with as soon as possible!" This and myriad variations of same were central to the mind and speech of everyone everywhere within the 24th Division. Clearly, something was brewing, and the men could hardly wait.

Recrossing the Naktong

One of the more interesting experiences at the brief rest near Kyongju was the opportunity to observe the integration of the KATUSAs into American units. At first, these solemn-faced youngsters hesitated to eat much American food. "Too much, too much," they would protest. "Too rich," their interpreters would say. This hesitation lasted only about a week. They soon began wolfing down American portions in the best GI manner and often stood in line for "seconds." They began gaining weight, causing real worry about their becoming too roly-poly to perform their jobs properly.

The primary duty of the artillery augmentations was that of manning perimeter defense positions, thereby permitting Americans formerly on the perimeter to concentrate on the more technical functions of the battery. However, after commanders had had a chance to observe the Koreans' willingness to work, some were assigned to technical sections where they were taught howitzer drill, radio and wire operations, and ammunition handling. Whole units fell to the task of becoming teachers and liking it.

KATUSAs in the infantry were assigned as integral members of squads. They not only carried ammunition for mortars and bazookas, but were trained to fire these weapons and the BAR as well. Some KATUSAs became full-fledged riflemen. One squad in B Company, 19th Regiment, later received considerable publicity as an "international squad." Its leader, Sfc. Arthur C. Dudley, was a Negro, and the squad contained white Americans, Negro-Americans and Koreans.[1] A group of KATUSAs in C Company became the point and flank guard for that unit while on the march.

Some mishandling of the Koreans was inevitable and particularly during pressure-type situations when the language barrier was most pronounced. There was often some shoving and kicking by Americans to enforce their will. Mostly, however, group pressure put a stop to such misconduct.

Proper Korean names were not learned well by the Americans, so new ones were often tendered. Such names as Salt and Pepper, Joe, PeeWee, Lefty, Hari, and Kari became part of the everyday chitchat in a typical howitzer position or infantry line. Two arrivals in the A Battery wire section were distinguished as Pete and Repeat. A KATUSA in the Service Battery became known as Moon.

The KATUSAs received only $2.00 per month for their services (American currency equivalent), but were quite satisfied about it all the same.[2] They were eating better, clothed better, and were in a cleaner environment than had been their lot in the towns and villages with their families.

On balance, except for the dangers involved, the KATUSAs had begun experiencing Western living, even under spartan-like conditions, and the experience would change their lives forever. They liked what they saw, liked what they experienced, and most, if not all, would carry the desire to continue these experiences in their home environments when the war ended. Korean culture would never again be what it was on Sunday, June 25, 1950.

A trace of restlessness was just beginning to be felt by the men after the few days of relative inactivity when, on the morning of September 15, the battery telephone rang, and Battalion informed all that the Marines had made their move. The First Marine Division had made a successful landing at Inch'on, the port city for Seoul. The Marines were accompanied by the 7th Infantry Division. The Seventh, filled with replacements from both the States and South Korea (KATUSAs), had been training in maneuver areas almost from the moment the other three Occupation divisions had been committed.

Within a minute, there was not a man who had not heard the news. Men slapped each other on the backs and grinned. There were more "goddamns," "We'll show those dirty bastards," and "It won't be long, now" that morning than in the many previous weeks.

That afternoon, as the Lieutenant stood by one of the howitzers, several truckloads of ROK soldiers began passing by, headed south, and to the accompaniment of a strange collection of sounds. As the Americans ran to look, a GI truck hove into view in which was seated a makeshift Korean brass band. The band was playing the South Korean *Victory March* or something closely resembling same. The tune seemed inharmonious, but the KATUSAs recognized what was being played. They smiled at one another, and one or two actually broke out in song, causing the GIs standing nearby to titter self-consciously.

Shortly, the word passed that this was the 17th Regiment, just relieved, and now on its way to Pusan where the unit would embark on LSTs for Inch'on and eventually Seoul. The regiment had been picked by President Syngman Rhee to participate in the fight for Seoul and would, once the battle ended, be the first South Korean unit to reenter the capital in triumph. This movement had been the gist, apparently, of the secret information Maj. Holt carried in his pocket.

Of all the ROK units deserving of the honor of participating in this last campaign against the NK, the 17th Regiment probably was the most deserving. It had fought hard and well. It was the most respected. The waves and smiles tendered by the men of the 13th Field Artillery Battalion as the 17th Regiment passed by that afternoon were occasioned by feelings of the highest regard.

Capt. Still received a message from Battalion the evening of the 16th for A Battery to leave the bivouac at 0700 the following morning. The 13th, along with the infantry, would organize a temporary bivouac along the Kumho River, near the recent Kyongsan rest area, and prepare for a river-crossing operation. The usually calm and taciturn captain became so excited about the Conflict approaching a final phase that he was seen to walk about the battery area long after most had gone to sleep.

A and B Batteries moved out promptly the morning of the 17th. C Battery would be along only after the Third Battalion, 19th Regiment, was relieved of its combat commitment. The remainder of the 19th was already on the road and being transported in part by an ROK army truck company, equipped with new Japanese-made trucks.

Japan had been supplying much replacement materiel for Eighth Army needs. Radio batteries, bulbs, and various mechanical parts of high wear-out composition were being manufactured in quantity by Japanese firms at a time when immediate resupply from the States was an impossibility.

The Japanese had also been contracted to provide much in the way of materiel resupply for the ROK army. The trucks were a case in point. Japanese trucks were easier to pilot on the narrow, pitted, dirt Korean roads and were more economical to operate than American models. The shortcoming, of course, was that these vehicles had a shorter wear-and-tear life than the larger, heavier American ones. Nevertheless, the Americans took pleasure at seeing their counterparts sport new equipment, such being in complete contrast to the dowdy and usually worn-out American trucks that had been theirs previously. The ROK truck drivers, it was noted, seemed to hold their heads a bit higher when passing through native villages.

The convoy moved rapidly. The new bivouac was reached about noon, and the men dismounted for a final rest and regrouping. Most guessed what was going to happen. There would be a river crossing under fire followed by a breakout up the main highway toward Taejon.

The 5th RCT, now attached to the 24th Division as the replacement regiment for the 34th RCT, had been brought up from the Masan front and was at that very moment attacking along the east river road toward Waegwan. Waegwan, the point of a major road and rail crossing across the Naktong River, had been a cavalry objective, but that division thus far had been unable to reach and clear it. If and when the 5th completed this clearing assignment, both the 19th and the 21st Regiments would move up for the crossing operation. Everyone now sat back to await the outcome.

With the bivouac reached, the observers went up immediately to join the infantry. The Lieutenant was assigned to C Company, and Totty went to A Company. B Company was placed in reserve. Coles was still the A Battery executive officer. C Company had been selected to spearhead the assault.

Plans had been made to move out that night, but nothing happened. This was fortunate for the Lieutenant because, for the second time since his arrival in Korea, he became sick. A severe headache caused by a stomach upset drove him to wandering about the bivouac in pain. He was particularly worried about his condition in view of the pending military operation. Finally, unable any longer to stand the misery, he jammed several fingers down his throat. Relieved at last, he lay down and slept away the weakness.

On the next afternoon, as the men still waited, loud explosions were heard from the direction of the river. Aircraft in formation buzzed overhead. An officer from battalion told the men that the Air Force was bombing likely defense positions across the Naktong. The men grew reticent after this announcement. There would be casualties resulting from this operation.

The regiment moved out of the bivouac on the morning of the nineteenth. This was it, the movement to attack. The 5th Regiment had retaken Waegwan in a two-day operation. The cavalry was still engaged in the hills northeast of the town. The 21st Regiment had already made a crossing that morning and was initiating action slowly up the main highway toward Kumch'on. The 19th had been ordered to effect a secondary crossing south of Waegwan.

In contrast to the many rainy and misty days around Kyongju, the nineteenth of September was bright, hot, and without a cloud. The Lieutenant, with his section, traveled behind the lead truck. He had Dear, Walsh, and Nezvensky. C Company officers, besides now-Capt. Rockwerk, were Lts. Ray Dowe (newly assigned from B Company), John Krasco,[3] Orlando Ortiz, Chester Van Orman, and the executive officer, Richard D. Haugen. M/Sgt. Ray Point, the grizzled veteran, was the field first sergeant.

As the convoy wound along the Taegu bypass, two enclosed Eighth Army Headquarters jeeps approached. Each jeep carried an elderly appearing civilian as a passenger, both men dressed in white or almond-colored outer wraps. The Lieutenant was puzzled. They weren't correspondents. They weren't foreign military officers, either. Then it came.

He had read in the *Stars and Stripes* about the arrival in Korea of the first Stateside entertainer to visit United Nations troops. He was Al Jolson, the singer. His pianist, Harry Akst, accompanied him. These were the two VIPs in the jeeps. No one got a good look, but a number commented later about seeing the jeeps pass by. Jolson had performed for cavalry troops in and around Taegu. None of the 24th Division personnel attended, so far as the Lieutenant knew.[4]

The jump-off point was reached in late afternoon. The observers dismounted and readied equipment. The Lieutenant carried one section of a SCR-610 radio, while Cpl. Walsh carried the other or battery pack. Nezvensky carried blankets and rations on another packboard. All was in order.

At the point where a ferry and a tiny Korean hamlet named Hasan-dong were located, near where the Naktong makes a bend, and where there is a wide, sandy beach, a crossing was already being made by the Second Battalion. The unit was encountering light sniper resistance and fire from several small NK artillery pieces.

Just after the trucks carrying First Battalion troops had been unloaded and were being turned around, several mortar shells exploded near the road, panicking the Eighth Army truck drivers into dashing madly for cover. When the mortar fire seemed to cease, the drivers ran to their trucks and gunned them at top speed toward the rear. The men in C Company merely chuckled.

The crossing not yet secure, the men moved up a little trail behind a rise to wait. Sounds of firing could be heard, and no one said much. Rockwerk moved from platoon to platoon checking equipment and giving instructions. Finally, a radio message ordered the company to the crossing site.

The company moved rapidly back down the trail and ahead into a marsh, just short of the site. A grove of trees and high bushes bordered the sandy beach. The regiment's heavy mortars were emplaced here, firing in support of the crossing units. The aid station was here also, and several wounded were lying on stretchers.

The company now filed onto the open beach. Fortunately, the sun was low in the sky, casting shadows that would complicate direct firing by the NK. A unit from the 3rd Engineer Battalion was waiting with small assault boats, metal tubs with oars. Men assigned to the boats would push them to free water where, fully loaded, the boats would float. Then all would climb aboard and paddling begin. Near the opposite shoreline, all would leap out and push the boats ashore.

Two engineers were assigned to each boat, and these brought the boats back after each assault wave. As the procedure called for each assault company to cross as a unit, the C Company men waited on the beach until a sufficient number of boats was gathered. While waiting, an NK small caliber shell exploded about thirty-five yards down the beach. Everyone hit the sand and stayed down until the engineer leader shouted, "Let's go!"

Walsh and the Lieutenant, with radio sections on their backs, were told to climb into their boat immediately, but the others waded into the water and began pushing. About midstream, the men climbed aboard, and the Lieutenant was afraid his boat would tip. It didn't. The far side of the river was reached without difficulty, although one man in the company took a bullet in the shoulder, the result of a stray sniper shot. Once on the far beach, everyone ran for cover. The Lieutenant and Walsh could only walk.

The C Company objective was the securing of a road leading west from the Naktong plus the occupation of a group of low-lying hills to the right of that road. The road was a continuation of the one on which the battalion traveled to the crossing site. The crossing site was actually a ford during the normal dry periods of the year.

It was growing dark. With the Second Battalion holding high ground on the left, it was decided that the First Battalion would remain in the brush along the shoreline for the night and attack in the morning. So in the middle of what appeared to be a damp cornfield, the men deployed and waited through the darkness.

At dawn, C Company moved to spearhead the attack on the hilly objective. Infantry-artillery cooperation was excellent throughout as, prior to the attack, a thunderous barrage, comprising both light and medium artillery, was laid down.

With the company ready to begin its advance, the artillery was asked to lift the barrage. Nothing happened. Finally, the Lieutenant radioed his S-3 controller and asked that the barrage be lifted. An answering voice stated that the barrage was covering an attack and therefore could not be lifted. The Lieutenant replied that he was in the attack and that the men could not move until artillery fire ceased. A moment later there was silence.

Capt. Rockwerk now ordered Dowe's platoon up the first hill. The men moved slowly, expecting resistance. A small land mine was tripped, but no one was hurt. No resistance was encountered. Within minutes, the objective was occupied.

The Second Battalion then started forward on the left. Seeing these men edge on, the Lieutenant asked for and received a one-round concentration on some flat land in front of the battalion line. The men in the advancing group, seeing the round explode, hesitated. Noting this, the Lieutenant called 1st Lt. Yates, the observer with E Company, explaining what he had done. E Company officers then moved up and the men, again, pushed on. There was no NK resistance.

With C Company on its objective, the Lieutenant was ordered to B Company for another hill assault. He stood with 1st Lt. Bailey watching as the men climbed the hill. There was no call or need for artillery close support.

It was back to C Company again, and this time for a foot operation over hills and ridges paralleling the river to the north. The regimental objective now was the clearing of enemy from the river's edge all the way to the Waegwan crossing and the main Seoul-Pusan highway. The regiment would then move to join the 21st Regiment, now several miles on the way toward Kumch'on.

The men struggled over mountain trails. The sandy soil and jutting rocks caused feet to slip and equipment to be dropped. Tempers grew short. The exhilaration that had gripped everyone the previous days faded completely. This was a mop-up operation that was proving more exhausting to the conquerors than to the conquered. Yet as none at the moment knew the extent of the NK withdrawal, this operation was necessary.

An evening halt was called at a point halfway to the final objective. The battalion spent the night on a low ridge, away from the river and above a burning village, fired deliberately on the chance that the huts could harbor NK snipers. This night, September 20, was the first really chilly night on the line. Men were granted permission to build fires, but only until dark. The Lieutenant fell asleep warm, but woke about 0300 shaking cold. Even his blanket proved of limited value. Many of the men without blankets spent a miserable night.

The hill-climbing resumed the following morning and tempers were even shorter, what with the general lack of rest. Men cursed at the slightest difficulty. Whenever they strained to the top of one hill, another just like it was always just ahead.

Regiment stopped the operation about noon. The movement was proving a useless expenditure of energy now that it was increasingly evident that the NK had departed this particular area. The companies would stay the night in position. Tempers abated and smiles returned. This phase was over and done with.

Immediately after breakfast, the two battalions moved in columns up the river road. Vehicles still had not reached the newly won side of the Naktong. Pontoon bridges were being constructed, both at Waegwan and at Pongch'ondong, the latter where the 19th had made the crossing. The British 27th Brigade crossed the Naktong after the 19th and was, at that moment, moving inland, supported by C Battery, 13th Field.

The town of Waegwan shortly came into view. Then the main north-south highway was discerned, a familiar sight to the "old men" of the 19th. Suddenly truck noises were heard, and a convoy of trucks appeared. A cheer went up. The men would walk no farther. The line-up began; no hurry, now. The men mounted, motors gunned, and the convoy set off with its load of "happy campers."

The convoy motored past the town of Yongmok and to a point about halfway to Kumch'on. Then, it moved off the road and into a nearly dry streambed. The men detrucked. The artillery had arrived earlier, less C Battery, of course. Dear appeared with the jeep, and the observer section was reunited.

The first order of business was a whore's bath and a shave. Later, the Lieutenant burned his map of the Waegwan area, following procedure. No need of the map, now. They were on their way to Taejon and victory.

Songju

The regiment was scheduled for the long-awaited jump-off toward Taejon the following morning, but for some reason or other there was a delay. The men lay about their bivouac waiting impatiently for the tanks to arrive, signaling the start of the march. Perhaps there had been a problem moving supplies across the river, particularly ammunition. Whatever, the men could wait. They had come this far. The rest of the way was a breeze.

It was just after the noon meal, the men continuing to rest, the only audible sounds emanating from the kitchen trucks, when a loud command was voiced: "Saddle up!"

"We're up," came answering voices from the brush piles and sandpits as the troops struggled to their feet. "Form companies, now!" Maybe this was it.

The Lieutenant, roused from his own somewhat fitful snooze, got to his feet just about the time a messenger drove up with news of a disaster. The Argyll and Sutherland unit with the British 27th Brigade had just been hit hard by a friendly air strike in the vicinity of the town of Songju, in direct line beyond the river crossing used by the 19th Regiment. The tragedy took place on Hill 282.

As a result of this mistake and the casualties resulting, the Argylls had been forced to withdraw from the hill. The NK then reoccupied it, beefing up their resistance and endangering the flanks of the 24th Division companies moving toward Kumch'on. The First Battalion of the 19th was being ordered to Songju immediately to flank the enemy and relieve the pressure, notably on the British, but on the 21st Regiment as well.

Reaching into his dispatch case, the Lieutenant realized shockingly that he had burned the relevant map. What a goof. Songju had been clearly outlined on that map.

He sent Dear to Battalion for a replacement map, meanwhile moving to round up the other section members. Dear returned shortly with another map, but said he almost wasn't given one. Lt. Col. Langlois was quite perturbed over the Lieutenant's disposing of the other one. The Lieutenant privately didn't blame him, but this was not the moment to reflect long on an error of commission.

The columns were forming. The tanks had arrived. C Company would be leading again. Rockwerk had once joked about the First Battalion's formation being like a "cab," a constant, stuck-in-the rut CAB, meaning, C Company leading out followed by A Company and B Company in reserve. The same formation constituted this operation. The joke had lost its freshness.

Totty and the Lieutenant would be the observers with the infantry. The artillery would follow closely and be ready for instant deployment. The infantry would walk this time, leaving the tanks free for quick maneuver.

The column began moving. Dear's jeep was the first vehicle. The tanks did not lead out. Two files of infantry marched at extended interval along the edges of the road. The Lieutenant soon became embarrassed riding and began walking with the men. The advancing companies passed the 52nd Field in position. The Lieutenant recognized several of the NCOs by their howitzers as former 48th Field men. Waves were exchanged.

A turnoff was reached, and the battalion left the main north-south road to head southwest and the virgin inland area around Songju. The 21st Regiment was about four miles further along the main road and near Kumch'on, expecting heavy resistance. That regiment would not advance too far until Songju was cleared.

The column moved steadily. The road distance to the objective was estimated at about twelve miles. Expected time of arrival was 2200 hours.

As they marched, the Lieutenant became acquainted with several who were marching with him. There was Sgt. Simington, Sgt. Major General Simington (his claimed names), the 81-mm mortar observer with C Company. Simington was a stocky lad from the Peach State, who never ceased expounding the glories of the South and particularly the pleasures from resting under peach trees in southern Georgia.

His witty loquaciousness made the going easier for those around him. He articulated well the thoughts of that mostly taciturn company of soldiers, and they repaid him by being ardent listeners. Simington had more friends and was known more widely throughout the First Battalion than most any other, officer or enlisted.

Another man who had become both popular and respected was the weapons platoon sergeant, Eliones Gant. Sgt. Gant was a tall Negro who had joined the company only a few weeks before. He was friendly, witty and above all efficient. His men swore by him. Where Simington's humor was outwardly inviting and neighborly, Gant's was pungent, reflecting perhaps the struggles of his race. Simington appealed to the homesickness and generally human instincts of the men. Gant magnified the imperfections of the Army and life proper. As the men were well versed in SNAFU, they heartily appreciated the latter's observations.[1]

The Lieutenant mused long over this juxtaposition of two races and cultures, each representative contributing something to the success of this particular military operation and to the morale of the men taking part. Neither seemed overtly aware of the other as products of racial and cultural antagonism in their home environments. They were simply two soldiers walking down the road toward Songju, doing their duty, helping where they could, Negro and southern white, Americans together in this hellhole of war.

It was obvious, as the combat team advanced through enemy-held countryside, that each village and hamlet had to be investigated, cursorily at least. Everyone had to move quietly, as any loud noise or firing would alert the NK, enabling the latter time to organize a line of resistance somewhere. Once, when a stream had to be crossed, the column stood in place a full hour while mine detectors were used along the stream's edge.

Finally, about midnight, an increasing number of huts denoted the outskirts of a larger town. Songju had been reached.

The column slowed and few words were spoken. Two tanks, by this time, were leading the battalion. The Lieutenant set his radio. The men moved onto a narrow part of the road or town street, along which were larger dwellings separated by areas of seemingly desolate space. It was all very eerie. The men had their rifles at the ready.

Suddenly the night was shattered by machine gun fire. Column silence was broken by the .50-caliber on the lead tank. The column halted. Men waited apprehensively. Then a forward movement began once more.

The Lieutenant soon learned what had happened. The lead tank, as it approached a road intersection, encountered several NK struggling to set up an antitank gun. The tank's machine gunner either cut the group down or scattered it. This incident indicated that the operation, thus far, had been successful. Hoped-for surprise had been achieved. The fact that no organized resistance had developed was comforting.

The company now moved slowly up a slight grade, the road leading through the western outskirts of the town. As he walked, the Lieutenant noticed that both sides of the road or street were lined with walls high enough to prevent a person from peering over while walking or standing. He thought for a moment how easily the column could be grenaded.

As he shuddered at the possibility, a loud explosion occurred just over the rise and at the head of the column. This was followed by a much larger explosion and then intermittent detonations. A fire broke out, and the sky was soon a reflection of bright light. The whirr of exploding mortar shells cut through the night. Everyone tensed and mentally began deploying in anticipation of engaging in a firefight.

However, word came back shortly that one of the lead platoon's launcher teams encountered an NK ammunition truck moving slowly along the road toward the UN force and had attacked it, setting it and several surrounding houses afire.[2] Although understood, the incident, by itself, was a tactical error. The presence of UN troops was now known and a battle could ensue.

The truck continued to burn and ammunition explode for about forty-five minutes. Then, with the fire dying out, the company readied to resume the advance. Just as the men began plodding forward, a two-and-a-half-ton truck came out of a side street or road about seventy-five yards behind the Lieutenant and turned onto the main road in the direction of the still-burning houses. The driver of the truck geared up quickly and sped forward without lights. As it definitely was a GI truck, no one challenged it, and it passed the Lieutenant and the men around him without slowing. There were no individuals in the truck's bed, but two men were noted riding in the cab.

Reaching the top of the rise, the truck's progress was blocked by a waiting tank. The driver sounded his horn, and one GI shouted for the tank to pull over. Then an unknown hero took a closer look. There was a yell and a cry, "They're gooks!"

The two truck occupants tumbled out and dashed for underbrush along the road. The tank's turret swung around and for a few moments the brush was raked with machine gun fire. When silence had returned, men looked at each other and laughed nervously. Not a few harbored some admiration for these two who had gambled boldly in their escape attempt. They almost succeeded. One was killed; the other captured.

The column now began edging over the rise. Houses on both sides of the road continued to burn, the flames curling lazily and reflecting in the faces of the men as they approached. It was about 0200. Many in the company had been up and on the go close to twenty hours without rest. A halt to the operation was now called.

Capt. Rockwerk ordered a company guard the remainder of the night; everyone on the alert, but every other man allowed to doze lightly. A and B Companies moved to a perimeter defense near the center of Songju. C Company would remain at the last point of advance.

As Dear slowed his jeep near the middle of the company perimeter, one of the tankers accidentally touched the trigger of a turret-mounted machine gun. A few rounds blasted out. In sudden panic, Dear started to leap out of his still-moving vehicle. In seconds, however, he realized what he had done and just as quickly edged back onto the seat, grabbing the steering wheel and jamming the brakes to keep the vehicle from heading into one of the burning houses. He mumbled something to himself. Those around him chuckled and kidded him. It had been a hard day.

With only three hours or so until the breaking of light, the observer group wrapped blankets about themselves and slept. The Lieutenant stretched out on the road in front of a former store, now being charred by persistent flames, and began dozing almost as he finished tucking a blanket about his shoulders.

Although it seemed but a short minute, the battalion rested about two and a half hours. Just at first light, 1st Lt. Haugen began moving about, rousing the men onto their feet. As he was so engaged, a group of battalion staff led by Lt. Col. Naudts walked into the area in the manner of a swift-moving combat patrol. The group was making a personal reconnaissance of the perimeter. As both Walsh and the Lieutenant were lying in the open on the street, covered in blankets, the staff may have thought them casualties. One officer prodded Walsh with a carbine and leaped back when the latter stirred.

The fires, begun hours earlier, were mostly burned out, but a smoky haze remained. The familiar dull scraping of C-ration cans being opened was beginning to be heard as was the inevitable coughing by men who had not covered themselves well during the few hours of rest.

More orders were issued. C Company would displace to a hill at the eastern approach to the town, overlooking the road leading to Hill 282. B Company would remain inside Songju as a security force, and A Company was placed in reserve. There was little time to lose before the general haze enveloping the town dissipated. C Company mounted tanks and jeeps and traveled to its new position.

The hill designated for occupation by the company was not a high one, but by the time the men began climbing the sun was up and the early heat, coupled with a general weariness, was almost too much for many. The men literally crawled up the hill trails. The Lieutenant passed one lad who was on his hands and knees, pulling his BAR. The Lieutenant was puffing alarmingly by the time he reached his OP and had to sit and rest a few minutes before orienting himself and performing necessary radio checks.

No one in or around Songju at that hour knew the NK strength or capability there. The town had been a vital communications center for the NK, and the Air Force, as one could see clearly now, virtually leveled it. Still, there were several small hamlets in the immediate vicinity which had probably been used by the NK as troop barracks and storage depots. These few hamlets looked untouched by the strafings and bombings.

B Company immediately began combing Songju, rounding up suspicious-looking men. The Lieutenant observed about seventy-five men dressed in surprisingly clean white clothing being lined up. Since the NK had often reverted to traditional garb to avoid capture, the sight of so many men of military age wearing clothing almost too clean for the circumstances aroused suspicion. These men were soon tagged and marked for further questioning and possible incarceration as prisoners of war.

It was at Songju that the Lieutenant first saw the narrow, tubular carrying cases which, according to some, were used by patrols and other elements of the NK army for storage of civilian clothing. Easily handled and just as easily discarded, the cases confirmed an assumption Americans had made all along, that many of the earlier infiltrations of friendly lines were carried out not by so-called Fifth Column Volunteers, but by NK dressed in civilian clothes.

The Lieutenant had now organized his OP on the hill overlooking the road leading east to the Naktong River. Another road, across and below a bare hill to his front, led diagonally to the southeast. Just at the foot of this bare hill and on the side away and out of sight from the Lieutenant, a small hamlet nestled, partially hidden by a grove of trees. It was a typical small Korean habitat, and as there were several other hamlets in the vicinity, each looking deserted, no one bothered to check it out.

About 1100, an A Company patrol began walking along this southeast road. At a point where a foot trail from the hidden hamlet intersected with the road, the patrol was fired on by NK camouflaged among the group of hamlet huts. A firefight seemed to be in the making. The patrol withdrew.

Before committing foot soldiers, however, it was decided to send a tank along the road for further reconnaissance. A Pershing tank from the 6th Tank

Battalion was seen to edge out slowly. Moments later, with a roar from its engine, the tank moved rapidly toward the danger area.

Then, as the tank neared the trail intersection, shells from a small NK field piece were seen to carom off the side of the tank. Far from being a harassing action, a major NK strong point had been flushed, potentially a formidable roadblock comprising both small arms and light artillery.

The tank eased a bit after this encounter, and the turret was seen to swing so as to point the 90-mm gun in the direction of NK fire. Still moving, two rounds were fired from the tank. Then the tank's driver stopped the tank. One more shot was fired.

Now the tank was observed reversing direction as if preparing for a turning maneuver. The vehicle veered to the left of the road when, suddenly, it listed into a sunken trail or trap. With a shudder noticeable to all who had been watching, the tank stopped. Two figures climbed out of the turret opening and dashed for cover in a nearby ditch.

Seeing what had happened, the Lieutenant radioed A Battery, alerting that unit for a fire mission. Meanwhile, the division artillery spotter plane pilot, who had been flying in the area, heard the fire mission request and buzzed over for a look. The pilot, 1st Lt. William F. Proncavage, radioed that he could see the hamlet clearly and would handle the mission. This intervention of a mission seemed perfectly logical. The Lieutenant had not been able to see the huts in question and would have to guess a destruction mission. But before Proncavage could transmit his initial data, an air strike got underway.

During the sojourn at Kyongsan, an Air Force liaison section was attached to the 19th Regiment. The section consisted of a jeep with driver and radio operator or controller, the latter in constant contact with Air Force spotter planes. Regiment or battalion, whichever happened to be the responsible unit, could request an air strike through this liaison section without having to clear with higher channels. The request would then be radioed to an area spotter who, in turn, after preliminary tactical flying, would call upon close-support aircraft flying in the immediate area or, if none were able to respond, message the nearest airfield for support. This air support request process was proving to be very successful at this stage of the fighting.

Two F-51s soon appeared over Songju. After circling several times to firm direction and target, they zoomed down on the hamlet. The planes strafed, rocketed, and napalmed, starting a fire. The strike lasted about five to ten minutes.

As soon as the planes completed their mission and flew away, a second tank began moving along the road toward the trail intersection. Gathering speed, the tank reached a point halfway to the other disabled tank when a tremendous explosion rent the air. The first tank had missed it, but the second struck an antitank mine buried there in the road. Black smoke curled up. Three crewmen were seen to emerge from the turret. The driver's hatch remained closed. The three, blackened by smoke, jumped off the tank and onto the road, to be picked up by an ambulance jeep that hurried to the scene. The driver, apparently killed by the blast, was left.

With two tanks out of action, it was decided to commit A Company on the hill opposite the hamlet. Commanding the company was Capt. Sam S. Walker, son of Eighth Army Commander, Lt. Gen. Walton H. Walker. The curious had asked about Sam when he arrived in the 19th while the regiment was near Chinju, wondering particularly about his attitude. It was reported that he was respected by his lieutenants and platoon sergeants, and that the men in the squads liked him.

The Lieutenant watched as the company moved up toward the crest of the slope. Then, as the lead squad reached the hilltop, an NK artillery shell exploded close by, killing one man. The squad backed off immediately, and the Lieutenant heard Totty, the observer with the company, call for artillery support.

Mortars began exploding on the hamlet, and by the time A Battery got its first round on the way, mortar shells had virtually covered the hamlet area. Both artillery and mortar shells fell for about ten minutes. Then, silence. The company regained the hilltop, and this time there was no enemy fire. Songju and its approaches were cleared.

First Lt. Proncavage, meanwhile, was observing what the ground observers could not—a major NK withdrawal through hill passes to the northwest. With Songju now completely in UN hands, the NK concluded that further resistance was futile and so began to retreat in the most expedient way possible. This meant traveling the hilly trails to the northwest.

As these retreating remnants neared the bare hilltops, Proncavage called for artillery volleys from both A Battery and a battery from the 11th Field, the latter having arrived belatedly as a general support unit. Intermittent firing at these NK groups continued for over an hour until no further ground movement could be seen.

All that remained was for the British to arrive and occupy Songju.

Darkness was approaching, earlier than in past weeks. Blankets were distributed to the company. The Lieutenant spread his poncho on the ground and arranged his blankets in the form of a bedroll. The air, hot during the day, had cooled considerably and would be crisp by morning. Before lying down, he fired two defensive concentrations on the road below. He would be ready for any surprise assault, although no one else expected this.

All was quiet that night and the next morning. The NK had completely withdrawn. The 19th began marking time, waiting for the 27th Brigade to arrive.

About 1400 that afternoon, the advance column of the 27th was spotted on the road approaching Songju. As the brigade column came into full view, the Lieutenant saw that 1st Lt. Delorimier was with them as the forward observer. (Delorimier later reported that he had left his position on Hill 282 minutes before American planes bombed and strafed it. He had had a close call and did not smile as he recounted his experience.)

First reports held that an entire British company was decimated, but Capt. Rockwerk said later that far fewer were actually killed.[3] The UN air assault had been a tragic error and one likely to have repercussions. But mistakes do occur in war, and the Lieutenant briefly recalled the incident of the South Korean F-

51 strafing escaping Americans running along the stream valley below the Kum River that Sunday afternoon of July 16.

With the arrival of the British, C Company was ordered back into Songju. A truck convoy had been observed snaking into the town a few hours before, and the vehicles were now parked on the road facing toward Kumch'on. The men walking toward the trucks were jovial. This had been an easy operation. There had been few casualties. The taste of approaching final victory was whetting the expective appetites of every man present.

As the Lieutenant waited in his jeep for the trucks to start moving, he heard a shot from one of the lead trucks and, in the next instant, saw a steel helmet fly up into the air. A GI came running yelling for a stretcher jeep. "A ROK killed himself," he said.

The Lieutenant got out of his jeep and walked forward. He soon learned that the shooting was an accident. So many of the troops sitting in trucks placed rifle butts on the truck beds and nozzles pointing almost under their chins. Such was the case with this unfortunate KATUSA. He had neglected to put his rifle on SAFE, and a jarring of the rifle detonated a shell, the bullet going completely through his head and sending the helmet into the air.

The convoy soon began moving, and a streambed bivouac was reached in short order. It was September 25. The men learned that the 21st Regiment had recaptured Kumch'on and was a few miles beyond, walking and with tank support. The job of these men was ferreting out any NK along the road and not bypass any pocket of resistance.

Now, however, it was opined that the NK, after initial resistance at the several Naktong River crossing points, had realized their hopeless predicament and were madly racing north, attempting to escape across the Parallel before advancing Marines and the 7th Infantry Division, with associated ROK units, could cut them off. Little rear-guard action by isolated pockets of NK was expected.

The men of the 19th Regiment knew they would be on the road in the morning. They also knew that they would pass through the lines of the 21st and continue alone to Taejon. Had the 34th Regiment still been operational within the division, it would have been given Taejon as a march objective. Excitement swept both the infantry companies and artillery batteries. Men could hardly contain themselves. The Lieutenant wandered out onto the road after dark with his section chief, Cpl. Walsh. They encountered Capt. Still. Still, also, was caught up in the emotion but so restrained that one had to know the man well to recognize the feeling. Later, Capt. Pate arrived with the news that B Company would lead out in the morning and the Lieutenant would accompany.

It was time to sleep, but few were serious about it. The Lieutenant must have dozed off about 2300.

Vengeance

The tanks arrived at first light. With the sound of the clanking armor, the infantry roused and struck tents. This was "the day." Men hurried to the mess lines. They ate and talked excitedly. The Conflict was ending. They would be home soon, perhaps within weeks.

This was the new breed chattering, the replacements. The older soldiers were more reticent. They sat quietly. If the Conflict ended, so be it. If it didn't, so be it. These veterans had seen too much to go hog wild with excitement. And yet their eyes were bright as they conversed among themselves. Hardly daring to show their emotions, they were equally hopeful, nevertheless.

The movement out was delayed several hours for some unknown reason. Then, with the men mounted on every available tank, truck, and jeep, and with B Company leading, the 19th Infantry Regiment motored out of the streambed and onto the main road. As the lead tank turned north, the men cheered.

Two tanks led the column, and then the Lieutenant and his observer crew were motioned to follow. If need demanded, he would be immediately available for artillery support. Another tank swept by and then came 1st Lt. Bailey, the company commander. Following Bailey were Lt. Col. Naudts and his S-2. More tanks and trucks entered the procession, all carrying the remainder of the First Battalion. The Second Battalion came after and with it the artillery, infantry on its trucks.

The column first passed the 52nd Field in position, just off the road and south of Kumch'on. The artillerymen were grouped about their howitzers. There was still some action ahead, and these men, gunners and cannoneers of the first artillery battalion in the Korean fighting, were standing ready to provide quick support for their infantry, if and when needed.

The town of Kumch'on was reached. The familiar landmarks were gone, of course. The town had mostly been leveled, first by the withdrawing cavalry, and later by the Air Force. Little other than a collection of hovels comprised evidence of inhabitants remaining.

Out of Kumch'on now and north, where a few miles along the road, two tanks were parked, their guns pointed up and north in a ceremonial gesture. A company of infantry was strung out along the berm of the road, resting. And there, just beyond the two tanks, the commanding officer of the 21st Infantry Regiment, Col. Richard W. Stephens, stood waving the advancing 19th Regiment forward. The 21st, assisted by the 5th Regiment, had forged the main bridgehead across the Naktong River at Waegwan and had cleared the main road up to this point. The 19th would carry the division insignia the rest of the way to Taejon.

With the advance point of the 21st now behind, the column grew serious. The lead tank slowed and ensuing progress became caterpillar-like. This was virgin territory. Many potential traps and NK roadblock opportunities existed. Well-placed antitank guns could do great damage. Nevertheless, the 19th was gambling that it could move along too quickly for any serious resistance to develop.

Through Kwan-ni and then into the rail junction of Hwanggan, the column edged. At Hwanggan, an enemy soldier was sighted, sprinting along a nearby hillside. The .50-caliber machine gun on one of the lead tanks zeroed in and spits of dust followed the running NK. The man made it to the top of the hill and safety but only by running practically straight up the hill at top speed.

The column now turned southwest toward Yongdong. Few civilians were seen along this stretch of the road and the countryside appeared mostly uninhabited.[1] An enemy hospital was discovered at the outskirts of Yongdong, housed in a relatively large building and courtyard just off the road. As the UN column approached, an NK officer ran from the courtyard and was immediately shot down by one of the men on the lead tank. Other NK, probably attendants, emerged from the station with their hands up. They were searched and then pointed to the rear.

The prisoner group went running back down the road, hands overheads, and each American group continued to point rearward as the group ran past. Several empty trucks were in the column, designated for prisoner pickup. As the column began to lumber forward again, NK wounded could be seen lying in the courtyard of the compound, their eyes closed. They were conscious, these men, but did not know what to expect and perhaps felt they would be killed, as indeed American wounded were killed following standard guerrilla warfare as practiced by the NK army. Closed eyes blot out terror very easily.

The column now swung into Yongdong proper, scene of a significant action involving the cavalry. There was a long halt and the men began to grow restless. Suddenly word was passed that several American prisoners had just been liberated. One of the lead tanks had rumbled up to the town jail in the center of the town, and three Americans were discovered there, locked in. A few moments work on the door and the men were freed. When the column began moving again, the three were observed sitting on a building porch eating from C-ration cans. The passing Americans waved. The three, formerly with the cavalry, waved their plastic spoons.

It was early evening and Naudts urged the column on. The vehicles swung out of Yongdong and toward the hill area where the cavalry had relieved the 21st Regiment. Reaching the location, the Lieutenant gazed at King Mountain once more. He was recollecting that the *Stars and Stripes* had listed a First Lieutenant

Reffner as being the recipient of a Silver Star medal, posthumously, and he wondered if this was the same officer who had relieved him at the King Mountain site on July 22.[2]

The Lieutenant had also been given to understand earlier that the NK had attacked the cavalry defenders here frontally, with flags and colors waving, and then resorting to the more familiar infiltration and encircling tactic, as at Taejon, until many of the cavalry were trapped. All was empty and serene now.

At the bridge, the forward defensive point of this former battlefield, a rickety wooden structure spanned the demolished concrete portions, a structure still in place despite repeated bombings by the Air Force. This temporary pile would hold jeeps and trucks, but not tanks. The tanks moved off the road and down onto the riverbed for their crossing.

It was decided that all available infantry vehicles (including tanks) would make the bridgehead crossing first, leaving the artillery until last. Lt. Col. Langlois and his forward party of battery commanders, at this juncture, were traveling almost with the lead infantry elements. At one point in the march, the group found itself in front of the infantry staff party. While the battery commander party acted to recede its position in the column, the Lieutenant, in the growing darkness, found he had slipped too far behind to be tactically useful, so Dear had to race the jeep and engage in some fancy driving to reach the original assigned march station.

From Yongdong north toward Okch'on, through the now darkened countryside, the sounds of tanks began rousing villagers from their beds. First a few, and then the many of each tiny village and hamlet gathered along the road as the UN column rumbled on. The KATUSAs on the lead tank shouted their identification, so that by the time the Lieutenant passed by, cheering and waving had reached a high crescendo. The villagers, in their white garments, reached out to the men as they passed. Many women were in tears.

Riding through these settlements, the Lieutenant concluded that the crowds along the roadside could not possibly be the result solely from the KATUSA's shouted words. There had to be some other form of communication. He listened carefully and, sure enough, he learned the secret. In one of the hamlets he heard the sound of a brass gong. He continued to hear it even after the hamlet was far behind. This was the communication. Whatever music, signal, or code was being rung out, civilians were interpreting the sounds as signaling the advance of the UN force and so were ready, when the lead elements approached, to greet the column in an appropriate manner.

The column was nearing Okch'on, although it would not pass directly through that town, but through Sinch'on, at the center of which was a vital intersection. The lead tank commander had been briefed not to turn right at the intersection, but continue straight ahead. The tanker followed instructions, partially. He did not turn to the right. He turned to the left.

Following this tank, the column roared into the center of Sinch'on and down a side road. Capt. Pate, who by this time was traveling just behind the Lieutenant, stopped. The Lieutenant stopped also, as did members of the infantry staff.

Someone tore after the tanks. In a short time, the lead elements returned, but the damage was done. From Sinch'on to Taejon the road wound narrowly between high mountains. The advancing column, now temporarily diverted, would almost certainly have been heard and the NK given time to organize anti-tank barriers, guns, or even T-34s to harass the UN force and attempt to stop its progress. Pate and the Lieutenant stood at the center of Sinch'on, on a corner sidewalk, as the confused mass of men and vehicles ground to a halt.

Into the center of this jumble stepped the regimental CO, Col. Moore. The regiment would halt here, disperse for perimeter security, gas up, and in general, rest in preparation for a resumed march in the morning. With daylight, aid from aircraft would be available should NK strongholds be encountered in this increasingly difficult terrain.

As order was being restored, the Lieutenant happened to glance through the window of a store there at the road corner and was a little startled to see human figures stretched out on the floor. Looking closer, he saw one of the figures move. Then he noticed bandages and other medical equipment strewn about. He motioned to Capt. Pate. Together, they continued to look, but could do nothing at the moment for or about the obviously wounded or sick NK lying there. These enemy patients would be checked in the morning and possible taken south in division medical ambulances.

B Company had dismounted from the tanks and trucks by this time, and the men were sitting or lying by the sides of buildings along the road. The artillery had stopped on the road near the town's entrance, but remaining in line and not in position to fire. The 19th Regimental Combat Team waited, watched and rested.

The men were up and about at dawn. C-ration cans were opened and contents half consumed when, with a blinding flash, a loud explosion rent the morning calm. This was followed by another crashing sound. There was a scurry of activity as men began taking cover or running to the tanks. None knew what was happening.

Then, shortly, an ambulance jeep approached carrying three blackened men. These were survivors from the lead tank. That tank, astride the main road out of Sinch'on, had just begun moving toward a small bridge, only about two hundred yards from where the NK Yak plane had bombed the rail line July 18, when it was struck by a shell from a T-34 tank. One of the American crew had been killed.

The Lieutenant, meanwhile, had already gone to his jeep to begin equipment preparation for a possible movement by foot. He was not to be disappointed. Just after the ambulance jeep went by, the call for an observer was passed along the line of waiting infantry. Walsh and Nezvensky came running. The packboards were readied with the Lieutenant carrying one radio section on his back. The three then began walking past the waiting vehicles toward the scene of the damaged American tank.

At the forward point of the column, the infantry staff had gathered in a strategy session. Pate stood nearby. As the Lieutenant approached, Pate informed him that an enemy tank was emplaced somewhere ahead, perhaps a few hundred yards away, but that no one could spot it because of a heavy mist that lay over the entire area. Pate told him to go up onto the hill on the right and report if anything could be seen. Upon reaching the crest of the hill, the Lieutenant saw another, higher hill mass to the front that blocked effective observation. He would have to climb that forward hill if any good was to result from this mission.

Meanwhile, a platoon from B Company climbed the hill where the Lieutenant was standing, providing a protective screen. While the men were thus engaged, an A-20 Air Force spotter arrived on the scene, circling overhead. Noting the Lieutenant with his radio and infantry busy about, the pilot prepared a message which he shortly dropped by small parachute.

The parachute was picked up by an infantry soldier and the attached message brought to the Lieutenant. The spotter was asking what was happening and if the NK were involved. As he could not contact the spotter with his radio, the Lieutenant sent Nezvensky down the hill with instructions to give the message sheet to the infantry leadership for further process.

B Company now began a forward movement to occupy the hill obstructing the Lieutenant's view. The company crested the hill mass in perfect skirmish formation. What everyone saw was an empty pastoral scene made ghost-like by the mist still clinging along the ground and particularly along the creek bed winding beside the road.

Scanning the panorama with his binoculars, the Lieutenant saw movement on the skyline along a hill just above the town, but too furtive for definitive identification. Whatever or whoever was out there was safe a few moments longer.

Suddenly, there was a call from the company's left platoon. The NK tank had been located just below the hill, but on the opposite side of the road, camouflaged by having been driven inside a substantial Korean hovel. The Lieutenant immediately called to Nezvensky to radio the tank's discovery and prepare for an adjustment. This was not going to be a grand march into Taejon. The NK appeared determined to stall the UN advance as long as possible, to the bitter end, perhaps.

When the lead U.S. tank had been hit earlier, Capt. Still began a reconnaissance mission to determine a proper battery position. Now, as the Lieutenant called for an adjustment on the newly discovered tank, two howitzers were being guided into the new position. It took several minutes for the howitzers to be laid and data placed on a firing chart. The distance between the howitzers and the target being quite short, a weak powder charge would most likely be used resulting in more inexact round dispersion.

The rounds were on the way shortly, and the Lieutenant adjusted further. But when he was ready for a final shift and the use of phosphorus, a plethora of mortar shells began exploding, so that it became difficult to distinguish whose shells were which. Nevertheless, he intended to take the chance of continuing with the mission. But just as he was about to call for a concentrated volley, shouts interrupted him. Looking down, he saw an infantry launcher team edging forward. These men were waving and shouting to the men on the hill to cease mortar and artillery fire.

The Lieutenant radioed this development and shut off his mission, angering Lt. Col. Langlois in the process. Mortar shelling soon ceased. The launcher team crept slowly along a sunken path leading to the hovel. And then they stopped. In seconds, there was a blast from the launcher, followed immediately by an explosion inside the hovel. The hull of the tank had been hit by the 3.5 projectile. Several brown-clad figures darted from the rear of the hovel and a machine gun opened up on them. One of the figures fell, but another kept racing until he disappeared along the creek bed.

The artillery spotter plane arrived. Quiet had descended on the scene, broken only by the buzzing engine of the L-5 when, suddenly, out of a house not a hundred yards from where the first NK T-34 tank had been disabled, another tank backed out with a roar, turned, and headed full speed away from the UN force and in the direction of the road and rail tunnels. The men on the line stood astonished, and more so as, in the next instant, a third T-34 broke out of another house, joining the second in a cloud of dust.

Whether the UN tank-infantry-artillery column was in full realization or not, the combat team had been tickled by fate when the lead tank made a wrong turning movement the night before. Had the advance continued, the probable confusion resulting from the tanks firing would have been considerable. Numerous infantry casualties could have been caused, and vehicles in the artillery group damaged or destroyed. As it was, the wrong turn and subsequent column halt limited casualties to only one life lost. Now, in the early morning light, continued action saw the disabling of one T-34 and the quick withdrawal of two others, all three obviously having been assigned the task of effecting a roadblock to cause maximum casualties and materiel damage, with delay of the advancing UN column the NK objective.

Almost a withdrawal, that is. One T-34 soon returned and, parking under a grove of trees at a bend in the road, began firing shells straight down the road into Sinch'on. Trucks and tanks still parked along the road awaiting the signal to resume the march were the targets.

In touch now with the L-5 spotter, the Lieutenant radioed the situation, asking if the spotter pilot could see the tank and giving approximate map coordinates. The plane zoomed ahead. Very shortly, adjusting rounds were being fired by A Battery. Ed Mattes was the air observer, and he was equal to the challenge. He adjusted a bracket and then called for phosphorus. None of the rounds scored a direct hit, as the dispersion effect was too great. But the tank was soon neutralized in that its crew abandoned it. A Battery was credited with a kill.

Soon, four F-51s burst into view, called to the scene by the Air Force liaison team. The planes circled momentarily, then flew up the valley. Sudden diving and rocketing indicated that they had cornered the remaining tank. The diving continued for several minutes until one plane came up and rolled over, the sign of a kill. Now, unless there were NK ground troops in the vicinity, the road to Taejon was seemingly clear.

But regiment was taking no chances. A Company was ordered to jump-off on the left and clear a settlement overlooking the road. The Lieutenant watched the advancing men firing their rifles as they probed houses and using a bazooka several times at suspected NK strong points. There were NK snipers about because the company sustained several wounded. However, the objective, a small tunnel on the rail line, was reached in short order. The company would sit astride the tunnel and await other battalion elements.

While watching the moving infantry, the Lieutenant caught a glimpse of white in the distance, just beyond the settlement. Peering carefully through his binoculars, he saw a large civilian group gathered in an open field, just out of effective rifle range. All in the group wore white garments. This discovery lent credence to his suspicions that the NK had been lying in wait for the advancing UN column had it continued through Sinch'on in the night. He recalled that he had not seen any civilians in Sinch'on standing out and greeting the column upon its arrival, contrary to experiences in villages prior to entering Sinch'on. The residents of that town obviously had been alerted to NK military preparations and so left their homes to bivouac in nearby open fields.

B Company now received orders to walk out onto the valley floor along the right of the road and occupy high ground near the rail tunnel. The objective place name was Sankyo-ri. The company proceeded immediately to advance.

On the way, the Lieutenant and his group paused at the edge of a stream and performed some quick ablutions. They were very close to the site where Headquarters Battery, 13th Field, had been from July 17 through the morning of July 21. It was also where the Lieutenant had bathed and washed his muddy clothes after the Kum River battle, and where the battery stood and gaped at the six Yak enemy planes flying down the valley to bomb the rail line and shower propaganda leaflets.

The sun, by this time, was dispersing the mist, and the Lieutenant recalled how impressed he had been with the valley as a potential camping site. He almost felt like flopping on the ground right then and there and relaxing, but he knew that he might be carried off as a "psycho" for doing so under present circumstances.

A waiting period was evolving. No one was quite sure what the next minute might bring. The valley ahead was quiet, outposts held secure by the First Battalion. Then news came that the Second Battalion would spearhead a night attack through to Taejon. The First Battalion would follow in the morning.

Some interdictory fire commenced with the 11th Field howitzers sending rounds over the hills into Taejon itself. Their steady blasts reminded the Lieutenant of the constant interdictory firing in France and Germany during WWII. Several tanks, also laid for indirect fire, joined the howitzers in further shattering the enemy-held city.

Late that afternoon, an infantry recon jeep that previously had been driven up the road beyond the line, came racing back to the sounds of rifle and machine gun fire. Green tracers revealed NK troops entrenched not too distant beyond the American outposts. The jeep came on full tilt, in second gear, and with several flat tires. The men in it survived without injury. Nevertheless, the continued presence of the NK was disturbing.

Following this incident, the Lieutenant called for defensive concentrations fronting B Company. One was slated at a spot near the main road while the other was scheduled across a narrow gully directly in front of the company position. Battalion refused to fire the one by the road, but permitted the firing of the other.

Soon after the concentration was fired, Bailey walked up to the OP position and told the Lieutenant that his KATUSAs had heard NK voices across the gully to the effect that there would be an attack later that evening. He, Bailey, was confident that his men could handle an attack. Expectantly, the Lieutenant went up on the high ground for the night leaving both Walsh and Nezvensky just below where they could hear his commands and transmit same.

That evening, just before nightfall, several F-51s appeared and began an air strike on the suspected NK position. The planes began their dives well back over friendly territory. As they finally buzzed down, the Lieutenant felt a sensation that must have been common among the NK, the fright at hearing the high-pitched whine of the engines, and then encountering a cloud of .50-caliber bullets, red tracer flames among them. The hiss of fired rockets was heard clearly by the Americans, the firing contacts made directly overhead. These were not hesitant pilots. They flew low, doing their jobs well.

The Second Battalion moved out at 2200 that evening. The Lieutenant had dozed off by that time so he hadn't heard the tanks approaching the outpost positions. But suddenly a firefight began. Tracers cut the night, seemingly from all directions. Tank guns exploded with flame as gunners aimed at the hillsides to the front, at NK entrenched there and firing on the advancing UN force. Machine guns chattered, and the sight of green tracers from NK gunners and riflemen made it plain that the NK, in one more desperate action, were attempting to halt that advance.

The Lieutenant rolled off his high point and dashed down to where he had left his two section members. Nezvensky, an old veteran of the withdrawals, was frantically scraping together the section's belongings. Walsh had picked up the radio and was ready to run down the hill with it. Then, the group stopped and looked at each other, grinning. This wasn't like before. Walsh put down the radio and Nezvensky turned it on.

As the radio warmed up, the voice of Capt. Maurice Slay, liaison officer with the Second Battalion, was heard trying to raise the battalion fire direction center. There was no answer. Finally, there was complete radio silence.

With the shooting exchange continuing, the Lieutenant radioed a volley request on the concentration fired earlier in front of B Company. Battalion responded quickly. Capt. Slay then came back on his radio to ask who was firing. The Lieutenant responded in code, volunteering to adjust further in defense of the halted column. Slay then requested fire further up on the hillside. After two adjustments, Slay broke in to say that the last adjustment was where the major source of enemy small arms fire was located and to repeat range several times. After observing three volleys, Slay requested that firing cease.[3]

The NK had begun to ease off when artillery started falling. Then, after the Lieutenant had zeroed in on the supposed center of NK resistance, their firing ceased altogether. He radioed Slay that he and his section would continue to be available in case of further need, but Slay answered that his observers could now handle the situation.

Moments after this last transmission, a platoon from F Company entered the B Company area. The platoon had been sent by Lt. Col. Kinney to protect the Lieutenant. Discovering that B Company was firmly entrenched, and that the latter needed no additional protection, the platoon withdrew. The Lieutenant then reported to his fire direction center the circumstances of the stalled attack column. The 19th Regiment remained in place through the night.

It was decided that the jump-off toward Taejon would resume at noon the next day. Patrols from the First Battalion, sent a short distance up the road, ascertained that no enemy force remained, so the noon jump-off time was kept. The infantry would walk this time, not ride on the tanks. The going would be slower, of course, but as the terrain was now quite rugged, and enemy roadblocks were always possible and easily manned, Regiment would take no chances.

The attack column resumed its forward movement on schedule and, as the last Second Battalion vehicle passed, B Company swung into line, leading the First Battalion. Dear guided his jeep in the middle of the road, between infantry files. The Lieutenant and Walsh walked with the others, as, also, did Nezvensky.

The men were on the last leg of their return to former areas of defeat. They tried to focus on roadside details, but for many, memories kept rushing back in such profusion that it was difficult to concentrate. The locomotive on which several GIs rode out of Taejon was still on the tracks where it was left late that July afternoon. No attempt had been made by the NK to repair it, the rail line, or both rail and road tunnels. A rocky trail had been fashioned over the blown road tunnel. The men looked down at the rail tunnel entrance and saw the T-34 that had been under air attack the day before. Napalm black was all over the tank and the area around it.

Up over the road tunnel the men trudged and then back to the main road and past the former positions of the 21st Regiment, emplaced to gather the withdrawing 19th and 34th regimental forces from Taejon. These positions had been organized as gates of safety. All was quiet now in deep contrast to the noisy turmoil on that afternoon of July 20, when the road churned with vehicles and men escaping a closing NK trap.

There were many halts and delays. Lt. Col. Kinney's men were taking no chances. Every hillside and suspicious roadside feature were investigated before proceeding.

Abandoned American Army vehicles and heavy equipment trucks remaining from the July debacle marked the last stretch preceding reentry into Taejon. Truck hulks and trailers of the 24th Medical Company were the first encountered. Off in a field, kitchen equipment and trailers of H Company, 19th Regiment, were noted. This had been the Second Battalion's service area, and a guerrilla attack had been mounted here on the early morning of the twentieth. Also nearby was a 155-mm howitzer, mired in a ditch, its barrel pointing skyward.

Then, at a point where the road turned sharply, where a massive NK roadblock had been in place, an antiaircraft half-track sat, burned out, its .50-caliber guns pointed at the hill where guerrillas had lain in wait. Silently acknowledged by the passing force, the track stood in mute testimony to the heroism of its crew, a crew who braved everything to help keep the lines of withdrawal open for their fellow soldiers.

Other trucks and jeeps were encountered scattered about, some damaged by the NK, but most probably abandoned and later wrecked by the Air Force.

No one could tell about grave mounds. Suggestive mounds were observed at intervals, but none could stop and investigate. Grave registration teams would be busy in this area for many, many weeks.

How did the men feel about all this? Well, there had been much in the way of backslapping and kidding at the start of this last march. But as the columns neared the environs of Taejon, the tragedy of that city and of the men who had attempted to defend it began to settle until, over the last mile or so, the men plodded in almost complete silence. Each man, including replacements, seemed to harbor some inner quieting thoughts about those three July days that constituted the Taejon battle. Each in his own way seemed to be silently acting out a measure of vengeance over the indignities imposed on the UN force during the recent weeks by the NK. And overall, a sense of quiet triumph pervaded the column stepping along. The UN fighting machine did prevail; the NK Army was conclusively prostrate.

And so, on this late September afternoon, without a cheer or loud noise of any kind, the columns, with accompanying tanks, swung down a slight grade and into what once had been a good-sized city but was now a hollow, burned-out shell. Taejon had been reached and recaptured.[4]

The Second Battalion took up positions within the city itself while the First Battalion moved through the city and out along the south road toward Kumsan. A roadblock would be established there for the night, a protective measure against any movement from that direction by stray NK.

Rising at dawn, the First Battalion marched back into the city and there, for the first clear moment, they glimpsed the center area, now little more than jumble of brick and stone. An MP was directing traffic at a main intersection, smiling as he did so. Various staff officers had stopped their jeeps and were engaged in earnest conferences.

Men waved and there were some shouts. Then trucks arrived to gather the battalion and convey it to the airfield, slated to be secured against guerrilla movements. This was to be the final mission of the First Battalion. The Second Battalion would remain in Taejon.

As the Lieutenant and his section rode along the streets, they encountered civilians walking about, some aimlessly, a pitifully few when compared to the throngs present on July 11. At one corner, a group of men with musical instruments had gathered and were performing with bells, cymbals, and a wind piece or two, while dancing in a circle. Others standing about were clapping their hands to the rhythm, occasionally turning to wave at the passing Americans.

A burned-out tractor prime mover, still coupled to a 155-mm howitzer, stood at an intersection. Some shattered American trucks were nearby, pushed together in a jumble. A little further on, near the original 24th Division cemetery, several disabled T-34 tanks stood. One of these was undergoing a hurried painting. The Lieutenant wondered why.[5]

With Taejon virtually leveled and few civilians or other native traffic on the streets, it didn't take long for the battalion convoy to reach the airfield. Once there, the companies took up positions on little earth mounds across the field from the Quonset huts that had been quarters for the regiment the night of July 11, just prior to the move to the Kum River line.

About 1400 that afternoon, the first large plane began circling the field preparatory to landing. The plane was an Army transport carrying Eighth United States Army Commander, Lt. Gen. Walton Walker. Walker was arriving to congratulate Col. Moore, the 19th Regiment CO, inspect the city of Taejon, and visit with his son who, at the moment, was seated by the A Company command tent, not far from the Lieutenant. That company shortly would move the twelve miles north to Taep'yong-ni as a guard unit to protect both the bridgehead and a company of division engineers, the latter scheduled to begin constructing a temporary vehicle crossing there over the Kum River.

Two tragic incidents were made known during that first day of occupation in and around Taejon. The most tragic was one that occurred the night previous, while the Second Battalion remained stalled on the road just outside Sinch'on. Forty American prisoners, the number given at the time, had been executed by the NK. Their bodies had been discovered by men from the Second Battalion. Few could be identified immediately. Men were reportedly so maddened by this discovery that enemy POW lives wouldn't have been worth a mouthful of spit.

The other incident was the discovery of several hundred civilian bodies, townspeople murdered by the retreating NK over a period of several days.[6]

Both atrocities had been prompted surely by the desire for revenge by the NK at the now perceived prospect of losing the war. These two incidents capped a cruel, vicious conflict, a final barbaric gesture by the NK at the site of a former victory, now the site of a well-deserved defeat.

The men were mostly quiet on this day, September 29, 1950, the eightieth day of the regiment's commitment. They pondered long over their experiences. When night fell, they lay on stunted hillsides and earth mounds or along the city's roads and streets and gazed at the clear, starry sky, brighter by far than the one into which many of these same men gazed the night of July 11.

And, as it was many times in many other places, prayers began to well up, prayers of thanksgiving now, but including expressions of sorrow over friends and buddies who didn't make it. These were being and would continue to be remembered in simple, direct fashion, remembrances bound to endure until the memory of the last survivor of the weeks and months preceding fades.

Then, in the relaxed atmosphere of a war drawing to a close, the men rested peacefully.

As It Must to All

Five artillerymen sat about on a high earth mound in the center of what had once been a frightening battlefield. It was mid-afternoon on a fair October day, the light rays slanting from a sun much lower in the sky than had been the case that Sunday, the previous July, the chatter of magpies breaking the pastoral stillness. A barely cool and tranquil breeze edged along the river valley in pleasant contrast to the burning, scorching heat of the past summer weeks. Cigarettes had been lit, and the men were engaged in the contented and lazy-like pastime of exhaling the smoke forcefully into the air, there to catch the river gusts and dissipate into the atmosphere.

These were members of A Battery, 13th Field Artillery Battalion, and they were grouped at the former artillery observation post within the defensive perimeter that C Company, 19th Infantry Regiment, had occupied during the battle of Kum River. They were preparing to make a final gesture of comradeship respecting one of their own, the removal from this battlefield of the remains of Private First Class Charles August Wallace, late of Hastings, Florida, and convey same to that temporary resting site of heroes, the 24th Infantry Division cemetery at Taejon.

None of the five said much as they shuffled their boots against the hard earth. All that could be said had been said in the weeks following that battle. Speculation and hope that Wallace and perhaps others with him had been captured and taken north to Seoul or more northern points had continuously been held forth. Many prisoners had indeed been taken, but relatively few had been positively identified by their captors.

This optimism had been stilled an hour before. When the group first came onto the scene, they noticed that the deep hole on the crest of the OP hill, where the machine gun had been emplaced during the Kum battle, and into which Wallace had jumped that morning of July 16, was now half-filled with dirt. It was likely that dirt had been shoveled in for a reason.

One of the five, a wireman named Cpl. David F. Peters, volunteered to probe. Taking a small trench shovel, he carefully dug at one end of the trench-hole until a hard object was struck. Scraping the dirt with his hand, he uncovered the top of a steel battle helmet.

As the others watched, he cleared small chunks of earth until it was established that the remains of a body were being uncovered. Sifting further, he located dogtags, still in place. He had to bend low to read the name, and then he announced that the remains were those of Charles Wallace.

Peters climbed out of the hole and sat down. The others continued to sit with him. After a few minutes, the Lieutenant sent back to the truck for the stretcher, shelter-half, and rope. When these were brought, the Lieutenant sensed the emotional intensity affecting them all. They would wait a bit, he decided, before doing what they had come to do.

Capt. Still had known that the Lieutenant wanted to return to the Kum River area as quickly as it was possible to do so. But while the infantry remained in a defensive stance around the airstrip, he would have to wait. On October 1, that mission terminated, the infantry moving to bivouac in the Quonset hut section across the field.

The Lieutenant at first was satisfied to just drive up to the Kum and look around. Then, on the morning of October 2, Capt. Tom Perkins, the 13th intelligence officer, called to say that a letter from division had been received authorizing commanders to initiate efforts to locate remains of men from their respective units who, to this date, were listed officially as missing in action both within the Kum River sector and at Taejon.

Capt. Still now agreed that the Lieutenant could take a three-quarter-ton truck and several men, particularly those who had known and were friends of Pfc. Wallace, and engage in a brief search of the C Company position for the latter's remains. (The Lieutenant had always felt that of the three missing men in his section, the chances of recovering the remains of Wallace— assuming he had not been captured—were greater than those respecting Thacker and Payne.) And so, amid quiet stares from others who had gathered to see them off, the party left the battery area.

The short ride from the airfield to Taep'yong-ni was a poignant one, full of memories for the Lieutenant. He recalled how confident, almost cocky many of the men had been that hot, dusty afternoon of July 12, and how shocked the survivors were when they crept back in the dead of night, leaving behind their wounded and the screaming soldier who begged for help that none could give.

Turning north now at Yusong, the road soon led past the initial artillery positions. The men in the truck noted, not without a trace of humor, ammunition still in place around the howitzer pits, particularly so where A Battery had been emplaced. Most had been under the impression all along that the NK used captured artillery ammunition in his assaults. They did use some, but apparently not the bulk. The NK depended mainly on their own weapons and shells. The partly rusted rounds laid neatly along the earthen pits attested to a fact that would soon puncture one of the more virile rumors of the conflict.

They now began passing the remains of trucks and jeeps. This was the site of the major July 16 roadblock, the one at Tuman-ni. Only twisted wreckage remained, of course. Vehicles not salvaged by the NK had been strafed and rocketed.

Off on the inner edge of the road, one of the men noticed a wrecked jeep with a marking on the front bumper. The driver stopped the truck and the men dismounted to look. They then noted a further identification: A-3. It was the Lieutenant's jeep, the one Pvt. Payne sought after he emerged from C Company's rear area CP the afternoon of July 16. Whoever had driven it away from Taep'yong-ni had probably died in it.

A few yards away, the lieutenant noticed a 19th Infantry jeep marked C-1. It was the same jeep 1st Lt. Aldridge was driving when he called out for the Lieutenant to accompany him to the rear that same afternoon. Aldridge apparently got only as far as this point in the withdrawal and had not been heard from or about since.

The group now continued on and soon passed the location where the stretcher party turned into the hills the night of the sixteenth. In the daylight, it looked but a brief distance to the plateau of that paddy-tiered hill, but on that fateful night it seemed not only high but a long way. The Lieutenant mused wonderingly why the NK hadn't charged up that hill after the Americans. All might have been captured without much of a fight.

Only a few of the vehicles overturned and abandoned by both the medical detachment and the 52nd Field battery remained along the road ditch. The NK probably worked quickly to salvage what they could. Perhaps this was why they delayed in following up their advantage. They were too busy looting and moving American vehicles back to their rear areas.

And then, the open space covered by the NK machine gun roadblock was reached. The whole area seemed contracted, in contrast to how it appeared on the afternoon of July 16, when tension and raw fear dominated the feelings and motions of the men trapped there. The bamboo hut was destroyed, burned to the ground. The Lieutenant peered across the valley. The paddy fields were seas of waving grain, the weaving grasses breathing life, not death. He could barely make out the stream dike, along which the ROK plane blazed its trail of American blood. There was nothing now to mark that incident. It would be emblazoned only in the memories of the dozen or so who survived there.

Taep'yong-ni was mostly leveled, burned out. Because of the many razed structures, the group almost drove by the place before the Lieutenant recognized it. Memory recounted the D Company machine gunners holding up the advancing NK, enabling the remnants of both A and C Companies to escape over the hill fronting the village, soon to form for the withdrawal. It was on the D Company hill that Capt. Prescott had remained. As befitting his professional calling, he had followed his superior's orders without question, either meeting death in doing so or taken prisoner. His was clearly a hero's destiny.

Out to the Kum River dike, now, and there the truck turned onto a cart trail, a truck's width, leading to the C Company position. At a turning point near the end of the dike, the truck stopped. The battleground had been reached.

For a long moment the Lieutenant, as did the others with him, looked about. They fixed their eyes on the battle site and on the OP mound that rose above it. Then, stiffly, in full view of several white-robed farmers working near by, the men began moving along the paddy walls leading to the old position. For these, the war, to use a phrase, had come full circle. It was here, along this river line, that the Korean Conflict began for the men in the 19th Regimental Combat Team and, if luck would have it, it would be here that the war would end.

So now, looking at his watch and then at the relaxing men, the Lieutenant felt the group could delay no longer. He stood up and, as he did, the others, watching, also stood. They converged above the trench hole, their faces reflecting an inner rigidity as they realized what they were about to do. No one moved for a moment, and then Peters took a small shovel and stepped down into the trench. The others crowded about, waiting. Their turn would come.

In all, the removal of earth took about twenty minutes. Details of how the men did it would be unseemly in the reporting. Each took his turn until finally only one task remained. It was the Lieutenant's to do. He had been Wallace's immediate CO.

He got down into the trench. Wallace probably had been killed or wounded outside the trench, perhaps as he was climbing out to make the break with the Lieutenant and the others. A cartridge belt, not his, had been fastened under the armpits, and someone, most likely a South Korean civilian, had used the belt as an aid to lower the body into the trench. The task had been done carefully. The legs were stretched out and the torso reclined gently against one side of the trench. Steel helmet and liner were still in place.

Forcing himself to breathe regularly, the Lieutenant called for the shelter-half. Then, placing the canvas as close to the body as possible, he moved the remains until they rested completely on the canvas. It was hot in the trench, and the air was sickening. The Lieutenant had to stand up once and lean over the side of the trench to retch, but only once.

Then, kneeling at first, the others began pulling on the canvas. Everyone was being careful. Each wanted to prevent unnecessary damage to the remains, not to treat them in the rough, almost unkind manner of a graves registration team, hardened by attending to hundreds of such casualties.

With a final effort, the canvas was lifted up and out of the trench and laid on the ground. The men relaxed noticeably. This was a new experience for them all, and they bore up well. This was no immature teenage group, although most were but twenty years of age and younger. They were men who could hide their feelings until well away by themselves. This experience would be remembered a lifetime.

One of the members of the group was the battery medic, Pfc. Dallas Stidd, of Fort McCoy, Florida. He examined the remains closely and saw that an enemy bullet that may have caused Wallace's death entered the body near the left shoulder, probably coursing deep into the chest. There was a dark stain on the left side of the fatigue jacket, and the jacket was slightly torn at the shoulder, near the shoulder socket.

No one mentioned it, but the thought was on everyone's mind. Unless the bullet coursed close to the heart, Wallace may have lain wounded and in pain for a time, possibly dying in the early evening of July 16.

The medic then began carefully to fold the shelter-half about the remains. The others watched at first but soon turned away. They would rather remember life than death. The call came for the rope. Produced, it looped the canvas and the covering was now secure. A knot was made, and then the canvas sack was lifted up and onto the stretcher. The work was done. The men again sat.

The sun now was considerably lower in the sky. The Lieutenant checked the time and realized it could be dark before they all would reach the division cemetery. Cigarettes had been lit. He would not give the order to leave until these had been completely smoked.

Leaving the resting men, the Lieutenant began walking once more about the former position. On the backside of the OP hill, where the mortars had been placed and the company headquarters stationed, there were half-filled trenches and open holes. It was here that NK mortaring and sniping had taken its greatest toll the morning of July 16. Rain, during the interim, had eroded the walls of several trenches, exposing parts of body remains. And on the east side of the OP hill, near where the Lieutenant had established his lookout position, the remains of an NK soldier lay uncovered. The South Koreans had not bothered to bury this, their enemy.

Still with a few minutes to go, he wandered down the forward hump of the OP hill as it stretched to the forward communication trench along the river. A number of mounds dotted the hump, but nothing unusual was noticeable in the forward trench except a few rusted C-ration cans. What had happened to the men who fled there following the fall-back order?

Standing by the forward trench, attempting to reason what may have happened as the NK began a closure operation, he deduced that some of the men had moved along the hump to provide protection for a majority to make a dash for the large river-front dike, the one he and two others had reached earlier, and beyond which Lts. Stavrakes and Orr and a platoon were waiting to provide escape support. The mounds along the forward hump were mute evidence that the protective strategy had failed as none of the men in that forward area, those under the immediate command of 1st Lt. MacGill, so far as the Lieutenant knew to the moment, had made it out safely.

It was time to go. He retraced his steps along the hump and called to the men. Cigarettes were flipped. The men, too, took a last look around, although none had been here previously and were not as emotionally tied to the place as was the Lieutenant.

With a slight effort, four of the men grasped the stretcher handles. They then, with the others, began walking down a draw, the same one down which the Lieutenant staggered in his withdrawal effort, and the one Wallace, too, would have taken had he remained unhurt. The Lieutenant continued to stand at the OP site while the stretcher group made its way toward the river dike and the truck. Upon reaching the vehicle, the four carriers carefully laid the stretcher on the truck bed and then turned to wait.

Feeling somehow that he would never return to this spot, the Lieutenant remained standing a moment longer, absorbing the scene so as to make it unforgettable. He gazed out toward the river as he had done many, many times before. Men sat along the forward trench along the river waiting for an enemy that never came from that direction. He then looked back along the escape trail, imagining 1st Lt. Aldridge swinging in rhythm with a group of native bearers, supplies in hand.

He recalled 2nd Lt. Maher and his first platoon. He could make out the trenches they had dug. Maher and many of his men were still over there, buried where they had fallen after struggling heroically to stem the initial NK onrush that Sunday morning.

Finally, looking close about him, his eye paused a fleeting moment to rest on a grave mound beside where he stood. It was at the exact location where the BAR gunner had been on the morning of the sixteenth, the lad who didn't fire his weapon and who continued to sit in his trench while the others broke off the hill.

Much further off to the left, by the main road, an engineer company was in position making repairs to the broken parts of the river bridge. Sam Walker's A Company was in bivouac nearby, providing protection should any guerrillas in the vicinity choose to attack and damage the bridge again. There was bound to be quite a number of those NK, cut off from escape north, either fearful or plain unwilling to be captives of the Americans in light of their own generally poor treatment of American prisoners. It would be a long time before complete tranquility would come to this embattled peninsula.

And was there peace now? It was reported that Lt. Gen. Walker had said there was. Although the Lieutenant had not actually seen it, he had been told that the *Stars and Stripes* had printed the general's pronouncement that the North Korean army had collapsed. There was little to worry about now.

Yet several South Korean divisions were reported rushing headlong toward the 38th Parallel, with every indication that they would cross and pursue NK remnants. Would these actions prompt renewed NK resistance, or would there finally be a grand victory march north to the Yalu River, with the purpose of uniting the two competing political entities?

For the moment, the Lieutenant was in no mood to care. He felt that the mission of the 24th Division had ended with the recapture of Taejon. The division would be returning to Japan shortly, and it would be nice, so nice to take a hot bath again. Let the ROKs beat a path to the Yalu. The 24th was ready to beat a path to Pusan.

This was it. The Lieutenant started off the hill. He would go down the same draw and walk along the same paddy walls on which he ran that afternoon of the sixteenth. He would retrace his steps one last time.

This time, however, unlike before, Pfc. Charles A. Wallace would "accompany." Of the many who yet "remained," Pfc. Wallace would be the first to "leave." The others would "leave" soon, when the jeeps and trailers of the quartermaster graves registration teams could get out here. Meanwhile, the fallen heroes of C Company, 19th Infantry Regiment, would lie together one last night on their field of honor.

The Lieutenant reached the top of the large earthen dike, the one he rolled over that early afternoon of July 16. Then, hesitating only slightly, he turned and began walking toward the truck and the end of the Conflict.

Epilogue

Well, the Conflict did not end with the recapture of Taejon nor with the liberation of Seoul by the Marines and the 17th ROK Regiment. Hostilities continued until July 27, 1953, three years, one month, and two days after it all began.

Although the Conflict initially was designed to cleanse South Korea only of NK troops and influence, pressure from that country's leadership prompted extension of hostilities beyond the 38th Parallel and into North Korea. The ROK Army began an incursion on October 1, and the remaining United Nations force, which included the Lieutenant, followed shortly afterward, with the First Cavalry Division beginning a penetration drive on October 9, the goal being the NK capital, P'yongyang.

It was not to be a glorious grand march up the peninsula to the Yalu River despite moments when the movement north seemed as such. The NK army, shattered and scattered, still managed point and roadblock defenses causing delays and associated casualties affecting the advancing UN units. But the Yalu was finally reached on October 26 by the ROK 6th Division and elements of the 17th Regiment, 7th Infantry Division, arrived at the river's edge on November 21.

Then, the hitherto unthinkable occurred: intervention by forces of the Peoples' Republic of China, identified militarily as CCF, Chinese Communist Forces. The first contact reportedly occurred on October 25, affecting ROK troops operating in the I Corps sector of the western front. Marine troops met CCF soldiers on November 2 while maneuvering within the X Corps sector to the northeast. CCF units had begun infiltrating North Korea as early as late September when it became evident that the latter might be invaded from the south. But except for isolated field reports and the taking of some few Chinese prisoners, there was little firm proof of a Chinese military presence. This was so even with aircraft surveillance.

Then came the night of November 1–2. The 8th Regiment of the First Cavalry Division received a crushing blow from Chinese forces. Chinese intervention in the Korean Conflict had become a reality, a dangerous reality.

From this point on, excepting for short periods of movement forward and limited withdrawals, both sides playing cat and mouse, Chinese pressure became such that the UN Army began a general withdrawal from North Korea proper.

Several notable rear-guard actions were fought. One took place in and around the Changjin (Chosin) Reservoir in the northeast by the Marines and the 7th Infantry Division. The other saw the 24th Division and associated ROK forces clash with advancing CCF units north of Uijongbu on New Year's Eve, 1950. Both the Marines and 7th Division units were evacuated by sea in a memorable operation while elsewhere the withdrawal continued until the narrow neck of South Korea was reached and contiguous defense line formed, defense line that included areas where American troops were first committed the previous July. It was during the pullback within the western portion of the UN battle area that the capital, Seoul, was abandoned a second time.

Beginning in January, 1951, United Nations troops engaged in a series of counterattacks that eventually forced the CCF back up the peninsula to roughly the original 38th Parallel line. There the two armies remained, slugging it out in competition for the best defensive sites until a cease-fire was declared in July 1953, the ensuing lull continuing to this day.

Casualty figures resulting from Conflict battles and other military operations are sourced in a 1954 report from the office of the Assistant Chief of Staff, G-1, titled *Battle Casualties of the Army.* Excerpts from this report were printed in tabular form in the *Army Almanac of 1959.*

(THE FOLLOWING FIGURES ARE **NOT** TO BE CONSIDERED AUTHORITATIVELY **FINAL.**)

As quoted in the *Almanac*, total casualties (all American services) occurring during the three-year span of the Conflict were 142,091. This figure is based on numbers derived from KIA (killed in action), WIA (wounded in action), MIA (missing in action), and POW (prisoner of war) data.[1]

Total combat-related deaths as reported by 1954 were 33,629. Included in this figure were 23,306 KIA; 2,501 DOW (died of wounds); 5,121 DOD (missing declared dead by the Department of Defense); and 2,701 DIE (those who died during internment by the enemy).

Total *Army* military combat-related deaths, again as reported by 1954, were 27,704. Included in this figure were 19,334 KIA; 1,930 DOW; 3,778 DOD; and 2,662 DIE.[2]

Marine Corps casualties are listed separately despite their units having served as ground forces under Army command. The Marines sustained 28,205 total casualties. Of this total, 4,267 died. Particularized: 3,308 were KIA; 537 DOW; 391 MIA (all later declared deceased); and 225 POW, 31 of this number reported as DIE.

Enduring the greater number of casualties among units participating during either the duration of the Conflict or a partial tour only was the First Marine Division. The Marines are followed in descending order of numbers by the 2nd Division, the First Cavalry Division, the 7th Division, the 25th Division, the 24th Division (figures do not include the 5th RCT), the 3rd Division, the 45th Division, the 187th RCT (airborne), and the 40th Division.

Casualties incurred by the 29th Regiment are included in the 25th Division totals. The 5th RCT suffered 4,052 KIA and WIA during the years of combat.

Marine division units suffered heavily during both battle commitments along the Naktong River. Later, with the X Corps in northeast Korea, both the Marines and the 7th Division incurred significant personnel loss.

The number of 2nd Division casualties most probably increased considerably as the result of (1) it being the major defending force during the Second Battle of the Naktong Pocket, September 1–9, 1950, and (2) from the disastrous November 30, 1950, withdrawal movement on the road between Kunu-ri and Sunch'on, North Korea, the stretch of road and accompanying deadly harassment by CCF forces sometimes referred to by military historians as "The Gauntlet."

The First Cavalry Division, as did the 24th Division earlier, felt the full impact of early NK frontal and roadblock maneuvers from Yongdong all the way back to Waegwan on the Naktong River. Later, this division was the first American unit to encounter the CCF in numbers sufficient to provoke battle. During this major encounter, the 8th Regiment was hit hard with its Third Battalion virtually destroyed as a functioning combat unit.

The American Eighth Army order of battle, at the outset of the invasion of North Korea, placed the 24th Division in the west coastal area and along roads leading to towns near to or adjoining the mouth of the Yalu river, to include the final NK capital city of Sinuiju, the site of a major road and bridge crossing into Manchuria. The terrain along these routes of march being less hilly or mountainous, the 24th escaped the core CCF infiltrations that first threatened then smashed into both American and ROK divisions advancing in the more mountainous interior. The division thus emerged from North Korea during the mass withdrawals of late November 1950, along with its sister 25th Division, relatively unscathed.

There has been no serious debate currently concerning the possibility of American soldiers listed as MIA as still being alive and residing behind what formerly was called the Iron Curtain, either in China or in the former Soviet Union. No credible evidence has surfaced verifying the existence currently of any American soldier in any of the former communist countries.

To this date, the North Korean government has discouraged searches throughout its domain for remains of American and other United Nations personnel, a number thought to total over 8,000. Although talks have begun between North Korea and the United States regarding the return of remains, North Korea continues to insist that a formal treaty between the two governments must replace the armistice agreement now existing before any large-scale effort is made to return remains. The United States, just as consistently, responds that such a treaty must be arranged between the two Koreas.

Eighteen hundred sets of remains were returned in 1954 during Operation Glory, 866 sets unidentifiable. During the 1990–1994 period, 208 sets were returned, only 5 sets positively identified.

The United States, in September 1993, appropriated $897,000 to the North Korean government for the return of forty-six sets of remains. North Korea then upped its payment demands, prompting American refusal to continue with this sort of bargaining, at least for the time being.[3]

By late August 1951, most who survived the first full year of the Conflict, of which the Lieutenant was one, had been rotated back to the States. And the 24th Division, as did the other American divisions positioned along Line Kansas, the relatively stable front in place as peace talks commenced, took on a different complexion with new leadership and fighting personnel.

During this stabilized but still aggressively hostile stance, the 24th was withdrawn to Japan where a reorganized and retrained 34th Regimental Combat Team rejoined it.

The division was returned to Korea just prior to cessation of hostilities in 1953. The 19th Regiment was assigned guard duty at the Cheju-do prison encampment; the 21st Regiment performed similar duties at the Koje-do camp; while the 34th Regiment furnished escort guard for released NK and Chinese prisoners. The 63rd Field had the honor of being the last divisional unit to fire in anger, ending the Conflict in general support of IX Corps.

Following Operation Big Switch, the main prisoner exchange procedure, the division engaged in battleground policing and then again withdrew to Japan. A third Korean tour took place later.

Although the 24th Division became an important element of the military's Rapid Deployment Force, it was not always part of the active duty establishment. The division was inactivated in Korea in 1957, then reactivated in Europe in 1958, seeing service in Lebanon and later in 1961 along the Berlin Wall. The division was transferred to the continental United States in 1968 for the first time, but was inactivated a second time in 1970.

A reformation of the division began at Ft. Stewart, Georgia, in 1974, with reactivation in 1975. Designated the 24th Infantry Division (Mechanized) in 1979, the division took part in Operation Desert Storm, engaging Iraqi forces in a memorable tank battle that effectively brought that campaign to a victorious close.

Unfortunately for the pride of WWII and Conflict veterans, most of the familiar combat team components are no longer part of the division's structure. This falling away probably occurred during those intervals when the division was inactivated.

On the other hand, many of the former components continue to survive within other divisions or special groupings. The three infantry regiments—the 19th, 21st, and 34th—have been retained and the 5th Regiment as well. Retained also are the 11th and 13th Field Artillery as artillery regiments. The 52nd Field continues as merged with the 52nd Artillery. A review of the listings reveals the absence of the 63rd Field, inactivated since 1958.

The current ongoing downsizing of the military has resulted in a planned reduction of active Army divisions from twelve to ten. Scheduled to be inactivated in 1996 were both the 7th and 24th Divisions. More recently, however, the 24th was reactivated as a training division, garrisoned at Ft. Riley, Kansas, and remains as such to date.

Finally, as a matter of appropriate interest for those who served during the early months of the Conflict, both the Argyll and Sutherland Highlanders and the Middlesex Regiments, a battalion of each making up two-thirds of the 27th

British Brigade, later the 27th British Commonwealth Brigade, have been united with other regiments, the process termed *amalgamation*. The Argyll and Sutherland Regiment was amalgamated into the Queen's Own Highlanders Regiment, the descriptive "Highlanders" thus assured continuity within British military traditions.[4]

Of the remaining men from the Lieutenant's original forward observation section listed as missing in action, the remains of Columbus Thacker were found soon after the recapture of Taejon and the surrounding area. His wound, as the Lieutenant had surmised that afternoon of July 16, was mortal. It is doubtful that members of the tank crew could or did anything other than make him comfortable as possible for the short period until his death.

Although he was struck down about the same time and under similar circumstances to Cpl. Thacker, the remains of JF Payne were not recovered until late winter 1951. There was a question about identification. A memo from Eighth Army was received stating that the remains of a certain second lieutenant were awaiting disposition, postponed because a casualty report bearing the officer's name had never been submitted. Eighth Army demanded an explanation.

Fortunately, the normal parental notification procedure had not been followed in this case due, of course, to the initial reporting irregularity. The Lieutenant was thus able to confirm quickly that he was a living person. Further, he informed the proper Eighth Army authority that on July 12, prior to going on the line along the Kum River, he had given his wallet to Pvt. Payne for safekeeping. Payne was apparently carrying the wallet, without other identification, when killed. The Lieutenant's first forward observation section finally was fully accounted for.

C Company, 19th Infantry Regiment, termed a "hard luck outfit" by author Clay Blair,[5] would be shattered twice more before a UN force line stabilization could be effected in May 1951. In the first encounter with the CCF, the action taking place November 4, 1950, C Company lost a number of men taken prisoner to include its commander and four other officers. And in an action on New Year's Eve 1950, that company would bear the brunt of a major Chinese assault, part of a general drive that hit neighboring ROK units particularly hard. American units were forced to withdraw to escape being flanked. The momentum of this Chinese attack caused Seoul to be evacuated a second time.

A strange twist of fate took place during the confrontation of November 4. A sudden roadblock mounted by the Chinese, particularly affecting the 19th's First Battalion, forced the capture, among others, of the regiment's Protestant chaplain, Capt. Kenneth C. Hyslop. Hyslop had been one of the two regimental chaplains accompanying the wounded on the night of July 16–17, 1950. He joined the emerging walking group after it was decided that the Catholic chaplain, Herman G. Felhoelter, would remain with the nonambulatory wounded. Felhoelter was killed, along with the wounded on stretchers, by the NK.

Now Hyslop, too, fell into enemy hands, albeit Chinese. And like his former colleague, although not in the same manner, he perished, the date being December 12, 1950, in a North Korean prison camp.

A memorial to the chaplains (there were four) of the United Nations force who succumbed in prison camps during the Conflict has been mounted and may be seen at Gloucester Cathedral, Gloucester, England. Chaplain Hyslop's name is one of the four inscribed on the memorial.

More than four decades have passed since that almost unbearable hot summer of 1950 in South Korea. Survivors of the battles fought during that summer are today living out their lives in such diverse locations as Breaux Bridge, Louisiana; Carrolton, Kentucky; Colorado Springs, Colorado; Council Bluffs, Iowa; Floyds Knobs, Indiana; Hicksville, New York; Lacey, Washington; Lake Forest, California; Livonia, Michigan; Onancock, Virginia; St. Petersburg, Florida; West Caldwell, New Jersey; Wright City, Oklahoma, and in myriad other cities and communities throughout the length and breadth of this nation.

And as each Conflict veteran, in his own manner, approaches the moment of his calling, not a day passes that some incident, place, or name from that first summer resurrects itself in the mind. For some—perhaps many—those few weeks are recalled now as being the most momentous of their lives, and memories of those days remain clear, notwithstanding the irreversible weakening of the body physical.

And then, there are a few, a very few now, for whom one segment of recall remains immeasurably tragic.[6]

By mid-afternoon of July 16, 1950, C Company, 19th Regiment, was shattered. Its first platoon, having taken the brunt of the NK attack earlier that morning, was nonexistent. Another platoon had been sent out to cover an anticipated company withdrawal. The headquarters and mortar sections, fully exposed to NK sniper fire and mortaring, remained in place, but resistance from this sector of the company's perimeter was dwindling. All that continued a viable resistance were one platoon strung along the river and remnants of other sections or squads scattered along the forward slope of the OP Hill, each man exchanging fire, albeit sporadically, with the NK rearward of the company position.

Having seen the NK begin a movement to envelop the position, 1st Lt. Henry MacGill, the commander, ordered a "Fire and fall back" maneuver to all who could hear and could obey. Shortly after 1400 hours, then, from all sides except that facing the river, the NK began entering the three-sided perimeter to face a platoon-sized remnant of the original company complement, gathered with their backs to the river.

Now the only officer left in the company position, 1st Lt. MacGill was overheard speaking shockingly of the disaster that had befallen his command. Noting the approaching NK, he began urging as many as could hear him to break away and get back to friendly lines.[7] But it was too late.

The platoon began disintegrating into small groups as each man struggled to find a way out, to return to the main road where safety with other regimental units lay. And in the process of this tangled activity, during which firing continued to be exchanged, several more men were killed and others wounded. Finally a remaining forty-odd, either within the position or nearby, were intercepted and taken prisoner. With this last act and after thirteen hours of resistance, making a truly heroic stand, most of the while cut off from cognate forces and written off by the battalion commander, C Company ceased to exist.

With the end of organized resistance, NK mopping up began. This was essentially a killing of the wounded and the herding together (snowballing) of the remaining able. There was pushing and shoving and the savage beating of several of the prisoners.

The C Company prisoners, a group that included 1st Lt. MacGill, began a northward march to the main NK POW collecting station. The march was not a forced one as a number of halts were called due to the presence of American fighter planes along the route. This slower-paced march allowed other POW groups to catch up so that by the time the collecting station was reached, many POWs from the 19th Regiment were marching as a unit.

Unfortunately, most of the American POWs had eaten little during the many hours of battle that preceded their capture. Now, en route in captivity, a number suffered severely from lack of nourishment. Also, as most of the march took place during daylight hours, thirst became a more severe problem.

NK frontline replacements were encountered as the POW group plodded along. Americans were often struck by one or another of the NK marching south. More often was the case of Americans being spit upon.

At one juncture during the march, a passing NK officer, whose responsibilities did not include transporting the POWs, threatened to assume that responsibility and then massacre the entire group. The officer was prevented from carrying out this threat by those in charge of the march.

And the marching men could not fail to notice, at intervals along the road, bodies of Americans, taken prisoner earlier, cause of death unknown, but suspicioned to be related to the psychology of guerrilla brutality as practiced by the NK.

First Lt. MacGill, meanwhile, made numerous attempts to prevent the NK from beating or otherwise harming Americans around him. One POW reported later that the NK were quite startled at MacGill's knowledge of spoken Japanese (which most adult Koreans at the time could understand) as well as a bit of the Korean language.[8]

At the collecting point finally, MacGill, on his own volition and in an absence of will on the part of American officers of higher rank who were present, moved to the forefront, endeavoring to assume protective charge of the enlisted men. Considerable animated discussion among the NK officer cluster followed, accompanied by pushing and shoving of prisoners, all of which took place in front of and around MacGill.

Then something was said by an NK officer, provoking MacGill to respond that "(he) would die first."

MacGill was taken immediately from the assembled group and placed in the sidecar of a waiting motorcycle. The cycle sped away followed by a small NK vehicle carrying a driver, an officer, and two enlisted men.[9] This was the last any American saw 1st Lt. Henry MacGill alive. It is assumed, lacking evidence to the contrary, that he was executed by his NK captors.

First Lt. Henry T. MacGill fought his share of the Kum River battle in the classic manner and with the highest degree of personal courage. He inspired the men in his company to stand against the NK until the very end. During the course of the siege, a total of perhaps thirteen hours, there was no panic or wholesale desertion, an extraordinary presence given the predicament of the American commitment at that moment.

If there was an operational fault, that fault can be charged to a higher authority that determined the defensive layout of the river line. C Company was too far out without adequate tie-ins. It also was deployed on a group of low-lying hills that both invited straight-on enemy attacks and stealthy flanking maneuvers.

During the lengthy NK siege, the C Company men remained continuously confident that they would be rescued. Certainly, in their minds, a headquarters that determined their battle position would stand ready to assist when that position became untenable. Like children with their parents, these men trusted the wisdom and military expertise of their betters. But the only response that was conveyed, that fortunately none in the position heard, was "every man for himself."

Buoyed by the defensive artillery curtain that halted the NK attack earlier that morning, the company maintained a viable defense despite a predicament that grew hopeless by the hour. The NK recognized and respected this steadfastness by not risking a second frontal assault, preferring to wait it out until the defenders' ammunition supply dwindled, as indeed happened. Only when NK feeler movements toward the position threatened encirclement did 1st Lt. MacGill order a fallback and then the cracking began. Nevertheless, there was no panic. Those who remained able at the moment of the fallback moved only on order from their commander.

In his exhaustive summary of the early Korean action, Roy E. Appleman sets 122 of an original strength figure of 177 of C Company personnel as killed, wounded, or missing (includes POWs) at or near their Kum battle site. This figure approximates 70 percent of the company roster.[10]

A more recent but unofficial accounting of the company lists a roster of 179 enlisted and 6 officers entering the Kum River line on July 12. Of this 185 total, 121, or about 65 percent of the company were killed, wounded, or missing (includes POWs). This unofficial record reveals enlisted losses as sixty-nine killed, six missing, and forty taken prisoner.[11] One known wounded survived.[12] Of the forty captives, twenty-nine died, one escaped, and ten were repatriated in 1953.[13]

The officer casualty total includes two killed, one wounded, and two taken prisoner. One of the captives was executed while the other was repatriated in 1953.[14]

First Lt. MacGill was awarded the Distinguished Service Cross posthumously for his outstanding leadership and sacrifice during the Kum River encounter. At the time the decoration was authorized, it was not known that he had been captured, then executed. As it turned out, his reported demeanor as a captive enhanced his stature as a military leader, with due credit to the institution that educated him, the United States Military Academy.

While 1st Lt. MacGill has been accorded appropriate deferential recognition, it might be suggested, and respectfully so, that each enlisted company member who died during the course of the battle action or, unhurt, remained with their commander and then taken prisoner, all relative to the exigencies of hostilities then being played out, merits acknowledgment that the duty of each during those long hours of July 16, 1950, was performed in a spirit of outstanding courageous willingness, a spirit consummately honorable as measured by standards of acceptable behavior before the enemy.

It was a behavior that all with whom these men had association ought identify with pride: their battalion, their regiment, their extended military peers, their families and, in the ultimate, the greater society they were sworn to represent and protect.

• • •

All is mostly quiet today along the dike facing the Kum River. The hills and earth mounds that overlook the river and paddy plain present the same serene, pastoral arena as first beheld by the men of the 19th Regiment when filing to their battle positions on July 12, 1950. The same may also be true of many other deployment sites of that 1950 summer, sites familiar to those in battalions of other, companion regiments, located, as most were, on the hills and along the valleys of a mainly rural nationhood.

While all this is so today in that Land of the Morning Calm, a different sort of quiet, half a world away, is gathering; reposeful evening reveries by a rapidly graying soldiery, deepening and enveloping, when strife's tumult from that long-ago summer is recalled and retraced and comrades from that time are remembered and venerated.

And in a future not too distant, those who yet remain, one by one, will join the stillness of those who have gone before; each, then all finally lying in uninterrupted peace; hopefully not forgotten.

Chapter Endnotes

Prelude

1 Robert Goralski, *World War I Almanac*, 1931–1945, p. 422. Pertinent figure quoted from information released by the U.S. Army Adjutant General's Office.

2 Earl L. Kinchner, ed., *Selective Service Under the 1948 Act*, p. 9.

3 *Ibid.*, p. 5.

4 *Army and Navy Journal*, Apr. 2, 1949, p. 894.

5 Kinchner, *Op. Cit.*, p. 9.

6 *Ibid.*

7 *Army and Navy Journal*, Feb. 21, 1948. Gen. Eisenhower's report is printed in full in this issue. Pertinent portions are on pg. 654.

8 *Ibid.*, Feb. 28, 1948, p. 666.

9 Kinchner, *Op. Cit.*, p. 25. Secretary of the Army Kenneth C. Royall, identified as the source for the newly authorized strength figures, used the phrase "might be increased to." A further reference to his remarks cites his caution that appropriations at the moment limited the strength figure to 790,000, at least until July 1, 1949. It would appear from this cautionary stance that pressures to economize were felt even at the pinnacle of the need to do something about Soviet gains in Europe.

10 *Army and Navy Journal*, July 3, 1948, p. 1197.

11 Kinchner, *Op. Cit.*, p. 16.

12 *Ibid.*

13 *Ibid.*, p. 131.

14 *Ibid.*

15 *Army and Navy Journal*, Jan. 15, 1949, p. 574. The national defense portion of the president's budget transmission is quoted in full.

16 Kinchner, *Op. Cit.*, p. 16.

17 *Army Times*, Aug. 27, 1949, p. 24.

18 Kinchner, *Op. Cit.*, p. 18.

19 *Army and Navy Journal*, Apr. 2, 1949, p. 894. The National Guard was authorized 325,000 and the Organized Reserve 230,000, both commissioned and enlisted.

20 *Ibid.*, Apr. 16, 1949, p. 947.
21 Kinchner, *Op. Cit.*, p. 17. Announcement of impending releases was made in a speech given to the National Guard Association. Gray stated that the releases were the result of budgetary concerns.
22 *Army and Navy Journal*, Oct. 29, 1949, p. 224.
23 *Ibid.*, June 24, 1950, p. 1168.
24 *Ibid.*, Mar. 4, 1950, p. 694.
25 *Ibid.*, Mar. 11, 1950, p. 734.
26 *Army Times*, Jan. 21, 1950, p. 4.
27 Gordon R. Young, ed., *The Army Almanac, 1959*, 2nd ed., p. 128. The *Almanac* affirms that 43,000 reserve officers were on active duty throughout the army's establishment at the outbreak of the Conflict. During the course of the fighting, 165,800 enlisted reservists and 78,500 reserve officers, the latter members of the newly identified Organized Reserve Corps (ORC), were counted as taking part.
28 *Army Times*, June 10, 1950, p. 4.
29 Kinchner, *Op. Cit.*, p. 134. The House passed the bill, identified as H.R. 6826, on May 24, 1950. The Senate did not take up discussion until June 21. It was the lag in the Senate that prompted the fifteen-day extension of Public Law 759.

On the Way

1 *Recruiting Journal*, vol. 2, no. 1, p. 4.
2 The combat team comprised the 5th Infantry Regiment and the 555th Field Artillery Battalion, ordered to permanent station in Hawaii.

Preparation

1 At the Camp Crawford military post.
2 Between the end of WWII and shortly after the commencement of the Korean Conflict, each of the military services was permitted to create its own qualifying test so as to determine the degree of value or competence of potential recruits. These new tests, including the one produced by the Army, followed closely the structure comprising the familiar AGCT (Army General Classification Test) administered to large numbers of entering servicemen during WWII. (See Bernard Karpinos, "Mental Test Failures," in *The Draft, Handbook of Facts and Alternatives*, Sol Tax ed., p. 36.)

A general understanding of AGCT analysis during WWII pointed to scores of 90 through 110 as ranging from low to high average.

Now, in the postwar atmosphere of peace and economic expansion with military recruitment, particularly Army, lagging, effort was made through a provision of the 1948 selective service act to make recruiting more successful by *lowering* the minimum acceptable classification scores. (Kinchner, *Op. Cit.*, p. 27.)

With seventy as the new score minimum for acceptance, twenty points lower than the lowest average score for WWII, it was hoped to attract men whose cognitive skills were open to question, given the prevailing requirements and obligations set by the several services, but whose contributions, after normally intensive basic training periods, would be sufficient to warrant retention over time.

Even so, recruiting pressures being what they are, some patently unqualified men slipped through with clearly falsified scores. A case in point was the alleged true AGCT score of one private driver in B Battery, 48th Field Artillery Battalion, 7th Infantry Division, which was said to be in the low forties.

3 Efforts were made periodically by Eighth Army to secure up-to-date data on road, rail, tunnel, and bridge conditions in areas of Japan deemed critical to Occupation military planning. This author headed a three-man survey detail in late 1949 that inspected roads and bridges in the Wakamatsu, Niigata, and Kashiwazaki area of west central Honshu, the report of inspection filed with the 7th Infantry Division Artillery headquarters at Camp Younghans, with copies to division, corps, and army.

4 Ian V. Hogg and John Weeks, *Illustrated Encyclopedia of Military Vehicles*, p. 123–124.

5 The *Army Times* issue of Aug. 27, 1949, p. 24, contains in detail the projected Army commissioned (reserve) reduction process. A total of 5,787 reserve officers would revert involuntarily to either inactive or enlisted (active duty) status. To reach this reduction goal, the following steps would be taken:
a. The age-in-grade policy (officers beyond the age bracket determined for the particular rank held) would be strictly enforced.
b. A total of 1,250 officers would be eliminated by December 1, 1949, after notification from theatre no later than October 1.
c. A total of 2,137 officers would be eliminated by April 1, 1950, after notification no later than January 1.
d. Normal attrition would constitute elimination of the remaining number.

It Begins

1 Fighting began on the morning of June 25 at about 0400 on the Ongjin Peninsula in the western segment of the Parallel and began rippling eastward about 0500. The city of Kaesong fell about 0930 without much resistance. (See Bruce Cumings, *Korea's Place in the Sun*, p. 260–261.)

With Bated Breath

1 Lt. Col. Roy Appleman, *South to the Naktong, North to the Yalu*, p. 113–17. An excellent survey of units and materiel available to the South Korean army at the onset of fighting may be found on these pages.

2 *Army Times*, Apr. 29, 1950, p. 10.

3 During the Korean Occupation and certainly throughout most if not the entirety of the Korean Conflict, American and other United Nations forces referred to Koreans and North Koreans in particular as "gooks." Many had the impression that the term's origin was connected with garments worn by

both men and women: a sort of white, Halloween-style garb, easily identifiable and just as easily fitted to spooky slang discourse.

The fact of the matter was, however, that the appellation was derived from part of the Korean language name for each of the two political entities within that divided land. In Korean, the Republic of Korea is *Taehan Min'guk*, while the name for the Democratic Peoples' Republic of Korea is *Choson Immin'guk*.

True to their reputation as masters of the contraction, American soldiers simply labeled *all* Koreans "guks" (gooks), an appellation bitterly resented by the average Korean national.

4 Judgment attributed to Brig. Gen. William L. Roberts, Chief of the Korean Military Advisory Group (KMAG), who left Korea just prior to the June 25 invasion. See article by Frank Gibney, "Korea, Progress Report," *Time*, June 5, 1950, p. 26. Brig. Gen. Roberts was also quoted in the *Army and Navy Journal* July 1, 1950, p. 1182, as touting the ROK army as the best fighting force on the Asiatic continent.

5 *Ibid.*

6 Marguerite Higgins, "The Terrible Days in Korea," *Saturday Evening Post*, Aug. 19, 1950, p. 110.

Pipeline

1 Conclusion based on an observed dearth of cavalry fillers during the early days of fighting.

2 On an evening in middle September 1949, during a visit to the Far East Command by the Army's Chief of Staff, Gen. J. Lawton Collins, a parade was held at the Tokyo Plaza, a parade ground near the moat and nearly opposite the Dai Ichi Building, Gen. Douglas MacArthur's headquarters. Cavalry units, including artillery, participated in the parade.

It was noted that the cavalrymen and their equipment both seemed in A-1 condition, conveying an excellent impression to Japanese and American spectators, this author being among the latter.

3 The *taro* is a large tropical plant native to the Pacific islands and Southeast Asia, cultivated particularly for its edible root. Widely found throughout the islands of Hawaii, the leaf of the taro came to symbolize, in part, that country's geopolitical stance. The taro leaf in turn was adopted as the symbol or emblem of one of the American military units stationed in Hawaii prior to WWII , the unit known as the Hawaiian Division. The Hawaiian Division later became the 24th Infantry Division, and the taro leaf was continued as that division's emblem.

4 The first combat units in Korea commanded by Maj. Gen. Dean, prior to the arrival of Eighth Army Headquarters, were identified by the acronym USAFIK: United States Army Forces in Korea.

5 This was the First Battalion, 21st Infantry Regiment, commanded by Lt. Col. Charles B. Smith.

Kublai Khan in Reverse

1 With the onset of the Conflict and the commitment of the Occupation divisions, organization of a Japanese indigenous force began immediately, bringing to an end Gen. MacArthur's program of forging a completely pacifistic postwar society. When this defense force was pronounced trained and ready in 1952, the American Occupation officially ended.

Assignment

1 Kenneth Shadrick's name as the first American killed in action was reported by Marguerite Higgins, one of the correspondents in Korea during the early actions. Later investigation casts doubt on the Shadrick casualty as being the first, although there has been no confirmed identification as to who that first KIA might have been.

Most at the time accepted the Shadrick identification and, despite continuing controversy, his name comes to mind whenever early battles in Korea are recounted.

Moving Up

1 Higgins, *Op. Cit.*, p. 8.

2 Orlando Ward, *Korea-1950*, p. 35. This publication by the Office of the Chief of Military History, Department of the Army, was the first to provide both text and pictures of the early action in Korea.

The picture on page thirty-five, lower, shows troops from the 19th Infantry Regiment lined up preparatory to boarding buses as described. Their first destination was an overnight bivouac. Many of these men would board the same buses the following morning, July 7, en route to Taegu.

3 See *Epilogue*, page 264 for more accurate company strength figures.

For Real

1 At the time, Americans in Korea were too busy adjusting to a troublesome topography, an unfriendly climate, and the tactics of a guerrilla-type military campaign to give careful thought to motives displayed by the NK in their treatment of prisoners. It was obvious, however, that through seemingly orchestrated incidents of outright brutality, acts that were callously in violation of acceptable international law, the NK were forcing the Americans to prove the depth of their commitment to battle.

None knew at the moment that a fair number of Americans had been taken prisoner early on by the NK and not harmed particularly. That this was so was somewhat contrary to normal guerrilla practice as affecting prisoners. For a variety of reasons, one of which is an unwillingness to house and otherwise care for prisoners, due to a refusal to allocate manpower and resources for their care, prisoners taken during guerrilla campaigns, more often than not, are eliminated immediately.

Since the first Americans in Korea anticipated, should it come to that, that their treatment as prisoners would generally be in line with the WWII

European experience, realization that surrender to the NK might very well be the equivalent of committing suicide came as a shock to line troops. In this respect, the NK scored first, and in a big way, in the push and pull of psychological warfare.

On the other hand, a judgment by a returned American POW regarding the general, initial NK POW operation is relevant here. Wilbert Estabrook, an enlistee detailed as a guard for the First Battalion, 19th Infantry Regiment, July 12–16, 1950, in attempting to evade NK thrusting during the late afternoon and evening of July 16, was forced away from the main escape road to Taejon and captured the next day.

In a letter dated March 17, 1995, reviewing the initial stage of his prisoner experience, he recollected that "…the NK people who had us seemed to have been trained for collection of POWs. They took care of us the best they could under front line conditions. Had this not been the case, we would have all been killed."

The Kum River Fight

1 The NK Third Division carried the assault against the First Battalion, 19th Infantry Regiment, along the Kum River at Taep'yong-ni.

2 The Americans were given to understand that ROK troops were in place beyond the river bend, but none were observed. The Second Battalion, 19th Regiment, had been given the mission of providing flank security for the First. No Second Battalion troops made contact with C Company personnel during the latter's stay in position.

3 First Lt. James C. Ruddell Jr. was wounded on July 16 and captured the following day. He is listed as having succumbed in an NK prison camp during February, 1951.

4 Maj. Arthur P. Lombardi, former executive officer of A Battery, 63rd Field, in a letter dated Aug. 9, 1961, confirmed the attack and resulting heavy loss suffered by the 63rd. He wrote that a large NK force advancing toward the battalion had been misidentified as ROK troops. This error permitted the NK to surround the battalion and launch a deadly strike at the Headquarters Battery, where was located the fire direction center (FDC).

The bulk of A Battery then began a withdrawal march along a predetermined escape road that led between two hills. An NK roadblock at this location forced the vehicle column to stop, exposing the men to enemy rifle and mortar fire. Among those killed was the battery commander, Capt. Lyndel Southerland.

A fired ammunition truck prevented Lombardi and several others from leaving the battery position with the rest of the convoy. When the exploding ammunition was mostly consumed, Lombardi and the men with him emerged from ground cover, came upon and disabled several howitzers in the stalled convoy, and left the scene on foot.

A second firing battery, commanded by Capt. Anthony F. Stahelski, also was exposed to NK roadblock fire preventing an orderly withdrawal. A number of vehicles and several howitzers were abandoned at this location. Roy Appleton has written that two howitzers only were salvaged from this artillery battalion debacle. See *Op. Cit.*, p. 126–8.

5 The gun carriages were most likely Soviet-built SU-76 models or a variant of same.

6 No one was sure at this stage where the F-80s were based. As the jets arrived within minutes after the attack began, the most likely take-off point was the Taegu airfield.

7 First Lt. MacGill earlier had dispatched a runner to the First Battalion CP with a request for food and more ammunition. The runner failed to return.

8 Sfc. Otis W. Loomis was captured by the NK somewhere between the First Battalion CP and the C Company positions. He was attempting to return to the company when confronted by the NK. In a letter dated Feb. 8, 1961, James Stavrakes confirmed that the battalion commander had spoken earlier with Sfc. Loomis. Had Loomis been able to return with the commander's message, C Company's withdrawal effort might have begun sooner with an outside possibility of success, certainly with fewer casualties.

9 Second Lt. Stavrakes accompanied the covering platoon, of which the Lieutenant was now part, to the foot of the hill fronting the diked plain and watched as the men merged with the withdrawing A Company. In a letter describing his part in the withdrawal action (Feb. 8, 1961) he recalled choosing to wait a bit longer in the Kum paddy area, hoping to meet MacGill and the remaining C Company men. Such was not to be, however.

Stavrakes was one of the last Americans to withdraw from the Taep'yong-ni locale, only to be cut off on the south escape road by an NK ambush. With thirteen others, he began a trek over the hills. NK harassment soon reduced the group to four, and these latter were captured on July 20. Stavrakes was one of the few Americans to survive forced marches and prison camps during a three-year ordeal and was repatriated during August 1953.

10 B Company withdrew from the Kum line in fairly good order. However, the relatively orderly withdrawal disintegrated at one or another of the NK roadblocks set up along the escape road. A number from this company were killed or wounded, and many were forced into surrounding hills to complete their escape.

11 The 19th Regiment's First Battalion commander was killed during one of the several engagements with the NK in and around Taep'yong-ni. So, also, were several members of his staff. Several were captured.

At some point during the early afternoon of the 16th, First Battalion staff organization and effectiveness ceased. Sufficient regimental authority remained, however, to continue a limited battalion command chain acting to authorize the withdrawals of A and B companies from the battle line.

Once the withdrawals began, authority descended to the company level, and then only until roadblocks were reached, at which sites authority more or less evaporated as bravery, ingenuity, or individual cowardice, whichever, all respecting the will or lack of same to survive, took hold.

Roadblock

1 The plane was quite high in the air and in view such a short time to the men on the ground in this narrow valley that identification as a B-29 may have been faulty. Regardless, it was a lone bomber, and its crew and mission were welcome at this difficult battle stage.

A picture of the "island" or wooded hamlet, the presumed target of the bombing, is on page 45 of the military history publication, *Korea-1950.*

A Night Never to Be Forgotten

1 The vehicles spotted by members of the tank crew constituted the afterpart of a column of backed-up equipment, the result of the NK's most effective roadblock, located at the most narrow point in the valley leading from the Kum River, and described in some detail by Appleman, *Op. Cit.*, p. 138 *ff.*

There were seemingly three roadblocks interposed by the NK that afternoon. The most damaging one was just south of Tuman-ni (first paragraph above), designed to trap the bulk of the withdrawing regiment and did wreak havoc on numbers of regimental vehicles and personnel riding in them.

The one machine gun-block just south of Taep'yong-ni effected a final structural disintegration of the withdrawing First Battalion, A and D Companies and the C Company platoon.

A third block, the one the 52nd Field was attempting to ride through, was probably a northward extension of the Tuman-ni block.

More positively, the NK obstruction affecting the 52nd Field column enabled withdrawing First Battalion infantry to survive their breakup in greater numbers than might have been the case otherwise. The continued sighting of the standing vehicles strengthened the will to survive at a time when mental and physical strains were close to being overwhelming.

2 One of the officers was identified as assigned to the 52nd Field while the other may have been either a chaplain or a medical officer.

3 Several audibly counted the number of stretchers bearing the wounded.

4 It was given to understand later that the men who remained on stretchers and a Roman Catholic chaplain, Capt. Herman G. Felhoelter of the 19th Regiment, and who continued ministering to the wounded men, were massacred by the NK close to daylight or three to four hours after the main group left for American lines.

5 The chaplain's name was Capt. Kenneth C. Hyslop, Protestant chaplain with the 19th Regiment. The conversation between the two men was heard clearly, conversation that included the remark about the coin toss. A later version has it that Chaplain Felhoelter urged Hyslop to leave because the latter was a family man.

As both chaplains died in Korea, Hyslop only five months later (see Epilogue, page 261), it is next to impossible to verify the exact nature of the decision-making on that early morning of July 17.

6 Chaplain (Capt.) Herman G. Felhoelter.

7 It was generally understood the Capt. Prescott was under 19th Regiment orders to remain on the hill above Taep'yong-ni, overlooking the diked plain

until relieved. Regimental authority may have eroded quickly during the afternoon of the sixteenth so that relief was never effected. It must be presumed that Prescott, a fine officer and professional in every respect, remained at his assigned position until the end.

Taejon

1 The North Korean 3rd and 4th Divisions carried the assault on Taejon against two battalions of the 34th Regiment and one battalion of the 19th Regiment.

2 Nugent survived the war in a prison camp. Upon release, he was court-martialed on the charge of giving aid and comfort to the enemy. He was acquitted, permitted to remain in the active service, and retired as a Lt. Col. Interestingly, his duty replacement with the 52nd Field was Capt. Paul Godsman, formerly with the 48th Field in Japan, and one of the officers who traveled with the Lieutenant in the pipeline to the 24th Division.

3 Letter dated Aug. 9, 1961.

4 Among those in vehicles withdrawing from Taejon the afternoon of July 20 was a young medical officer from this narrator's former hometown of Altoona, Pennsylvania. He was 1st Lt. Dale W. McDowell, an acquaintance and member of the same high school graduating class (1940), assigned to the 34th Regiment on July 18, having been flown from the States and his position as a resident at the Western Pennsylvania Hospital in Pittsburgh, Pennsylvania.

First Lt. McDowell was in a medical three-quarter-ton, probably somewhere in the column led by the 13th Field's B Battery, when a mortar shell exploded, either close to or on the vehicle, killing all personnel riding in it.

5 Col. (Ret.) Ernest P. Terrell, in a summary draft reviewing his participation in the Taejon battle of July 20, rejects a previously published assertion that infantry and engineer elements were responsible for retrieving the 11th Field howitzers and accompanying equipment. The retrieval was accomplished by battery personnel as described above.

6 Then-2nd Lt. Terrell was not previously aware of the observation made by then-1st Lt. Arthur Lombardi regarding the state of mind of Maj. Gen. William Dean on the early morning of July 20. Terrell's own observation of the general's actions and responses later that day and evening, although he declined to use the word, led him to conclude that his (general's) behavior could be construed as bordering on the irrational.

Limited proof of this conclusion was that, although the walking group of which Gen. Dean was part did cross a streambed en route to the ridge destination, *no water was seen flowing*. The general's breaking away alone to search for water was explained later by his Aide as an act of succor for the wounded among the group. Terrell does not remember hearing Gen. Dean tell anyone in the group that he was leaving to search for water.

A short time later, as the general would write some years later, he fell and injured himself, rendering him unable to rejoin the safety of the walking group and vulnerable to capture by the enemy. The latter happened, as we know, and he sat out the remainder of the war in solitary confinement, officially unreported as a POW until early 1953.

It would be grossly unfair to comment adversely or make a firm judgment concerning the mental state of the general on the evening of July 20, 1950. However, it does seem clear that the course of battle played out by the 24th Division, up to and including the stand at Taejon, weighed heavily. The division had not anticipated nor was it prepared for the kind of combat waged by the NK. The early unsuccessful defensive efforts, regardless of circumstances or reason, and culminating in the almost chaotic troop withdrawal from Taejon, may have effected permanent damage to the general's psyche.

There are only two fragmentary observations supporting the damage thesis. Nevertheless, Dean's leaving a withdrawing group to become a "loner" in indisputably enemy territory, despite the high-minded explanation made later by another, the purpose of which may or may not have been voiced by the general, and ignoring the presence within the group of able-bodied soldiers who might willingly have undertaken the water chore, was not the sort of rational duty performance one would normally expect from a higher ranking leader.

Whatever, no one ever doubted that Maj. Gen. William Dean, a Medal of Honor recipient, tried his damnedest. Sadly, through July 20, 1950, held hostage first by a parsimonious American public, then by an imposed battle plan not initially considered winnable, and thirdly by a temporarily ineffectual soldiery, he failed.

Relief

1 Grave mounds were one of the more curious sights encountered by American soldiers in Korea, but not that they were all that noticeably numerous. Many, those stationed in urban settings, never saw one. Others caught fleeting glimpses of oddly pimpled, uncultivated fields extending from rural roads and not understanding that what they were seeing were cemeteries. It remained mostly for line troops and their direct support to both happen upon and use these mounds on higher elevations as part of line defensive measures. The Rev. Hyoung Dock Yoo, a Methodist minister in Morristown, New Jersey, born and raised in South Korea, has provided an explanation for the mounds as a funerary practice, particularly among rural Koreans.

The grave mound is a fact of *naturalism* as a religious practice. It is an experience comprising (1) worship of the natural law and (2) a heaven to be attained through obedience to natural processes.

The funerary process calls for the deceased to be buried in a coffin beneath the earth's surface. A mound of soil is then raised over the coffin, four to six feet in diameter and two to four feet in height and roughly oblong. The mound represents the shape of heaven and the universe. The spirit of the deceased may then ascend to heaven through the mound.

The terminal function of the mound is to erode over time, returning the soil to its original (natural) flat appearance and purpose.

2 The 8th Regiment, the first cavalry regiment to go on line in relief of the 24th Division, would also be the first American regiment to engage the Chinese "Volunteer" force, the CCF. This contact took place at Unsan, North Korea, on November 1, 1950.

3 The tactical amphibious operation reported by 1st Lt. Reffner was not considered a combat confrontation. No arrowhead award was authorized to be worn by the men involved. See the *Army Almanac*, p. 638.

4 *Time*, July 31, 1950, p. 16.

No Rest for the Weary

1 Unknown to this narrator at the time, Brig. Gen. Church, Gen. MacArthur's personal representative and liaison to the forces in Korea, including the ROK force, had received his promotion to Maj. Gen. prior to assuming command of the 24th Division.

Maj. Gen. Dean survived the war as an NK prisoner.

Back to the Naktong

1 The North Korean 4th Division faced one battalion of the 34th Regiment at Koch'ang and both the First and Third Battalions of the 34th later at Kwanbin-ni. Two battalions of the 21st regiment relieved the 34th after the Kwanbin-ni stand. The 17th ROK Regiment entered the fighting on the second day of the Kwanbin-ni battle.

2 The bell sound emanated from a small church near the command post. Whether as part of a religious exercise or as a signal, the sound triggered fire from NK positions and the beginning of an enveloping assault.

3 For some reason, the 34th Regiment may have reported the engagement at Kwanbin-ni as having taken place on July 29, the date that saw the regiment's Third Battalion withdraw from Koch'ang without contesting the town. The inference that the regiment so reported is deduced from the number of regimental KIAs listed on that date: twenty-seven. Only one KIA is listed for July 30.

The deaths of 1st Lt. Christine and his driver, Pfc. Hanford K. Maeda, on the other hand, were reported as occurring on July 30. It can only be conjectured that the 34th command may have been embarrassed over giving up Koch'ang without a fight and sought to cover the loss by reporting fighting and casualties in that town, the fighting and casualties actually occurring one day later at another place.

Appleman, *Op. Cit.*, p. 249, has written that the 34th was driven from Koch'ang and later set up a defensive position at Sanje-ri. As he was privy to official records when compiling his excellent book, deliberately falsified information made official would seem to be the case here, unfortunately.

4 Despite the glaring headlines and images of "last stands" that, together, acted to convey the general's words to the world, his message, basically, was misinterpreted. What he meant to emphasize was: There would be no

Dunkirk. American forces would have to make a determined effort in place to hold back further NK attempts to advance, but that some maneuvering, even some withdrawals may prove necessary to effect a successful defensive effort.

Most within hearing by this narrator, upon becoming aware of Gen. Walker's message, looked about their present positions and concluded, "No way."

Later, of course, with the bulk of American units behind the Naktong River, and the Pusan Perimeter a defensive reality, the phrase "determined effort" described accurately what took place along the battle line, to the credit of both the American soldiers who made the effort a successful one and to the general whose job it was to prod.

Manning the Perimeter

1 Nelsen, letter, dated Aug. 21, 1959; Cody, letter, dated July 7, 1961; Bailey, letter, dated June 21, 1961.

2 The 29th currently survives as a parent regiment in the combat arms regimental system.

3 Lacking information to the contrary, it was understood that units of the 29th Infantry Regiment were officially parceled to the 25th Division.

4 Bill Gibbons was wounded about this time. He was evacuated for hospitalization.

5 These locations, simply situated in small rural communities but more amply arranged in urban settlements, carry the name *Ma-Dang*. The Ma-Dang, meaning public round garden, is the center place where community bonds are forged, where decisions affecting the community are made, and depending on the occasion and season, where community activities and feasts are held.

Into the Jaws Again

1 Pfc. Koppelman received the Silver Star decoration for his plain disregard of self during the rescue operation. Second Lt. Hoover, an outstanding and dedicated officer, suffered injuries that led ultimately to his being retired on disability.

2 Summary excerpts by Nelsen in letter, dated Aug. 21, 1959.

The First Battle of the Naktong Pocket

1 The North Korean 4th Division carried the assault in this area of the Perimeter against two battalions of the 19th Regiment, two battalions of the 34th Regiment, one battalion of the 23rd Regiment, two battalions of the 15th Regiment, units of the 5th Marine Regiment (a component of the First Provisional Marine Brigade), and peripherally against one battalion of the 21st Regiment. Also, various other elements of the 25th Division were involved. The American units were not committed simultaneously, but as need dictated.

2 Second Lt. Nattras was with one of the cut off companies. Injured, he was evacuated for medical treatment after rescue was effected.

3 The red cloth ID panels, roughly two feet by six feet, distributed on company levels to mark lines of advance, would become invaluable aids for both artillery and close-in air support. Occasionally, however, the NK utilized

captured panels to confuse airmen.

4 One of the deeply regretted oversights was not securing names of these two young men. Both continued in C Company at least until November 4, 1950.

5 Second Lt. Coles had been designated as the next A Battery executive officer and left to assume this new duty.

6 This attack maneuver by the 34th Regiment was the last executed by that unit prior to its dissolution as a cognate component of the 24th Division. The regiment was destined to be reorganized and retrained, eventually rejoining the division.

7 Division, corps, and Army headquarters requests for body counts, although seemingly unreasonable, represented a certain settling-in of military planning and maneuver. There no longer was emphasis on containment. New emphasis was on attacking, killing, and/or capturing. The unit reporting success in either of the three categories, particularly of the first two categories, was doing its job well.

Pressure on units for continuous reporting of tactical successes (body counting), unfortunately, as is often the case in a military setting, leads to exaggerated accounting. Such exaggeration, during all phases of the Korean Conflict, was more the rule than the exception, both on the ground and from the air.

Rest, at Last

1 On page 120 of the booklet, *Korea-1950*, there is a picture of soldiers on Hill 311. The caption strongly infers that the men, some using binoculars, are on the alert for enemy activity.

To the contrary. This is a picture of the *backside* of Hill 311, and the men are facing the rear or pocket area, in and around which the battle of the Naktong Pocket was fought.

Faintly seen in the picture's background is the curving Naktong River as it brushes the right flank of the 25th Division sector.

Reflections While at Rest

1 Gen. Eisenhower is quoted in the *Army Almanac*, p. 228, as declaring "Food is part of a soldier's pay; none of it should be counterfeit."

2 Col. (Ret.) Ernest P. Terrell Jr., in a summary brief recalling events affecting the 11th Field just prior to Conflict commitment, wrote that an IG (Inspector General) inspection of the battalion about a month before the war began found "all our vehicles, all of the howitzers, and about 90 percent of small arms and crew-served weapons to be combat unserviceable." In Terrell's words: "This was the equipment we took to Korea." Brief received from Terrell, Feb. 7, 1995.

3 The *Army and Navy Journal* of October 29, 1949, p. 223, reported Secretary of Defense Louis Johnson as projecting a saving of $20 million involving maintenance, operation, and replacement of military motor vehicles. His promises were made to members of the House Armed Service Committee.

The saving would be effected by June 30, 1950. Included in his projection was the release to other duties of 2,136 men then engaged in either operation or maintenance of vehicles.

4 *The Clan*, Organizational Day Booklet of the 13th Field Artillery Battalion, APO Camp Hakata, Japan, May 1947.

The Kyongsan Bivouac

1 Concurrence as to the tactics used is contained in a letter from Maj. Jerry Fly, dated Mar. 13, 1961.

2 Books was taken prisoner. Several group pictures of American POWs, circulated to news media during the summer of 1950, groupings that included commissioned officers, showed Books as one of the captives. He did not survive imprisonment. The date of his death was December 31, 1950.

3 Bruce Cumings identifies the English-speaker as Anne Wallace Suhr, a former Methodist missionary and wife of a Korean leftist. See Cumings, *Op. Cit.*, p. 270.

4 One KP, presumable Japanese and named Kiyohito Tsutsui, survived. He was taken to Korea by a unit of the 63rd Field and was known in an NK prison camp as "Mike." Confirmation of his survival was contained in a letter dated May 8, 1953, written by Pfc. Robert L. Edson, then an incarcerated POW in North Korea. Name and exact spelling of same has been provided by Homer E. Dailey, a former member of C Company, 19th Infantry Regiment.

5 The 34th Regimental Combat Team underwent reorganization and retraining at Camp Zama, Japan, with replacement officers and enlisted personnel.

Recrossing the Naktong

1 Bill Stapleton, "Fourth Squad, Third Platoon," *Collier's*, Jan. 13, 1951, p. 127.

2 This was the pay rate most understood the KATUSAs were receiving. Other accounts differ in the amount, but by one or two dollars only.

3 First Lt. John Krasco later changed his name to John H. Hastings. He was a West Point graduate. Source for the name change may be found in USMA records.

4 Al Jolson died shortly after returning from this Korean entertainment tour.

Songju

1 Sgt. Joseph Eliones Gant was later tendered a battlefield commission. During fighting in the early spring of 1951, 2nd Lt. Gant was taken prisoner. He survived a POW camp and was released during August 1953.

2 The rocket launcher (bazooka) team member who aimed and fired the missile was identified as Pfc. John I. Sullivan. Identification was provided by Homer E. Dailey, a member of C Company during the Songju operation.

3 Appleman, *Op. Cit.*, p. 583, reported that the Argyll company suffered thirteen KIA, seventy-four WIA, and two MIA during both the air attack and the effort to retain control of the hill. The Argylls were not driven from the

hill by the NK, but relinquished it voluntarily as a tactical maneuver.

Vengeance

1 It had long been rumored that the NK used civilians as human shields against the cavalry in and around Yongdong. Whether this tactic accounted in part for the dearth of civilians along this part of the returning route traveled by the Americans is not really known, but suspicioned, nevertheless.

2 First Lt. Emerson L. Reffner, artillery observer with C Troop, 8th Cavalry Regiment, and assigned to A Battery, 99th Field, was killed in action on or about July 25. His death occurred somewhere near the main road, not on King Mountain. He was awarded the Silver Star decoration posthumously. Letter from his brother, Wendell Reffner, dated Jan. 10, 1961.

3 This tactical artillery mission proved to be the last fired by the 24th Division artillery during the first phase of the Korean Conflict. Fire in anger would not resume until the 38th Parallel was crossed and North Korean territory entered.

4 Breakout action initiated by the First Cavalry Division met with greater success than that mounted by the 24th Division. Beginning at a point north of its long-held Perimeter battle line, the cavalry was able to organize a drive parallel to the 24th Division's sector, a drive that extended north of Taejon, enveloping the initial battle sites of Choch'iwon, Chonui, and Ch'onan. The cavalry became the first of the original Eighth Army-committed divisions to effect a linkup with units of the 7th Infantry Division that had come ashore at Inch'on as part of the X Corps.

The highlight of this preeminent breakout maneuver was a forced road march against light enemy opposition by a grouping designated as Taskforce Lynch. This taskforce covered a distance of 106.4 miles in eleven hours on September 26. The grouping, essentially the Third Battalion, 7th Cavalry Regiment, was commanded by Lt. Col. James H. Lynch.

In his comprehensive study of the Korean campaign, Clay Blair comments dryly that as a result of this road march maneuver and the subsequent linkage of the Eighth Army with the newly landed X Corps, the First Cavalry Division "had finally and fully regained the honor lost during the retreat to the Naktong and the defense of Taegu." Clay Blair, *The Forgotten War – America in Korea*, p. 317.

5 A group of military, of which Maj. Gen. Dean was one, disabled an NK tank. Word that Gen. Dean had participated in this action had circulated throughout the division for some time prior to the recapture of Taejon. The enemy tank being painted the day after the city's recapture was pointed out as the one the general had helped disable.

6 This figure was soon expanded to over several thousand.

Epilogue

1 *Army Almanac*, 279. Major unit casualty figures may be found on pgs. 652, 656, 659, 692, and 695. Casualty information and numbers for the 29th

Regiment and the 5th RCT, also derived from the 1954 report, were reprinted in the *Taro Leaf,* the 24th Infantry Division Association Newsmagazine, vol. 47, no. 6, p. 27.

2 The Korean Conflict data board, posted at Arlington National Cemetery (1995), shows the *Army* death in combat total as 27,709. The total combat death figure for all *services* during the Conflict is shown as 33,652. The Marine combat death total on the Arlington data board is 4,270. As the difference in *total* figures between the data supplied in 1954 and that of 1995 is noticeably limited, particularly affecting the Army and Marine Corps, figures supplied in the 1954 report, complete with appropriate categories, would seem to be sufficient for current common usage.

3 A summary of diplomatic maneuvering between the United States and the North Korean government affecting the problem of recovering remains of American soldiers in North Korea proper is contained on page 4, the Newark (NJ) *Star-Ledger,* Jan. 12, 1996.

4 Fitzroy, MacLean, *Highlanders, A History of the Scottish Clans,* p. 246.

5 Blair, *Op. Cit.,* p. 385.

6 The sequence of events respecting the capture of remaining C Company men and incidents immediately following have been related, either through interview or by letter, by the following returned POWs: William M. Allen, Wilbert "Shorty" Estabrook, and Herman Naville.

7 William M. Allen, letter, dated Mar. 14, 1993.

8 Ibid.

9 Wilbert "Shorty" Estabrook, letter, dated Sept. 10, 1993.

10 Appleman, *Op. Cit.,* p. 144

11 The unofficial roster of C Company personnel was provided by Richard A. Stuben, a later member of the company. Additional input, particularly respecting the status of company POWs, was contributed by Wilbert Estabrook. The roster compiled by Stuben and others working with him is representative of a very considerable amount of time and effort, evidence of the emotional impact the tragedy had on both the immediate survivors and those who came later to the company.

12 One of the two enlisted men who followed the Lieutenant out of the company position and whose name remains unknown.

13 Reference the unofficial Stuben company roster, pgs. 303-307.

14 Second Lt. James Stavrakes survived the three-year period of internment.

Appendices

Rosters

Following are selected rosters of commissioned and enlisted personnel, names of men who were assigned to the 13th Field Artillery Battalion and to certain companies of the 19th Infantry Regiment, 24th Infantry Division, during the summer of 1950.

The primary source for these rosters is the National Personnel Records Center, St. Louis, Missouri. Maj. Charles T. Bailey, USA-Ret., a former company commander with the 19th Regiment, and Richard A. Stuben, a former member of C Company, 19th Regiment, provided additional names and valuable status information.

Unfortunately, unit rosters from the Korean Conflict period are retained biannually only, January 31 and July 31 of a year in question. Thus some individuals, particularly those assigned to infantry companies, whose assignments were transitory for whatever reason, may not appear on any retained official roster.

The ultimate casualty status of certain individuals is included *where known*. The basic source for battle and prisoner of war deaths is the record maintained by the National Personnel Records Center. POW status listings, other than deceased notations, have been provided by Wilbert Estabrook, a former long-term POW, and Richard Stuben. Corroborative information regarding POW listings was provided by Robert L. Edson and Herman Naville, both long-term POWs.

ABSOLUTE ACCURACY RESPECTING BOTH ROSTER NAMES AND ASSOCIATED STATUSES, WHERE NOTED, CANNOT BE ASSERTED.

APPENDIX A
COMMISSIONED PERSONNEL: 13th Field Artillery Battalion, July 1950

LIEUTENANT COLONEL
Stratton, Charles W.

MAJOR
Cheek, Leon B. Jr.
Kron, Jack J.

CAPTAIN
Goode, James C.
Mayer, George E.
Morris, Cecil E.
Prescott, Coleman L. (KIA 7/16/50)
Still, Edgar E.
Thomas, Daniel L.

FIRST LIEUTENANT
Ball, Robert D.
Canfield, Morris H.
Dexter, Donald M. Jr.
Fullen, Robert L. (KIA 7/16/50)
Guier, David H.
Holton, Clarence A.
Monsour, Thomas B.
Pate, William A.
Perkins, Tom J.
Proncavage, William
Seem, Donald L.

SECOND LIEUTENANT
Bordley, James E.
Cody, Raymond J. (WIA 8/2/50)
Coles, Dewey L. Jr.
Coomer, Joseph A.
Delorimier, Charles
Gibbons, William J. (WIA 8/50)
Harrity, Ralph D.
Hoover, Samuel E. (WIA 8/6/50)
Mattes, Edwin L.
Nattras, Edward D. (WIA 8/50)
Nelson, Ellsworth (WIA 7/20/50)
Ring, Alfred D.

WARRANT
Cox, J. A. (CWO)
Gomez, Angel L. (JWI)
Tucker, Joseph (JWI)

Additional C Battery, August 31, 1950
Sullivan, Loren W. (CAPT)
Lombardi, Arthur P. (1LT)
Mabry, William (1LT)
Maxson, Kenneth (1LT)
Yates, Arnold R. (1LT)

APPENDIX B
ENLISTED PERSONNEL: 13th Field Artillery Battalion, July 1950
Headquarters and Headquarters Battery

MASTER SERGEANT
Farmer, Traver H.
Nelson, David A.
Thorstensen, Roy F.
Totty, Robert A. (KIA 1/1/51)

SERGEANT FIRST CLASS
Collins, Elmore D.
Heath, Doyle L.
Misdorf, Bernard M.
Ray, Joe L.
Smith, Earl
Smith, William E.
Sullivan, Daniel P.

SERGEANT
Clegg, Arthur L.
Flood, Merlin C.
Morales, Manzor
Powell, Brince A.
Slaughter, Francis
Slazenik, Adam J.
Wollesen, Frederick

CORPORAL
Agristi, Angelo T.
Blouin, Leslie L.
Boulden, Roger D.
Caputo, Michael R.
Clark, Bobby C.
Coveny, William E.
Cranford, Billie F.
Daniel, Jerry E.
Dehaven, Major C.
Does, Ersel A.
Ellis, Billie E.
Folds, Bobby S.
Fosberg, Raymond O.
Golnick, Harold H.
Gordon, Frank E.
Hall, Edward J.

Hall, James V.
Hall, Wayne T.
Hernet, Donald F.
Hughes, John Jr.
James, Albert H.
Jones, Rudolph
Kinser, Paul L.
Kralapp, William
Lewis, Dale
Love, Eugene R.
McCord, James G.
McGurdy, Helmuth
Mortz, Paul C.
Myers, William P.
Nelson, Ted A.
Paladino, Louis
Pittman, Arzo C.
Reid, Alton
Schuth, Richard
Sebben, Albert J.
Shanan, Vernon
Slater, William
Smeck, William E.
Smith William H.
Stoddert, Norman I.
Supat, Richard S.
Taylor, Max R.
Valasquez, Robert
Vaughn, James Jr.

PRIVATE FIRST CLASS
Adcox, Harold R.
Dobbins, Ernest L.
Ferenchak, George
Ferrell, Thomas L.
German, William B.
Hensley, Edward F.
Hirschkopf, Benjamin
Hurst, John L. (POW 11/4/50)
Jones, Joseph C. Jr.
Koenig, Charles M.
Kyle, Leland (POW 11/4/50)
Lazar, Peter H.
McDaniel, James E.
Mentz, Walter J.

Overfield, James
Owens, Charles W.
Perry, Harold B.
Phillips, Bobby R.
Phillips, Charles
Rux, John C.
Tenario, Sam F.
Thornton, Beverly L.
Toney, Charles E.
Van Horn, Clayton Jr.
Von Thauen, Edward
Wildeson, David
Wilson, Durell
Witwer, Jack J. (KIA 7/16/50)
Woodley, William

PRIVATE
Bayns, Ernest E.
Bishop, John L.
Canales, Jose O.
Carroll, Duwayne O.
Fairchild, Robert C.
Fletcher, Norman C.
Hill, James E.
Kettenring, John E.
Kirkland, James (KIA 7/16/50)
Leaf, Charles L.
Lee, William C. (KIA 7/30/50)
Longbard, Frank
Martinez, Fernando
Messer, Lester
Somerlott, Stevenson
Strickland, Robert
Stricklen, Earnest
RANK UNKNOWN: Green, Eugene

Service Battery
SERGEANT FIRST CLASS
Dolbow, Thomas B.
Killian, Chester S.
McLean, Oscar J.
Rust, William D.

SERGEANT
Kenealy, William E.

Sweeney, John W.
Tokuda, Seiko

CORPORAL
Basham, Carl L.
Carson, Albert
Dobson, Clyde E.
Engel, George L.
Fruzyna, Francis T.
Gentile, Ernest C.
Graddy, Vexter P.
Keeran, Harvey W.
Kennen, Donald F.
Martinez, Ramond
Mireles, Oscar L.
Morgan, James P.
Muska, Steve
Oxendine, Grover C.
Radcliff, Forrest
Riley, Jasper O.
Sharp, Lawrence M.
Smith, Howard L.
Sweeney, William J.

PRIVATE FIRST CLASS
Ames, Dewey Z.
Anderson, Gerald E.
Carroll, Ronald E.
Corson, Harold G.
Fluty, John E.
Kiser, Bobby R.
Kotake, Kazuo H.
Patterson, Henry C.
Penney, Allan N.
Teller, Russell M.
Weidt, William B.
Welch, Gene J.
Whitmire, James A.
Wooten, Alfred F.

PRIVATE
Betts, Donald T.
Borgin, Lynn R.
Haney, Clarence J.
Kreiling, Frank O.

Lake, Orval W.
McDonald, Grady L.
McNichol, Kenneth
Hills, William H.
Rambaur, Frederick
Range, Nolan L.
Rush, James R.
Singleton, Charles (KIA 8/12/50)
Smith, Melvin F.
Stafford, Zollie E.
Stanberry, Alvin C.
Stinnett, Charles
Valles, Daniel
Werkweiser, Herbert

A Battery
MASTER SERGEANT
Knott, William E.

SERGEANT FIRST CLASS
Davis, James A.
Guthrie, William B.
Lucero, Antonio E.
Morgan, Harold H.
Wood Lonnie

SERGEANT
Counts, G. C. Jr.
Mayo, Gerald F.
Rubek, Charles R.
Skinner, Abner H.
Warfle, William K.
Zann, George

CORPORAL
Adamson, Roger M.
Adkinson, M. L.
Anderson, Billy H. (POW 1/1/51 DIE 3/29/51)
Bank, Joseph
Barnard, Robert L.
Baugher, Ralph
Brown, Harold R.
Burks, Willie H.
Carter, James A.
Chavez, Juan B.

Churchill, Ernest
Dabrawalski, Joseph
Duich, George J.
Finley, Fondo Jr.
Fitzgerald, Cletus
Garcia, Frank
Hammons, James F.
Hodge, Richard J.
Jackson, Reymond E.
Locke, Lynwood
Millsapps, Elmer E.
Oakman, Jules J.
Parullo, Charles R.
Thacker, Columbus (KIA 7/16/50)
Thompson, Earnest H.
Wallace, Glen L.
Walsh, Robert
Wilson, James C.

PRIVATE FIRST CLASS
Akers, Samuel C.
Bergeron, Paul
Blackmon, Bobby J.
Bonyer, Emory J.
Bowlin, James R.
Brenker, Raymond
Canfield, Lloyd R.
Cockrell, Hubert
Davis, John W.
Dear, Charles H.
Dietz, Charles Jr.
Digmon, John H.
Ducharme, Normand
Edson, Robert L. (POW 11/4/50)
Foreman, William H.
Garcia, Vircilig
Hackney, Billy H.
Hanks, James F.
Hayward, Charles W.
Hefferson, George
Hill, David C.
Huey, James M.
Hulbert, George H.
Hyman, John E.
Kaschak, Francis T.

King, Miles J.
Laprade, William J. (KIA 7/16/50)
Love, Lawrence
Middleton, Tilford
Miyashiro, Minosuke
Moore, Kenneth W.
Morton, Charles F.
Mosely, Charles O.
Nakashima, S.
Nezvensky, Marvin C.
Remetch, John K.
Steckley, Steward
Tester, John L.
Throneberry, Billy
Traycoff, Stephen S.
Walker, Jake W.
Wallace, Charles A. (KIA 7/16/50)
Watkins, Floyd H.
Wurzer, Paul J.
Young, Richard J.

PRIVATE
Baker, Ralph P.
Duckworth, Lynn E.
Francis, Jimmie H.
Haynes, Eugene T.
Henson, Clint M.
Huffman, Ronald L.
King, Charles E
Miller, James N.
Montez, Carmen A.
Munsey, Jack H.
Oglesby, Jack H.
Payne, J F (KIA 7/16/50)
Rosen, Charles R.
Schlosser, Lyman L.
Schmidt, Ronald
Shallo, August
Stacy, Maurice
Van Fleet, Gardner
Williams, Houston

MEDIC
Stidd, Dallas (PFC)

B Battery

MASTER SERGEANT
Schmidt, Leroy
Toner, James E.

SERGEANT FIRST CLASS
Andrews, James D.
Butler, James O.
Chepaitis, A.L.
Springer, Frank D.
Williams, Albert W.

SERGEANT
Adair, Thurman
Alanix, Miquel
Halsey, Walter V.
Lowe, George E.
Pigg, Bennie
Polson, Earl H.
White, David J. (KIA 8/6/50)

CORPORAL
Boudreaux, John H.
Brown, Earl D.
Cooper, Harold L.
Davis, Ronald K.
Dennis, Alvin F.
Edwards, Billy J.
Edwards, William
Field, Edgar F.
Hall, David E.
Jiminez, Pedro Jr.
Lindsley, Raymond
Malone, Benjamin M.
Marquiss, Stanley R.
Mendoza, Manuel
Miller, Joseph
Milliman, Douglas
Obermein, Stanley
Pina, Donald A. (KIA 8/10/50)
Reed, Donald C.
Speakman, Johnny, J.
Strehel, Raymond F.
Twiss, Harold J.
Williams, Charles K. (KIA 8/12/50)

PRIVATE FIRST-CLASS
Adkins, William F.
Atkins, Edward J.
Boronka, Walter Jr.
Brown, William M.
Carlstrom, William
Croy, Bertis L.
DuBose, Charles
Eppard, Divis
Fathergill, Chester
Fauro, Martin A.
Fitzgerald, Harvey
Freeze, John C. Jr.
Gaffrey, William O.
Hoak, Jack T.
Kean, William O.
Koppelman, Marvin
Lange, Elmer R. (DOW 7/23/50)
Lay, Charlie M. Jr.
Lee, Morton L.
Leisure, Harley Jr.
Littlejohn, Lawrence
Lockart, Lilburn L. (WIA 8/6/50)
McNeal, Robert P.
Medlin, Marshall S.
Montgomery, Buddy
Myers, Jesse Jr.
Nolan, Lawrence E.
Plotkin, Sidney
Rogers, Mack C.
Russell, Raymond L.
Schoenman, Robert
Smith, Harold D.
Smith, Jacques D.
Solomon, Francis L.
Stuart, Dewey L.
Switzer, Marvin
Thatcher, William C.
Thompson, Arthur L.
Tillman, Willard C.
Vaine, Howard, (WIA 8/6/50)
Wahl, John H.
Walker, Robert S.
Webster, James P.
Wilcox, Fay L.

Wiley, Robert L

PRIVATE
Bagi, Gustav Jr.
Clark, Charles F.
Creasia, Nicholas F.
Crisp, Charles J.
Funden, Lawrence
Higden, James O.
Horvath, Joseph III
Humphrey, James R.
Kumalae, Alfred L.
Livorsi, Frank J.
May, Kerton D.
Nedved, Frederick E. (KIA 4/18/51)
Roberts, Leroy R.
Robinson, Bernard W.
Sheehan, Paul A.
Smith, Dannie E.
Spencer, Norman
Weaver, Philip G.

APPENDIX C
COMMISSIONED PERSONNEL: 19th Infantry Regiment, July 1950

COLONEL
Meloy, Guy S. Jr. WIA 7/16/50)
Moore, Ned D.

LIEUTENANT COLONEL
Chandler, Homer J.
McGrail, Thomas A.
Winstead, Otho T. (KIA 7/16/50)

MAJOR
Cook. John M. (KIA 7/16/50)
Emery, Jack R.
Kleinman, Forest K.
Logan, Edward O.
Miller, Robert M. (WIA 8/50)
Pohl, Glyn W.
Sewell, Milton R.

CAPTAIN
Barscz, Michael
Clark, Samuel G. (KIA 7/16/50)
Cutler, Elliott C.
Dover, George J. Jr.
Elliott, Orin B. (KIA 7/20/50)
Felhoelter, Herman (KIA 7/17/50)
Fenstermacher, Edgar
Hackett, Allan P. (KIA 7/16/50)
Hyslop, Kenneth C. (POW 11/4/50 DIE 12/12/50)
Jones, Llewellyn R.
Lundberg, Earl A. (KIA 7/20/50)
Macomber, Wayne B. (POW 7/16/50 DIE 7/31/51)
McSweeney, Michael
Peacock, Donald F.
Slack, George D. (KIA 8/16/50)
Woods, Kenneth J.

FIRST LIEUTENANT
Aldridge, Edward F. (KIA 7/16/50)
Anderson, Monroe
Androsko, Frank J.
Armstrong, Louis W. (KIA 7/16/50)
Blankenship, Herman (KIA 7/31/50)

Cannon, Jack D.
Chitty, John M. Jr.
Christie, William K. (KIA 7/20/50)
Coones, James A. Jr.
Crozier, Bruce U.
Davis, Cecil R.
DuPuis, James R. (KIA 8/2/50)
Fisher, George W.
Fossum, Adolph C.
Grady, Albert W. (KIA 7/16/50)
Hall, Charles E.
Hennigan, Franklin
Hotchkiss, William (KIA 7/16/50)
Jenkins, Charles H.
Kaiser, William J.
Kimball, Hunter H. (MIA 7/16/50 Death Decl. DOD)
Lindsey, Robert (KIA 8/10/50)
Lowe, George A. (WIA 7/16/50)
Maple, John C.
McDougell, Oliver
McGill, Henry T. (POW 7/16/50 EXECUTED *ca* 7/20/70)
Norton, Alvin
Peterson, Richard
Rainey, Herbert W.
Reagan, Paul F.
Ruddell, James C. (POW 7/16/50 DIE 2/28/51)
Siegel, Kenneth I.
Smith, James E. Jr.
Souza, Lawrence P.
Tabor, Stanley E. (KIA 7/20/50)
Taylor, John W.
Wygal, William
Yerka, Jay H.

SECOND LIEUTENANT
Bailey, Charles T.
Baker, Ray L.
Boll, John M.
Byron, Kenneth M.
Catharine, Harry O.
Chaney, Robert B. Jr.
Clark, Felix G. Jr.
Crowe, William H. (KIA 7/20/50)
Dianda, Alfred (KIA 8/17/50)
Dower, Frank J.

Early, Charles C.
Ebbs, Joseph M.
Eberhart, Guy A.
English, John N. (WIA 8/15/50)
Fry, Louis C
Funchess, William N. (POW 11/4/50)
Gansky, Michael J.
Greer, Andrew K.
Herbert, Robert L.
Hill, James F.
Horacek, Clifford L.
Jacobs, Howard Jr.
Johnson, Dale N.
Karwoski, John N.
Kijek, Walter A.
Kille, Bruce R.
Longenecki, George (KIA 10/10/50)
Maher, Thomas A.M. (KIA 7/16/50)
Matlach, Charles A. (KIA 7/20/50)
McKinney, Jack M. (KIA 7/20/50)
Moment, William E. (KIA 7/16/50)
Nash, Robert E.
Orr, Augustus B. (WIA 7/20/50)
Perry, Marvin R.
Silberberg, Jules W.
Smith, Harold L. (KIA 7/16/50)
Smith, Lloyd D.
Stavrakes, James (POW 7/16/50)
Stickney, Louis E.
Vass, Marshall B.

WARRANT (JW-I)
Asner, Owen S.
Garrett, Charles E.
Norman, James R.
Scott, Ray C.
Weinshelbaum, Samuel
Worzel, Herbert R.

REPLACEMENT COMMISSIONED PERSONNEL: C COMPANY, Summer 1950
Rockwerk, Louis B. (CAPT) (POW 11/4/50)
Haugen, Richard D. (1LT) (POW 11/4/50 DIE 3/8/51)
Dowe, Ray M. (2LT) (POW 11/4/50)
Funchess Wm. H. (1LT) (POW 11/4/50)

Goodspeed, George (1LT)
Van Orman, Chester (2LT) (POW 1/1/51)
Ortiz, Orlando (ILT) (POW 11/4/50)
Krasco, John (1LT)

ENLISTED PERSONNEL: 19th Infantry Regiment, July 1950
B Company

MASTER SERGEANT
Mixon, Quinton
Roberts, Hobson (KIA 8/2/50)
Smith, Kenneth H.
Stowell, Patrick J.
Ward, Carl M.

SERGEANT FIRST-CLASS
Burrow, Lonnie E.
Cantrell, Olin N.
Clark, Walter E.
Gray, Max I.
Hale, Alfred B.
Hamric, Clifford D.
Lang, Joseph D.
Lupton, Leo
Matchett, Edward W. (KIA 7/16/50)
McAlhany, Wade T.
McGalliard, Joseph
Streetman, James S. (KIA 8/14/50)
Willis, Gordon B.

SERGEANT
Abel, Fred
Amacker, Alfred
Asari, Koichi
Blakemore, John E. (KIA 8/2/50)
Guzniczak, Joseph D.
Ives, Kenneth C.

CORPORAL
Bellflower, Edward (KIA 7/16/50)
Boggs, Raymond S.
Coghlan, Hardy
Dood, Arthur Jr.
Estabrook, Wilbert (POW 7/17/50)

Gravel, Joseph S.
Hartley, Robert L.
Hysong, James R.
Mainor, Charles
Melzer, Ernest (KIA 4/24/51)
Olzewski, Paul R.
Payton, Malcolm B.
Witherspoon, Bernard

PRIVATE FIRST-CLASS
Akers, Robert D.
Allen, Robert E.
Allred, Ace L.
Babin, Robert A. (KIA 8/2/50)
Barber, Ralph
Berce, Gunder O.
Blano, Henry L.
Boroznoff, Walter
Brecht, Albert E.
Bremer, James R.
Brennon, Francis
Brown, James A. (KIA 8/2/50)
Carter, James M. (KIA 7/16/50)
Chumley, Louis B.
Churney, Robert A.
Clark, Lee R.
Clark, Luther W.
Connell, Melvin F.
Cooley, Raymond D.
Culotta, Joseph V.
Dilley, Gerald L.
Doxtator, James L.
Doyon, Paul M.
Driver, Eugene T.
Dumas, James H.
Eckart, Nilson S.
Estela, Enrique
Floyd, Daniel D.
Foddrill, Homer E.
Frederick, Harvey L.
Fulmer, William F.
Gallegos, Polito G. (KIA 8/17/50)
Gaskin, Richard L.
Giroux, Jean P.
Gluvna, David E.

Golden, Richard R.
Griggs, Allen D.
Griggs, Virgil L. (DOW 1/30/51)
Gross, John R.
Hahn, William W.
Hakes, Harry H.
Hankamer, Fred A (KIA 1/30/51)
Hanson, George
Harbour, William F.
Hubbard, Richard L.
Hunter, Bobby C.
Jennings, Elmer D.
Jewett, Arthur F.
Johnson, Leonard C.
Johnson, Merlin E. (KIA 7/16/50)
Kami______, Matthew
Kimble, Richard L.
Knight, Everett
Kosheba, Joseph
Lewis, Eugene L.
Lopez, Luis B.
McGinty, John J. (KIA 7/16/50)
McIlveen, Andrew J.
Mortensen, Roy S.
Mullen, Alfred E. (KIA 4/24/51)
Newman, Marvin L. (KIA 8/2//50)
Olson, Norman E.(POW 1/1/51 DIE 6/23/51)
Orr, Donald A.
Owens, Myles S.
Pearce, Louis R.
Quillen, Harold H.
Ramirez, Antonio B.
Reed, Howard R. (KIA 7/16/50)
Rice, James (KIA 7/16/50)
Robertson, Charles (KIA 7/16/50)
Robinett, Bill B.
Schatz, Raymond H. (KIA 8/10/50
Schneider, Clifford
Searcy, James L.
Sheridan, Frank H. (KIA 7/16/50)
Snedden, David R.
Strouse, Francis
Thompson, Robert F. (KIA 8/2/50)
Uhl, Jack W.
Van Gundy, Julius L. (KIA 9/2/50)

Weatherly, Gilbert
Williams, John S.
Willrich, Gene W. (KIA 7/16/50)
Wilson, Donald J. (KIA 8/2/50)
Wojesky, Richard L. (KIA 3/8/51)
Worley, Donald B. (KIA 7/16/50)
Zippiere, William

PRIVATE
Albertson, John R.
Allen, James L.
Bloomquist, Russell
Carlson, Herbert C.
Clow, David R.
Davidson, Edward E. (KIA 7/16/50)
Dilling, Ernest E.
Dusoblom, Walter (KIA 7/16/50)
Dyer, Dale E.
Eggelston, Donald
Ethridge, Hal E.
Fabrize, Donald (KIA 7/16/50)
Fleming, Wilbur A.
Follini, William W.
Greco, Edward L.
Hall, Abner C. (KIA 7/16/50)
Heasley, Johnnie D.
Hershiser, Marvin L.
Hoffert, Joseph B.
Holder, Larry L.
Kimble, Richard L.
Kleso, Thomas J.
Lehrman, Fred E.
Lile, Melvin C.
Long, Simon P.
Lutes, Raymond E.
Maderas, Daniel D.
Maidens, Thomas J.
McDonough, Thomas
Mims, Robert F.
Mitchell, Earl
Musnicky, Steve S.
Myers, Luther W.
Naegele, William J.
Nowosielski, Daniel
Ormsby, Wendell D.

Osborne, Dale B.
Palm, Merle R.
Parisi, Joseph
Rasnick, Woodrow
Riedy, Edward R. (KIA 9/24/50)
Rissman, Girard T.
Robson, Charles R.
Roll, Anthony A.
Scott, Carl L.
Shaw, Wesley R.
Smith, Daniel S.
Spencer, Lawrence D.
Stranahan, Ashle
Swinford, Hillis E.
Taube, Thomas H.
Thompson, Harold M.
Tuggle, Roy F.
Tukarski, Chester M.
VanOrden, Velfred
Vanover, Franklin D.
Vaughn, Carl D. (KIA 1/1/51)
Vorel, Charles A. (MIA 7/16/50 Death Decl. DOD)
Wadding, Harry J.
Wagener, Harvey A.
Walker, Walter W.
York, Edward E.

RECRUIT
Burgher, Robert R.
Greene, Leon A.
Lemaster, Robert C.
Rubid, Richard A.
Tugman, Richard A.
Wescott, Jasper A.

APPENDIX E
ENLISTED PERSONNEL: 19th Infantry Regiment, July 1950
C Company

MASTER SERGEANT
Martin, James H. (KIA 7/16/50)
Oleyar, Frank J. (KIA 7/16/50)
Point, Ray (KIA 11/4/50)

SERGEANT FIRST-CLASS
Baker, Charlie C. (KIA 7/16/50)
Brown, Chester H.
Byers, Ernest E.
Loomis, Otis W. (POW 7/16/50 DIE 12/31/50)
Moynihan, John T. (KIA 7/16/50)
Nicodemus, James R. (KIA 7/16/50)
Pixley, George A. (MIA 7/16/50 Death Decl DOD)
Stewart, Graham (KIA 11/4/50)
Stone, Herbert E.
Van Orman, Chester (POW 1/1/51)

SERGEANT
Hood, William P.
Kawich, Harry
McKinney, Arnold E. (KIA 11/4/50)
Polka, Francis (POW 7/16/50 DIE 2/28/51)
Rowland, Carl W. (KIA 7/16/50)
Turner, Cooper T. (KIA 2/4/51)

CORPORAL
Allen, Leo (KIA 7/16/50)
Couch, Samuel H. (KIA 7/16/50)
Garrison, William H.
Inman, William L.
Jaso, Joe (KIA 7/16/50)
Jiminez, Victor P. (POW 7/16/50 DIE 4/16/51)
Jinks, Leonard W. (MIA 7/16/50 Death Decl. DOD)
Landrum, I.L. (KIA 7/16/50)
Lenz, Robert G. (MIA 7/16/50 Death Decl. DOD)
Sanzi, Robert D. (KIA 7/16./50)
Schoonover, George (POW 1/1/51/DIE 4/30/51)
Stewart, Roland F.
*Smith, Herbert B. (POW 7/16/50 Reported DIE)
Stidham, Henry (POW 7/16/50 DIE 10/20/50)
Sumpter, Bill A. (POW 7/16/50 DIE 11/7/50)

Thompson, William H. (KIA 7/16/50)
Warrick, John L. (POW 7/16/50 DIE 12/31/50)

PRIVATE FIRST-CLASS
Anderson, James E. (KIA 7/16/50)
Anderson, Johnnie
Angell, Eugene L. (POW 7/16/50 DIE 9/25/50)
Arakawa, Jack C. (POW 7/16/50 Escaped)
Barron, George L. (KIA 7/16/50)
Bogan, Vincent J.
Calaway, William E. (POW 7/16/50 DIE 1/26/51)
Clevenger, Bruce W. (KIA 7/16/50)
Coultress, Alfred G.
Cropper, Robert D. (KIA 7/16/50)
Cummins, Zolton (POW 7/16/50 DIE 10/31/50)
Dalton, Edmond F. (KIA 7/16/50)
Dampier, Bill A.
Dobbs, Lee A.
Dupuis, Raymond J. (KIA 7/16/50)
Englehart, Robert M. (POW 11/4/50 DIE 8/17/51)
Faleshock, Michael (KIA 7/16/50)
Francis, Robert B.
Frey, Stanley W.(KIA 7/16/50)
Goff, Howard W. Jr. (KIA 7/16/50)
Gravley, Thomas J.
Green, Donald L.
Guerrero, Moses G. (POW 7/16/50 Reported DIE)
Hamel, Harold K.
Harris, James C. (KIA 7/16/50)
Hernandez, Francisco (KIA 7/16/50)
High, Benjamin F. (KIA 7/16/50)
Holencik, Joseph P. (POW 7/16/50 DIE 4/30/51)
Hylton, Lonnie Jr. (KIA 7/16/50)
Knapp, Peter
Kogel, Frederick J. (KIA 7/16/50)
Legay, Donald (POW Date Unk)
Lukitsch, John J. (POW 7/16/50 DIE 2/28/51)
Marty, Albert E. (KIA 7/16/50)
Maudlin, Sidney E. (KIA 7/16/50)
Mayes, James D. (KIA 7/16/50)
Mills, Carroll E. (KIA 11/4/50)
Mills, Donald F. (KIA 7/16/50)
Mitchell, Rudus Jr. (KIA 11/4/50)
Monroe, James H. (KIA 11/4/50)
Myers, Russell L.

Naville, Herman F. (POW 7/16/50)
Ochoa, Arnold (KIA 7/16/50)
Ollero, Luciano F. (POW 7/16/50 DIE 5/23/51)
Pacleb, Pantolion M. (KIA 7/16/50)
Peterson, Donwin R. (POW 7/16/50 DIE 8/5/51)
Pettis, Gilbert L. (POW 7/16/50 DIE 11/1/50)
Powers, John F.
Pillow, Wade M. (POW 7/16/50 DIE 11/6/50)
Radford, Johnnie E. (MIA 7/16/50 Death Decl. DOD)
Ramos, Joseph
Ream, Gilbert E. (POW 7/16/50)
Reney, Edward S. (POW 7/16/50 Death Decl. DOD)
Richmond, Charles R. (KIA 7/16/50)
Saldama, Roberto (KIA 7/16/50)
Sands, William T. (KIA 7/16/50)
Sciluffo, Santo
Slagle, Donald L.
Smith, Clifton E. (KIA 7/16/50)
Smith, Fred (KIA 7/16/50)
Sorrentino, Anthony (KIA 7/16/50)
Sutherland, Kenneth (KIA 7/16/50)
Sweet, Richard L. (POW 7/16/50 DIE 12/19/50)
Tabor, Charles A. (KIA 7/16/50)
Thompson, Jeremiah
Vega, Gilberto
Wagner, Charles W.
Walton, Bobby B. (KIA 7/16/50)
Ward, Samuel E. (KIA 7/16/50)
Weaver, Donald A.
Williams, Lowell R.

PRIVATE
Abercrombie, Wherry (KIA 7/16/50)
Ancensio, Alejandro
Aldridge, Harry H. (KIA 7/16/50)
Allen, William M. (POW 7/16/50)
Baulk, Richard E. (POW 7/16/50 DIE 8/31/50)
Beckham, Larry E. (POW 7/16/50 DIE 2/24/51)
Bennett, Earl (KIA 7/16/50)
Bernier, Stephen L. (KIA 7/16/50)
Coyne, Ronald B. (KIA 7/16/50)
Creel, Shelby C. (POW 7/16/50)
Creshine, Frank J. (KIA 7/16/50)
Davis, Charles R. (POW 7/16/50)
Evans, Robert M. (KIA 7/16/50)

Funkhouser, Peter
Hallahan, George R.
Hegg, Arnold (KIA 7/16/50)
Hemenway, John HJ. (KIA 7/16/50)
Hess, Kenneth L. (POW 7/16/50 DIE 2/28/51)
Hoit, Freddie G. (KIA 7/16/50)
Hunt, James R. (POW 7/16/50)
Iwao, Eddie E.
Jablonski, George W.
Jaecke, William A.
King, George R. (POW 1/1/51 DIE 12/6/51)
Komorowski, Richard J.
Kutters, William (KIA 1/1/51)
Kwallek, James
Lahm, Leonard E. (KIA 7/16/50)
*Langevin, Alcide G. (POW 7/16/50 Reported DIE)
*Langley, Alton R. (POW 7/16/50 Reported DIE)
Larson, Charles E.
Lashley, Marvin J. (KIA 7/16/50)
Lawrence, James W.
Leftwich, Robert M.
Lindley, John Z.
Livingston, Marvin J.
Loper, George D.
Luebbers, Daniel E. POW 7/16/50 DIE 7/18/50)
May, Donald A. (KIA 7/16/50)
McAdams, Ronald L. (KIA 7/16/50)
McCutcheon, James E. (KIA 7/16/50)
McKeown, Joseph T. (MIA 7/16/50 Death Decl. DOD
Merriett, Anthony G. (KIA 7/16/50)
Murphy, O.G.
Nelson, Clayburn E. (KIA 7/16/50)
Oles, Peter (POW 7/16/50 DIE 12/31/50)
Oresto, James V. (POW 7/16/50)
Pfouts, Darrell D.
Pope, John R.
Schleker, Robert P.
Schmidt, Charles C. (POW 7/16/50)
Shaw, Richard B.
Smith, Gerald J. (POW 7/16/50)
Smith, Ray (KIA 7/16/50)
Smith, Robert L.
Springston, Clyde (KIA 7/16/50)
Sunsdahl, Roy L. (POW 7/16/50 DIE 12/5/50)
Tatro, Richard D. (KIA 7/16/50)

Tepakeyah, Julius (KIA 7/16/50)
Thomas, Garland C. (KIA 7/16/50)
Thorsteinson, Duncan (KIA 7/16/50)
Titus, Robert E. (POW 7/16/50 DIE 12/31/50)
Toney, Clarence (KIA 7/16/50)
Trent, Ira V. (KIA 11/4/50)
Turner, Charles J.
Varvel, Patrick J. (KIA 7/16/50)
Wallace, Willard D. (KIA 7/16/50)
Weldon, Harold D. (POW 7/16/59 DIE 2/13/51)
Wolfe, Charles J. (POW 7/16/50)
Wright, Robert A. (MIA 7/16/50 Death Decl. DOD)

* Individuals reported as POWs and later succumbing while incarcerated. Their names do not appear on the listing of 19th Infantry Regiment KIA, MIA or DIE deaths as compiled by the Department of Defense.
# The Department of Defense lists PFC Moses Guerrero as having been KIA on July 16, 1950. Guerrero has been identified by returning POW Wilbert Estabrook as having been taken prisoner on July 16, succumbing at some point in time while incarcerated.

APPENDIX F

This additional appendix is a listing of newly appointed field artillery officers, all in the grade of second lieutenant, who reported to Fort Sill, Oklahoma, on December 1, 1948, under the provisions of Circular 330, Department of the Army 1948, for attendance at the Special Associate Basic Artillery Officers' Course # 1.

Ankrom, Kenneth F.
Bardwell, Welburn C.
Barker, Elbert S.
Battle, Morris F.
Bauman, Walter J.
Danley, Noah N.
Dillingham, Clarence
Gibbons, William J. Jr. (WIA 8/50)
Golden, Peter T. (KIA 11/30/50)
Hager, Richard M.
Harrity, Ralph D.
Haugerud, Howard E.
Juedes, Roger J.
Krohn, Thomas F.
McCanlies, Hiram Jr.
Nicholas, Billy B.
Osburn. Lawrence S.
Redgate, Thomas J.
Rogers, Carl E.
Shircliff, Edward C.
Somerville, George Jr.

BIBLIOGRAPHY

Selected Sources

Appleman, Lt. Col. Roy E. *South to the Naktong, North to the Yalu, June–November, 1950,* (U.S. Army in the Korean War). Washington, D.C.: US. Government Printing office, 1961.

Blair, Clay. *The Forgotten War – America in Korea, 1950–1953.* New York: Random House (Times Books), 1987.

Cumings, Bruce. *Korea's Place in the Sun, A Modern History.* New York: W.W. Norton & Co, 1997.

Goralski, Robert. *World War II Almanac, 1931–1945.* New York: G.R. Putnam Sons, 1981.

Hogg, Ian V. and John Weeks. *The Illustrated Encyclopedia of Military Vehicles.* London: Quarto (New Burlington Books).

Kinchner, Earl L. ed. *Selective Service Under the 1948 Act; Selective Service Act of 1948.* Washington, D.C.: U.S. Government Printing Office, 1951.

Maclean, Fitzroy. *Highlanders, A History of the Scottish Clans.* New York: Penguin (Viking Studio Books), 1995.

Sowicki, James A. *Field Artillery Battalions of the U.S. Army,* vol. 1, 1st ed. Dumfries, Va.: Centaur Publications, 1977.

———. *Infantry Regiments of the U.S. Army.* Dumfries, Va.: Wyvern Publications, 1981.

Spurr, Russell. *Enter the Dragon: China's Undeclared War Against the US. in Korea, 1950—51.* New York: Newmarket, 1988.

Tax, Sol ed. *The Draft, Handbook of Facts and Alternatives.* Chicago: University of Chicago Press, 1967.

Ward, Orlando, Chief of Military History. *Korea-1950.* Department of the Army. Washington, D.C.: U.S. Government Printing Office.

Young, Gordon R. ed. *The Army Almanac,* 2nd ed. Harrisburg, PA: The Stackpole Co., 1959.

MAGAZINES

The following listed magazine titles were searched for relevant information providing both sequential guidance and incident/background specificities.

Army and Navy Journal, vols. 85, 86, 87
Army Times, vols. 8, 9, 10
Colliers, vol. 127
Newsweek, vol. 36
Saturday Evening Post, vol. 223
Time, vols. 55, 56

INDEX OF NAMES (less Rosters)

Y